# HOLLYWOOD'S IMPERIAL WARS

# Hollywood's Imperial Wars

## *The Vietnam Generation and the American Myth of Heroic Continuity*

ARMANDO JOSÉ PRATS

University of Oklahoma Press : Norman

This book is published with the generous assistance of the McCasland Foundation, Duncan, Oklahoma.

**Library of Congress Cataloging-in-Publication Data**

Names: Prats, A. J., 1948– author.
Title: Hollywood's imperial wars : the Vietnam generation and the American myth of heroic continuity / Armando José Prats.
Description: Norman : University of Oklahoma Press, [2024] | Includes bibliographical
references, filmography, and index. | Summary: "The history of Hollywood depictions, and the historical context in which they were created, of US military involvement with racial 'others' from the Indian Wars through Vietnam to the War on Terror"—Provided by publisher.
Identifiers: LCCN 2023043161 | ISBN 978-0-8061-9375-5 (hardcover)
ISBN 978-0-8061-9748-7 (paperback)
Subjects: LCSH: Vietnam War, 1961–1975—Motion pictures and the war. | War films—United States—History and criticism. | Heroes in motion pictures. | National characteristics, American, in motion pictures. | BISAC: History / United States / 20th Century | ART / Popular Culture
Classification: LCC DS557.73 .P73 2024 | DDC 959.704/3—dc23/eng/20231214
LC record available at https://lccn.loc.gov/2023043161



The paper in this book meets the guidelines for permanence and durability of the Committee on Production Guidelines for Book Longevity of the Council on Library Resources, Inc. ∞

The manufacturer's authorized representative in the EU for product safety is Mare Nostrum Group B.V., Mauritskade 21D, 1091 GC Amsterdam, The Netherlands, email: gpsr@mare-nostrum.co.uk

In memoriam:
Olga A. Rodriguez-Cáceres
Clara Avendaño y Quintero
and for
Ana Prats Alvord,
who ever keeps, pure and undiminished, their legacy of devotion

# Contents

# Preface

*Hollywood's Imperial Wars* addresses and explores two distinct types of Hollywood war narratives. The difference between these two types arises chiefly from the more or less settled historical assessment of each war's outcome. All of them had been victories except for that murky, execrable, and unremittingly tragic American war in Vietnam. History, or at least the force of collective wishful thinking throughout the centuries, had accommodatingly declared and recurringly confirmed the record of American triumphs. Brought by drift or drag into the orbits of the myriad themes and ideals held to be peculiar to the triumphal nation—for instance, manifest destinies and exceptionalisms, errands into the wilderness, and cities upon a hill—the chronicles of American victories could be made to reveal and attest to the familiar emergence of America's heroic myth. Generation after generation, the American hero unfailingly embodied the enduring American values, his might an instrument of his right, his victory the sole source of his heroic identity. Yet, the victorious hero evinced an even higher achievement, namely the affirmed and enforced continuity, measured in victories past and projected, of a heroic America.

The seemingly simple pattern whereby the hero and his heroic inheritance secured the continuity of America's special privilege concealed, however, an insidiously subversive complication. This anomaly dwelt in abeyance, perhaps even unsuspected, throughout the centuries of triumph and glory. After the loss in Vietnam, however, the erstwhile oddity stepped out of the shadows of the myth and into historical prominence, and its many narrative expressions never ceased to locate their birth in the patterns and cycles that had long since produced the investment and installation of the hero as the concomitant of the victory. The myth, in short, held within it the harsh proscription that losers could not be heroes. If indeed our American war heroes had, each and all and without quibble or cavil, embodied the nation's triumphalism—if their very existence gave proof that victory both confers and safeguards an extraordinary national privilege, a privilege, as some had imagined, divinely bestowed and superintended—how then do we respond to the once unthinkable, to the now so sudden and grim actuality that America had lost a war? Each generation had heretofore inherited the heroic virtue of the fathers, and the victory itself was the deeded thing. Heroes were heroes because they were winners. Each generation conveyed and proffered its own exalted status as victors. And the victory itself made possible the transfer, the legacy. In this way, the continuity of the heroic legacy designated something akin to the immortality of both nation and hero. When victory did not materialize, continuity failed, and the intrusion caused by the loss, the peremptory, unapologetically urgent, and not-to-be-ignored crashing of it, would accordingly alter not only the heroic myth but also the foundational assumptions of American exceptionalism that underlay it. The myth would come to be known for the shocking intrusion—the *rupture*, as I call it throughout—wrought by the one loss.

One of these two types of American war narratives all but defined the childhood and adolescence of the so-called baby boomers and in many ways shaped the patriotic ideal that drove many to Vietnam. Many of these movies feature heroes of preceding American generations, from those who fought in the centuries of the Indian Wars to the one, now enshrined as the archetypal American war, that their fathers had recently fought in Europe and the Pacific. These are the American epics of manifest destiny, the national tales of empire and triumph wherein the children beheld the promise of their own future heroism. And they are primarily Indian Westerns and World War II movies. The other war narrative, the tale that others the American hero, features the Vietnam generation and emerges about half a decade after the last American soldiers returned from service in Vietnam in 1973.

The first of these two narrative types proclaims and promotes a mythic America, the peerless nation eminently represented by the hero. This mythic narrative, moreover, claims historical authenticity (the ever-implied "based on a true story"). The mythic account is what really happened, and the "reality" is to be confirmed in the victory. The second type of American war narrative aspires to the status of history but a history that inherently subverts the mythic, infusing it with irony. As befits the narrative of loss—of what William Faulkner in the short story "Barn Burning" (1939) called "the waste and extravagance of war"—history narrates tragedy. Military defeat, however, is not the full measure of loss. Taken in a broader cultural context, that unique experience of defeat, convulsive, dystopic, apocalyptic even, becomes unrecognizable, disorienting in its very newness. Here is not a loss merely but rather *the* Loss (capitalized, in context, hereafter)—often presumed to be America's first—that bares the irrecoverable innocence and reveals instead a pervasive national disquiet, the obstinate anxieties about national destiny and perhaps even divine judgment, as if spawned of the primordial Fall.

In the mythic narratives, the American hero high up on the screen radiated the bold spirit that would shape and all too often drive the fate of many children of the heroes of World War II. In the dark of the movie house, the witnesses became the hero's inheritors, his covenanted beneficiaries, by the simple privilege of being "Americans." The second of these war narratives, however, the tragic one, had been all but unforeseeable in the hero's heyday, unanticipated in his deeds, his courage, and above all his undoubted embodiment of victory. And so, the young viewers' own American war narrative would be a continuation of the first. Who better than these young witnesses to claim an intimacy with the intricate rules and recondite solemnities of the American heroic? All that lore and that patriotic passion—and, of course, the skill wherewith to validate it—would be, nay had to be, transferable to their own war. Yet, soon after their return from Vietnam, they had occasion to rail, justly though in vain, against the Hollywood images purporting to place them—broken, traduced, and disowned—up where they might once have expected to see themselves in full possession of their own mythic legacy.

Unembarrassed by the excesses of delusion that it long fobbed off as history, Hollywood war movies beguiled the children who grew up during the first two decades or so of the Cold War, inventing for their benefit (and their uncritical consumption) a special mythic past, a heroic and exalted past to be sure but one that also continually reminded them of their own pending inheritance, of the sacred patrimony that would soon enough be theirs to lay undisputed claim to even as a war of their own came ever closer into view. And how could they fail in their contest when the very form and model of American heroism called to them to join the company of heroes indomitable and triumphant, waging righteous war up there on the Saturday matinee movie screen? But the fervor that they so innocently, so devotedly, lavished on the heroic myth became in time demurral, then discord, and at last moral outrage and resistance. (Was there a Vietnam War protestor more righteous than the returned veteran who now knew the myth for the tragedy that it had always meant to conceal?) Thus, the second defining phase of their development initiated, enacted, and consummated the grim transformation of the myth into tragic history. And so, looking from the other side of the Vietnam War—that is, from the historic side, from the losing, the tragic, side—*Hollywood's Imperial Wars* turns to the ways in which an exuberant faith driven and sustained by a stubborn and seemingly unassailable myth yielded to a historic national calamity, one that Hollywood, in its often self-serving and dilatory fashion, at last consented to narrate. All throughout the Vietnam War's duration, Hollywood had dodged direct encounters with it; this is well known and incontestable. Hollywood's erstwhile affirmations of America's exceptionalist vaunt could not easily adapt to narratives of the war even if none other than John Wayne, in *The Green Berets* (Wayne and Kellogg, 1968), managed to produce and exhibit the single major Hollywood movie of the Vietnam War released during the time of the war itself, thereby attempting, despite an orgy of ideological posturing, to foist stale and fusty heroics on an irremediably tragic tale. And the testimony from Vietnam denied Hollywood any plausible recourse to the worn tropes of World War II movies. The daily documented experiences of Americans in Vietnam disavowed those tropes and often recast them into occasions of just reproach for Hollywood's great generational deception.

Principally, however, the irrefutable fact of America's Vietnam War, in its history as in its narrative representations, was the Loss, and Hollywood had long since embraced the fundamental premise of America's heroic myth, namely that losers could never be heroes. And so, correspondingly, defeat rescinded the heroic inheritance. If Hollywood was at last to take on the Vietnam War, it would have to destroy (or, more tenderly, deconstruct) the very myth it had done so much to present as history. This narrative conundrum echoes a famous paradox dating to the time of the Tet Offensive in early 1968, when a high-placed US Army officer at the ruined city of Ben Tre explained that it had become necessary to destroy the city in order to save it.

As the de facto narrative of "containment," the Cold War still too clearly adverted to infernal horrors to come: World War III, Armageddon, end times. One important iteration of the national disquiet arising from the prospect of such seemingly inescapable catastrophes took shape as *the anxiety of legacy*, the unsettling doubt that America, though yet in the full flush of victory in World War II and in plenary enjoyment of its unmatched global ascendancy, might somehow cease to transmit its heroic birthright to a new generation. In other words, the narratives that modeled the requisite heroism for the benefit of the young—*Fort Apache* (Ford, 1948), for instance, and *Sands of Iwo Jima* (Dwan, 1949), movies chiefly about the urgent transfer of heroic virtue—were also and at the same time urgent responses, sometimes desperately shrill reactions, to Cold War disquiet. The anxiety of legacy explained what I will call the *heroic imperative*, that is, the young generation's redoubtable response to the call of duty, a response that, consciously or not, would mitigate or at least mask their consternation.

After the delay and the deferral, Hollywood came to the Vietnam War at last. Once there, however, it could not ignore the too recent time of dissent and protest, of deceptions and atrocities, that found little in the way of complement or counterpart in its narratives of World War II. More important, it could not ignore the historical fact of America's Loss. Thus, Hollywood had to abandon the mythic certitudes that it had promoted in Westerns and war movies alike. Wayne's *The Green Berets* notwithstanding, there could be no other Vietnam War but the historically tragic one. Hollywood would accordingly have to find ways to shape a generation's now frazzled passion, the innocent patriotic devotion now burdened by the faithlessness that denied them their heroic birthright for so insistently casting them as incarnations of the Loss.

To note that Hollywood eventually attempted a different war movie is hardly to suggest that it succeeded in faithfully holding the mirror up to the American combat veteran's experience in Vietnam. This book makes no pretense of ascertaining whether Hollywood's Vietnam War movies faithfully portray a historical experience common to the American soldier of that generation. Some things are too sacred, and the painful memories remain, ghosts and all, etched in the soul of the individual soldier, and we must allow them to chasten and temper the rest of us. Instead, *Hollywood's*

*Imperial Wars* assigns a central role to the historical Loss as the principal source of difference between the narratives of the heroic legacy and those of the Vietnam War. This difference promotes the elucidation, throughout this study, of the rupture, that is, the historically necessary break with both the heroic legacy and the continuity of the heroic myth. What sort of American war movie, Hollywood may have asked, is credibly possible in this unwonted site created and inhabited by the rupture?

# Acknowledgments

First, I thank Judith G. Prats for almost everything but mostly in enduring gratitude for and constant wonder at her generosity of soul. Emily Rose Prats, she of the brilliant and expansive and loving spirit, cheerfully softens the world's asperities even as she inspires. Lily K. Prats Bobbitt, luminous and ever-loving, contributes bounteously to the needful wellsprings of joy. She and her gallant husband, USAF Capt. Jonathan G. Bobbitt, have graced the world with Julian B. Bobbitt, who is himself to be acknowledged as a source of pure joy and reverent hope, of grace "unprevented, unimplored, unsought."

At times during the years of research and writing, it seemed as if I could well measure my slow progress by the passing of so many dear friends and colleagues. And none dearer in this bunch is C. Patrick "Pat" White, who opposed the war as ardently as he loved his country. But the list rightly includes Joseph Bryant, J. Douglas Canfield, Joseph G. Gardner, W. R. Robinson, Jane Gentry Vance, Lucy Combs, Thomas Blues, Larry Swingle, John G. Cawelti, Art Wrobel, Joan Blythe, Steve Weisenburger, Gurney Norman, and George C. Herring. I include two special former undergraduate students: Jerome "Jerry" Wurmser, World War II veteran of sixty-six sorties in the south of France in a P-47, and Larry Froelich, a witness to the Kent State tragedy who served well during the Vietnam War era.

I am indebted to Andy Johnson for a cherished and constant friendship and to Michelle Sizemore, a student many years ago who became a formidable scholar, teacher, and colleague. I thank Jonathan Allison, who never ceased to encourage me and to ask about the progress of the book. I am grateful to Pearl James, who read my chapter on *Sands of Iwo Jima* and thought well enough of it to share it with her graduate students; this double generosity, added to the years of fellowship and collegiality, encouraged me to air out the whole manuscript.

I wish to acknowledge the gentle influence of dear friends over many years: Dan Howell, Greg Waller, Bill Campbell, David Durant, Anibal Biglieri, Ana Rueda, and Yanira Paz.

Kristen Pickett and Robin LaMer Rahija of the University of Kentucky English Department are to be thanked for the graciousness with which they unravel the arcana of departmental matters large and small. I would also like to acknowledge the generous assistance through the years of the following colleagues at my university's William T. Young Library: Gordon Hogg, Shawn Livingston, Jennifer Bartlett, Peter Hesseldenz, Jay-Marie Bravent, and Terri Brown.

I thank Josh Reid for not only a magnanimous contribution to my university in my name but also his talents: the best graduate student has long since become a renowned teacher and researcher.

For the indispensable friendship of fifty years—the friendship that erases the line between the personal and the professional, that freely provides a seemingly inexhaustible fund of wisdom about so many different things, and that even in its everyday manifestations dazzles and inspires—for all this bounty and ever so much more I acknowledge the genius of my dear friend Walter C. Foreman.

I thank Cassie Blake and May Haduong of the Pickford Center for Motion Picture Study in Hollywood for kindly granting me access to the DVD of *Oscar Presents: The War Movies and John Wayne*.

My association with the University of Oklahoma Press has been characterized by not only a cordial professionalism but also the genuine interest of its staff in publishing the best possible version of the manuscript. I am grateful to Joe Schiller, who on more than one occasion turned his appreciation for the book into the work of seeing it through. I thank Yvonne Ramsey for the intensive labor of editing the manuscript and for teaching me just how much I needed to learn about things I didn't think I still had to know. Thanks also to Helen Robertson for laying out all the steps from manuscript to book and to Amy Hernandez for the kindness with which she makes her requests.

# Introduction

"There are already three, among us, who have also names derived from that scout."

"A name, did you say!" exclaimed the old man, starting; "what, the name, of the solitary, unl'arned hunter! Do the great, and the rich, and the honored, and what is better, still, the just, do they bear his very, actual name!"

—James Fenimore Cooper, *The Prairie, a Tale*

(The deed of gift was many deeds of war)

—Robert Frost, "The Gift Outright"

All of us, I suppose, like to believe that in a moral emergency we will behave like the heroes of our youth, bravely and forthrightly, without thought of personal loss or discredit.

—Tim O'Brien, "On the Rainy River," *The Things They Carried*

[Vietnam] was my chance to be the star of my own John Wayne movie.

—Bill Ehrhart, *The Vietnam War*

## America's Heroic Legacy and the Vietnam War

The Vietnam generation grew up in tacit embrace of the *myth of heroic continuity.* This essential myth came to them, or so it may have once seemed, as a cultural legacy, auspicious and reassuring, the cynosure of the exceptional nation. The myth of heroic continuity held implicitly that Americans had never lost a war. American heroism was therefore a continuum, evidence of not only global preeminence but also divine favor. Certainly many of the young men who fought in Vietnam took this continuity for historical fact, and so, ironically, they also took it as an article of faith. Beginning with the proto-Americans of the New England and Virginia wildernesses, every generation of European ancestry had won its war, and appeals to disputed history about who "really" won this war or lost (if at all) this other war were merely academic quibbles. But as the nightmare prospect of Loss in Vietnam loomed ever larger, the war managers seemed unable to awaken from the spell of the myth of heroic continuity. Victory, however ill defined, was still the goal if only because losing was unthinkable. And yet, no less eminent a figure than George F. Kennan—author of the "Long Telegram" (1946) and of the article, authored by "X," in *Foreign Affairs* (1947),[1] two bedrock documents of America's Cold War policy of containment—fairly sneered at the wobbly myth of victory supporting American policy and strategy in Vietnam. Testifying live on national TV on February 10, 1966, before the Senate Foreign Relations Committee, Kennan stated that he could think of "several reasons why we should wish not to be" involved in Vietnam. Then, committee chairman J. William Fulbright summarized what he took to be Kennan's basic position, namely that Vietnam presented no "practicable objective" that the United States could attain "even with the best of will." "This is correct," Kennan confidently replied, "And I have a fear that our thinking about this whole problem is still affected by some sort of illusions about invincibility on our part."[2]

America's many and undoubted victories had long enabled narratives meant to sustain such illusions as Kennan adduces. Taken in the aggregate—and thus requiring no small measure of historical fudging—these illusions took shape as the myth of heroic continuity. As the American presence in Vietnam obdurately persisted in validating this sacrosanct source of America's exceptional identity, it transformed that identity into a national tragedy. The possibility arises, no doubt, that the myth of heroic continuity emerged post-Vietnam, that the Loss in effect antedated the myth in relation to its own historical occurrence. In other words, the myth, which had lain in quiet abeyance throughout the centuries as a more or less unchallenged historical precept, now became something like a foundational principle with which to set apart and thus condemn the war in Vietnam. The Loss itself, so galling to the nation, urged a backward look, and the uneasy retrospect produced the facile assessment that yes, all previous American wars but this one in Vietnam were victories. Accordingly, it became possible to isolate the Loss and concomitantly to cast the Vietnam veteran as a loser, the scapegoat denied a righteous rank in America's heroic epic. America would still be heroic—a winner, then—if it could somehow forget Vietnam. A feature of every Vietnam War movie treated in *Hollywood's Imperial Wars* is that their openings tend to affirm, indeed proclaim, the myth of heroic continuity. Vietnam will be that generation's Indian Wars, even its World War II. Then, with the patriotic fervor of a whole generation clearly established, we witness the turn, gradual or abrupt, toward the utter undoing of the myth.

In every American war, as in many American war movies, common dogface soldiers readily became heroes. Proof of their heroism lies in not only some phenomenal deed in battle but also the historical fact of their victory. Such, then, is the stern injunction: first victory, then—but only after victory—the hero. After World War II, a new generation, impatient for its own turn at heroism, would rise inexorably and enthusiastically to claim its exalted patrimony. But in the aftermath of Vietnam, the Loss came to signify the end of the myth of heroic continuity. Thus, this book is also about the ironic modes and tropes whereby Hollywood came at last to narrate the rupture by subverting its own tropes and themes. In this way, *Hollywood's Imperial Wars* provides an account of the cultural history and the myths invoked both before and during three particular eras not only consecutive but also interrelated: the Cold War, whose first decade and a half circumscribed and supervised the Vietnam generation's fraught ascent toward young manhood, the period of their military activity in Vietnam (roughly 1965–1973), and the post-Vietnam era, when the Loss looms over all putative reaffirmations of heroic war narratives (e.g., Clint Eastwood's *American Sniper* [2014], which I treat in chapter 7). I have, however, appealed throughout to a wider array of sources than those specifically concerned with these time periods. Many of these sources far predate the Cold War and the Vietnam War as well as the fictional and historical narratives of those times. Yet, they also enrich our understanding of them. For instance, my reading of certain early passages in James Fenimore Cooper's *The Pioneers* (1823) provides an important context for my inquiry into *The Deer Hunter* (Cimino, 1978). Cooper may not "explain" Cimino, and surely the narrative power of *The Deer Hunter* stands, whole and independent, without a prop from Cooper and his Old Leatherstocking. Nevertheless, the link suggests Cooper's importance in shaping the character of the American hero roaming the hostile American frontier; and it validates and qualifies the urge of Cimino's protagonist to affirm American heroism as if Vietnam were no different from the Indian frontier in the first three decades of the nineteenth century. Thus, Cooper's implied influence functions to not only certify the heroic pedigree of *The Deer Hunter* but also highlight the devastating irony of the protagonist's blind faith in the universality—temporal, spatial, cultural, historical—of the American wilderness and its hero.

In a few instances, I found it instructive to address a movie released before World War II narrating an event that occurred between the Indian Wars and World War I. This movie, *The Real Glory* (Hathaway, 1939), dramatizes America's unexpected struggles against the Moro rebels—Rudyard Kipling would confidently place it among empire's "savage wars of peace"—in the southern islands of the Philippine archipelago. I have placed the analysis of *The Real Glory* after that of *Fort Apache* (Ford, 1948), released three years after the end of World War II. This seeming slight to film history is rather an assent to basic demands of historical inquiry, as found in the historical setting of the narratives: first the Apache Wars, then the Moro Wars. But this predilection for historical chronology never overrides this book's abiding concern with the continuity of—and the eventual rupture in—the heroic myth.

## Troubled Convergences: Racial Reckonings and Gender Restraints

Racism, the perennial American scandal so often unacknowledged and as often disavowed, courses grimly and unrepentant through the heroic myth. Hollywood's wars demonstrate an undeviating affirmation of the whiteness of America's heroic narrative. Early Hollywood assigned a specific time and place for its own story of the myth's whiteness, as well as for the concomitant narrative of sustained and brutally enforced suppression of the racial Other's presence at the feast of American liberty. To this narrative of heroic greatness achieved through genocidal violence,

Hollywood gave no less august a title than "the birth of a nation." And that same "birth" would always remind us that Hollywood was all but midwifed, only a half century after the American Civil War, by a devout heir of the so-called Lost Cause. That such a birth could presume to dispense with or minimize the labor of women only begins to suggest the limits of the woman's place and her role in the myth of heroic continuity. I assert therefore that racism and misogyny inhere in the heroic myth and that as they emerge and reemerge, they can be readily taken for granted. These ingrained and distinctly American features of the heroic myth require exposition, illustration, but as to their actual presence in the narratives of the heroic myth, they are altogether past requiring proof. Throughout the ages they have lain in plain sight, as much in the heroic myth and American history as in the daily woes of American life. And willful blindness and denialism are only their own forms of evidence, the deafening testimony of their inveterateness.

In the vision of triumphal racist whiteness at the end of D. W. Griffith's *The Birth of a Nation* (1915), the Ku Klux Klan has become sole arbiter of both whiteness and the meaning of "America." And the implied bequeathals of racial privilege as well as the reclaimed birthrights that are sure to follow augur the unrepentant persistence of such whiteness as a formidable power, that is, the power of legacy itself. Such a stunted sense of "nation" endures, its vehemence and virulence preserving and sustaining the racist animus that remains all but intact into our own time. The racial angst that drives *Birth of a Nation*—and through which, in turn, Griffith presumes to justify an all but genocidal violence against Black Americans—has remained unaltered for the full century and more since the movie's release in 1915, its quantum of racism, so to put it, a reliable constant, even if the various configurations differ in accordance with the exigencies of political power and the imperatives of cultural hegemony. In an essay titled "The Birtherism of a Nation," Adam Serwer has noted the insidiousness of the birtherism that haunted the presidency of Barack Obama, a birtherism that, though hardly invented by Donald Trump, was still inarguably co-opted by him with the view of confounding the very possibility of a Black president of the United States: "Birtherism was a statement of values, a way to express allegiance to a particular notion of American identity, one that became the central theme of the Trump campaign itself: To Make America Great Again, to turn back the clock to an era where white political and cultural hegemony was unthreatened by black people, by immigrants, by people of a different faith. By people like Barack Obama."[3]

Timothy Egan's *A Fever in the Heartland* cites the telltale boast of the ruthless and depraved David C. Stephenson, Grand Dragon of the Ku Klux Klan in Indiana during the 1920s: "I did not sell the Klan in Indiana on hatreds. I sold it on Americanism."[4] Here is an ancestral branch of "America First" and not least of MAGA (Make America Great Again), whose "again," vague yet dogged, nurtures a morbidly aggrieved whiteness even as it wistfully promotes the allure of a bygone time when "America" meant "white." A full century after Stephenson's boast, amid the fallout of the April 21, 2023, firing of right-wing Fox News prevaricator Tucker Carlson, some of us learned for the first time of his frequent use of the term "legacy Americans"—"a dog-whistle term," Nicholas Confessore wrote in the *New York Times* in 2022, "that, before [Carlson] began using it on his show, . . . appeared almost exclusively in white nationalist outlets."[5] "Legacy" defines "American" defines "white," and if you did not inherit that gift, it may well be because you are not really an American.

This persistent, ingrained, systemic racism supports the idea of continuity in the myth. Continuity expresses much more than mere ubiquity in time, as if marking the mere passage of empty chronological time between America's imperial wars. So, the stouthearted white paladin of freedom and democracy is also and always the stalwart defender of the white race—and not least the white woman—against any and all racial Others. Accordingly, the white hero must ensure the virginity of the white woman, who precisely because of this gendered hierarchy never superintends her own reproduction or even affirms her own racial affiliation. In a paradigmatic scene in *The Searchers* (Ford, 1956), Ethan Edwards (John Wayne) and his sidekick Martin Pawley (Jeffrey Hunter) stop at a remote fort looking for Ethan's niece Debbie (played as a child by Lana Wood and as a young woman by Natalie Wood), taken captive years earlier in a Comanche raid against white cattle ranchers. The fort's doctor brings the two searchers into the presence of several white women recently rescued from the Comanches. Two of these women, perhaps sisters, present only vacuous simpers and dull stares, as befits those presumed to have suffered "a fate worse than death." But one nameless white woman (Ruth Clifford), older than the other two and in any case much older than Debbie would be, is seated on the floor, and as Martin goes by her, she snatches a rag doll (named Topsy) that Martin had brought with him hoping that Debbie would recognize it from her girlhood. Holding Topsy tight, the woman shrieks and coos and rocks herself and her "baby." Disappointed that they have not found Debbie, the searchers head out, almost fleeing in horror before the unendurable spectacle of racial trauma. But now Ethan, horrified and revolted, stops at the door to look once more at the woman, and the doctor remarks, "It's hard to believe they're white." Ethan's response, in a close-up that registers his unmitigated disgust, lays bare the white hero's power to legislate and adjudicate in matters concerning racial identity. Staring at the mad captive, he says that "they ain't white, anymore" and then snarls, "They're Comanch." Ethan denies these poor wretches the white hero's own authenticating gaze, a single validating gesture that might acknowledge the trauma that humanizes them. Ethan Edwards's status as "hero"—and "hero" unfailingly means white—enables him to revoke something so seemingly settled as the woman's race itself. And the cause of his baleful wrath is not merely the white woman's lost virginity to an Other but rather the indelible stain that defiles the white race.

In the climactic scene of *Birth of a Nation*, the Ku Klux Klan rides furiously to the rescue of the little white community (North and South together, old and young, a woman and a girl, and two or three "faithful" Black people) seeking refuge from rampaging "Negroes" in a little two-room cabin. Many of these Black men are in Union uniforms, but it is their Blackness that threatens the white people inside. Earlier we saw the brave "Little Sister" (Flora Cameron, played by Mae Marsh) fleeing from Gus (Walter Long), the "Renegade Negro," who tells her, to her horror, that "now" that he is free, he can marry her. (Both the Emancipation Proclamation and the first use of the word "miscegenation" date from the same year, 1863.) So suddenly alone in the dark woods, what is the Little Sister to do but flee aimlessly, hopeless of hearth and home? Soon enough—and through the relentless, even malevolent efficacy of Griffith's intercutting—Gus closes the distance. But it is Flora's shrill and highly emoted agitation, not Gus's halting overtures, that identifies just what it is that the white woman should fear. (A similar scenario of impending sexual assault, its horror punctuated more by the white woman's outlandish histrionics than by the maddened cupidity of the pursuing assailant, unfolds in the Stoneman home, when the biracial villain Silas Lynch, played by George Siegmann, chases the northern ingenue, Elsie Stoneman, played by Lillian Gish, round and round a table until the Klansmen burst in and subdue him). With Gus now at arm's length, still half pleading, half menacing, what else is she to do but cheat the "fate worse than death"? She jumps off a cliff to her death. Brother Ben is too late, though he will avenge her death by castrating and killing Gus.

In the climactic scene, Griffith presents a tableau of doomed defiance: Dr. Cameron (Spottiswoode Aitken), the southern patriarch, stands over his kneeling, praying daughter Margaret (Miriam Cooper), gripping an empty revolver by the barrel and raising it high above his head, ready to drive the gun's grip, hammer-like, into Margaret's skull if the assailants should burst through. But the Klan arrives in the nick of time, and the siege of the cabin is soon over, the routed foe in full chaotic retreat. As if transformed by mystical powers suddenly set loose by the Klan's timely intervention, Margaret now instantly becomes the embodiment of southern womanhood, the white virgin through whom the heroic legacy ensures the continuity of white supremacy. Her purity shall not mitigate but shall instead foment the no doubt sublime ascendance of the heroic myth and of the heroic legacy itself, the legacy of white American masculinity and its heavy, existential investment in racism and misogyny.

At the end following the triumph of the myth, no wider, deeper, more inclusive vision of America emerges. The Other merely vanishes, as do those itinerant and ever-fungible Others who, dragooned by the genre itself into doomed complicities against themselves, will once again enable the white myth to proclaim itself historically, which is to say racially, justified. Thus, the racial Others' unresisting participation in America's white heroic narrative serves mostly to illuminate the need for their exclusion (or their submission). In short, the Other (likely at the behest of the Same) mounts a resistance while anticipating already yet another disappearance into some narrative doldrums, there to brood and lament in near oblivion. Before too long, however, the myth shall summon them again to force them to enact, with a sort of hapless and hopeless ferocity, their well-rehearsed, feckless rancor.

Even after it became institutionally possible for an American woman to serve in Iraq or Afghanistan and even if she behaved more or less heroically in combat, her return stateside sternly demanded a resumption of her domestic prewar duties just as if the war had not happened. (The general pattern of sudden disempowerment following the soldiers' homecoming was already familiar to the women of the World War II generation, many of whom returned to their appointed domestic duties after performing magnificently in the factory jobs vacated by the men serving abroad.) Such in brief is the story of Kelli (Linda Cardellini) in Liza Johnson's *Return* (2011). Back in her hometown from a tour in Iraq, Kelli seems to be adrift. Following several domestic arguments and a palpably widening distance with virtually everyone, she drops off her daughter at practice on the wrong day. Her husband, Mike (Michael Shannon), scolds her: "You're here, okay? You're back! Be a goddamned mother!" Being back means that Kelli is to resume her culturally assigned role even as she buries her experiences in Iraq. Thus, when her group counselor suggests to her that "telling your trauma can be an important step," Kelli replies that "I don't really have a story for you" and says nothing else at the meeting. At the end of the movie she returns to Iraq, only this time divorced, estranged from her children, and without a story for us or for the heroic myth.

Kelli's narrative (the story of not having a story) addresses implicitly the unheroic aftermath of the Loss in Vietnam. Set in the context of September 11, the wars in Afghanistan and Iraq, whatever the political rhetoric told us they were about, were to avoid at all cost "another Vietnam." In other words, as American empire looked once more to familiar lands overseas, there was public anxiety about "another Vietnam." (The pre-9/11 Persian Gulf War had been a resounding victory, however, perhaps the start of a new winning streak.) Between the myth's affinity for the compliant, homebound wife of the white hero and the institutional presence of enlisted women in combat zones, there had been Vietnam, the iconoclasm, the subversion of norms and of gender expectations, and, not least, the indisputable laying bare of the heart of darkness in the heroic myth. Vietnam, the Loss, had produced the rupture in the continuity of the myth. And the rupture made possible a focused and determined challenge to the myth's idea of the woman and the white hero: "Vietnam was full of strange stories."[6] So begins the framing narrator in Tim O'Brien's incandescent short story "The Sweetheart of the Song Tra Bong" in *The Things They Carried*. And the strangeness of the stories—about their special truths that, paradoxically, promote the puzzling and the preposterous—emerges from the breakdown of the heroic myth. If the principles and values of America's heroic narrative constituted in themselves an inheritance, then Vietnam in "The Sweetheart of the Song Tra Bong" represents something close to a radical abrogation of the legacy.

Implausibly arriving in Vietnam after her boyfriend arranges the most convoluted flight schedule imaginable—from Cleveland Heights to Chu Lai—a young white American woman all of seventeen, fresh-faced Mary Anne Bell, gradually yet grimly becomes the scourge of the Viet Cong. Mary Anne arrives at the post wearing culottes and a pink sweater and carrying her suitcase and "one of those plastic cosmetic bags."[7] Her transformation into a guerrilla fighter becomes all the more engrossing the less credible it may seem. At the end, "she had crossed to the other side. She was part of the land. She was wearing her culottes, her pink sweater, and a necklace of human tongues. She was dangerous. She was ready for the kill."[8] One feels that Mary Anne could have won the Vietnam War on her own, as much so as Rambo could have had he been left to his own deadly devices. And it seems possible that Mary Anne's transformation presupposes the Loss in Vietnam: the break, the rupture, in the continuity of the heroic myth in effect releases her, as a woman, from compliance with traditional roles. In the context of the rupture Mary Anne, now a lethal force in the jungle, is no less plausible a phenomenon than the collapse of the heroic myth might have seemed before Vietnam. She has run the gamut from dewy-eyed innocent to grim warrior. One extreme may well bind her to the typology of the Little Sister in *Birth of a Nation*, but the opposite one, liberating already by her actions' inherent repudiation of gendered roles, makes her not the male hero's equal but rather the exultant aberration who shows him the way out of the myth's ruins. But perhaps so much freedom is dangerous. Certainly Mary Anne cannot go back to any form of home, least of all to the slow-burn despair that consumes Kelli in *Return*. Mary Anne lives in the jungle in a sustained ecstasy of freedom. Here, she says to her boyfriend, "'I know exactly who I am. You can't feel like that anywhere else.'" And there she will stay. It may be significant that Mary Anne's story is so heavily mediated by male narrators even if some of them, such as Rat Kiley, are unreliable. Perhaps the men's vestigial connection with the absent male white hero can take the form of control over her story. Better still, however, if only for the frayed sensibilities of the nation's post-Vietnam convalescence, that, like Kelli in *Return*, Mary Anne have no story at all.

HALF A CENTURY AGO AND MORE, James Baldwin exposed the white heroic myth for its delusions of racial privilege. "The American Negro," he wrote, "has the great advantage of having never believed that collection of myths to which white Americans cling: that their ancestors were all freedom-loving heroes, that they were born in the greatest country the world has ever seen, or that Americans are invincible in battle and wise in peace, that Americans have always dealt honorably with Mexicans and Indians and all other neighbors or inferiors, that American men are the world's most direct and virile, that American women are pure."[9] Baldwin transforms the exclusion of the "American Negro" from the white myth into the Other's "great advantage." His keen skepticism produces a liberated critical space from which to expose the myth as white America's great self-flattering racist fantasy. Moreover, he implicitly speaks not just for Black America but also for every nationality and ethnicity and skin color historically made to play the abject and doomed foil to the white American hero, for American Indians, Mexicans and Filipinos, Japanese and Koreans, Vietnamese, and Iraqis. Despite his genius in describing and identifying the white heroic myth and its racist presumptions, Baldwin here at least seems to revel a bit too much in his own clear-eyed understanding of the Black American's status as outsider to the myth. Surely his acuity allows him to understand, if only implicitly, the imminent threat—visceral, vindictive, rancorous, and in so many different ways cruel—that the myth, both because of and despite its delusions, poses to Black Americans.

The centuries of white antagonism against Black Americans enact at home what the myth seeks to achieve abroad, namely the radical defenselessness of the Other. In an essay on white racist interpretations of "self-defense" and how the term itself tends to favor white over Black, historian Carol Anderson analyzes the contrast between the 2014 case of Jessie Murray Jr., a Black Georgia man who shot one of the five white racists pummeling him outside a bar, with two notorious cases of white men wounding or killing Black youths. One of these white men is Bernhard Goetz, dubbed by the press the "Subway Vigilante." In 1984 Goetz shot four Black youths whom he claimed were threatening him on the train. The second is George Zimmerman, of Hispanic American descent, who stalked, accosted, and fatally shot seventeen-year-old Trayvon Martin in Sanford, Florida, in 2012. Neither white man was found guilty of murder (Zimmerman) or of attempted murder (Goetz). Almost three years after the shooting in Georgia, Murray was allowed to plead guilty to a lesser charge and was given five years' probation. Anderson concludes that "behind the cases of Bernhard Goetz, George Zimmerman, and Jessie Murray, Jr., is a legacy of laws originally created to make it easier for white people to defend themselves against the Black people they enslaved, who were defined as 'dangerous' because they wanted desperately to be free."[10]

Marked and perverted by centuries of disempowerment, the Black legacy is one in which, in the words of journalist Trymaine Lee, "instead of wealth, millions of Black families have passed down something else from one generation to the next: the mental and emotional stress that results from the constant threat of white violence and financial insecurity."[11] The grossly unjust treatment of America's Black citizens and the laws and rulings themselves that presume to enforce such treatment are readily recognizable in the imperial narratives of the white myth. Indeed, the inherited defenselessness of Black Americans, such as Anderson presents it in her essay, fits as but a species within the larger class of mythic narratives that of themselves produce, promote, and determine—that always and already inaugurate—the inherent and ineradicable doom of the Other. The iterations of the myth require a more formidable weapon than even the firearm, namely the "war machine," as Viet Thanh Nguyen calls the Hollywood film production enterprise: "In war machines, the bristling armaments are on display, but more important are the ideas, ideologies, fantasies and words that justify war, the sacrifices of our side, and the death of others."[12] This "war machine," moreover, produces myth and calls it history. It generates American "memory," which is first and last white memory. "Likewise," Nguyen continues, "an industry of memory includes the material and ideological forces that determine how and why memories are produced and circulated, and who has access to, and control of, the memory industries."[13]

James Q. Whitman's research shows the extent to which American race laws and extralegal practices, especially in the form of Jim Crow laws, influenced the Nazis as they came together in the spring of 1934 to draft the framework for the virulently anti-Semitic documents that would come to be known as the Nuremberg Laws. "Indeed," Whitman writes, "Nazis almost never mentioned the American treatment of blacks without also mentioning the American treatment of other groups, in particular Asians and Native Americans: To them what 'Nordic' America faced, was not just the 'Negro problem,' but the problems of 'Mongols,' of Indians, of Filipinos, and of innumerable other non-'Nordic' groups trying to 'push their way in.'"[14] The near century of abused rights suffered by Black Americans during Jim Crow easily enough accommodated, so to say, other ethnic groups that had historically endured a recognizably similar outrage. But perhaps a kindred if unacknowledged scandal stemmed from the bleak, disheartening irony implicit in such an all-encompassing hostility, namely that America's "exceptional" character, especially as projected by the heroic myth, somehow modeled and indeed provided an epistemic foundation for Nazism, the most virulent racism that the world would ever know. A nation yet young, one that had passionately defined itself as an exception to the grotesque moral excesses of two millennia of European history, suddenly found its own narrative heavily referenced in evil's ambitious desiderata.

In a fundamental way, then, whiteness itself is the legacy, the authorizing and empowering legacy. In William Faulkner's masterpiece *Absalom, Absalom!*, Henry Sutpen, son of the patriarch Thomas Sutpen with his white wife Ellen, urges his sister Judith's marriage to their half brother Charles Bon almost as soon as he makes Charles's acquaintance. Incest is no obstacle, if only because Henry so desperately loves Charles. But when Thomas tells Henry that Charles is "part negro," Henry kills Charles to prevent the marriage.[15] Toni Morrison took Henry Sutpen's "choice" as the clear sign of white America's obsession with race and racial purity. "Unlike any nation in Europe," she wrote in the *New Yorker* soon after the presidential election of 2016, "the United States holds whiteness as the unifying force. Here, for many people, the definition of 'Americanness' is color."[16] And the white obsession with color, she maintained, was born of and sustained by racial fear. "William Faulkner," Morrison concluded, "understood this better than almost any other American writer. In 'Absalom, Absalom' incest is less of a taboo for an upper-class Southern family than acknowledging the one drop of black blood that would clearly soil the family line. Rather than lose its 'whiteness' (once again), the family chooses murder."

As a legacy in itself, whiteness must be zealously safeguarded. In contrast with the gilded if overripe racial zeal that compels Henry to murder Charles, Morrison's protagonist, Sethe, in *Beloved* obeys the compulsion—an imperative morally inaccessible to the Sutpen men—to murder her own baby daughter in order to save her from the horrors of slavery. "I won't never let her go," Sethe says in the great interior monologue that casts the brutal murder of her baby as an act of supreme love. "I'll explain to her, even though I don't have to. Why I did it. How if I hadn't killed her she would have died and that is something I could not bear to happen to her."[17] The memory—or in this case rememory—of slavery produces the Black woman's own dread version of "the fate worse than death."

Henry's murder of Charles Bon for his racial "impurity" speaks therefore to the perversity that undergirds the whiteness of the myth: even your own brother—whom you love dearly—can be sacrificed on the altar of white "purity." The same perversity, moreover, stands as a dire warning to all racial Others. Sethe, however, chooses—however dark and dispiriting, it is still a choice, still the affirmation of an undiminished devotion—her baby daughter's freedom from the only "legacy" available to her as a Black child, the legacy of slavery. Sethe's choice becomes thereby the devastatingly and unspeakably tragic donation, the only freedom available to the enslaved. "Chattel slavery," as Nikole Hannah-Jones reminds us, "was not conditional but racial. It was *heritable* and permanent, not temporary, meaning generations of Black people were born into it and passed their enslaved status on to their children."[18] Enslaved Black people were to be known by this thorough inversion of white privilege so that we would come to know the enslaved not only by the color of their skin but also by their obligation to the very opposite of the entitlements that defined white preeminence. "Enslaved people," Hannah-Jones reminds us, "had no claim to their own children" unless, as in Sethe's case, murder would have to do for a claim.

The heroic myth sublimates white rage (Morrison might say "white fear") into righteousness, violence into justice, and power into racial prerogative. And history, according to the myth (which poses as history), only reiterates the ascendance of white America over the diverse host of conquered Others. The City on a Hill, American exceptionalism, manifest destiny, westward expansion, America First, and of course "MAGA" are all notions, whether invoked as guiding doctrines or tossed about as coded buzzwords, enigmatic gestures, or partisan shibboleths, that imply a foreordained fulfillment of the heroic legacy by each successive American generation so long as the nation remains "white." Thus, whiteness presumes to sustain the sundry delusions of the heroic myth, its delusion of moral right, for example, or of divinely sanctioned socioeconomic privilege, or of that primal innocence by which the myth would ignore its many wrongs and enfold them into higher national purposes, would transmute its sins into self-vindicating errands into the wilderness.

## Heroic Destinies and the Anxiety of Legacy

Each successive American generation narrates the account of its own heroic time, thus earning its own distinctive place and identity in the myth of heroic continuity. But place and identity became merely the deed and testament of participation, of inclusion, say, in the one all-encompassing vision that subsumed possibility, change, and novelty to a continuity that inherently resisted the freshness of the very impulse that revived it and that carried it to a new historical reality. The heroic myth scorns all avowals of the differences between history and myth: every new generation would take the myth for the history, without any but the most insignificant distinctions. It is the hallmark of exceptionalism that American history should be the stuff and essence of the heroic, of the epic, of the transcendent. This blurring of the differences between myth and history demonstrates the steady and unerring guidance of a divine dispensation. Yet, that which might have seemed settled at the end of the most recent mythic triumph still somehow failed to prevent the reemergence of the familiar national disquiet, of the haunting, enervating doubt. The victory that had lately seemed so fair and righteous and so entitling suddenly appeared as if implicated in the rise of the new, the unforeseen crisis, almost as if America's millenarian purpose, invoked in every one of its wars, was now somehow a spiteful deception, the inscrutable, cruel drollery of divine Providence. Considered in its ironic mode, then, the myth of heroic continuity contained a fatal and yet defining paradox: it unfolded toward a destiny that it could fulfill only by in effect failing to do so. A generation's heroic work is never done until it has passed its own legacy to the younger generation, and if there is indeed a legacy to pass on, then the older generation's work of establishing the millennial dispensation has in fact failed.

America's heroic destiny was the irresistible current that bore the generations to the fulfillment of their patriotic obligation. Yet, somehow this destiny remained only partly consummated. Once loose in Vietnam, America's offenses would reveal both the moral ambiguity and the conceptual fallacies of the narratives that the new generation had taken on faith. In Vietnam the myth of heroic continuity foundered, and for the first time in American history, a generation earned its identity not for a destined victory but instead for an unaccountable Loss. This breach in the continuity of the heroic myth is the great distinguishing feature of American Vietnam War narratives. Broadly speaking, part 2 addresses narratives of the rupture, analyses supported by both literary and historical texts of the historic break with the heroic myth. Thus, the movies that I address in part 1—*Fort Apache* and *The Real Glory* in chapter 1 and *Sands of Iwo Jima* in chapter 2—unfold the master narrative of a heroic America. When arranged by their represented historical eras—from the frontier West immediately after the Civil War to the Philippine-American War to World War II—these movies give a clear sense of the terms, values, and ideals that Hollywood movies of the Vietnam War tend to break from. Taken, however, in the order of their release, *Fort Apache* and *Sands of Iwo Jima* commemorate America's heroic triumphs even as they narrate reactions to a world much different from the one at the end of World War II. The release of *The Real Glory* predates that of both *Fort Apache* and *Sands*; but it comes at the end of more than four decades of Hollywood Westerns and, more important, unabashedly presents the American war against the Moros in the southernmost islands of the Philippine archipelago as an Indian Western. Aside from their release dates or even the historical wars that they claim to represent, these movies would continue to play in America's theaters well into the late 1950s and beyond. They thus acquired a liturgical, sacramental character that entitled the new generation as it grew up to take them as nostrums for the anticipated end times and to embrace them as promises of their own heroic birthright. Unapologetic epics, these movies nonetheless aspired to the condition of history: American history, they implied, is the stuff of myth. But the very effusiveness of their triumphalism conveyed the anxiety that they imagined themselves at once denying and contesting. And the more acclaimed and uncontested the victory in these narratives, the more intensely felt the disquiet of their subtext at the heart of which lies what I term the "anxiety of legacy."

## The President, the Duke, and Their "Superb Children"

In the first minute or so of Ken Burns and Lynn Novick's eighteen-hour documentary *The Vietnam War* (2017), a film clip of a small-town America Fourth of July parade in the late 1950s or early 1960s shows a float on which half a dozen boys in combat uniforms, even though they seem short of draft age, lean forward together to right the Stars and Stripes attached to a pole. The wheeled tableau, unmistakably evoking Joe Rosenthal's famous photograph atop Mount Suribachi on February 23, 1945, commemorates the American victory on Iwo Jima even as it introduces the community to its future heroes. Perhaps these young innocents are hoping for glory atop a Suribachi of their own. But the reenactment suggests a more complex relation to America's past than the boys might have gleaned from such a moment. Although they eagerly remind us of the glorious moment, they themselves know nothing of the horrors that the moment conceals. Having skipped the hell that was Iwo Jima, they nonetheless lay claim to a hero's renown. Such is, in condensed form, the heroic vision promoted by Hollywood movies of the Cold War era for the eager and compliant consumption of youngsters such as the parading flag raisers. Anything like the pain or the terror or the grief that gave context to that original moment on February 23, 1945, was certain to be drowned out in cheers of victory. In Vietnam, however, far from flags and parades and from anything resembling jubilation, the boys' dear myth, having proved a fraud in the fields of fire, turned against them and heaped upon them—and then luridly illuminated—a great shame, for they had lost their war.

At the beginning of a new decade, President John F. Kennedy declared that Americans were "proud of our ancient heritage." Spurred as insistently by American ascendancy following World War II as by the dangers of the Cold War, the president seemed justifiably compelled to "let every nation know" that the "torch had been passed" to the sons and daughters of our latest heroes. Kennedy inspired the Vietnam generation to "pay any price, bear any burden, meet any hardship." This inaugural America fanned a generation's hopes for a contest recognizably like its fathers' own. World War II would be their cynosure, and they would fight heroically in an equally just war. Those boys on the small-town parade float were not just reenacting; they were training.

Even as Kennedy warned youths that the world "was very different now," he appointed them "heirs of that first revolution." The heroic myth, moreover, sustained their desire for war; theirs was accordingly a longing heedless of historical tragedy and utterly bereft of foresight. This mystified history inspired, authorized, and promoted what I call the "heroic imperative" (discussed chiefly in chapter 4): young Americans would bear witness to history with a zealot's faith. Only time could show them what neither history nor myth could, namely that their essential and distinct achievement would itself source their own generational tragedy. And the enduring woe of even the most righteous war would soon enough expose the persistent hubris of American history and of American myth alike, all of it, unsurprisingly, as their lifelong burden.

But Kennedy's inaugural address merely endorsed the values that the new heirs had repeatedly seen defended and upheld in Hollywood's Westerns and war movies. That which we more or less compliantly term "generic convention" offered a generation the model and pattern of the indispensable affirmations, the measured ceremonies of righteous violence, and the solemnities of grief that portended a final exultation—rituals all at once oracular, exemplary, and paradoxical—through which the young heirs innocently prefigured their own heroic deeds. To those who came of draft age during the Vietnam War, Hollywood's West and its World War II far surpassed their cultural role as "entertainment." They incited the young to deeds worthy of their birthright and held out the promise, as Walt Whitman had described seven decades earlier, "of superb children and therein superb grown people."[19]

It is impossible to overestimate the influence of John Wayne on the Vietnam generation. Christian G. Appy is only among the latest cultural historians to note "just how important John Wayne was as a boyhood fantasy figure among soldiers who fought in Vietnam."[20] But more than half a century earlier, Joan Didion recalled, as if in a child's openhearted rapture, an apotheosized, transcendent Wayne, the hero as artificer of dreams and destiny both: "when John Wayne rode through my childhood," Didion wrote, "and perhaps through yours, he determined forever the shape of certain of our dreams."[21] For many of the Vietnam generation, Wayne provided an otherwise absent model of American heroism. He enacted that which the young fathers couldn't or wouldn't, either because they did not survive the war or because they were too traumatized to talk about it (hence, perhaps, the origin of that notorious silence characteristic of the veterans of World War II). In their impressionable childhood, many who grew up to serve in Vietnam could not have imagined that Wayne had never enlisted, let alone seen actual combat. Yet, Wayne's movie heroism radiated a sense of America's righteous might, and the young, in token of their innocence, found in it a force that justified their own heroic aspirations. Moreover, Wayne's heroic figure projected something like a historical ubiquity, an American hero coeval with just that moment before "we were the land's" (as the Robert Frost poem puts it) and thereafter present in every subsequent historic victory.[22] Wayne therefore, alone among all the Hollywood male stars, personifies the continuity of the heroic legacy. And even as the younger generation shipped to Vietnam, Wayne played the hero in the only major American movie of the Vietnam War to be exhibited during the years of the war, *The Green Berets.*

Yet, Wayne's personification (and performance) of the mythic virtues seems forever tarnished by the historical fact of his failure to serve in his own generation's war. In this way, he embodies not only the mythic virtues but also, at the same time, the scandalously ironic turn that those virtues took in Vietnam when the long-since betrayed grunts came to know Wayne's "legacy" for a craven deception. "Even in Vietnam," notes Christian Appy, "many GIs turned on their childhood hero. They saw [Wayne] as a dangerous and fraudulent model of swaggering bravado."[23] Before Vietnam, the testimony of the children would consistently and repeatedly summon up Wayne as their chief heroic muse. After Vietnam, they would attest to their dismay and their bitterness, and then they would inveigh against the erstwhile hero now turned Moloch.

All of this is true enough, but none of it, neither the deception nor the betrayal nor the bitterness, makes Wayne any less important to the Vietnam generation or to this book.

## Victory and the Hero, Loss and the Scapegoat

Winning without ever once losing, we never knew whether Americans, once they lost a war—a *war*, mind you, not just this or that battle—could still be anointed as heroes. Amassing the spoils of war and decreeing the terms of peace are as nothing in the afterglow of victory to the crucial prize, namely the restored cultural faith in the providential dispensation that graced the previous generations. Winning, at least in the vivid flush of victory, tended to dispel national self-doubt. But winning also veiled (or presumed to veil) all that was bleak and despairing and calamitous in war. Taken not as an outcome but as an essential feature of national identity, victory transmuted historical tragedy into a reaffirmation of America's foundational myth. Privileged over everything else in the heroic myth, victory determined right. Victory therefore amounted to a providential avowal of America's exceptional status among the nations of the world. Divine acquiescence in America's successes in war revealed not only a bounteous and everlasting testator of the heroic legacy but also the actual originator of that legacy. As well might have America's heroic identity, along with its imperial privilege, been prefigured in the Creation itself.

But what about *losing* a war? So unthinkable an outcome would in turn produce conspiracies to unearth, cabals to identify, portents to interpret, and sins to atone for. Losing a war meant nothing less than divine censure. During the decade and a half that began with Kennedy's inaugural address in 1961, successive American presidents agonized more about being held politically and historically accountable for the Loss than for the lives lost or wrecked or the treasure spent in the war. "I don't think anything is going to be as bad as losing,"[24] President Lyndon Johnson said in late February 1965, mere days before he ordered the bombing of North Vietnam (Operation Rolling Thunder, begun March 2). Less than a week later, the first two combat battalions of US marines landed in Da Nang (March 8, 1965). In a draft memorandum of March 24, 1965, Assistant Secretary of Defense John McNaughton wondered whether the "situation inside" South Vietnam could be "bottomed out" short of the "deployment of large numbers of US (and other) combat troops inside SVN." McNaughton then tried to "get closer to an answer . . . by restating U.S. objectives in Vietnam, and by attempting to weigh these objectives by their relative importance."[25] Hence his grim reckoning of American priorities in Vietnam, early in 1965:

> 70%—To avoid a humiliating US defeat (to our reputation as a guarantor).
> 20%—To keep SVN [South Vietnam] (and then adjacent) territory from Chinese hands.
> 10%—To permit the people of SVN to enjoy a better, freer way of life.
> ALSO—To emerge from crisis without unacceptable taint from methods used.
> NOT—To "help a friend," although it would be hard to stay in if asked out.[26]

And America's young soldiers in Vietnam had no inkling of the crass calculus that aimed to measure their devotion to the heroic myth by the grotesque indignity of a loss deferred.

## The One Lost War

Throughout much of the time spent with my topic, I found it increasingly impossible not to suspect that a perverse sort of efficacy animates postwar declarations that, except for Vietnam, America had never lost a war. The Loss named a forsworn birthright, and its implicit censure of a generation would so plague Vietnam's aftermath as to attempt to reinstate and reauthorize the myth of heroic continuity, that is, invoking the myth's integrity in the era before Vietnam and then after, Vietnam alluding fearfully and ominously to the Loss even as the nation rushed to new wars of dubious purpose that would themselves inevitably recall Vietnam. At all costs we were to avoid "another Vietnam" in Afghanistan and Iraq, and the more we did so the more the new wars recalled it so that the warnings themselves became the thing warned against. Thus, if America's Vietnam marked the end of a glorious past, it also animated the hope of reinstating, however tendentiously, heroic continuity. Hence, a typical expression of Vietnam's ironies after Vietnam: if we were going to avoid it, we would have to invoke it, remember it.

In one of the fundamental ironies of an already too ironic war, the Loss itself animates the triumphal tale of consecutive victories. The Loss casts them as many triumphs to its own singular tragedy. In its role as foil—as the narrative of the rupture, then—the Loss tells of its own exclusion from an exalted history and of the tragic estrangement of a generation from its heroic patrimony. Vietnam would accordingly play a pivotal role in the professed resumptions of continuity in subsequent wars. No longer agonizing about the war's outcome, as Kennedy, Johnson, and Nixon had, each post-Vietnam president seems to have inhabited his own echo chamber of revisionist history—or rather of resurrected myth—regarding Vietnam. President Ronald Reagan anointed Rambo as a Republican—meaning, one assumes, that in the reprise of the Vietnam War in *Rambo: First Blood Part II* (Cosmatos, 1985) America had in fact gotten "to win this time," as Rambo puts it at the beginning. A few years earlier, however, during the presidential campaign of 1980 (only five years after the collapse of South Vietnam), Reagan declared at the national convention of the Veterans of Foreign Wars that "it is time we recognized that ours was, in truth, a noble cause."[27] We ask, however, had it ever been necessary to *say* of any previous American war that it had been a noble cause? Had noble causes not defined all American wars, if only because they could be justified by the resulting victories? Why call it a "noble cause" if not because the Loss always and already determined Vietnam's unique identity? But "why" is ever the loser's question. Winners never ask why except to exult in the will of the gods. If a war is not victory, then at least it is a noble cause.

America would therefore remember Vietnam by clumsy calls to national amnesia. "By God, we've kicked the Vietnam syndrome once and for all," crowed President George H. W. Bush just after the 1991 Persian Gulf War as if a victory in Kuwait would forever erase Vietnam, the "syndrome," from American history. If the myth of heroic continuity was to undergo rehabilitation in American culture, Vietnam would still be the revenant ghoul demanding a reckoning, and the greater the compulsion to put it out of mind the more lurid its presence. The cruel invidiousness of Bush's reference to Vietnam reaffirmed the rupture precisely for trying to consign it to oblivion. On May 1, 2003, more than a decade after his father's proclaimed success in exorcising the demons of Vietnam, George W. Bush, arrayed in full flight uniform and helmet, rode along in a Lockheed Viking S-3 that landed on the aircraft carrier USS *Abraham Lincoln.*

Bush approached the news cameras and proceeded to announce the end of "major combat operations in Iraq." Waving conspicuously over him, a gigantic banner hanging from the carrier's bridge declared "Mission Accomplished." This latest American war, begun only six weeks earlier, had been lightning quick, and victory had been decisive according to both the banner and the speech. Here at last was the desired "closure," and the American public, which had feared another Vietnam, could rest easy. Yet, the son's gasconade, far more grandiose than his father's own, veiled the gross deception and the dubious alchemy claiming to have wrought a "mission accomplished" out of six weeks' worth of war that yielded, in time, only the leaden realization that here again in Iraq (as in Afghanistan, now eighteen months in) America faced something very much like another Vietnam. In the years after May 2003, the rupture seems to have claimed an essential role in American war narratives. In a way, the rupture manifested a continuity of its own. Its language and its tropes pervaded the justificatory rhetoric of Iraq and Afghanistan, insinuating themselves into their every phase from the blind headlong drive toward yet more imperial wars to the dark portents, as in John McNaughton's memo expressing the dread of a national "humiliation."

In general, Hollywood's pre-Vietnam wars, taken up not only with World War II but also in allusions to that war in Indian Westerns, demonstrate the persistence of the heroic myth and stress the crucial role of a heroic inheritance in the continual unfolding of America's special destiny. Broadly considered, these are narratives of what one might call generational entitlement as well as of the struggle to preserve it and transfer it. The parallels between *Fort Apache* (chapter 1) and *Sands of Iwo Jima* (chapter 2) extend far beyond the mere presence in both movies of the basic dramatic relationship between actors John Wayne and John Agar. Both narratives underscore the essential need of their time (the Cold War) to both envision and ensure the continuity of American exceptionalism. It seems beyond coincidence that in the four decades of the Cold War, Hollywood turned repeatedly to America's wars against people of color that it might thereby extol and promote the heroic myth. Not surprisingly, a pre–World War II war movie, Henry Hathaway's *The Real Glory* (chapter 2), about America's war against the Filipino Moros, takes up the trope of heroic inheritance but only to establish the absurdity that a child of color (and a Muslim at that) should be a proper heir. In this way, *The Real Glory* presages America's imperial condescension toward the Other in *The Green Berets* (see chapter 3).

History contests the mythic narratives that presume to chronicle it faithfully. Thus, one of the uses of history in this book involves examining the documented events that the movies purport to narrate: the Apache Wars of the late 1880s in *Fort Apache* and the struggle for Iwo Jima toward the end of World War II. But these mythic narratives urge us to consider them also in light of important events, both foreign and domestic, unfolding even as they were playing at a theater near you, in other words, some four or five years after the end of World War II. For example, the sheer quantity of near-cataclysmic events in 1949, at the end of which *Sands of Iwo Jima* was released, informs the representation of the battle in that year. The film defines America's resolve against the communist threat even as it narrates the prevailing national anxiety of the time. The battle that in 1945 vitally advanced America's cause against the Japanese aggressor is the battle that, in the context of 1949, might look very much like the model of America's imperial wars on the Indian frontiers or in the Philippines—or later in Vietnam—against a people said to threaten Anglo-American hegemony. Thus, the historical battle redirects the victory over Japan toward a now (and new) foreshadowed "twilight struggle," as President Kennedy put it, against global communism. What was it, then, to screen *Sands of Iwo Jima* against the background of its own historical references (including the famous photograph of the second flag raising and the nearly neglected photograph of the first one)? How did such a movie, released almost half a decade after the battle, assert the need for a new generation of heroes? And how did that generation, still not quite weaned from dreams of heroic deeds, find inspiration in this display of America's virtues?

Vietnam War movies as different from each other as *The Green Berets* and *Full Metal Jacket* (Kubrick, 1987) reflect the historical verdict: even the clumsily triumphalist *Green Berets* made American anxiety and lack of national resolve an integral part of its story, things all but absent from John Wayne's versions of World War II. Also, the Hollywood Vietnam narrative denies Americans the victory so inevitably expected in movies of previous wars: think, for example, of the climactic confrontation in *Apocalypse Now* (Coppola, 1979), where the American protagonist/narrator hacks the disgraced American hero to pieces on orders from his commanders; or of the final face-off with the enemy in *Full Metal Jacket*, which pits a Viet Cong sniper against a squad of young US marines, all of them stunned to realize that the deadly enemy, already responsible for three American deaths, is in fact an English-speaking teenage girl. Consider, moreover, that the American flag, so prominent and potent a symbol in *Fort Apache, The Real Glory*, and, of course, *Sands of Iwo Jima*, is not memorably present, let alone explicitly exalted, in movies of the Vietnam War. And scarce as the American flag is in Vietnam narratives, the mythic hero, Wayne in *Green Berets* notwithstanding, is far more so. Vietnam, one might say, is where John Wayne becomes Marlon Brando.

## A Note on "History" and "Myth"

The appeal to history for the sake of debunking national myths assumes uncritically the most naive senses of both history and myth. And the same critical strategy often betrays a willful indifference to their interactions. Such a mode of criticism takes on dubious faith the authority of a master narrative deployed solely for the sake of rendering all others inferior, deceptive, frivolous, superfluous. My study of the heroic legacy begins by referencing Richard Slotkin's magisterial three-volume account of America's "regeneration through violence." "Myth," Slotkin writes late in the third volume, *Gunfighter Nation*, "is the language in which a society remembers its history."[28] I take the statement not on faith, though it has long struck me as especially fruitful, but as a working definition enabling me to announce my method as the sustained exploration of the intertwined expressions of its principal terms, "myth" and "history."

Myth and history, then, cannot stand in relation to each other only as narrative to counternarrative, for we meet them always and already in a process of reciprocal influence, and as the one seems to tease out the one thread from the other, so it also spins its own narrative strands, thus refreshing, redirecting, and redefining a new unfolding pattern continually in a process of becoming. We can appeal to history's function as either corrective or corroborative of a myth, or we can invoke history as a source of irony: this book gives ample evidence of such uses. But we had best not conclude that by doing so we have exploded the myth or revised the history. A myth that persists through a nation's memory is all too often a myth taken, if often at great peril, for gospel history. Moreover, mythologies are perfectly capable of generating their own historical consequences. The danger of taking myth for history is seldom apparent before the tragedy of doing so has come to pass, hence America's Vietnam War.

*The Real Glory*, which I discuss in chapter 1, shapes the myth by its exclusion of a racial Other from any possible heroic legacy. At the end, the Filipino Muslim boy, despite his sacrifices on behalf of the white community, can aspire only to the condition of abject servitude, which, not surprisingly, he undertakes all too cheerfully. Soon after World War II, however, and in the context of the Cold War, the heroic legacy takes on a new urgency. *Fort Apache* and *Sands of Iwo Jima* stress not only the necessity of the heroic inheritance but also the requisite terms of its fulfillment.

Chapter 3 addresses the persistence of John Wayne and the heroic legacy during the time of the war. *The Green Berets*, released in the tumultuous year 1968, narrates not a later iteration of the relation between the hero and his heir but rather a condemnation, thinly veiled if at all, of the younger generation. At the end Wayne remains the hero, vampirically haunting the heroic myth, and an infantilized Other remains the mocking wisp of the young would-be American who never inherited his heroic due.

Chapter 4 traces the post–World War II generation's innocent enthusiasm for its heroic birthright, only to suffer the crushing sense of tragedy reflected in the resisting, unreconciled yet decisive repudiation of that birthright hard upon the irrefragable Loss. The movies I treat in chapters 5 and 6 narrate the Vietnam War as and through their own antimyth, recombining the elemental tropes of the myth of heroic continuity and yielding instead a clear and palpable sense of the Vietnam War's historical (and historic) tragedy. The Loss is therefore not so much a military defeat as a fall from the providential benediction that the heroic myth lays claim to. Chapter 7 begins with a critique of a late November 1977 two-hour documentary that aired on ABC TV titled *Oscar Presents: The War Movies and John Wayne* in which Wayne, who had already made his last movie (*The Shootist*, 1976), assumes the triple task of host, Hollywood historian, and hero. This documentary, a last-gasp attempt to relive the glory of Hollywood's World War II, narrated the anxiety of an industry that had released but one movie of the Vietnam War. Hollywood war glory, loudly enough trumpeted in the documentary, might remind us that we could wallow in war nostalgia and happily forget Vietnam.

*Oscar Presents: The War Movies and John Wayne* aired less than a year before the first wave of important Vietnam movies, in 1978. One of them, *The Deer Hunter*, which Wayne is said to have hated, won the Oscar for best picture in 1979; then, in a sort of supplementary irony, Wayne, here in his last public appearance, handed the Oscar for that same objectionably un-American movie to the winning filmmakers. Earlier in the same ceremony, Jane Fonda, once roundly reviled for the photos showing her cheerily behind a North Vietnamese antiaircraft battery, won the Oscar for best actress in *Coming Home*, that is, for portraying a marine's unfaithful wife who turns against the war. Wayne's kind of war movie—even perhaps his kind of Western—had predeceased him.

Laconic, often dispassionate, almost always cynical (in a way that Wayne seldom is), ever deadly, and for the most part nihilistically unconcerned with the transfer of a heroic legacy, Clint Eastwood's heroic persona arrives at its most improbable moment in *Gran Torino* (Eastwood, 2008), in which a cancer-ridden veteran of the Korean War must urgently and radically reenvision his idea of the Other, an Other, it stands noting, with roots in Vietnam and the Vietnam War. In a way, Eastwood's *American Sniper* (2014) evokes the trail of dead bodies that the Eastwood hero can look back upon after half a century's worth of movie-made carnage. *American Sniper* attempts to reconnect with the mythic origins of the American hero principally by establishing a heroic lineage for the protagonist, Chris Kyle, in the Iraq War, a war meant in part to redeem the Loss. But in presuming to ignore the persistence of the rupture beginning with the Loss, *American Sniper* instead recalls it. In its own unavoidable convergence of history and myth—and specifically in the connections between the personal and the public Chris Kyle—*American Sniper* echoes the Vietnam War's dark judgment on the American soul.

# PART I

# CHAPTER 1

# "Heirs of Natty Bumppo"; or, What Mrs. Collingwood Saw

## Westering Empires and the Heroic Inheritance in *Fort Apache* and *The Real Glory*

> We are all heirs of Natty Bumppo, and cannot escape our heritage.
>
> —Perry Miller, *Errand into the Wilderness*

> I, for one, hope that Uncle Sam will apply the chastening rod, good, hard, and plenty . . . until [the Filipinos] come into the reservation and promise to be good "Injuns."
>
> —Brig. Gen. Frederick Funston

> It was merely a piece of public work much as the Army has had to do many times in our own west.
>
> —Rowland Thomas, veteran of the Massacre at Bud Dajo, 1906

> The Philippines . . . was finally subdued after a protracted "pacification" campaign that foreshadowed U.S. strategy in Vietnam.
>
> —Stanley Karnow, *Vietnam: A History*

## *Fort Apache* (1948) and the Heroic Patrimony

*Fort Apache*, like the two other Indian Westerns that followed it in John Ford's cavalry trilogy—*She Wore a Yellow Ribbon* (1949) and *Rio Grande* (1950)—dramatizes the Cold War era's deep anxiety about the new generation of Americans. In this respect, *Fort Apache* asks whether, like the honored American ancestry, the young scions of World War II heroes will earn their heroic inheritance. In *Fort Apache*'s historical timeline—1861–1886, that is, the quarter century of the Apache Wars—the latest inheritance will reprise the previous struggle: just as the older generation fought Cochise, the younger will soon ride out in pursuit of Geronimo. Thus, in the final scene, when the cavalry goes after Geronimo, any renewal—any "regeneration" wrought of "violence" in the form, say, of new nuptials, a newborn, and new promotions up the ranks—remains complicit with a tradition of wars of questionable moral purpose. Still, for the white community now assembled as if in a tableau of racial federation, there shall be no doubt of the coming war's righteousness or of its outcome. Right and privilege and the assurance of triumph are themselves the inheritance.

In *Fort Apache*, two American generations contest the Apaches for possession of the desert Southwest. The generational trope becomes vital to the movie's vision, at once mirrored and projected, of America moving ever into the next one of those "successive frontiers" whose three hundred–year sweep Frederick Jackson Turner described as America's "national character."[1] In the last decade of the nineteenth century, the deep tracks of conquest over the continental empire pointed reassuringly to transpacific realms, and a young nation still and again "fac[ed] West from California's shores," as Walt Whitman put it.[2] And still and again it was a nation eager, unfaltering, high-minded, and all too ambitious, its promulgated innocence itself a portent of its tragedy. Westward expansion had been only the spatial and temporal manifestation of a recurrent claim to the abiding enjoyment of grace and favor manifested not only as a divine predilection for America over other nations but also as an outright prepossession. And now in 1948 following the victory over Japan, it was possible to look back across what had once been howling wastes and affirm the providential dispensation that again seemed to tender its special favor to a heroic people. History itself seemed to confirm the benediction. America had never lost a war, and "all" that was needed for the continuation of so high a privilege was the transmission and transference of that blessing to the next generation. And heroic continuity—history transcendent yet abiding as the birthright of a "peculiar people"—would, as always before, inspire all young heirs to mythic deeds fully worthy of their fathers' own.

The last nineteenth-century phase of the genocide of North America's indigenous population, culminating in the massacre at Wounded Knee in late December 1890, cannot have been incidental upon the official announcement that America's frontier settlement was irreversibly closed. The Indian had been in large measure the living definition of frontier. Now, however, the *Extra Census Bulletin* (no. 2, 1891) of the eleventh census (1890) concluded with a grave pronouncement: "In the discussion of its extent, its westward movement, etc. it can not, therefore, any longer have a place in the census reports."[3] Without a frontier—which is to say in human terms without the Indian—there could be no heroic succession. Frontiers past had always been alive in the current frontier, directing the drive toward the continual fulfillment of a special destiny, ever at the expense of the "vanished" Indian. So, myth—taken as the special and privileged narrative of foundation—was to be America's response to the historical crisis created by the closing of the frontier. Myth would appropriate history and transcend it, would refashion it into a sort of national rapture. The rise of the frontier myth in the last half decade of the nineteenth century found both expression and confirmation in the expansion of the frontier across the Pacific. And the movies, though in their most primitive form, were already there, not so much to document historical events as to reanimate the heroic myth. At the very time that America seemed resigned to abandon the western frontier as the narrative site of a thriving national identity, the movies established their readiness to reinvigorate and exalt the tropes that had long sustained the so-called American character.

Considered in the historical context of its 1948 release, however, when the Cold War, so soon after World War II, was already an epochal reality, *Fort Apache* elucidates and models the urgent need for a distinctively American response to the dangers that now bedeviled the nation. This pressing renewal of the heroic myth—the reconsecration of not only American heroism but also its continuity—remains palpably evident, indeed, thematically dominant, in *Fort Apache.* It is perhaps because *Fort Apache* implicitly looks to America's struggles ahead more than to its past glories that Michael Herr determined it to be "more a war movie than a Western, Nam Paradigm, Vietnam."[4]

The action unfolds as follows: Lt. Col. Owen Thursday (Henry Fonda), irascible martinet and American Civil War general by brevet—a "West

Point aristo wounded in his career and his pride," as Herr puts it—travels westward with his daughter Philadelphia (Shirley Temple) to take command of Fort Apache, a posting that he considers beneath his dignity.[5] In the absence of a senior officer, Capt. Kirby York (John Wayne) has commanded this hinterland outpost of manifest destiny. Arriving at the fort at about the same time as the Thursdays is young 2nd Lt. Michael Shannon "Mickey" O'Rourke (John Agar), fresh from West Point. Mickey is the son of Sgt. Maj. Michael O'Rourke (Ward Bond), a Medal of Honor recipient of Irish descent who is joined in the fort by his wife (Irene Rich). The only other commissioned officer of prominence in the narrative is Capt. Sam Collingwood (George O'Brien). Collingwood, whose wife Emily (Anna Lee) has joined him in Fort Apache, has been consistently denied transfer, most likely for drunkenness in the line of duty back during the Civil War. Sgt. Beaufort (Pedro Armendáriz) translates from the Spanish in parleys with Cochise (Miguel Inclán), and a group of noncoms of Irish descent, chief among them Sgt. Festus Mulcahy (Victor McLaglen), completes the roster of the older generation. The Civil War thus becomes to the Apache Wars as World War II became to the Cold War. There are also fresh recruits, most of them from the generation too young to have fought in the Civil War. One of them, an Irish private named Flaherty (Ray Hyke), will rise in the ranks to replace Sgt. Maj. O'Rourke. Once married to Mickey O'Rourke, Philadelphia Thursday, all frippery and frivolity at first, shall inherit the patient, fraught existence of the older army wives. More important, Philadelphia shall give birth to a son, a third-generation heir of the heroic legacy.

The Apaches here are little more than temporary obstacles in the way of America's westward expansion. Perhaps, as we are often told, *Fort Apache*'s Cochise appears more dignified than most Indians in Westerns of that time, but the cloud of dust that covers the victorious Apaches' ride from the battlefield indicates not so much their victory as it does the generic Indian's complicity in his preordained condition as "Vanishing American." It is worth noting that but for Thursday's incorrigible bigotry, the narrative spares the Apaches its most virulent moral judgment and lays it upon the corrupt Indian agent, Silas Meacham (Grant Withers), who cheats the Apaches of their government-allotted beef and sells them rotgut whiskey. Acting on Cochise's complaints, both York and Thursday censure Meacham and warn him about further crimes against the Apaches. The

US Army itself, however, as we are to believe, wants only to return the Apaches to the reservation, even if it has to exterminate them to do so.

## The Ending of *Fort Apache*

The ending of *Fort Apache* reveals the Western's enduringly ambiguous play of myth and history.[6] And much of the critical writing on the ending has tended to focus on that moment when York, lying egregiously, confirms the historical accuracy of Thursday's "last stand" in a painting hanging in Washington, D.C. "That was a magnificent work," remarks one of the four reporters in the scene. "There were these massed columns of Apaches in their war paint and feather bonnets; and here was Thursday, leading his men in that heroic charge." York, in close-up, vacantly deadpans, "Correct in every detail." Of course, we have just witnessed a much different battle, one in which Thursday's incompetence, sourced in his racist contempt for the Apaches, causes the death of all the men under his command. York's lie at the end becomes important not only because he acquiesces in the painting's misrepresentations but also because York's own dealings with Thursday are so strained throughout that we may well doubt the sincerity of his vindication of the now-martyred martinet.

Moments before the battle, the two men clash over the meaning of a cloud of dust far away. Thursday believes it is dust kicked up by the Apaches' horses; York knows it is Apache women and children dragging mesquite branches as a decoy. Thursday accuses York of cowardice; York, outraged, gallops away a bit from Thursday, then whirls his horse around and throws down the gage. Thursday acknowledges the challenge and tells York he will give him satisfaction after the battle. Thursday then leads the charge to his doom, while York, on orders, stays behind with his companies. Moments later, however, when York sees that Thursday is alone, wounded, and dismounted, he rides down to extricate him from the fight. But Thursday commandeers York's horse and saber and rides off to meet his doom beside his men. Before he goes, however, he issues his last order to York: "When you command this regiment, and you probably will, command it." We witness the transfer of a heroic legacy. Thursday, odiously racist and insufferably abrasive, nonetheless dies well, "with his boots on." In the final scene, York exalts Thursday and so integrates him fully, if only by falsifying his memory, into the myth of the regiment; and the sustained glory of the regiment brooks no disharmony.

And truth be told, Thursday, who in life was roundly and condignly despised, manages nonetheless a gracious reconciliation with those he has insulted. Once he rejoins his doomed command, he apologizes to Collingwood for delaying his transfer and to the senior O'Rourke for repeatedly disparaging his Irish ancestry. In this context, York's lie about the "correctness" of the painting integrates the acerbic elitist Thursday into an America that can now claim national unity and identity not only because the Indian is no more but also because the heroic inheritance has been safeguarded. The model for righteous action against the looming communist menace has been laid out for a young generation in the form of an exalted history no different from a foundational myth. The regiment represents an idealized America, its generations reconciled, as are North and South, myth and history, and past, present, and future; hence, for example, York's care in correcting the reporter who refers to Captain Collingwood as "Collingworth" and York's tribute to "the regiment" when another reporter remarks that "we always remember the Thursdays, but the others are forgotten." "You're wrong there," York remonstrates. "They aren't forgotten because they haven't died, Collingwood and the rest. They'll keep on living as long as the regiment lives. The pay is $13.00 a month, their diet beans and hay, maybe horse meat before this campaign is over. . . . The faces may change, and the names; but they're there. They're the regiment, the regular army, now and fifty years from now. They're better men than they used to be. Thursday did that. He made it a command to be proud of." The hero thus lives chiefly through the martyrdom of the numberless unknowns, of "the rest." York in effect promulgates the mythic faith that Walt Whitman attested in the darkest days of the Civil War: "One falls, and another falls. The soldier drops, sinks like a wave—but the ranks of the ocean eternally press on. Death does its work, obliterates a hundred, a thousand—President, general, captain, private—but the Nation is immortal."[7] To be sure, the lie that exalts Thursday and proclaims the regiment's unity also sustains the compromised, self-delusory remembrance that satisfies the nation's appetite for a heroic history. Accordingly, the lie itself invests events with a self-authorizing, self-justifying deception that becomes an exhaustless source of American history. York casts the last moments of Thursday's command in the familiarly mythic terms of Whitman's eulogy for Custer: "The Indian ambuscade, the craft, the fatal environment, / The cavalry companies fighting in sternest heroism."[8] Is it, then, that some such lie or, better yet, *legacy of lies* sustains America's dearest values? And did such lies seduce the children and thus cast them, both and at once, as the hero's exalted successors *and* the dupes of his deceptions?

After York ends his conference with the reporters, he walks out, and there, in the outer office, as if in a tableau of American domestic virtues, stand Mickey O'Rourke, Philadelphia Thursday O'Rourke, Mrs. Michael O'Rourke, and the boy, no older than two here in 1948 and therefore a baby boomer. And now, as if deliberately invoking a baptismal trope, York lifts the toddler up high, pronounces his full name—Michael Thursday York O'Rourke—and declares him "the best man in the regiment." The boy's name reflects the lineage composed of both Irish American and Anglo-American as well as his descent from both a noncommissioned officer and a West Point graduate. Thus, the ending of *Fort Apache* presents the toddler as the inheritor of a birthright that seems suddenly washed clean of blood, appearing before us as if imbued in innocence. And yet, all his names and namesakes are ineluctably bound to blood and guilt. Does he atone for these sins? Can he, when his names already destine him to repeat the deeds of his fathers? For now, though, myth reverses history's course, producing, out of the great genocidal slaughter of the Indian in the howling wilderness, a new prelapsed Adam in the "virgin land."

Heroic continuity, though it may appear necessarily to unfold in time, affirms not so much a process as an enduring bond and celebrates not an evolving, growing, ever-inclusive vision of America but instead a declaration of unrestricted—and unexpired—white generational entitlement. Time passes but to reassert, indeed to emblaze, the primal bestowal. The legacy of the heroic American on the western frontier thus appears as if delivered from history's subversive possibilities. Heroic America has been rendered mythic not only by virtue of its supposedly fabulous origins or because of the unsurpassed strength, moral as well as physical, of its various heroes but also because of the legacy's own indefeasible claim to the prerogatives of innocence, to the high-most privilege, that is, whereby America's tradition of violent deeds against the Indian bears down as lightly on the hero's soul as it does on the nation's own. Having introduced the boy Michael Thursday York O'Rourke to the reporters, York hands the toddler over to the older of the mesdames O'Rourke and then dons a forage cap with havelock and slips on a pair of white gloves, dons, that is, the identifying accoutrements of Thursday's uniform. The sartorial gestures confirm a transferred legacy. But the enthusiastic children, those innocent witnesses in the movie theater, never could have imagined that York's mythic artifice had always contained the moment when they would curse those deeds meant to satisfy their blameless desires.

## The Westward View; or, What Mrs. Collingwood Saw

The women of the fort—Mrs. O'Rourke, Mrs. Collingwood, Philadelphia, and a few others—gather on a rooftop balcony, a sort of Arizona desert widow's walk, to see the regiment ride out after Cochise. No sooner does the last cavalry company leave the fort than a messenger hands Mrs. Collingwood a letter from Washington, D.C. The letter grants her husband, Sam, his long-hoped-for transfer to West Point. Mrs. Collingwood knows that she can send out a rider to bring her husband back, and the other women encourage her to do so, but she also knows that he is too proud a soldier to abandon his unit in the face of the impending battle, and so forgoes the opportunity to recall him. Instead, she looks out at the column, now far in the distance, and in the most piteous tone exclaims, "I can't see him. All I can see is the flags" (figure 1.1).[9]

Tender and doleful and even elegiac as the moment is, it nonetheless nestles a disquieting vision of American empire. Historical signposts no less than emblems of destined doom, the receding flags chart the nation's westward advance. Old Glory, flanked and protected by the regimental flag and the guidons of the individual companies, leads the nation toward its manifestly destined conquest of the West. Thus, Mrs. Collingwood's view of the flags suggests their transcendent status. Moving as if by themselves, the flags specify the inevitability of America's imperial ascendancy.

Mrs. Collingwood envisions a heroic legacy in the very process of affirming its continuity. In the climactic battle, Cochise and his warriors charge at the cluster of soldiers arrayed in the last-stand pose made familiar by visual representations of Custer's Last Stand (June 25, 1876). Thursday, calm and resolute in the center, carefully aims his pistol at the

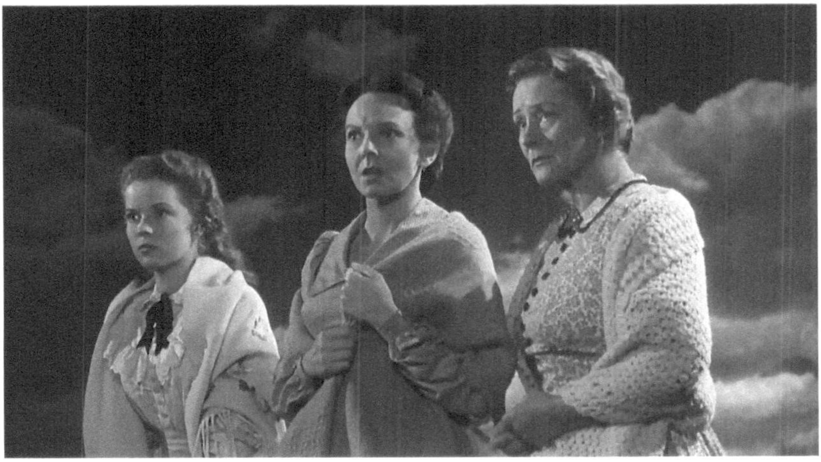

Figure 1.1. *Fort Apache*. Mrs. Collingwood (Anna Lee), center: "All I can see is the flags." Left, Philadelphia Thursday (Shirley Temple) and Mrs. O'Rourke (Irene Rich).

galloping mass of Apaches. In a long shot that follows scenes of the "fatal environment," Cochise himself rides through the broken circle of soldiers and carries away Company B's guidon. All the troopers and their officers are dead, and now the action returns to the ridge where York, following his attempted rescue of Thursday, again takes his place with his men and the supply wagons. The Apaches now ride toward York's position, an unrelenting menace enfolded in a gigantic cloud of dust. Emerging from the billowing dust, Cochise rides slowly toward York, who walks alone and unarmed to face him. Cochise impales the captured guidon and flagpole in the ground, right before York's feet. York stands undaunted. Cochise whirls his pony around and rejoins his warriors, and they all ride away, engulfed by the cloud of dust. Although Cochise is the clear victor in the battle, he has performed an ironic deed of validation, of endorsement. The act of hurling the guidon and the pole at York's feet implicitly acknowledges York as Thursday's successor. The Indian's ironic agency in confirming the continuity of the myth fulfills Thursday's prediction just before the massacre that York shall command the regiment. In the final scene, York and Mickey O'Rourke's mission to capture Geronimo assures us that Cochise has met the tragic fate that the heroic myth reserves for the enemies of westward expansion.

The last scene of *Fort Apache* opens with a fade-in, at once complement and counterpart of the fade-out that marked Cochise's ride away from York. The first image of this scene is a center-screen close-up of the guidon. As the camera pulls back slightly and pans right, the portrait of Owen Thursday in full army regalia comes into view. Hanging above the mantelpiece, the portrait is itself framed by the same rough rocks that make up the face of the mantel and the fireplace. Just below the portrait, resting at an angle on the mantelpiece, a wooden board holds a saber and a plaque under it. The flags that Mrs. Collingwood saw signaled the tragic outcome of Thursday's hubris, with Custer's own blunder being its historical source and counterpart. But now the flags have come at least this much farther westward, and the guidon in the shrine identifies and authorizes not only the history of American expansion but also the mythic nation's readiness for yet more wars. Moreover, the guidon also confirms the transferred command and thus also refers us to the reconstitution of the regiment, now under York. The national myth depended for its very existence on a self-authorized, self-promulgated presence of successive frontiers. But now, as it again faced westward, America transcended geography. Where America gazed, there the new frontier appeared. And there loomed as well the Indian or, rather, some sort of postfrontier "Indian," hence the pattern and the method of westward expansion even beyond America's westernmost shores: the imperial gaze again rekindles the naked greed that must be swaddled in the rhetoric of righteous purpose. And as if by a kind of derivative alchemy, the myth would invest the tragic and violent end of the Indian with an all-absolving melancholy that ministered to the conqueror's battered conscience (if only after he had killed the "last" Indian). Only a spurious memory could vindicate the hero's years of devotion to the workaday business of genocidal violence. In perhaps the most perverse turn of this false memory, the Indian's postmortem acquiescence in his own inevitable demise—this profound understanding of the historical necessity of his vanishment—produces in turn the wistful gloaming of the white hero's musings, the sham history that remembers the Indian's blameless best even back in the days when the hero was slaughtering "savages." If the hero's all-consuming westward drive could overwhelm the authority of conscience, if it allowed him somehow to ignore the counsels of a reflective humanity, and if indeed the errand into the wilderness, the very fervor of it, did not shrivel up before the unfolding horror of it, was it not because the Indian, even if now vanished, could still somehow be relied on to acknowledge, to yield, and then to absolve? And was it not, even beyond the absolution itself, the Indian's return—as savage, as enemy, and then once more as Vanishing American—that sustained the illusion of an innocent white hero whose compliance with the mythic gestures and rituals already and always spare him the Indian's censure? In the scheme of America's heroic myth, the Indian had a legacy of his own: his was an inheritance of doom.

## Continuity as Reiteration: The Moro Wars as Indian Western

Among the many imposing structures at the St. Louis World's Fair of 1904 was an unassuming exhibit of Philippine natives and their various cultural artifacts, practices, and rituals. Situated significantly enough in the western-most part of the fair, the "Philippine Reservation" (or "Encampment" or "Village," depending on the particular guidebook) beckoned curious visitors even as Americans were fighting the Muslim Filipinos—the Moros[10]—in the southern islands of the archipelago. The very reference to the "village/encampment" as a reservation already bound the Moros to the historical process that had continually brought the American Indian from wilderness freedom to abject dependence. The exhibit claimed to portray "the advancement of the barbarian Filipino to the ranks of civilization under the paternal guidance of the American government."[11] Wishing to satisfy his interest in "the races of men," the old Bedonkohe/Chiricahua chief Geronimo, now almost two decades after his surrender, was allowed to visit some of these natives. Geronimo remarked that they

> did not wear much clothing, and I think that they should not have been allowed to come to the Fair. But they themselves did not seem to know any better. They had some little brass plates, and they tried to play music with these, but I did not think it was music—it was only a rattle. However, they danced to this noise and seemed to think they were giving a fine show. I do not know how true the report was, but I heard that the President sent them to the Fair so that they could learn some manners, and when they went home teach their people how to dress and how to behave.[12]

The great Apache chief frames his disparagement in terms that clearly echo the four centuries of opprobrium that white America heaped on American Indians. Geronimo's scorn invoked the binaries that, according to Roy Harvey Pearce, characterized the centuries of white American attitudes toward Indians: pity and censure. "[White] Americans who were setting out to make a new society could find a place in it for the Indian only if he would become what they were—settled, steady, civilized. Yet somehow he would not be anything but what he was—roaming, unreliable, savage. So they concluded that they were destined to try to civilize him and, in trying, to destroy him, because he could not and would not be civilized. He was to be pitied for this, and also to be censured."[13]

Thus, Geronimo implicitly—and ironically—authorizes the American assault on the Philippines and through this unacknowledged complicity with the conqueror appears to revoke the deep-rooted and abiding historical guilt that suffuses the conqueror's narrative of his first transpacific crime. In film or at the World's Fair, the Indian ironically sponsors America's heroic birthright even though—or really because—it was the heroic legacy that compelled his expulsion from the West. Beginning as early as 1901, three years after its first foray into the Philippines, the US Army would face a decade and more of war, this time not against the Catholic Filipinos but instead against the Moros of the southern islands. Yet, as the US Army moved southward along the archipelago, it would encounter a wilderness daunting enough and an enemy unnerving enough, to recall—and thus to reenact—the Indian Wars that had ended a mere decade earlier.

## Oblivion as Portent

Even as the United States was fighting its first transpacific war, Thomas Edison's New Jersey–made reenactments of the ongoing conflict offered brief and unsurprisingly biased glimpses of the military action. The dearth of post-Edison movies about the Philippine-American War may well suggest the extent of America's devotion to unhistory. Yet, Hollywood's inattention to the Philippine-American War also suggests the effects of the national obliviousness starting with the moment when President

Theodore Roosevelt declared America's victory in the Philippines eleven years before the hostilities ceased. "President Roosevelt," writes Stuart Creighton Miller, "best reflected imperialist amnesia when he declared on July 4, 1902, that not only was the war over, but that it had been the most glorious war in the nation's history."[14]

Filmmaker Nick Deocampo has drawn attention to the prominence and persistence of the American flag in Edison's patriotic "reenactments" of the Philippine-American War. In *Advance of Kansas Volunteers at Caloocan* (June 5, 1899), Deocampo notes, "a phalanx of American soldiers springs from the direction of the camera and assaults the . . . Filipino [soldiers]. Prominently displayed is the American flag which is being held by a soldier seen at center frame. . . . As an emotional highlight of the film, the American flag bearer is shot and falls to the ground. The American officer, brandishing his sword, picks up the fallen flag, lifts it high up, and waves it patriotically."[15]

Indeed, the officer carries the flag close upon the advance of his troops and into the background so that the flag, as if in an excess of allegorical reference, recedes into the vanishing point. In another Edison reenactment, *Col. Funstan Swimming the Baglag River* (corrected in later prints to *Col. Funston Swimming the Bagbag River*), the uncredited actor playing Funston stands on the edge of a tiny river raft crowded with another five US soldiers, one of whom carries a large American flag.[16] Funston then drops his saber and belt, doffs his coat, grabs the loose end of a rope tied to the raft, and jumps head-first in the water. He swims toward the opposite shore, where a group of hostile Filipino soldiers (played by Black actors) await. Some wave their bolos perfunctorily, but only three of them use firearms, and not one of them, it seems, even considers shooting at Funston, though he is now no more than five feet away. Standing waist-deep in the river, Funston turns his back to the Filipinos and begins to pull the raft toward him. Soon the natives scurry away, and as Deocampo writes, "the U.S. flag . . . is unfurled once more. . . . [T]he Filipinos are once again chased out to the farthermost margins on the left side of the frame. They reappear and hover over the outline of the hill (like Indians in later-day Hollywood cowboy movies) as they scuttle away, offscreen right, never to be seen again."[17]

How far "westward" could the flag continue in the vanguard of American empire? President William McKinley, Stanley Karnow has noted, could not locate the Philippines on the map,[18] yet surely he might have been at least slightly aware of just how far "west" the Flag had come. The burning question, however, was one not of elementary geography but rather of law, or of justice: Does the Constitution follow the flag? Such was in essence the question before the US Supreme Court in the so-called Insular Cases, beginning with *DeLima v. Bidwell* (1901). Contemporary legal scholars, writes James Q. Whitman in his disconcertingly persuasive *Hitler's American Model*, "highlight" the Insular Cases "as a key development in American race law and the making of an 'American Empire.'"[19] Thus, Whitman reminds us, "When America acquired new territories, the inhabitants were supposed to become citizens. Nevertheless there was widespread sentiment against granting the inhabitants of the new territories full citizenship. The Philippines in particular, which became the site of a nasty American war, was home to a Pacific population that Americans regarded as belonging to an inferior, or at least for the moment hopelessly backward race." In the Insular Cases, then, "the Supreme Court consented to the creation of a de jure form of second-class citizenship for the newly conquered populations: the Constitution, held the Court, permitted these colonial subjects to be treated as mere 'non-citizen nationals.'"[20] The Supreme Court had in effect granted legal status to "otherness," which does not mean of course that it had thereby invested the Other with equal rights. To the question "Does the Constitution follow the Flag?," the high court consistently decided in the negative. That Old Glory yet waved preeminent in lands heretofore claimed by rude and benighted peoples—inhabitants of a "howling wilderness" no less implacable or defiant than the one that bedeviled the New England Puritans—hardly meant that it thereby extended American freedoms to "savages." Thus, the Insular Cases licensed the American flag not as an extension of American freedoms but instead as a warrant for the great grab at everything that was somehow still not America, soil and souls alike.

At the far "westward" limit of Mrs. Collingwood's fatal vision, the flags signaled America's manic hunger for dominion, a hankering sourced not in the pieties and bromides of "benevolent assimilation" but instead in an unconcealed and even boastful racist animus virulent enough to deny the Filipinos and the Moros anything like a heroic inheritance of their own, least of all one fashioned after the conqueror's own mythology.

## Moros as Indians

In 1939, Americans could barely remember their first war for transoceanic empire, let alone identify it as the beginning of a new epoch. When *The Real Glory* (Hathaway, 1939) was released, America, at once chastened and self-assured by its immersion in World War I and already a decade into the Great Depression, cast a nostalgic glance at its early imperial adventures. Hollywood reclaimed the Philippine-American War in 1939, the first of two consecutive years said by film historians to mark the revival of the Western.[21] But Hollywood also chose to do this two years before the United States would have to go to war against another formidable "Asian" Other. The war in the Philippines was, after all, America's only experience fighting a transcontinental Other. Yet, America seems to have acted on the conviction that it possessed an eminently serviceable model of action against any and all "Others." And so, the spirit and character of the Indian fighter of old reemerged to take on the enemy Other in a reenacted "Indian" war.

Contemporaneous accounts of the Philippine-American War almost offhandedly note the similarities with the Indian campaigns of the American West. At the urging of President Theodore Roosevelt, Secretary of War Elihu Root delivered a eulogy to the Eighth Army Corps, which had done much of the fighting against the Filipinos. Root stated that the American troops, "utilizing the lessons of the Indian wars," had "relentlessly followed the guerrilla bands to their fastness in mountains and jungles and crushed them."[22] And Roosevelt himself, in his letter accepting his party's vice presidential nomination, forced an analogy between the Moros and the American Indians. To not subdue the Moros, he stated, would be to grant "self-government to an Apache reservation under some local chief."[23] Poor Geronimo. In the eyes of the white man, he was no different from the Igorots he would deride in St. Louis only three years later.

Filipino scholar Patricio Abinales has noted the influence of concepts and terms derived from America's frontier experience—"savagery," "vacant land," "manifest destiny"—on the Americans who fought in the Philippines. Abinales also notes that the distance (some five hundred miles) of the southern island of Mindanao "from Manila was only made complicated by the inaccessibility of its interiors. Much of [the southern island of] Mindanao was, therefore, imagined as 'empty' or 'dark,' evoking memories of the Western frontier of settlers, cowboys, armies, and carpetbaggers."[24] The characterization of the Moros as "savages" enabled American authorities to censure them. Yet, true to Roy Harvey Pearce's formulation, "censure" coexisted with "pity." "Alongside this odium, . . ." Abinales observes, "was a kind of paternalism that regarded the Muslims and other groups as people in need of protection, not unlike some of the American Indian tribes at the opening of the Western frontier."[25] Thus, imperialist ideology and revisionist history collude to promote a mythological sequencing whereby the culture of the Indian Wars—in the form of scandalous assumptions about the character of the enemy, no less than of the lore and practice of exterminationist rancor—passes wholly and uninterruptedly into the war against the Filipinos and the Moros. This link between myth and history is evident in the conduct of US Army officers who served in the Philippines after seeing action in the waning days of the Indian Wars.[26]

John J. "Black Jack" Pershing, who would become commander of the American Expeditionary Forces in World War I, began his military career in the desert Southwest chasing the ragged remnants of the Apache Wars following Geronimo's surrender. In late 1890 during the time of the Ghost Dance, Pershing served in South Dakota as a second lieutenant in the Sixth Cavalry. Soon after the massacre at Wounded Knee (December 29, 1890), he briefly led "four companies of [Oglala] Sioux Indian Scouts."[27] Without acknowledging even the smallest difference between Indian and Moro or between the Great Plains and the southern Philippine archipelago, Pershing could boast that he had "'many very strong personal friends among the Moros. . . . Some of them will do anything for me.'" "If I should say," he added, "'Go and kill this man or that,' the next day they would appear in camp with his head."[28] Pershing casts himself as the transpacific iteration of the archetypal figure dating back to the New England frontier that Richard Slotkin defines as "the 'man who knows Indians,' the frontier hero [who] stands between the opposed worlds of savagery and civilization, acting sometimes as mediator or interpreter between races and cultures but more often as civilization's most effective instrument against savagery—a man who knows how to think and fight like the Indian, to turn their own methods against them."[29] The cultural hubris that frames Pershing's avowals of (br)Other(hood) with the indigenous people enforces difference as not only conspicuous degradation but also the Other's tacit obedience of imperatives presumed to arise from his own—that is, the Indian's or the Moro's own—eager subservience. In the presence of such a hero, the rebellious Moros were but "children," simple-minded, acquiescent, complaisant, and ever awed by the white hero's eminence.

For the most part, however, Pershing's Moro "children" remained refractory; indeed, they dared the "father" to "come on and fight."[30] In June 1913, reports reached Pershing that the Moros, who had massed in the crater of an extinct volcano named Bud Bagsak, "held five or six times as many women and children as Moro warriors."[31] Bent on war yet wishing to spare the women and children, Pershing feigned an elaborate withdrawal intended to draw the noncombatants out of the stronghold and back to the fields.[32] The stratagem served Pershing's purposes well enough, and when the four-day battle was over on June 15, the American forces and their Moro scouts had killed more than five hundred Moros.[33] "Only" 5–10 percent of the dead were women and children, and Pershing congratulated himself on his restraint. Many years later, President Franklin D. Roosevelt awarded Pershing the Distinguished Service Cross for his "splendid example of personal heroism" at Bud Bagsak.[34]

But the "Bagsak massacre," as the voice-over narrator of the documentary *Memories of a Forgotten War* notes, "was not the worst atrocity of the war." That distinction belonged instead to the earlier massacre at Bud Dajo (March 1906), often referred to in contemporaneous accounts as "Moro Crater," an extinct volcano on the island of Jolo in the Sulu archipelago. This massacre was led by Gen. Leonard Wood, a medical doctor turned Indian fighter who had been Theodore Roosevelt's superior officer in the Rough Riders. "No prisoners were taken," informs the voice-over, "no wounded remained alive." Some nine hundred Moro men, women, and children were reported dead.[35] As unfazed by the grotesque body count as by the age and gender of the slain, Roosevelt sent a telegram to Wood praising him for the "brilliant feat of arms wherein you and they so well upheld the honor of the American flag."[36] So, the flag flew proudly atop the latest American-made abattoir. "Pacification," which is often genocide by another name, came unsuspectingly to the Moros out of the centuries of successive American frontiers even if it also came to them as a new euphemism: "benevolent assimilation."

Late in 1969, just as the American public began to learn of the atrocities that came to be known as the My Lai Massacre (March 16, 1968), in which US troops slaughtered at least 504 Vietnamese villagers, Americans who thought that this enormity was a unique event in their history might have listened to a grizzled veteran of the Samar campaign in the Philippines. In 1901, in reprisal for the deaths of American troops at Balangiga, Gen. Jacob "Hell Roaring Jake" Smith, himself once an Indian fighter, had ordered US Marine Corps Maj. Littleton "Tony" Waller to turn the island of Samar into a "howling wilderness" (thus invoking the phrase favored by the old Puritans to depict the American forests as the "Devil's Territories," as Cotton Mather called them). And now in late 1969, seven decades later, a hoary veteran of Samar under Waller's command "protested to a reporter in Los Angeles that there had been 'earlier Mylais' and described his own 'search and destroy' mission against a harmless fishing village. 'We snuck through the grass as high as a man's head,' the veteran asserted, 'until both platoons had flanked them. We opened fire and killed all but one. They were unarmed.'"[37]

For nearly three centuries, white Americans sought in vain to justify their brutality against the Indian as a necessary expedient for eliminating savagery. It was the Indian's own savagery, so went the incontrovertibly ironic argument, that compelled the Americans' retributory savagery. And so as the hopeless hope would have it, their expedient savagery would be easily abjured and atoned for after the "vanishment" of the Indian. Savagery itself, its essential Indianness, as it were, was too dark a thing to admit of having its origin anywhere but in the dark heart of the Other. The Indian thus became the very means of denying that the dark thing inhabited all human hearts alike. So long as there were Indians to kill, there would also be Indians to credit with the dire agency, the ruthless tutelage, that begat white savagery. But the attribution of savagery, the projection of it, always returned to its actual and primal source in the white man's heart: he could foist it upon the Indian only because he knew it so intimately in himself. Thus would savagery come to figure prominently in the "American character."

Purporting to narrate the pacification of the Moros in 1906, *The Real Glory* turned to Hollywood's Indian Western for its plot and thereby perforce for its ideological assumptions. In a list of twenty-three relevant subjects appended to the *American Film Institute Catalog* summary of *The Real Glory*—right after the first three entries, "Bandits," "Courage," and "Officers (Military)"—the fourth entry reads "Moro Indians."[38] Were the villain ever so much the Moro born and bred, he would be an Indian first and last. The hero, though operating in the "Far East," could not be anything less than the Indian fighter of the American West.

That the hero of *The Real Glory*, Lt. Bill Canavan (Gary Cooper), is a US Army physician in the Philippines in 1906 might seem not to have a strong kinship with the hero of the Western. But by 1939, Gary Cooper had long since earned full credentials as a Western hero. A decade earlier he had starred in *The Virginian* (Fleming, 1929), adapted from Owen Wister's seminal novel of 1902. Cooper's first movie after *The Real Glory* was *The Westerner* (Wyler, 1940), and he would go on to star in many Westerns for two more decades, most memorably in *High Noon* (Zinnemann, 1952) and notably in Anthony Mann's *Man of the West* (1958); Delmer Daves's *The Hanging Tree* (1959), in which he again plays a frontier doctor though one quite different from the uncomplicated Canavan; and *They Came to Cordura* (Rossen, 1959).

The source novel, *The Real Glory* (1937), by Charles L. Clifford, presents Canavan's American frontier inheritance as the prerequisite for heroic action in the jungles of the southern Philippine islands. Fittingly, then, Canavan (in the novel he is never a doctor, and in the Philippines he is a captain and not, as in the movie, a lieutenant) "was raised on a ranch in Wyoming."[39] His mother died when he was a child, and when he was sixteen his father was killed by a horse. Canavan leaves school and sells "what was left of a none too prosperous ranch." Bored with cowboy life, the restless young man reads "avidly of the Spanish war: the sinking of the *Maine*, the Battle of Santiago and the charge up San Juan Hill." The "charge" in particular breathes into his pliable soul the vision of his destined heroism: "it aroused all the heritage of adventurous blood in him." Where, however, might such a young man claim his inheritance now, almost two decades after the closing of the frontier? *The Real Glory* (novel and movie alike) seems to take it on faith that the frontier abides, that it transcends geography, that it comes into being wherever the Other resists American empire.

Released in mid-September 1939, *The Real Glory* went through production as *The Last Frontier*. As Larry Swindell notes, "*The Real Glory* was set in the Philippines but Sam Goldwyn called it a Western."[40] Howard Bares of the *New York Herald Tribune* called it "essentially . . . a cowboy-and-Indian show."[41] And in 1942 Goldwyn, in a tawdry attempt to connect the movie to US and Filipino reversals in Bataan and Corregidor, considered rereleasing *The Real Glory* as "A Yank in the Philippines,"[42] but by this time the Philippine Moros were the allies of the United States in the war against Japan.

Its bloated ideological gravity mocked by its own historical speciousness, *The Real Glory* presumes that the early twentieth-century American occupation of the Philippines consisted of disinterestedly empowering the Philippine Constabulary to become a self-sufficient police force in the service of democracy. Whatever the movie's shortcomings as history, however, its ideology is disturbingly familiar to those with a memory of the American wars in Vietnam, Afghanistan, and Iraq. The Americans of *The Real Glory* will leave the Philippines as soon as the native constabulary can provide nationwide security. So tidy a plan therefore implies that the Philippines—the war, the nation, the imperial possession, the narrative—can have its origin only in American imperial designs and fantasies. To be sure, *The Real Glory* is set in the bloody year 1906—the year of the massacre at Bud Dajo—but smugly limits its historical references to a mention of the San Francisco earthquake. Here, accordingly, the Philippines barely exists until the mythic hero's arrival.

The film's dedication to the Philippine Constabulary assures us that this force "struggled valiantly to wrest their independence from forces that sought to enslave them." The proposed account of a struggle for freedom from a yet unidentified enemy shall be "history" enough—whether imperial history of three decades before the movie's theatrical release or presentist history or perhaps both. Out of this historical half-light, a long shot shows scores of Moro vintas (small square-sail vessels with catamaran-like outriggers), led by a chieftain named Alipang (Tetsu Komai), approaching the defenseless village of Misang. The opening scene all but denies the glaring historical fact of an American invasion of the Philippines, beginning in 1898, as an extension of the Spanish-American War. Thus utterly without historical or cultural context, native aggression reveals only the inscrutable motives of savage passions. Before we learn of the American mission in Misang or about the paramount importance of Misang as if through an archaic version of the toppling domino trope made familiar by American policy in Vietnam, before the American officers define Misang as a "test" of Philippine independence, and before we meet the hero, there are only the pusillanimous Catholic Filipinos, their constabulary a sorry excuse for a military force.

*The Real Glory* identifies each major native group by its religion, though religion here is only a way of othering: the Filipinos are Catholics, and the Moros are Muslims of an unspecified branch of Islam. The Filipinos have Padre Felipe (Charles Waldron), an ineffectual fatalist almost eager to die as a martyr. The Moros have Datu (Vladimir Sokoloff), a character given a proper name out of the traditional title for a ruler, *datu* (also *datto*). Datu, familiar "oriental" unctuousness and all, poses as a smart and trusted adviser to the unsuspecting Americans while actually spying for Alipang. In *The Real Glory*, as we will see, Islam figures only as the rudimentary sorcery that the Americans must explicitly discredit.

After the early shots of the fiendish Moros looting, carrying away the women, and even gutting a Filipino, the action cuts to an office in the Manila headquarters of the Philippine Constabulary. Yet, there is hardly a Filipino in sight, and such Filipinos as do appear—dimly, in the background—remain stone silent throughout. The chatter is consumed with strategies to withdraw American soldiers and turn the fight against the Moros over to native Filipino troops (a policy that during the Vietnam War came to be called "Vietnamization"). Colonel Hatch (Roy Gordon), however, pleads with his fellow officers. "But gentlemen, this is Misang, the heart of the Moro country, the poison spot of the Philippines. To take the army out of there at this time is suicide. And what happens to those poor Philippine natives?" The general, however, is unmoved, so when he orders his officers to train the constabularies "to defend themselves," Hatch is incredulous:

**Hatch:** Against Alipang? I couldn't get them ready in ten years; and I'm afraid Alipang won't wait that long. He's got thousands of Moro bandits in the jungle, just waiting for the American army to leave. It'll be slaughter.

**General:** You'll have to stop him, Colonel Hatch.

**Hatch:** With what? Raw native troops?

**General:** Yes, with native troops. As long as our army is there, the Filipinos will depend on them. Sooner or later they'll have to take care of themselves. It's your job to prepare them. We're making Misang a sort of test. If it works out there, it's bound to work out in the rest of the islands.

**Hatch:** Well, I can tell you now. As soon as Alipang knows we've left, he'll pounce on us. In forty-eight hours I'll be screaming for help.
**General:** There'll be no one listening, Colonel.

Eventually, however, Canavan's decisive victory over the Moros will in effect demand the absence of the Philippine Constabulary from the crucial battle.

## Retreat, Advent, and Conspiracy

Following the officers' meeting in Manila, the action returns to Misang, where the US soldiers are still evacuating, leaving Colonel Hatch in command of a tiny force for the defense of the outpost. Besides Hatch, we have met the other handful of Americans charged with training the Philippine Constabulary. Each one is quirky enough to qualify as an integral part of the American counterinsurgency group of misfits that would become familiar to moviegoers three decades later in, for example, *The Dirty Dozen* (Aldrich, 1967). Lieutenant Larsen (Broderick Crawford), among those who remain in Misang, breeds orchids and is delighted to have been posted on the edge of a tropical jungle. Another, Lieutenant McCool (David Niven), "never took an order in his life, but he's the best one-man army in the Philippines," says the general at the meeting in Manila. A third, Captain Hartley (Reginald Owen), is a martinet and a veteran of earlier encounters in the Philippines. More important, however, Hartley is the father of Linda Hartley (Andrea Leeds), who arrives in Misang on the same boat as Canavan and at the end leaves in it with him. Just before Canavan's arrival in Misang, Padre Felipe greets Hatch with a vision of the inevitable destruction of Misang once American troops complete their withdrawal. "Alipang is bringing together all the Moro tribes on Mindanao," the padre says. "As soon as the American troops are gone, the Moros will come down from the hills; they will kill all the men and carry away all the women and children." Padre Felipe thus articulates the Western's common perception of the Indian threat, namely that all Indians surrender their tribal affiliation in order to unite in a grand apocalyptic conspiracy that will wipe out the white settlements.

The implacable pandemonic force of wild-eyed "savages" riding hard to Armageddon would sacrifice all to their unjustified rancor toward white America.

Chroniclers of the frontier, many of whom held that Indians were capable of only crude forms of social organization, somehow also believed that all Indian nations, spurred by a shared hatred of white Americans, could easily unite against the white settlements. The early Indian fighter Benjamin Church (1639–1716), hero of King Philip's War (1675–1677), "had it daily suggested to him that the Indians were plotting a bloody design. That *Philip* [i.e., Wampanoag chief Metacom] the great *Mount-hope* Sachem was Leader therein: and so it prov'd, he was sending his Messengers to all the Neighbouring Sachems, to ingage them in a Confederacy with him in the War."[43] More than two centuries after Church's exploits, Theodore Roosevelt's *The Winning of the West* made similar assertions about Indian "conspiracies" during the time of the early US republic. Indigenous nations, inflamed by a century and more of unsatisfied grievances, had plotted to eliminate white settlements. On July 1, 1791, natives long aggrieved by the persistent disappearance of their hunting grounds gathered at the Miami Rapids. "They were all assembled," Roosevelt writes, "not only the Shawnees, Delawares, Wyandots, Ottawas, Pottawatamies and others who had openly taken the hatchet against the Americans, but also representatives of the Six Nations, and tribes of savages from lands so remote that they carried no guns, but warred with bows, spears, and tomahawks, and were clad in buffalo-robes instead of blankets."[44] Whether on the eve of the republic or a century and a half earlier in the Puritans' "Devil's Territories," the "paranoid style,"[45] in Richard Hofstadter's enduringly apt phrase, still shaped the myth of heroic continuity.

When Datu explains to Alipang that the Americans will keep only "a handful" of soldiers, Alipang orders him to begin eliminating the remaining Americans. Datu sends a juramentado (from Spanish *juramento*: oath, vow) to kill Colonel Hatch.[46] Even as Canavan's boat is docking in Misang, the juramentado, barong in hand, makes his way to the post from the mountains that surround it, and Canavan unexpectedly finds himself emptying his service revolver into the back of the juramentado who, though shot many times, still hacks away at Hatch, who falls by the base of the flagpole and thus becomes the latest martyr of American imperialism. The next scene opens with a shot of the first of three American flags—this first one, at half-mast, in Hatch's honor—that wave at several crucial moments in *The Real Glory*. The command of Misang's puny force devolves to Captain Manning, but a juramentado soon beheads him. In the next scene the American flag flies again, prominently, almost defiantly, yet again at half-mast. The near-blind Hartley now assumes command.

## Otherness as Degradation: The Juramentado and the Moro Sidekick

Canavan knows the Moro enemy as thoroughly as the white Indian fighter knows his Indian nemesis. After the assassination of Hatch, for example, only Canavan notices that the juramentado did not kill "the first Christian" he met, as juramentados supposedly do, and deliberately selected Hatch. Later in an episode as memorable for its outrageous cultural pretensions as for its tasteless and misplaced mummeries, Canavan implicitly declares all Islam so much humbug. Then after Padre Felipe tells him that Moros are "mortally afraid of being buried in a pigskin," Canavan announces with Archimedean enthusiasm that he has found a "cure" for the Filipinos' paralyzing fear of the Moros. He proceeds to pervert the Qur'anic injunction against eating "the flesh of swine" (5.3) into a mere superstition. With the help of his Moro sidekick, Miguel (Benny Inocencio), Canavan ventures into the jungle and straight into Alipang's camp, where he summarily captures a juramentado. Canavan then frogmarches him to the fort's parade grounds, where he orders Lieutenant Yabo (Rudy Robles) to fetch a pigskin. When the captured juramentado, who has so far stood defiant, understands Canavan's threat, he goes into a wild panic.[47] The juramentado shouts his desperate prayers and rants his curses, falls to his knees and grovels before the cool and composed tormentor. Canavan's is thus the inevitable triumph of Western science over "orientalist" superstition, the fulfillment of the American promise of freedom and light in the heart of darkness.

Perhaps, however, no moment so affirms Canavan's exclusive fitness for the heroic inheritance as does his first encounter with Miguel, or "Mike," as Canavan insists on calling him. As soon as Canavan's boat docks at Misang, some half dozen native boys swim up to it and scamper aboard, seeking to find favor with the arriving Americans. One of the boys, older and more muscular than the rest, boards the boat last, but when he barks a command (or a curse), all the others, terrified, jump ship. Canavan, of course, is not intimidated. As he calmly finishes rolling a cigarette, he says with mock concern, "Hey, you haven't by any chance got leprosy." The boy, now flashing the first of his many idiotic grins, nods no. Then Canavan, affecting curiosity, asks, "What's the Indian sign [that is, the "hex"] you've got on those other kids, anyway? You're not Filipino, are you?"

> **Miguel** [*smiling stupidly*]: No.
> **Canavan:** Moro? [*Miguel nods yes*] Oh, so that's it. What's your name?
> **Miguel:** Miguel.
> **Canavan:** All right, Mike, you can take my bags to headquarters.
> **Miguel:** You bet your life.

Already in his first appearance before the white hero, Miguel—the name he gives himself—is minimized the moment Canavan implicitly translates the name (Michael) only to opt for its diminutive (Mike). Moreover, Canavan immediately renders him harmless, ridiculous even, and not a bit contemptible, a born factotum, though moments earlier he was a proud Moro ordering the Catholic boys about. As an extension of America's "civilizing" mission in Misang, Canavan's deeds acquire a compelling metaphorical value by virtue of his early relation to Miguel: he tames the boy's presumed savagery while reaffirming his ineluctable Otherness. So, similarly, shall Canavan subdue the Moros of Misang—those that survive the final battle, at any rate—while implicitly condemning them to the role of strangers in their own land.

The last time we see Miguel, he is wearing a white suit, a collar and tie, a Panama hat, and a lei around his neck, an outfit in every way betokening his new status as poster child of "benevolent assimilation," the "before-and-after" picture that validates imperial intervention in the heart of darkness. The *American Film Institute Catalog* summary of *The Real Glory* assures us that Miguel leaves Misang for America with Canavan even though we never see Miguel board the riverboat out. But whether or not Miguel leaves with Canavan, the "ethnic cleansing" of Misang still leaves an inexhaustible supply of "Mikes," all of them sorted and stored under the sign of the now safely diminished Other, each one a ready-made reification of American imperial desires in Asia.

Having so far failed to lure the Americans out of the fort and into the jungle, Datu and Alipang decide to dam the river that flows through Misang: the Americans, the villains believe, will have to venture into the jungle to release the water, and there the Moros will destroy them. Soon the waters of the river begin to recede, and Misang finds itself in the grip of a cholera epidemic. As Canavan is vaccinating Linda (a too-obvious stab at sexual nuance), he lectures her. "A man named Krag invented the repeating rifle; a man named [Edward] Jenner invented vaccination. If the Philippines ever becomes a nation of its own, who'll get the credit? Krag. But who'll live longer? Jenner. The whole post is in an uproar about a few Moros when all around them are billions of enemies, whole regiments of disease." The conqueror may seek to vindicate himself through medical science, but mythology insists on another sort of lore for dazzling the benighted brutes: the hero's wilderness wisdom. However devoutly Canavan may believe in the benefits that science confers on the "little brown brothers" (the historical euphemism), he must go forth into the wilderness and decisively claim his heroic inheritance. Culture, myth, and genre all determine that his noblest errand, his "real glory," lies thither. But if the nation now being built is not America but rather the Philippines—if America is already fully formed and its unfolding destiny in successive frontiers merely reaffirms its exceptional history—then Philippine nationhood seems far less dependent on cultural integrity and political sovereignty than on a sort of acquiescence, enforced or benevolent, in assimilation not so much of a "greater" culture but rather of empire. As for the Moros in *The Real Glory*, their choice in the matter of nationhood seems to be just about as clear as it was of old for the American Indian: assimilate or die.

When the village's freshwater well becomes polluted, Hartley has no choice but to send his men into the jungle to blow up the dam the Moros have built. First he sends Larsen, with Miguel as guide, along with a small detachment of constabularies. When Larsen is late returning to Misang, Hartley, at Datu's suggestion, sends out thirty-two constabularies accompanied by three presumably friendly Moros. Each of these three Moros carries a wooden crate of dynamite strapped to his back. Almost completely blind now, Hartley allows Datu to guide him and his Filipino troops to the mountains. Just before this detachment leaves Misang, however, Miguel arrives, wounded; he is the sole survivor of the Larsen expedition. He manages only one word, "Ambush," before he faints from his wounds. Nonetheless, Hartley leaves with Datu and the constabularies. Moments later, Miguel, already recovering under Canavan's care, manages to say, "Datu kill Larsen." In an instant, Canavan straps on his gun belt and six-gun and sets out for the mountains alone.

As if instinctively (for he is new to the area), Canavan takes a path different from the one through which Datu leads Hartley and the constabularies and soon overtakes them. Canavan challenges Datu, who pulls a kris on Canavan, only to have it shot out of his hand by the unerring, ever-magical six-gun. Even in the Philippine jungle, American mythology reenacts the Western's ritual shootout. The six-gun is no less a weapon of a vastly superior imperial technology than the cholera vaccine.

Though still under Canavan's gun, Datu shouts an order to the three Moro bearers. In an act that could not have yielded at the time one drop's worth of warning or of foresight to our twenty-first century, the bearers, willing to sacrifice themselves to keep the explosives from the Americans, rush off the cliff. Canavan shoots one of them, however, wounding him, and saves the remaining dynamite for the dam. His shirt now stuffed with sticks of dynamite, Canavan forces Datu to lead him to the site of the dam. But Datu instead leads him to a punji trap, except that he halts suspiciously before it, and when Canavan prods him to go on, Datu falls in. Though once again alone in the jungle, Canavan fearlessly finds his way to the dam and single-handedly blows it up. Cut to the water flowing again in Misang and then to the amazed Filipinos, all now made joyous by the unseen power that has released the life-giving waters from an inaccessible height. "A man named Jenner" may have indeed invented the modern-day vaccine, but it is the American hero who delivers yet one more dark place into the light of civilization.

With Misang imperiled by Alipang's second invasion, Canavan now rides a makeshift raft down the turbid river rapids. (The two constabularies with him fall off and are thus expediently sacrificed to the reaffirmation of the hero's essential self-sufficiency.) While Hartley and the constabularies follow in their own rafts, Canavan, who has saved some of the dynamite, undertakes the defense of the fort as the Moro invaders catapult off the tops of trees and fly over the walls of the fort, their own bodies airborne weapons. At this moment before Canavan arrives, Linda finds herself in the predicament of the forsaken white maiden threatened by dusky devils. But she proves herself worthy of the hero's heritage: she holds the fort, even barking orders at terrified constabularies. Though the fort has run out of ammunition by the time Canavan arrives, we hardly fret. He has his woman, who greets him with a passionate embrace. And he has his dynamite. His arrival inspires the constabularies to action. Hartley's waterborne "cavalry" arrives in time only for the generic mopping-up. In only a little while, the smiling Filipino women are placing farewell leis on Hartley, Canavan, and Linda. The "test" that was Misang has been passed, the errand into the wilderness has been once again fulfilled, and as a happy concomitant, the Philippines shall be a democracy, or something like it, some day.

## The Reclaimed Other and the American Flag

In the last scene, Miguel, clownishly dapper in western togs, affirms his abject subjection. He has suffered severe, debilitating wounds, yet consistent with his generic servility, he alone loads all the Americans' suitcases aboard the riverboat leaving Misang. Although we see the three Americans board—and although Miguel too, like the departing Americans, wears a lei around his neck (suggesting that he also is leaving Misang)—we never see him actually board. Perhaps it is a careless oversight on the part of the filmmakers that they fail to show Miguel standing beside the three Americans and waving goodbye at Misang as the riverboat pulls away. Surely Miguel, a Muslim in a long-ago slightly better day for Islam in America, shall emigrate to the United States with the blessed couple and become an American, fully and all too benevolently "assimilated." He will become Mike, then—perhaps Mike Canavan—however deracinated, however unschooled in "the Language"—but still and despite all assuredly one of us or at least the perpetual child of one of us. Maybe the filmmakers, reflecting the very biases that they uncritically narrate, thought it a thing of no consequence whether Miguel left or stayed. Could it be, though, that Miguel, having outlived his days as guide, sidekick, and factotum remains in Misang as a testament to America's civilizing influence? Could it be that this infantilized Other, now so completely drained of the spunk that he showed when we first met him, can somehow become a model of how

America could subdue, in the tough times soon to follow the 1939 release of *The Real Glory*, even the most militaristic of Asian nations?

As "American" as Miguel may become in time, however, he will never be Canavan's heir, not even with Canavan's blessing. Enduringly the child of empire, Miguel lives only to surrender his indigenousness to his unalterable status as abject subordinate. The heroic myth does not vouchsafe the likes of Miguel anything akin to the opportunity to lead America's errand into the wilderness. Miguel can never be to Canavan what, for example, *Fort Apache*'s Mickey O'Rourke (though burdened with his own diminutive of the name Michael) is to Captain York. The very continuity of America's heroic myth would thus depend as much on denying the legacy to the Other as on finding a suitably heroic white successor. Hence, the dilemma of the heroic myth in America's transpacific venture in *The Real Glory* is that it must continue to narrate the part of the myth that has the white hero fighting selflessly for freedom and equality while at the same time denying a genuine, let alone autochthonous, inheritance to the very people meant to reap the benefits of that struggle. The greater the success of the American hero in his ever-expanding frontier empire—that is, the more Others his success brings into the great imperial fold—the more attenuated the line of heroic inheritance. If the myth of heroic continuity is irredeemably racist and if inevitably the empire fairly teems with racial Otherness, who is to be the next protagonist of America's heroic myth if not he who inherits the age-old animus toward these very Others? That Old Glory waved supreme and unchallenged in heretofore "savage" lands did not mean that America extended its freedoms to the natives. The Insular Cases licensed and enfranchised the American flag only as a warrant for the great grab of all that was not America. The flags that Mrs. Collingwood saw driving relentlessly westward manifested America's imperial will without in the least recognizing, let alone realizing, the dreams of benighted and "huddled masses yearning to breathe free."

In the last scene of *The Real Glory*, the American flag, which had so far flown only at half-mast, flies high up on the flagpole at the parade grounds, or rather, a flag flies high. It is difficult to tell what country's flag it is, since we see it in a long shot, and, more irksome still, the flag flies so far up against the upper frame of the screen as to be almost entirely out of it. Perhaps this partial flag is the product of nothing more significant than a cameraman's indifferent framing. Or it could well be the result of poor film-to-video transfer. Still, it is so indistinct a flag that it could be the flag of the Philippines. After all, if Misang was the "test" of Filipino ability to establish and sustain a democracy, should it not be the flag of the Philippines that waves on high now that the Philippine Constabulary has become an effective fighting force? Lt. General R. L. Bullard, who as Colonel Bullard in the Philippines in 1906 took great pride in having pacified the region designated since Spanish times as "Moro Province" (Provincia Mora), relates an incident in which two dattos go off on a slave-taking expedition against Filipinos "under the American flag, which they had somehow managed to get hold of!"[48] Bullard sentences each datto to seventeen years in prison and concludes the brief tale of empire's retributive wrath by assuring us that the American flag will never again "cover a slave-taking expedition." There was a time, well within the memory of many an American officer then serving in the Philippines, when the enslavement of Black men and women had very much existed "under the American flag." Bullard never considers that the two dattos may have availed themselves of the American flag not as a deception but instead as a potent certification of their own imperial enterprise.

Even so, this hallowed Old Glory, though soiled by a Moro slave-taking expedition, was the only national flag allowed to fly in the Philippines until 1919.[49] "During the first years of American occupation," we read in an official history of the Philippine flag, "the display of the Philippine colors produced such repercussions that on August 23, 1907, the Philippine Commission [run by Americans] passed the Flag Law, which forbade the display of the Philippine flag anywhere, even in Filipino homes."[50] A photograph in Orosa's *The Sulu Archipelago and Its People* adds an accusatory postscript to the act of imperial benevolence that at last consented to let the flag of the Philippines fly free in 1919. The occasion was the dedication of a monument to the apostle of Filipino nationalism, José Rizal (1861–1896). The place was Jolo, now six years after the pacification of Moro Province (in 1913, after the massacre of Bud Bagsak). The date was June 19, 1921. The flag of the Philippines flies over the proceedings, yet the American flag—the real (Old) Glory—flies above it from the same pole; it is the true source of trickle-down Filipino sovereignty.[51] *The Real Glory*, recall, is set in 1906. Historically, then (bad camera framing or indifferent video transfer), only the American flag can fly high over Misang at the end.

President Theodore Roosevelt brought the triumphalism of America's frontier mythology to bear on the Philippines when, in his General Orders 66 (July 4, 1902), he declared victory in the war against the Filipinos. He asserted that the US Army in the Philippines, "utilizing the lessons of the Indian wars, . . . ha[d] relentlessly followed the guerrilla bands to their fastnesses in mountains and jungles and crushed them."[52] So did he, then, however much against instinct or intention, bring the war against the Filipinos and the Moros to share in the historical shame that had previously defined the Indian Wars. If the points of comparison between the two conflicts did not produce a near-precise correspondence of the impetus, motives, and methods of conquest, they at least proved that America had again grounded its narratives of an exalted past on a tragic history for which the only pattern available to cultural memory was that of the Indian Wars. In its own way of prevaricating about the end of the war, *The Real Glory*, though driven by myth, exhibits a correspondence of its own with the "history" of Roosevelt's version of the Philippine-American War in his General Orders 66. Not only does the film promote an ending that falsifies the narrative of the war in 1906, it also perpetuates the shame that a genocidal war against the Moros had brought democracy to the Philippines and "real glory" to the United States of America. Whichever flag, American or Filipino, waves at the end of *The Real Glory*, it yet waves as an expression of a dishonor shared with the official account of the war. Thus, history and myth find common ground in this dark way of remembering the past. Long after Bud Dajo and Bud Bagsak—long even after Bataan and Corregidor (December 1941–May 1942)—Hollywood would take to the Philippines as a favorite location for movies about America's Vietnam War, likely never suspecting that its Vietnam War reenacted the earlier war that it had long since forgotten.

## CHAPTER 2

# Heroic Genealogies and the Anxiety of Legacy

## The Two Flag Raisings, *Sands of Iwo Jima*, and the "Year of Shocks"

> 'Tis not the concern of the day, a year, or an age; posterity are virtually involved in the contest, and will be more or less affected even to the end of time, by the proceedings now.
>
> —Thomas Paine, *Common Sense*

> Wars produce many stories of fiction, some of which are told until they are believed to be true.
>
> —Ulysses S. Grant, *Personal Memoirs*

### The Photograph, the Suribachi Imaginary, and the Anxiety of Legacy

In the captured instant, six US marines—helmeted and in combat fatigues, none of their faces clearly visible—wrestle a heavy makeshift flagstaff and its unfurling Old Glory to within some forty-five degrees of the battle-ravaged ground atop Mount Suribachi, the volcano on the southernmost tip of the Japanese-held island of Iwo Jima (figure 2.1). Moments earlier, Associated Press photographer Joe Rosenthal had finally made it to the top of Mount Suribachi, hours after other photographers covering the taking of the volcano. All was now quiet, but Rosenthal decided not to waste the trip up. Standing on some rocks, he took a picture of the six

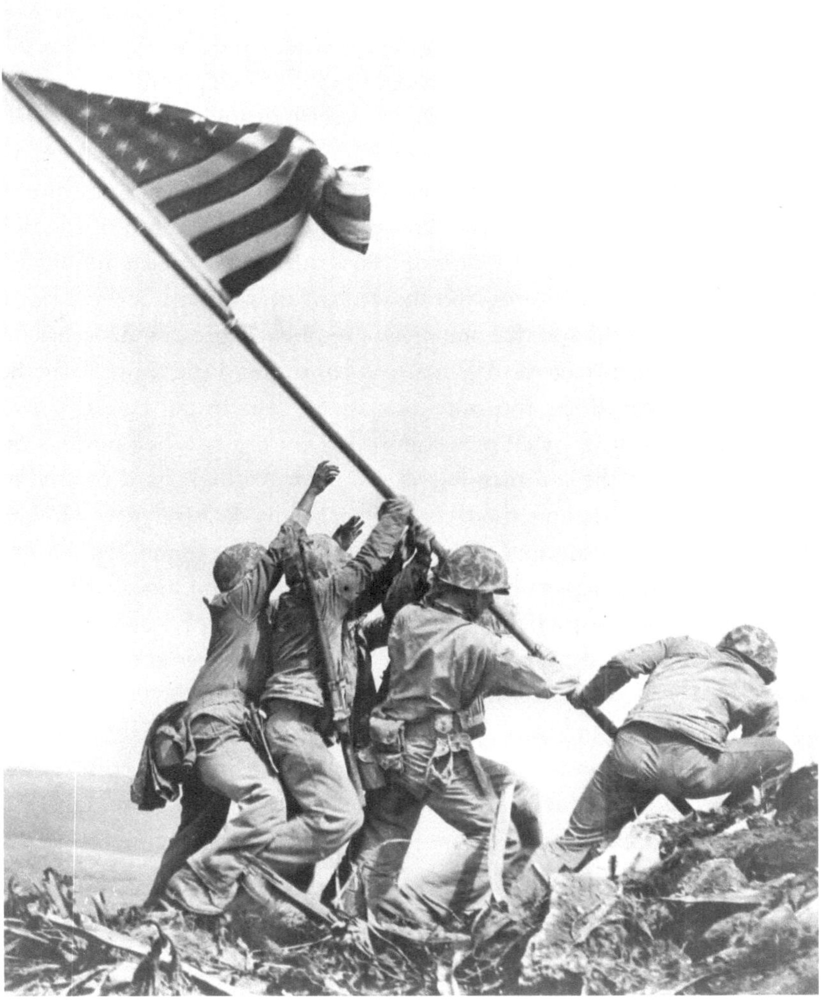

Figure 2.1. *Sands of Iwo Jima.* Photograph by Joseph Rosenthal of the second flag raising on Mount Suribachi on Iwo Jima, February 23, 1945. Courtesy Library of Congress.

marines, little suspecting that he had taken the most iconic war photograph in the history of the US military.

In 1945 and even well after the war, the American public did not know that the six men in the photograph were raising only a replacement flag. The battalion commander had demanded the original (hoisted some three hours earlier) for the battalion and had ordered that a larger flag be put up in its place. But if Americans knew little of the photograph's provenance, it was mostly because the account of the first flag raising—and of the photograph that showed the marines celebrating it—had been well-nigh suppressed. Since its first appearance in American newspapers on February 25, the photograph seemed uniquely suited for promoting the mystique of US Marine Corps heroism. Throughout the rest of the war and well beyond it, Marine Corps officials hailed and hyped a double fiction, namely that the photograph showed the very instant of the capture of Mount Suribachi and that the precise moment represented victory on Iwo Jima when in fact the US marines controlled little more than the southwestern tip of the five-mile-long island. The brutal Battle of Iwo Jima would go on for well over a month after the two flag raisings on February 23, and the commanders would be increasingly hard-pressed to explain to the public how there could have been a decisive victory in late February when the number of American dead on the island kept climbing in appallingly high numbers all through March and into April.

Aware of the photograph's possibilities as a morale booster at home, President Franklin Roosevelt ordered three of the marines—the three others had been killed in combat in the days following the flag raising—to return stateside and tour the nation from coast to coast. They were to be the stars of the Seventh War Loan Drive, the "Mighty Seventh" as the promoters called it. One of the three flag raisers, Ira Hayes, would have to be sent back to the fighting before the end of the tour because his persistent drunkenness threatened to tarnish his heroism. Another flag raiser, Pharmacist's Mate 2nd Class John H. "Doc" Bradley, insisted throughout his life that he was no hero, perhaps trying to deflect attention from himself or perhaps doubting that he had been in the photograph at all.[1] The third marine, Rene Gagnon, though his fame suddenly allowed him to rub elbows with the powerful, would end his days still trying to cash in on his ever-fading fame. He died of a heart attack at age fifty-four in 1979, not long after he was fired for drinking on the job.

The commanders never felt compelled to explain the strategic importance of Iwo Jima to the American public, at least not until after the end of the battle, once the scale of the slaughter demanded a plausibly vindicating account of the reasoning behind their initial predictions of easy victory. The US Navy's casualty reports just after the flag raising on February 23 would have easily led the public to believe that the marines were merely mopping up after capturing Mount Suribachi. In order to sustain this fiction, a high-placed admiral officially claimed that four Japanese soldiers were dying for every American casualty. Yet, historians would eventually determine that the Americans suffered more casualties than the Japanese on Iwo Jima. (Casualties comprises not only the dead but also the wounded, the missing, the captured, and those suffering from "combat fatigue," as the condition known in our time as post-traumatic stress disorder was then known.)

Almost five years after the war, the juggling of the public response to both the photograph and the battle itself found its way into *Sands of Iwo Jima*, directed by Alan Dwan and released in mid-December 1949. Toward the end of the movie, immediately after the death of the protagonist, Sgt. John M. Stryker (John Wayne), *Sands* seems to declare total American victory in the battle by staging the hoisting of the flag. The three surviving marines participate in the reenactment, as do still others present on Mount Suribachi when the flag went up. Now, however, in 1949 in a world so suddenly and strangely transformed since the end of the war, *Sands of Iwo Jima* appropriated the photograph, uncritically accepting and tendentiously promoting the deceptions about its origin, its history, and its meaning. Be it ever the apocrypha of the American heroic, however, the photograph nonetheless stands as the telos of *Sands of Iwo Jima*: the narrative process aims at the reenactment of the second flag raising but also at the complicity of image and heroic myth. Like the photograph itself, *Sands of Iwo Jima* elides the narrative process that accounts for the second flag raising. Moreover, in the historical and cultural contexts of the Cold War and of the convulsive events rumbling ominously through all of 1949, the photograph becomes a transcendent, ahistorical force, present at the climacteric of American heroism and then abiding forever as the highest possible attestation of righteous dominion. That *Sands of Iwo Jima* aspires to a share of the photograph's otherworldliness, however, hardly shields it—or for that matter the photograph itself—from the destabilizing effects of the presiding anxieties of the time.

In order to construct a narrative out of the photograph, *Sands of Iwo Jima* had to not only project the narrative possibilities of an arrested moment but also acquiesce in the falsification of the narrative action—amounting almost to its erasure—that had led to the event that the photograph freezes in time. Therefore, the film implicitly and uncritically embraces the counterfeit tale that the US Marine Corps foisted on the photograph from its first appearance. Accordingly, the unfolding matrix consists of the historical battle, the flag raisings, the photograph itself, the bond drive, and *Sands of Iwo Jima.*[2] Moreover, the matrix also comprises the colossal US Marine Corps War Memorial adjacent to Arlington Cemetery (unveiled in 1954), the tiny three-cent stamp issued by the US Post Office in July 1945, and the innumerable reproductions, reenactments, trinkets, and small-town monuments representing the photograph, all copies of the photograph that was itself, if not quite a copy, then two removes from the first flag and the first flag raising. This narrative matrix constitutes what I call the *Suribachi imaginary.*

The photograph, not the battle itself, inhabits the center of the Suribachi imaginary. It is the photograph that abstracts the carnage and the tragedy into an easy triumphalist exuberance. The photograph generates a comfortable, fatuous acquiescence in a sort of fuzzy, foggy national blessedness that enables if not amnesia then a turn from the blood, sweat, and tears that might just spoil the easeful contemplation of so reassuring a moment. *Sands of Iwo Jima*, for its part, unfolds as a way of explaining how the photograph came to be. The film purports to provide an uncontested historical narrative in which the second flag raising is the only flag raising.[3] For suggesting that the photograph marks the moment of victory on Iwo Jima, the film also promotes the photograph's implicit dismissal of the ironic complications and the ambiguities of the Suribachi imaginary. To sum up, then, *Sands of Iwo Jima* provides the presumed historical context for the photograph and concomitantly proffers that image as an enduring icon of American heroism, a national talisman of sorts for the Cold War.

But precisely because it presumes to explain the origin of the photograph, *Sands of Iwo Jima* also references the anxieties of its own time. As the film drives toward the stirring moment atop Mount Suribachi, it also reassures us that victory on Iwo Jima is but prelude to a final triumph in the dark *postwar* postwar struggles. Yet, the seeming confidence with which *Sands of Iwo Jima* promotes the vision of enduring and unassailable triumph discloses already the underlying disquiet, the compelling urgency. And the greater the insistence on and pursuit of that vision, the more glaringly foregrounded the anxiety of legacy becomes. The transfer and consequent affirmation of the heroic legacy shape the essential preconditions of the flag raising. Driven by such anxiety, however, the victory—on Iwo Jima and in the Cold War—remains ambiguous, unresolved, unable to dispel the ruling anxiety for so obsessively invoking it.

Throughout most of the action, Pete Conway (John Agar), abrasively irreverent toward the Marine Corps, casts doubt on whether he is worthy of his father's heroic legacy. Stryker's reverence for the dead Col. Sam Conway (under whom he served at Guadalcanal) casts him as Pete's surrogate father. The youngest of the three generations are Stryker's ten-year-old estranged son Sam (whom we never meet), Conway's newborn boy (also Sam), and the child of an unwed mother, Mary—a boy whom Stryker refers to as "Mac." Pete Conway comes to understand the need to put aside his peevishness if these children are to have a chance at their own heroic birthright. Thus, the narrative that leads to the flag raising concerns itself chiefly, indeed obsessively, with this intergenerational legacy and thus reflects the problem of its own cultural time, namely whether America, so recently emergent as the world's unrivaled power, could count on the legacy of the World War II generation to help it surmount the evils that beset the nation right after the war. The anxiety of legacy finds its clearest and, at the same time, most ironic expression in this seemingly most exultant of national narratives. The anxiety of legacy is present in *Sands of Iwo Jima* not only as the dramatic conflict between generations but also in the narrative itself, that is to say, in its necessary existence as an unacknowledged reaction to the dread upheavals of its time

## Iwo Jima: American History, American Myth

As it came to be defined by the photograph, the second flag raising reawakened visions of a nation made heroic by providential favor. America had faced west from the shores of Virginia and New England, and now, an exact century after John L. O'Sullivan teased the chaste and elemental vision of "manifest destiny" out of a notoriously tangled and intemperate sentence, the young nation stood poised to claim a righteous global dominion: the Pax Americana. Secretary of War James V. Forrestal, ashore on the "Green Beach" sector of Iwo Jima, from which he witnessed the first flag raising, allegedly said to General Holland "Howlin' Mad" Smith that "the raising of that flag on Suribachi means a Marine Corps for another five hundred years."[4] By contrast, the hoisting of the replacement flag on Suribachi was unremarkable to anyone close to the action that day; yet, it soon enough provided the image that seemed to transform Forrestal's prediction about the life expectancy of the Marine Corps into a millenarian vision of American empire everlastingly sustained by the heroic legacy. Less than five years after the flag raising, the photograph again served to promote heroic continuity when *Sands of Iwo Jima*, presenting the reenactment of the flag raising as the high point of the narrative, produced the apotheosis of both the photograph and John Wayne. Yet, if only because it so uncritically, so deferentially, privileges the second flag raising, the film implicitly endorses the institutional prevarications that had sought to transform the photograph into a symbol of American heroism.

A close reading of contemporaneous *New York Times* reports of the battle establishes the milieu of cultural and political abuse out of which the photograph emerged not only as the defining moment of the Battle of Iwo Jima but also as the luminous symbol, rich with totemic possibilities, of the heroic myth. The paragraphs that follow pay particular attention to reports of the first ten days of the land battle (which began on February 19) and focus especially on the relation between the stateside appearance of the photograph and the reports—and after the first ten days or so the *paucity* of reports—of American casualties on Iwo Jima.

On February 20, 1945, *New York Times* reporter Warren Moscow stated, based on a US Navy communiqué from Admiral Chester W. Nimitz, that "American casualties suffered at the hands of the Japanese were described as 'moderate,' though the operation was viewed in advance as possibly one of the toughest nuts an amphibious force has ever tried to crack, tougher than Tarawa and Saipan."[5] However difficult the first day's chaos may have made it for the US Navy and the US Marine Corps to determine American casualties, Nimitz's "moderate" stands as a monstrous misnomer for the actual numbers of February 19: 566 dead, 1,775 wounded, and 99 suffering from combat fatigue.[6] On February 21, the *New York Times* reported that "the Japanese are fighting fiercely, especially on the flanks, and it has been impossible as yet to estimate our casualties."[7] Yet, military historians George W. Garand and Truman R.

Strobridge note that "by the evening of 21 February the combat efficiency of the 28th Marines had declined to 75 percent."[8]

The February 22 *New York Times* headlines read, "Marines Halted on Iwo, New Division Lands: . . . U.S. Casualties 3,650." From "moderate" and not "so heavy as expected" and "impossible as yet to determine," the casualty count jumped suddenly to a demoralizingly precise 3,650. Perhaps even more dispiriting, the marines had "halted" before Mount Suribachi, and a fresh division (the Third), meant to be held in reserve, had to be thrown into the fight. Warren Moscow reported the grim official total of the first forty-eight hours: "150 officers and 3,500 men wounded, missing and killed, according to the communiqué, which announced that 3,063 had been evacuated."[9]

On the next day (February 23), when the marines hoisted the flag on Suribachi's summit, a sizable American readership had reason to believe that the Battle for Iwo Jima was all but over. The *New York Times* headlines raved with optimism: "Marines Take Suribachi, Chief Point on Iwo." Such glad tidings might have lured the hasty reader away from the last two subtitles in that same column: "Japanese Hit Back: One of 2 Heavy Blows Believed Repulsed—Our Casualties at 5,372."[10] The encouraging news notwithstanding, then, American casualties from one day to the next had risen by almost 50 percent. In his front-page article, Warren Moscow prudently warned that "reaching the summit of Suribachi does not mean immediate capture [of the island]." A separate article in the same issue cited a dour if determined General Smith: "'We expect to take this island[,] and while it will be at a severe cost, it is our assigned mission.'"[11] Iwo Jima, a third article announced, was the Corps' "Hardest Fight in 168 Years," that is, since the Marine Corps' very inception, shortly after Lexington and Concord.[12] Historians would come to understand that the generals and admirals had overestimated the importance of Mount Suribachi: its capture on February 23 meant, as Garand and Strobridge note, only that "one phase of the Iwo Jima campaign had ended. . . . The Marines of VAC [V Amphibious Corps] had established a solid foothold ashore, and there no longer was any chance for the Japanese on the island to dislodge them. *Yet the most bitter and bloody part of the campaign was just about to begin.*"[13]

The February 24 *New York Times* published no new casualty report from Admiral Nimitz's command. The US marines, the headlines declared, had made small gains "in Center of Iwo." The column's subtitle announced that the Fourth Division had registered some "gains," while the "5th Held." Instead of reporting new numbers of American casualties, however, the *New York Times* provided its first report of Japanese losses—all deaths, no wounded, no prisoners—in the defense of Mount Suribachi: 717.[14] Yet, the continuation of the front page reported that the day's "communiqué made no further addition to [American] casualty figures, which up to Wednesday night had totaled 5,372." But "as D plus 5 ended, American casualties on Iwo Jima had risen to 7,758, an increase of 5,388 since the end of D-Day."[15] Whoever cared to total the figures so far published could have determined that American casualties outpaced those of the Japanese at an unacceptable—and unsustainable—ratio of eight to one.

The three-row headline in the *New York Times* for February 25 dropped the fight on Iwo Jima to third place (Eisenhower's advance to the Roer tops the other two, and the raids on Tokyo appear in the middle): "Marines Win Half of Iwo's Central Airfield," the third-row headline announces. But the photograph, which appears for the first time (to the immediate right of the Warren Moscow column "Japanese Overrun/Marines Smash through Maze of Defenses"), would have undoubtedly caught the readers' attention. Just above the photograph's frame, the caption, in all capitals, proclaims "OLD GLORY GOES UP OVER IWO." The caption below the photograph reads "Marines of the Fifth Division hoist the American flag atop Mount Suribachi." Significantly, the top caption declares that the flag has been raised *on Iwo Jima* (or "on Iwo"), and from this, photograph and caption together, the public might have justifiably inferred that the marines had captured the entire island. But the battle would go on for another month.

Dateline: "By Wireless to *The New York Times*, Guam, Monday, February 26." On the day following the report of the flag raising and the photograph, the third of another three-tiered headline announced that the marines had captured "Most of Second Iwo Airfield." On the front page, right under the headlines, the title of the fourth column (from Guam, "by wireless to *The New York Times*") announced that the runway had been "won," and the subtitle below it reported that the marines had seized "Two-thirds of Other [a second runway]." A third heading said simply "Fleet Paves the Way," while the fourth (and last) heading read "Ship Guns and Carrier Plane Lash Japanese—Foe's Dead at 2,827." And once again, as on the previous day's reporting, the commanders, abetted by the press, credited the capture of Suribachi for such progress as the marines were in fact making: "Beach supply conditions continued to show improvement, Admiral Nimitz reported. . . . This was made possible when Mount Suribachi, [the] volcano at the south end of the island, was taken and the beaches freed of Japanese fire from the rear."[16] Meanwhile, Nimitz's communiqués continued to direct public attention to Japanese casualties: "Admiral Nimitz disclosed that 2,827 enemy dead had been counted on the bloody little island." There was, by contrast, "no further report on American casualties, estimated [by an earlier count] at 5,372, including more than 500 dead, up to 6 P. M. Wednesday [February 21]." As we have seen, American dead had reached 566 on the first day of the land battle, February 19. Yet now, on the seventh day, Monday, February 26, the admiral, as if by some grim sleight of hand, had in effect reduced the reported number of total American deaths. Thus, the conquest of Suribachi continued to serve the commanders as a smoke screen for the relative lack of progress.

Also on February 26, the *New York Times* published a photograph—dateline "Feb. 23 (Delayed)"—of Secretary Forrestal looking at Iwo Jima from the bridge of Admiral Richmond Kelly Turner's ship.[17] "Forrestal," the caption reads, "pays tribute to Marines; he hit Iwo beach behind them." Forrestal did not "hit the beach" just behind the first wave of marines. He did, however, as noted earlier, come ashore with General Smith on February 23rd to witness the hoisting of the flag. The subtitle heading (column 5) reads "[Forrestal] Says Fight May Last Weeks," but in the article itself the secretary affirms not that the marines will fight for weeks to come but that they will be "'digging dead Japs, and some live Japs even out of Iwo probably for weeks to come." But Forrestal's next statement muddles the account of American casualties even more: "'In spite of all the skill of the Japanese defense,' the secretary says, 'the Marines went ashore, and they have exacted a 4-to-1 toll in death from our enemies.'" Those figures yield a ratio of almost six Japanese deaths for every one dead American, thus making Forrestal's "4-to-1 toll" seem positively prudent. Accordingly, the key element in Forrestal's statement—the equivocal calculus wherein to swathe the naked lie—is not the kill ratio of "4-to-1" but rather the phrase "toll in death." The secretary knew that virtually all the Japanese casualties had so far been—and would in fact continue to be—deaths. The Battle for Iwo Jima, as we now know, would produce more American casualties—dead, wounded, missing, captured, and battle-fatigued—than Japanese. Total American casualties were 28,696 (6,821 killed, 19,217 wounded, and 2,648 suffering from combat fatigue), while the estimate of Japanese casualties falls between 18,061 and 18,591 (all dead except for 216 prisoners). If the final reckoning of American to Japanese casualties—yielding a ratio of 1:0.64—had been made public at the time, the American commanders might well have been shamed out of their jobs or worse.[18] Still, on February 27, General Smith declared that all of Iwo Jima would belong to the US marines "'In a Few More Days.'"[19]

As February came to a close, Iwo Jima had begun to fade from the headlines. The front page of the *New York Times* included only a small article (an Associated Press release) on the battle. The Associated Press stated that the marines were winning "More of Iwo."[20] Reading on to the continuation of the article, on page 3, however, the reader might have paused before the photo spread on that same page 3. The first of five photos shows US Marine Corps "Amtracks" and tanks stuck in the island's volcanic ash. The next photo, however, shows a marine flamethrower moving "against an enemy pillbox," as the caption explains. The other three photos in the spread appear under the top two. The first one from the left shows wounded marines being evacuated "immediately from the danger zone." In the next photo, a helmeted Secretary Forrestal stands defiantly on the beach and "watches the Marines wage their fierce struggle." And next to these two photos, eighteen jubilant marines from Easy Company raise their helmets and rifles in celebration, the second (i.e., replacement) flag waving amply and proudly behind them. (This latter photograph was one of only three that Rosenthal took on February 23 atop Suribachi.) The *New York Times* caption refers to the men indifferently as the marines who "placed our flag atop Mount Suribachi after a bitter uphill battle with the Japanese in caves and pillboxes."[21] Most conspicuous, however, was the heavy-letter caption over the five photographs: "The Fighting Was Bitter and Bloody on the Iwo Beachhead, but at the End Old Glory Flew Over the Island."

While the fighting was indeed bitter, at the end the flag flew and not on Suribachi alone but instead over the island. Who would not have expressed surprise when told that the fighting and the dying were far from over? Who that read on to page 5 would not have thought that Nimitz was being overcautious? The photo spread omits all dates. Thus, if only for failing to establish even the most rudimentary chronology for the five photos, the spread as a whole more than hints at a syntax of its own, encouraging a top-to-bottom, left-to-right "reading." Aided by the top caption, the five photos tell a tale of unequivocal and complete American victory in Iwo Jima.

On March 1, the nation might have been wholly oblivious of Iwo Jima. President Roosevelt, though exhausted from Yalta (he had been back little more than a full day) and was in failing health, was to address Congress at noon. Earlier, however, as biographer Jim Bishop records, Roosevelt had audibly gasped "in horror" when "he was given the news that Iwo Jima had cost 27,000 American lives *and had not yet been secured*."[22] But now, addressing Congress and the nation, the president boasted. "'The Japs,' the president declared, 'know what it means . . . that the United States Marines have landed.'"[23] Roosevelt's "succeeding words," Bishop writes, "were drowned by applause." The president had said, "'And I think I may add, having Iwo Jima in mind, that the situation is well in hand.'" On Iwo Jima at that moment, it was a few minutes past midnight of the day when one of the flag raisers in the photograph, Sgt. Michael Strank, would die of his wounds. Another flag raiser in the photograph, Cpl. Harlon Block, died a few hours later, and on that same day Sgt. Henry "Hank" Hansen (who had been mistakenly identified as a flag raiser in the photograph) was killed by small-arms fire.[24] Also on that day, Lt. Col. Chandler Johnson, who had ordered both flags raised on Suribachi, was, as James Bradley coarsely puts it, "blown to bits, a collarbone here, another fragment there."[25] "Boots" Thomas and Louis Charlo, both present at the first flag raising, died two days later.

Perhaps the presidential shamming emboldened Admiral Nimitz to declare on March 14 "that Iwo Jima had been conquered." Bill D. Ross notes that "marines, from privates to generals, later cynically and understandably questioned [Nimitz's] timing as tragically premature; they would suffer more than *six thousand additional casualties* before leaving the island."[26] Still, two days later on March 15, Adm. Richmond Kelly Turner, who commanded all the amphibious forces in the Pacific, asserted "that Marine death casualties were 'less than one-fifth those of the defenders.'"[27] The appalling count would show that US marine deaths were closer to one-third of Japanese deaths. Nonetheless, Turner boasted that the final kill ratio was "'almost unbelievable and deserves the highest rank in military history; *the economy of losses can reach no higher perfection*'" (emphasis added).

"Pacific Fleet communiqué 300," issued on March 16, declared succinctly that "the battle of Iwo Island has been won."[28] The second paragraph of the communiqué declared that "organized resistance on Iwo Island ceased at 1800 (6 P.M.) on March 16 (East longitude date)." Between the initial sentence of each paragraph there was nothing in the way of casualties, American or Japanese; nothing about the staggering American losses; and nothing about a home front so dismayed even at such numbers as the military had already admitted to that there were urgent calls for turning over "the supreme command of the Pacific war" to General Douglas MacArthur.[29]

"History," so adroitly juggled, had become myth. By distortion and deceit, the implied scorn for truth and public alike, and the Olympian indifference to loss of life that compelled the commanders' rhetoric of sacrifice and heroism, more than by the undoubted courage of the marines, the official casualty figures tendered by the commanders in effect sublimated the Battle of Iwo Jima, transmuting the carnage into nothing less than a foundational cultural myth.[30] The casualty figures themselves—which is to say the numbers in their raw actuality—had given the commanders motive enough to submit not only different numbers but also a different narrative, one that exalted the marines on Iwo Jima even as it exonerated the battle planners.

On March 17, three days after first declaring the end of the fighting on Iwo Jima, Nimitz's command again proclaimed the end of the battle. "Announcing the end of organized resistance on Iwo Island," wrote Robert Trumbull, "Advanced Pacific Fleet Headquarters revealed that the Marines lost 4,189 officers and men killed in the twenty-six-day action. The wounded totaled 15,308 and the missing 441, bringing the overall casualties on Iwo to 19,938."[31] Trumbull's choice of verb tense—"lost," "killed," and "totaled," all of them lacking a qualifying "have" or a "so far" to hint at the ongoing battle—implicitly complied with the will of the commanders for closure, and the truth be damned. In this second and no less misleading declaration of the battle's "end," the commanders were reporting only 60 percent of the eventual total of American deaths (nearly 7,000) and only 70 percent of the total American casualties (about 28,000). On parts of the island already secured, battlefield cemeteries were dedicated as early as March 14. Yet, on March 21, Franklin Sousley, credited as being among the six flag raisers in the photograph, was killed by a Japanese sniper.

On March 26, Gen. Harry Schmidt, commander of the Landing Force at Iwo Jima, closed the Fifth Corps command post. Earlier that day, however, approximately 300 Japanese launched a well-organized predawn suicide raid against a roughly equal number of unsuspecting Americans in "a complex of tents." This was not, Ross notes, "a drunken, shouting banzai charge, but a well-organized and silent raid that bore every sign of [Gen. Tadamichi] Kuribayashi's cunning and determination."[32] When US forces finally repulsed the raid, 53 Americans were dead, and 119 were wounded. Among them lay 262 dead Japanese soldiers. No communiqué reported this event. After all, why report these belated and unexpected losses when, at Iwo Jima, the marines had attained to an "economy of losses" that could "reach no higher perfection"?

## The Anxiety of Legacy in 1949

*Sands of Iwo Jima* proposes to commemorate the bravery and the defiance that the photograph appeared to have captured almost four years earlier. But even as—indeed because—it seeks to memorialize and exalt the event, the film also and at the same time alludes to the anxiety of legacy as the event's proper counterpart. The year 1949 has been rightly called "the year of shocks."[33] America in 1949 found itself in that time "of continual crisis," as Richard Hofstadter put it, "from which the future promises no relief. In no foreign war in our history, did we fight so long or make such sacrifices as in the Second World War." Yet now that the war "was over, instead of being able to resume our peacetime preoccupations, we were promptly confronted with another war [in Korea]."[34] Consider, then, a brief account of some—only some—of the causes of America's consternation in 1949. On October 1, Mao Zedong proclaimed the birth of the People's Republic of China. Within a week of that earth-shaking event, the Democratic Republic of Germany (communist East Germany) was founded. The Federal Republic of Germany (West Germany) had been established earlier that year on May 23, and seven weeks earlier on April 4, the United States and ten western European nations, hoping to present a united front to the Soviet Union and communist eastern Europe, signed the charter of the North Atlantic Treaty Organization. By 1949, George F. Kennan's "Long Telegram" of February 22, 1946, had become the foundational expression of what I have termed America's "anxiety of legacy." In 1946, Kennan, serving in Moscow, had warned that "at bottom of Kremlin's neurotic view of world affairs is traditional and instinctive Russian sense of insecurity."[35] America's insecurities, however, matched the Soviets' own, for as Kennan warned, the Soviets intended to undermine American democracy from within. "Whereas formerly foreign communist parties represented a curious . . . mixture of conspiracy and legitimate activity, now the conspiratorial element has been neatly concentrated in [an] inner circle and ordered underground." Alluding to the American penchant for conspiracies, Kennan resorted to a metaphor of sexual seduction to explain the Soviet strategy. "A wide variety of national associations or bodies which can be dominated or influenced by such penetration. These include: labor unions, youth leagues, womens [*sic*] organizations, racial societies, religious societies, social organizations, cultural groups, liberal magazines, publishing houses, etc." America was in clear and present danger of surrender to the insidious "penetration."[36] In July 1947, when Kennan, writing anonymously (as "X"), published the famous article "The Sources of Soviet Conduct," "containment"—"firm and vigilant containment of Russian expansive tendencies"[37]—became the watchword of the US stance toward the Soviet Union. So single-mindedly devoted to "vigilance," the nation in effect incorporated anxiety into its foreign policy.

Against this background of suspicion and hypervigilance, the American distress over postwar global alignments became even more aggravated on August 29, when the Soviet Union detonated its first nuclear bomb (President Harry Truman did not make the announcement to the Free World until September 23). The Soviet bomb, by itself, may as well have marked the birth—or rather rebirth—of what Hofstadter identified as the "paranoid style," an idea that finds an apt historical description in this passage: "The distinguishing thing about the paranoid style is not that its exponents see conspiracies or plots here and there in history, but that they regard a 'vast' or 'gigantic' conspiracy as *the motive force* in historical events. History *is* a conspiracy, set in motion by demonic forces of almost transcendent power, and what is felt to be needed to defeat it is not the usual methods of political give-and-take, but an all-out crusade."[38] The typical proponent of the paranoid style, Hofstadter writes, sees "the fate of this conspiracy in apocalyptic terms—he traffics in the birth and death of whole worlds, whole political orders, whole systems of human values. He is always manning the barricades of civilization. He constantly lives at a turning point: it is now or never in organizing resistance to conspiracy. Time is forever just running out. Like religious millenarians, he expresses the anxiety of those who are living through the last days and he is sometimes disposed to set a date for the apocalypse."[39] Perhaps America in 1949 was not clearly aware of such subtle ironies and contradictions as had so suddenly emerged from and arrayed themselves around the threat of total annihilation, but there should be no doubt that the anxiety pervading American life at the time could take the shape of ideologies and precepts, of sentiments and affiliations, intended to conceal or displace the dread wherein they were all sourced. Already in 1949, as Robbie Lieberman notes, "Proponents of the cold war consensus in the United States argued that Americans must 'live in crisis—prepared for war.'"[40]

Well primed for paranoia by daily events, Americans who read George Orwell's *Nineteen Eighty-Four*, published in June 1949, could easily decipher therein the nightmares to be visited even on the nation's slumbers. Surely the author had tendered this story as a gloomy warning of an imminent dystopic future so as to avoid the same dismal destiny that it augured. Americans might have seen their anxieties over the red menace mirrored as well in Marion Starkey's *The Devil in Massachusetts*, a narrative of the dubious battle between the Pilgrim ancestors and the satanic powers at large in the New World. "Who in my day," Starkey asks rhetorically in her preface, "has a right to be indignant with people in Salem of 1692?"[41] The year and the time confirmed at every turn the deep moral ambivalence chronicled in Starkey's narrative. America's earliest "frontier," hopeful site and source of hallowed civil liberties and individual freedoms and visions of cities upon hills, also revealed a benighted, obdurate, and petty people, a people at home in ignorance, tolerant of cruelty, and predisposed to see revenge as a divinely allotted recompense for their own pharisaical canting.

In October 1949, RKO Studios released *I Married a Communist* (dir. Robert Stevenson), a noir piece about the thuggery rampant on the docks of San Francisco. "The [Communist] party," *Time* noted in its account of the victimized wife, played by Laraine Day, "has . . . killed her husband, run a sports convertible over her brother [played by John Agar], and pushed her prospective sister-in-law out of a window."[42] Communists swarmed all around us, and Hollywood would teach us to identify them, ward them off, and destroy them. It was a compellingly ironic feature of the paranoid style that filmgoers could so readily detect communists while the film's characters remained so perilously in the dark as to their neighbors' allegiances.

The national alarm over communism rendered the late-summer riots at Peekskill, in New York's Westchester County, in the sharp chiaroscuros of good and evil, each side claiming the former as its exclusive own. The riots, as James P. Shenton put it in 1976, "'opened up what was to become extensive public endorsement of the prosecution and persecution of so-called Communists.'"[43] On August 27, Paul Robeson—singer, actor, athlete, lawyer, activist (*Time* dismissed his genius and settled for "Communist-turned Singer")[44]—was scheduled to perform at Lakeland Acres picnic grounds to benefit the Harlem chapter of the Civil Rights Congress. Four days before the concert, the *Peekskill Evening Star* declared that "the time . . . for tolerant silence that signifies approval is running out."[45] The *Evening Star* did not make clear just why the clock had run out on tolerance in Peekskill or why a silent tolerance would have meant only consent for Robeson's pro-Soviet statements, made in April at the Paris Peace Conference.[46] Still, on August 27, members of the Council of Veterans' Organizations sought to "spoil the concert by having members march up and down before the picnic grounds and drown out the voice of Mr. Robeson with the music of their bands." An article in the *Washington Post* stated that "as the marchers neared the concert platform they broke ranks and, after some fighting, captured it by storm."[47] *Time* reported that some five hundred veterans "smashed the stage, set fire to the camp chairs lined up around it and burned the sheet music."[48] "The lynch spirit arrived in Westchester [County]," heralded *The Nation*, "complete down to the burning of crosses."[49]

Robeson's performance was rescheduled for the Sunday (September 4) of Labor Day weekend. Although "veterans' groups [were] allowed to stage a counter-demonstration in front of the concert grounds,"[50] the performance went on, with the concertgoers protected this time by union men forming a cordon between protestors and the audience. After the concert, however, every exit out of the venue at Hollow Brock led to a hellish trap. "Men and women along the roadsides," writes Roger M. Williams, "began stoning the buses and cars. Stone throwers seemed to be everywhere, forming gauntlets that the concertgoers had to run no matter which route they followed."[51] Mobs of local teenagers joined the veterans against the departing concertgoers. *The Nation* noted with dismay the "revelation of Nazi-like violence in the teen-agers" and also said what needed saying, namely that "the explosion at Peekskill was not merely anti-Communist. It was anti-Negro and anti-Semitic as well."[52] According to the blacklisted novelist Howard Fast, who was present at Peekskill, half of the concertgoers who fought the veterans that late August day at Lakeland Acres "had been in some part of the war, the Bulge, the Pacific, Africa, the C.B.I., but we learned about fascism here."[53] The alien abominations that Americans had died to crush only five years earlier now arose from native soil.

In the immediate postwar, the South's old ineradicable odium struck with perverse acrimony against returning Black veterans, many of whom had dared to imagine that their service in the US armed forces would reward them with increased opportunities at home. Instead, as John Egerton notes in his magisterial *Speak Now against the Day*, "an epidemic of random murder and mayhem was sweeping like a fever through the region, fueled by white fears that Black veterans might become a revolutionary force, and that Blacks in general would no longer stay 'in their place.' It would be too much to suggest that a massive conspiracy to drive out or eliminate the African-American minority was lurking in the postwar South. No such master plan was necessary; fear and ignorance were enough to loose the vigilante mobs."[54] In the face of all evidence to the contrary—from the military service of African Americans (both free and enslaved) during the Revolutionary War through to World War I—America's heroic myth had implicitly insisted that its heroes could never be but white. The time after World War II was no different. Indeed, the animus against returning Black veterans, especially in the South, seemed unprecedentedly virulent. Almost two decades after the end of the war, James Baldwin gave Americans an extended reflection on the fate of Black American soldiers both in wartime and following their homecoming:

> The treatment accorded the Negro during the Second World War marks, for me, a turning point in the Negro's relation to America. To put it briefly, and somewhat too simply, a certain hope died, a certain respect for white Americans faded. One began to pity them, or to hate them. You must put yourself in the skin of a man who is wearing the uniform of his country, is a candidate for death in its defense, and who is called "nigger" by his comrades-in-arms and his officers; who is almost always given the hardest, ugliest, most menial work to do; who knows that the white G.I. has informed the Europeans that he is subhuman (so much for the American male's sexual security); who does not dance at the U.S.O. the night white soldiers dance there, and does not drink in the same bars white soldiers drink in; and who watches German prisoners of war being treated by Americans with more human dignity than he has ever received at their hands. And who, at the same time, as a human being, is far freer in a strange land than he has ever been at home. *Home!* The very word begins to have a despairing and diabolical ring. You must consider what happens to this citizen, after all he has endured, when he returns—home: search, in his shoes, for a job, for a place to live; ride, in his skin, on segregated buses; see, with his eyes, the signs saying "White" and "Colored," and especially the signs that say "White Ladies" and "Colored *Women.*"[55]

The local events that I sketch in the next few paragraphs instantiate Baldwin's reflections on Black soldiers "home" from the war. I note, however, that the outrages of 1949 had an infamous precedent, the beating and blinding of World War II veteran Sgt. Isaac Woodard—who was wearing his army uniform—in South Carolina in March 1946.[56]

In Lake County, Florida, on the night of July 15, 1949, two Black army veterans, Samuel Shepherd and Walter Irvin, had driven Samuel's brother's car to Eatonville for a night out on the town. Sometime past midnight on July 16, Shepherd and Irvin drove by a young white couple, Willie Padgett and his young but estranged wife Norma Lee Padgett—"both of them roaring drunk," Gilbert King notes—whose disabled car was stopped by the side of the road.[57] Shepherd and Irvin offered to help push the car to get it started. With Padgett at the wheel, Shepherd and Irvin started to push, but when they stopped to rest, Padgett stuck his head out the window and snarled, "'Get to pushin'.'" Shepherd "didn't appreciate being bossed around by Padgett," and soon the two friends had had enough of Padgett's venom.[58] "[Shepherd] grabbed Willie by the shirt. Willie tried fighting back, but, drunk and scrawny, he was no match for Samuel. In a few seconds Willie was flat on his back, either knocked out or passed out, in the ditch."

The tragedy's next act concerns Norma Padgett's allegation that she had been kidnapped and raped. The white community called for lynchings, and the houses of African Americans in the area—including that of Shepherd's parents—were set ablaze. The National Guard was brought in. On July 29, when civil rights attorney Franklin Williams visited Shepherd and Irvin, he "was profoundly shocked. . . . It had been nearly two weeks since they had been transported to Raiford [State Prison], but their faces and bodies still bore the effects of the beatings that they'd suffered in Lake County."[59] On September 3, the accused were found guilty. Shepherd and Irvin received the mandatory death penalty. (A third codefendant, Charles Greenlee, was charged along with Irvin and Shepherd even though he had never met them. Greenlee had been arrested in Groveland for carrying his friend Ernest Thomas's pistol and had then been transferred to the jail in Tavares, where Irvin and Shepherd, now badly beaten, were being held. Willie Padgett himself told the sheriff that Greenlee was not one of the men from the previous night's encounter. Still, Greenlee was sentenced to life in prison. He had avoided the death penalty only because he was sixteen years old at the time. A fourth "Groveland Boy," Ernest Thomas, had arrived in Groveland with Charles Greenlee and so had nothing to do with the Padgetts or with Irvin and Shepherd, but having heard that Mabel Padgett was claiming she had been raped by four Black men and knowing that his friend Charles had been framed, Thomas got on a north-bound bus. A posse of about a thousand white men hunted him down and eventually found him asleep at the edge of a swamp. They shot at him with buckshot, pistols, and rifles. Later it was determined that he had been shot some four hundred times.)

Some two and a half years after the original incident, Sheriff Willis McCall, transporting Shepherd and Irvin south to Tavares, pulled over with a flat tire. Moments later Shepherd had been shot dead, and Irvin lay on the ground, grievously wounded. McCall would maintain that the two men had assaulted him and had tried to escape. Five or ten minutes after that incident, McCall's deputy, James Yates, arrived on the scene and shot Walter Irvin at point-blank range in the neck, though Irvin was to survive this outrage as well.

In the postwar South, the long-suffering, resigned, and tragic wisdom of an older generation of African Americans had foreseen such attacks against their own sons, against these doomed heirs of the rancor inherent in the heroic myth. "Fathers of black soldiers," Gilbert King writes, "warned their sons not to come home in their uniforms because police had made a practice of searching and beating Black military men."[60] Henry Shepherd, Samuel's father, spoke with the old fatalistic vision of African Americans in the South. "'Sammy is a good boy,'" he told Franklin Williams after the arrests. "'All the white people will say he was before he went to the army. Since he come back people didn't like Sammy and the Irvin boy driving James's [Shepherd] car around. They didn't like no veterans' attitude.'" Heroism in the South was also a "whites-only" privilege. In justice's own good time, the Groveland Four (to spare them the scurrilous "Boys") were exonerated more than seven decades after the initial crime against them.[61]

Early in 1949, Audie Leon Murphy published his ghostwritten memoir of World War II, *To Hell and Back.* Child of the Texas hardscrabble, Murphy was only twenty-five years old at the time. His unsparing accounts of battle are as vivid as they are horrific and consistently deny the reader's impulse to bask in the liquid noon of the heroic myth. All that Murphy achieves as a combat soldier—all, accordingly, that might serve as fodder for the heroic myth—takes place in the teeth of a constant and freely acknowledged state of terror. Only two months after the surrender of Germany, *Life* magazine featured Murphy on its cover and devoted a photo essay to him.[62] The cover photo, showing a freckle-faced, blue-eyed, beaming boy in army cap tilted raffishly, belies the man credited with killing more than two hundred German soldiers during his two years in the battlegrounds of north Africa, Sicily, Italy, and France. In the cover photo, Murphy wears the badges, the ribbons, and the fourragère that seem more like a child's playthings than institutional affirmations of extraordinary courage and sacrifice.

The bitter squalor of Murphy's prewar life in Texas controverted *Life*'s treacly piece. "The Murphy family," his biographer Don Graham notes, "could have posed for any of the documentary photographers of the thirties: Walker Evans, Dorothea Lange, Margaret Bourke-White."[63]

A blighting hopelessness, deep, endemic, had made Murphy's youth all but impervious to any and all varieties of the American dream. In his postwar life, he would look back upon his youth and find there nothing recognizably American or Texan. "'I am one Texan boy who never had a pair of cowboy boots. I am one native-bred American male who actually doesn't know the rules of our national pastime—baseball. . . . I never had a bike. It was a full-time job just existing.'"[64] To such a boy, the US Army—even in the time of war—might not have seemed a bad bargain, especially since most of what he knew about combat came from not only the yarns of those who had served in World War I but also the movies. "He went to the movies whenever he could," Graham writes. But there was only one he saw twice. "It was about a favorite subject, war, and it starred his favorite actor, Gary Cooper. The movie was *Sergeant York*. . . . This film . . . touched him deeply, and why not? Its true-life story of a poor Southern farmer who loved his mother and rose from rural obscurity through feats in battle to become the most decorated soldier of World War I was virtually a prophecy of Audie's fate."[65] Small surprise that one seemingly so foredoomed would have obeyed the heroic imperative. Howard Hawks's *Sergeant York* (1941) could consecrate the misery of York's—or Murphy's—life to make of it fertile ground for more heroics "over there," Horatio Alger behind Hawkeye's long rifle.

Now in 1949, Murphy's autobiography debunked the wholesome Boy Scout image that *Life* magazine had carefully crafted and promoted four years earlier. Murphy remains throughout bent on chronicling the nightmares of combat, on documenting the pervasive terror, the overwhelming grief, and, not least, the monstrous metamorphoses that combat wreaks in the human heart, as in his memorable account of house-to-house fighting in the town of Montélimar. "Leaping from the sunlight into the dim rooms we must wait for our eyes to become adjusted to the change. As we stand in one house, the door of a room creaks open. Suddenly I find myself faced by a terrible looking creature with a tommy gun. His face is black; his eyes are red and glaring. I give him a burst and see the flash of his own gun, which is followed by the sound of shattering glass. The horrible being that I shot at was the reflection of my own smoke-blackened self in a mirror."[66]

The moment controverts the culturally constructed notion of heroic virtue in the service of a clear cause with clearly defined sides, hero and enemy, good and evil. Even the famous action that earned him the Medal of Honor failed to compel Murphy to claim a heroic inheritance. "Except for a vague pain in my leg," he notes, "I feel nothing: no sense of triumph; no exhilaration at being alive. Even the weariness seems to have passed. Existence has taken on the quality of a dream in which I am detached from all that is present. I hear the shells bursting among the trees, see the dead scattered on the ground; but I do not connect them with anything that particularly concerns me."[67] Soon after the war, the moral lassitude of one who has seen altogether too much would explain both blind rage and dispassionate cynicism, or his preoccupation with firearms (to protect himself from unseen enemies and from himself). This would explain the obsessive womanizing, the fraught marriages, the drug addiction, and the addictive gambling, the vigilant restlessness that often pervades apathy.

But the movie, based on the autobiography and bearing its title, "cleaned up World War II, repackaged it, and made it seem like anything *but* 'to hell and back.' . . . The film altered certain facts in the book to refocus our attention away from cynicism and psychological wounds."[68] It had taken a good deal of cajoling to get Murphy to play himself in the movie, but when it came to his assessment of its fidelity to the book and to his own experiences, he agreed with his longtime friend and ghost-writer Spec McClure: "I don't give a damn if this movie makes seventeen million dollars. You were right. We missed by a mile."[69] Missing by a mile perhaps meant failing to realize that heroism cannot erase the terror in the act itself. Missing by a mile meant, moreover, that the public anointment of Murphy served primarily to diminish and dilute, while only seeming to honor, the concomitant realization of utter perdition, even in the service of God and country. Hollywood made sure that war's hell would never obtrude on the heroic myth, even as it ensured that its self-serving investitures of heroic status on tragically and irreparably broken souls would signal its sorry estrangement from the very experiences that it presumed to represent.

Plagued by demons similar to those that beset Audie Murphy and so many other returning veterans, Howard B. Unruh, "a mild, soft-spoken veteran of many armored artillery battles in Italy, France, Austria, Belgium and Germany," as Meyer Berger reported in the *New York Times* in September 1949,[70] had returned home from the war to the same shabby apartment in East Camden, New Jersey, that he had shared with his mother before the war. Unemployed, Unruh seems to have divided most of his waking hours between target practice (in his building's basement) and reading scripture. *Newsweek* noted that "the war had seemed to do great things for Howard. . . . He won medals as a marksman and was counted a good soldier."[71] But "he had not seemed quite the same" since his return. On the morning of September 6, Unruh left his apartment with his German Luger pistol and began his killing rampage at a shoe repair store, where he shot the owner in the stomach, and for the next twelve minutes went on to terrorize the 3200 block of East Camden. In one of the photos in *Life*, Maurice Cohen, a neighbor with whom Unruh had had many petty quarrels, lies dead in a gutter. Unruh also killed Cohen's wife and mother.[72] Three of Unruh's victims were children. One of them, six-year-old Orris "Brux" Smith, was straddling a white carousel horse getting a haircut for the start of school when Unruh shot him at point-blank range. Two-year-old Tommy Hamilton was peering through a window of his home when Unruh walked up to him and shot him between the eyes. Unruh also killed a ten-year-old boy and his mother. The neighbors, Unruh eventually revealed, "'ha[d] been making derogatory remarks about my character.'" In complicity with war's horrors, Unruh had produced the first "spree" or "rampage" crime in modern American history. At the time, it was "the most concentrated series of crimes ever committed in the U.S."[73] Unruh was declared insane.[74] He died, hardly a familiar figure, in October 2009, a full six decades after the rampage.

In the early morning of May 22, 1949, James V. Forrestal, who as secretary of the navy had fudged the kill ratios in the Battle of Iwo Jima and had resigned from his position as the nation's first-ever secretary of defense less than two months earlier, jumped to his death from the sixteenth floor window of a diet kitchen at Bethesda Naval Hospital, where he had been recovering from a nervous breakdown. If Forrestal had not directly experienced combat, he had certainly seen a fair copy of it at Iwo Jima. In an article that appeared only two months before the suicide, Admiral Ellis M. Zacharias, who had served under Forrestal in the Office of Naval Intelligence, wrote that Iwo Jima had been the pivotal experience of Forrestal's life. Forrestal, Zacharias wrote, "watched with his own eyes young Americans die by the hundreds despite the most painstaking material preparations and determination to cut human losses to a minimum."[75] Before Iwo Jima, Forrestal "had always scorned war with the groping peace-mindedness of the average American. . . . But in the bloody battle for Iwo, his civilized dislike of war suddenly hardened into hatred. After this brutal show his mind was not again to be free of its effect. It even left physical marks on him—a new brassy petulance, deeper furrows in his brow, a grimmer and grittier look to his face."[76] Doctors who admitted Forrestal to Bethesda "concluded that [he] was suffering from 'reactive depression'—essentially the condition of combat fatigue seen with such frequency during World War II—which results from an accumulation of intense external pressures that overwhelm the mind and the nervous system."[77] Now two months later, the president of the United States, unable to fathom the depths of Forrestal's despair, could only echo the doctors whose diagnoses, however accurate, had so fatally failed of a cure: "'This able and devoted public servant,' President Harry Truman said, 'was as truly a casualty of the war as if he had died on the firing line.'" Forrestal, who had promoted the mythology of Iwo Jima, had become one of its historical casualties.

The year 1949 stood as astonished witness to events that urged an incessant, indeed slavish preparation against an imminent undoing at the hands of oppressed races or communists or both. Thus, the nation found itself caught in a cycle of imaginative affirmations followed—or stalked, as befits the paranoid style—by subversive self-interrogations. In the most critical times and despite the proclaimed glory of its most recent and perhaps greatest triumph, America in 1949 could not make its heroic legacy stop the wildly unfolding events that imperiled its newly minted, unmatched ascendancy. And then midway through the fateful year, there was this, which no doubt would have seemed at the time only a mild by-product of the national paranoia. "In June 1949," as historian George C. Herring wrote, "the United States issued a statement of support for the Bao Dai government [of Vietnam], a hugely significant first step toward active involvement in the war."[78]

## *Sands of Iwo Jima* at the End of 1949

Did *Sands of Iwo Jima* merely pander to the American heroic, fawn before it and flatter it in vacuous adulation? Or did its very excess of nationalistic fervor reveal, albeit unwittingly, the anxieties that seemed to undermine the triumph that had so recently reaffirmed America's heroic inheritance? The ideological complacency that characterizes the film's fables of American heroism does not preclude a critique based on the complications inherent in a narrative so single-mindedly invested in its own vapid rhapsodizing over the national pieties. Its shrill insistence on the historical truth of the myth reveals already its implicit recognition of and reaction to the anxiety of legacy. The thematic weight and import of the anxiety of legacy is evident in an early scene. Sgt. John Stryker (John Wayne) has been leading his squad on a march through the woods. Once the march is over, he summons Pvt. Pete Conway:

> **Stryker:** I was checking over the records last night. Your father was Colonel Sam Conway.
> **Conway** [*petulant*]: What if he was?
> **Stryker:** I was with him ten months ago in the Canal [i.e., Guadalcanal]. He was my C.O. before he got killed. One of the best officers and finest men I ever served under, and I thought if you . . .
> **Conway** [*interrupting*]: Thanks, I'll keep it in mind [walks away].

The exchange establishes a genealogy only to destabilize a legacy, for Conway scorns his own heroic ancestry. When the march resumes, with the men walking in columns of two, Cpl. Robert Dunne (Arthur Franz) picks up the thread of the exchange above between Conway and Stryker. Conway explains to Dunne that he "shipped in" not because his father died in Guadalcanal but instead "because [he] was expected to ship in." "Every time there's a war," he explains, "the men in my family join the marines. I'm the last of the Conways, so here I am." When Dunne remarks that the colonel would be "proud to know you're carrying on the tradition," Conway sneeringly replies, "Not my father. He would have expected me to find some soft duty somewhere. In fact, he told me so." The rest of Conway's diatribe in this scene might have seemed especially disturbing here in late 1949, when the outbreak of war in Korea was only half a year away. "I embarrassed my father. I wasn't tough enough for him—too soft. 'No guts' was the phrase he used. Now Stryker—he's the type of man my father wanted me to be. [*Parodying Stryker, on Colonel Conway*] 'The finest man I ever served under.' Yeah, I bet they got along just fine together.

Both of them with ramrods strapped on their backs. But not me. I'm a civilian, not a marine. They're not going to strap one on mine. I'm here strictly for tradition." At this point Conway knows tradition merely, living, as it were, in the Marine Corps' *semper* but without the *fidelis*.

Two consecutive scenes, still early in *Sands of Iwo Jima*, help illuminate the anxiety of legacy. The first unfolds in the training grounds in New Zealand, where Stryker has been drilling his squad. A day earlier while on leave, most of Stryker's men attended a dance, where Conway meets and quickly falls in love with Allison Bromley (Adele Mara). The day after the dance, Stryker leads his tired and hungover men on a twenty-two-mile hike, and eventually the weary marines turn in, two to a pup tent (Dunne is Conway's tent mate), except for Stryker, who is alone in his tent, which is pitched next to Conway and Dunne's. The cross-cutting between the interiors of the two tents has Conway spilling out his romantic hopes to Dunne, who is exhausted and barely responsive. But Stryker is wide awake, and he eavesdrops. Toward the end of the scene, Conway, in the indefinite "you" and heedless of Dunne's inattention, babbles on: "You realize way down inside, no matter how much you try not to think about it, that maybe something's got your number on it, and you want to leave a little bit of yourself behind. [*CUT*: *close-up; Stryker eavesdropping*] It doesn't matter whether it's a boy or a girl, just so long as you know you won't be forgotten. There's got to be someone who would never have lived if it hadn't been for you. [*CUT*: *Dunne fast asleep, snoring*] Am I right? [*To himself*] I think I'm right. [*CUT*: *Stryker, pensive still, lies down to sleep.*]"

Out of the end-of-scene dissolve, Conway is walking to town on a dusty road. Stryker comes up behind him in a jeep and offers him a ride into town. As soon as Conway hops in, Stryker urges him to desist from pursuing Allison: wartime, he counsels, is no time for romance. Conway stops Stryker. "Listen, Stryker, if it's in the line of duty, you can tell me to do something and I'll do it. But as far as my personal life goes, keep your hands off." But Stryker persists, and the rest of the exchange only widens the generational gap.

**Stryker:** It's the same thing your father would have told you.
**Conway:** I wouldn't listen to him either.
**Stryker:** That's right. You never did.

**Conway:** How do you know?
**Stryker:** He told me.
**Conway:** What did he say? Never mind. I'll tell you what he said. He said I was a disappointment, right? He said I didn't have what it takes, right? He said I wouldn't be able to stand up for myself, right?
**Stryker:** You're doing the talking.
**Conway:** No, Stryker. My father's doing the talking. Every time you open your mouth, my father's doing the talking. Every thought you think is my father's thought. It's as though he were standing on my shoulder all the time. But he didn't always say the right thing, and he didn't always think the right thing. You're going to find that out. When the time comes, you're going to find that out. But until then, leave me alone.

Himself a son of sorts to Col. Sam Conway, Stryker presumes to know what the colonel might say to his son Pete about romance in a time of war. But the exchange above also anticipates Stryker's admission of his own estrangement from his ten-year-old son Sam (named after Pete's father).

Stryker, however unwelcome his advice, must nonetheless instruct Conway in the greater duty, namely the moral obligation to recast his romantic and familial hopes in the crucible of the two critical contests with which the narrative is vitally concerned: the looming fight for Iwo Jima and the disasters (with their attendant anxieties) portended by postwar upheavals.

The anxiety of legacy manifests itself not so much through Pete Conway's impatient wish for children as through the bitterness that keeps him from recognizing the urgency with which his desires must be fulfilled. In time, the self-absorption at the core of Conway's scorn for the Marine Corps relents. Yet, the repeatedly foretokened surrender of his puerile hubris affirms not so much pride in the unit, everlasting fidelity to the Marine Corps, or selfless love of the imperiled nation as it does the reaffirmation of the heroic lineage. On the night before the assault on Mount Suribachi, the reiteration of the name Sam (linking past, present, and future), the harmony between Stryker and Conway, and the surrender of self to the Marine Corps all come together in the following exchange:

**Conway:** Stryker, it's going to start getting rough tomorrow when we go against Suribachi.

**Stryker:** It started getting rough when you put on that uniform.

**Conway** [*reaching inside his shirt*]: Stryker, . . . you want to see a good-looking kid?

**Stryker** [*over a close-up of little boy's photo*]: Husky little boot. What'd you name him?

**Conway:** I'm going to name him Sam, Sam Conway.

**Stryker:** A name that's been awarded the Navy Cross ought to be good enough for any kid.

**Conway:** Yeah. [*Haltingly*] Look here, Stryker, there's something I've been trying to say, but I just can't seem to find the words.

**Stryker:** You mean you've been to two universities and still can't find the words to say you've been out of line?

**Conway:** Okay, I'm out of line.

**Stryker:** No, you *were* out of line. There's a difference. . . . You know, everybody gets out of line once in a while.

**Conway:** Thanks, Gyrene.[79]

The scene above immediately precedes the fight for Mount Suribachi. The reconciliation now guarantees not only the victory on Iwo Jima but also the continuity of the heroic legacy. We are confident that Conway will show himself fully worthy of his ancient patrimony. The heroic inheritance shall be determined, proclaimed, and fulfilled by the progression from the first of "the Conways" (some original *ur*-Conway) to Col. Sam Conway (and his proxy, Stryker) and now to Pete Conway. "Conway," then, designates not so much a biogenetic lineage as it does the very name and essence of the American heroic, the anointed pedigree wherein genesis commingles with destiny, and the foreordained accession both requires and confirms a freely tendered fidelity to nation, destiny, and the heroic myth itself.

In the second of two brief but crucial scenes with "Mary" (Julie Bishop), a barfly coquette in a seedy off-base joint, Stryker finds a surrogate Sam Stryker and something like parental redemption. In the preceding scene at the saloon, Stryker rudely rebuffs Mary, who approached him for companionship, but her name reminds him of his estranged wife, herself named Mary. Now softened somewhat, he follows Mary to her apartment for a drink, but her one bottle is empty, so Stryker gives her money to buy a full one. While Mary is gone, Stryker discovers an infant in its crib and casually refers to him as "Mac." Soon Mary returns with not only the whiskey but also Pablum, the impecunious would-be whore somehow a loving mother Mary. Moments earlier Stryker had referred to the child as "she," but Mary emphatically retorted "*He*," as if Stryker had somehow insulted the child. Gender is invested with a redemptive role not only because this bond with a male child so clearly mitigates Stryker's parental anguish but also because maleness, which here is indistinct from manliness, becomes the means for extending the inheritance of World War II into the Cold War era. (Just before the battle, Stryker tells Conway that "a fellow always gets more kick out of a boy.") Let Allison and Mary and all other American women "bring forth men-children only" (as Macbeth says to his dear wife in that other tale of inheritance), for only so can the nation's nurseries replenish the requisite legions to win the wars to come.

The anxiety of legacy in *Sands of Iwo Jima* promotes an almost laughable, though nonetheless significant, lack of variety in the names of the several characters, male and female, present and absent. The strategy succeeds to the extent that characters become types, and types and their recurrence signalize the continuity of the American heroic. Allison's letter to Pete announcing the birth of their son ends with something like an anxiety over naming: "I still don't know what to call him. We never discussed that, you know." We have already learned that Stryker has a ten-year-old son named Sam. And Pete names his own son Sam, so that now two boys are named after Col. Sam Conway. Moreover, Mary's toddler functions as a substitute for the ten-year-old Sam Stryker even as he embodies Stryker's reclaimed fatherhood. If Stryker recovers his estranged Sam through "Mac," he also receives a sort of absolution from Mary. "You're a very good man," she says as Stryker leaves, adding, "I'll pray for you." Stryker's feigned cynicism in response to Mary's benedictions (to the first, "You can get odds on that in the Marine Corps," and to the second, "Let's not get religion") fails to attenuate their sanctifying effect. This "other" Mary, it turns out, is not just a tatty whore with a crummy come-on but a hard-bitten American Madonna doing her duty by son and hero alike.

The second encounter between Conway and Allison ends by dispelling our anxiety over his fitness for heroic action, but it begins by baring his doubts about his own manliness. Alone with Allison, Conway responds at last to her concern about his brooding silence:

**Conway:** Honey, do you think I'm a brave man?
**Allison:** What a funny question to ask.
**Conway:** Do you?
**Allison:** I don't know. Why?
**Conway:** I've got to prove something to somebody.
**Allison:** Who?
**Conway:** You don't know him. He's dead now.
**Allison:** Yes, Pete, I think you're brave.
**Conway:** That helps. You don't know how much that helps.

Conway's worry, an anxiety voiced so pitiably that it practically *forces* Allison's reassurance, shows him for the first time responsive to the demands of the heroic myth. The ghosts of his father, of his heroic lineage, and of the Marine Corps—all of them embodied in Stryker—urge him to embrace his obligations to the heroic ideal. Conway understands that if only in the lap of easeful love, as he is in this scene, he must "prove something to somebody." And we understand that this "somebody" is none other than Colonel Conway (or his ever-importunate ghost), though we also understand that Allison's perfunctory endorsement (what else could she have replied?) establishes her own worth as American wife and mother. Before the scene closes, she accepts Pete's marriage proposal. Pete's ill will toward Stryker appears now in a different light: the early grumblings of a self-entitled, effete marine brat were all along the vital demurrals of a red-blooded American youth.

## History and Myth: Three Brief Encounters

Almost as soon as the fight for Mount Suribachi begins, Stryker's unit suffers the loss of several characters from the original squad. Also, *Sands of Iwo Jima* registers the staggering casualty numbers of the historical battle by showing the swift deaths of three young replacements. Their minimal screen time and their unmourned deaths only intensify our already dismaying sense of the ghastly, grisly waste, the mounds of the dead, faceless and defaced, that null and mock individual tragedy: Fowler (stabbed in the back), Stein (praying in Hebrew as he dies), and McHugh (in his pocket a copy of *Our Hearts Were Young and Gay*). Each death implicitly acknowledges the Marine Corps' historic losses in Iwo Jima but also serves as a narrative strategy for linking Stryker and his squad to some of the real-life marines who raised the flags on Suribachi.

As Stryker and Conway huddle against a dune to avoid Japanese machine-gun fire, a runner comes up and tells Stryker that "Lieutenant Schrier" wants "to see" him. Stryker scampers a few yards off and reports. "Your platoon has been hit pretty hard," woodenly says Lt. Harold G. "Hal" Schrier, one of the actual historical marines who raised the first flag. "What's left of it has been assigned to me." Schrier's order authenticates Stryker/Wayne's presence in, or at least his engagement with, the flag raising and therefore casts him as a historical witness. At the same time, however, Stryker's heroic status is sorely diminished the moment Wayne appears before Schrier. For Schrier is very much the historical witness—witness to not only the flag raisings but also the myriad horrors of Iwo Jima.[80] Still, Stryker is now brother in arms to the unimpeachable witness. And yet, neither Stryker nor Wayne have been merely superadded to Hal Schrier's presence. By virtue of sharing the screen with Schrier, Stryker—a fictional character—is himself suddenly empowered to authenticate the Suribachi imaginary (since Schrier will entrust the actual first flag to him) and to codify it (since Stryker himself and by himself, having received the hallowed relic, can permissibly embody American heroism).

The anointment of Pete Conway, which occurs almost immediately, follows from Stryker's certified status as a mythic hero. Stryker can now pronounce—ordain, really—a full-fledged brave, patriotic marine. How else would *Sands of Iwo Jima* bear out Allison's faith in her man's courage in battle but by having Conway savagely kill a Japanese attacker? And how much more fitting could such a killing be than in defense of Stryker? As a Japanese soldier raises his sword against Stryker, Conway hits him across the belly with the shovel part of an entrenching tool and then falls on the soldier with his knife, stabbing and slashing frenziedly. "Thanks, Marine," Stryker says, and both his gratitude and his designation for Conway as "Marine" amount to a ritual anointment of a new hero, the instauration that remedies the lapse. In the calm after the fight, Conway shows Stryker a photo of his infant boy. Stryker assumes that the boy already has a name: "What'd you name him?" But Conway's reply suggests otherwise: "I'm going to name him Sam, Sam Conway." Only now has Conway earned the right to name his son, his heir. Before the scene closes, Conway volunteers for the first watch, and we never doubt his wide-awake vigilance.

Now, Lieutenant Schrier summons Stryker a second time and directs him to get his men "squared away." Schrier will be "taking a patrol up Suribachi in the morning." Moments later, we see Schrier shooting into the mouth of a cave and Stryker tossing a grenade in. The scene, perhaps superfluously, authenticates the mythic by mixing it with the historical but also prepares us for the third and most important of these authenticating pairings. Schrier calls for Stryker a third time. "The colonel," Schrier tells him, "has ordered that we put up this flag as soon as the top is secured. Be sure that it gets there." Schrier hands Stryker the flag, the actual first flag, the one that Schrier himself helped hoist atop Suribachi and as such the same one that, together with the flag in the photograph, are even today "perhaps the most important artifacts in the care of the National Museum of the Marine Corps."[81] What greater irony—and yet, what more succinct display of the power of the heroic myth—than that the historical figure (Schrier) should entrust the historic flag to the movie hero (Stryker) played by the actor (Wayne) who never served in his generation's war.

Despite the opening "historical note" announcing that "The First American Flag Was Raised on Mount Suribachi by the Late Sgt. Ernest I. ["Boots"] Thomas, Jr. U.S.M.C. on The Morning of February 23, 1945," *Sands of Iwo Jima* seems only too glad to conflate the first and second flag raisings. Stryker does hand the first flag to the three survivors and stateside protagonists of the "Mighty Seventh": Gagnon, Bradley,[82] and Hayes (figure 2.2). But these are the survivors of the second flag raising, hence part of the confusion. Then, Stryker orders the three marines to "find something for a standard, and we'll put this up."

There follows the reenactment of the second flag raising, an event now in *Sands of Iwo Jima* seemingly oblivious of the first flag raising, an event therefore purportedly without precedent. So fudged, this raising of the first flag as both the first (and only) and as the flag in the photograph

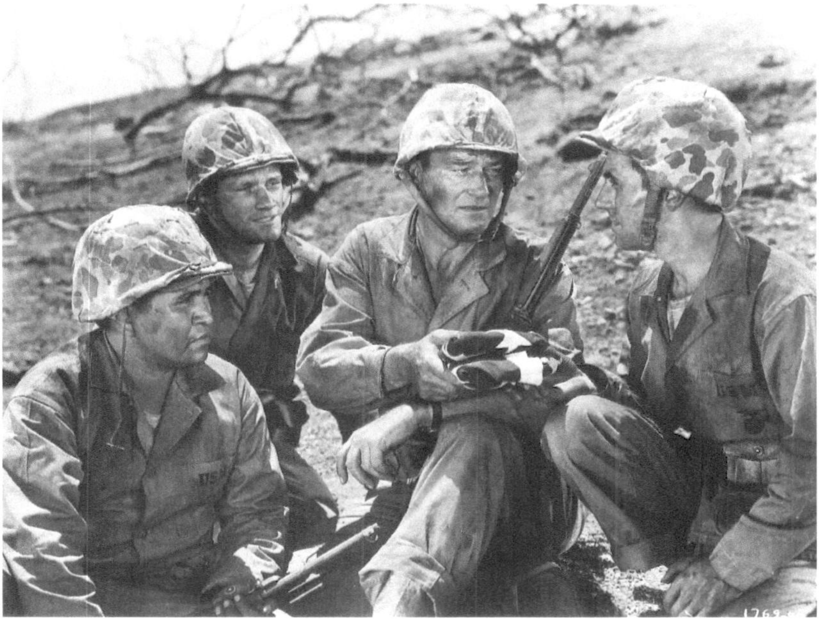

Figure 2.2. *Sands of Iwo Jima.* Sergeant Stryker (John Wayne), third from left, hands actual Iwo Jima flag to marines present at the flag raising. Left to right, Ira Hayes, John "Doc" Bradley, and Rene Gagnon.

would make this 1949 moment the original itself, the impossible source, of that 1945 photograph. And the witnesses—Gagnon, Bradley, and Hayes—themselves replacement flag raisers in 1945 and now in 1949 bit-part players ordered about by Stryker, are to re-create only the one flag raising by using the first flag (which Stryker has just handed them) while assuming, as ordered, the pose of the second flag raising. As *Sands of Iwo Jima* appropriates the Suribachi imaginary, so too does Stryker inaugurate the full-fledged Wayne persona. Roberts and Olson can hardly exaggerate when they maintain that the film identified the moment when Wayne began "to live in the shadow of his own image. He had never served a day in the military and he was America's ideal Marine. . . . From the disappearance of the flags of a cavalry regiment [in *Fort Apache*] to the raising of the flag on Mount Suribachi, John Wayne's image had become tightly intertwined with the destiny of the United States."[83] Wayne's presence in a mythic version of the historical record has him in effect becoming, or at least plausibly replacing, Hal Schrier himself. But if we turn our attention instead to the men to whom he hands the flag—that is, to Gagnon, Hayes, and Bradley—Wayne becomes more properly Sgt. Mike Strank, who commanded the squad that raised the replacement flag and was himself one of the six men in the photograph. In this way the name "Stryker," by itself so suggestive of effective might and unwavering resolve, also evokes the anagrammatic abridgement that calls forth both patronymics, one from each flag raising: *Strank* and Schri*er*. Here, moreover, Wayne becomes more than just another legator. He becomes the legacy itself. No longer a mere character in the film, he is John Wayne, as he would be in virtually every movie thereafter—Western or war movie—undaunted and invincible (Conway calls him "indestructible"), patriotic and patriarchal, killing Indians and Japanese indifferently and (in time) Vietnamese, all in affirmation of the true and only order of things "American," things imperial, things racial. In solemn earnest of such wondrous cultural realities, though no less in tacit surrender to the anxieties that would continue to summon up the cultural prodigy, many an "heir" of John Wayne would follow his mythic trail all the way to Vietnam.

## The Stryker-Wayne Legacy

The death of Stryker marks a defining moment in the theogony of John Wayne, a sort of ascension, for Stryker becomes Wayne, America's preeminent Cold War warrior. Henceforth, the character onscreen shall be one more iteration of the uncompounded cultural essence, John Wayne. Thus, Stryker can die only because John Wayne already lives on. In the end, it is Wayne, not Stryker, who is "indestructible," immortal, as befits a true hero. Wayne is not merely the sum of America's heroic virtues but also the abidingly self-sustaining being, the unquestioned protagonist of his own metanarrative. The three young heirs—the two Sams (Stryker and Conway) and "Mac"—represent the faithful millions of their generation whose heroic model would become not the historical flag raisers but rather Wayne himself, indeed Wayne only or at least Wayne self-sufficiently.

The taking of Mount Suribachi at the end of *Sands of Iwo Jima* brings a brief respite to the squad. In an earlier scene, Conway had told Dunne of a "feeling" he kept having, "like a voice in my ear," that he was "not going to come out of this [military] operation." Now, however, after the capture of the volcano, a much-relieved Conway tells Stryker, "I guess that little voice was wrong. I feel better." Stryker agrees: "I feel a lot better, too. As a matter of fact, I never felt so good in my life." But right away Stryker is shot dead by an unseen sniper. In the resulting silence of the squad's shock, Pfc. Al Thomas (Forrest Tucker) finds a letter in Stryker's pocket. "It's a letter to his kid," Thomas announces, and he begins to read it out loud. The letter begins by excusing the boy's silence: "I guess none of my letters have reached you." Soon, however, it brings up the basic terms of the legacy, especially (for Sam Stryker is only ten) in the form of parental pieties. First, "you've got to take care of your mother and love her and make her happy. Never hurt her or anyone as I did." But directly Stryker adds, "Always do what your heart tells you is right." In so spurring the boy to the free exercise of his will, the letter clearly bares Stryker's fear of a fatherless boy too fastidiously nurtured by a single mother as well as of the disadvantaged condition, evident in the scene with Mary and "Mac," of fatherless American boys. The rueful wisdom that exhorts Sam Stryker to take counsel with his heart barely hides Sergeant Stryker's hope that his son will someday do as the errant husband and father has himself done and put country and the Marine Corps above all. "Maybe," the letter continues, "someone will write you someday and tell you about me." Here the cut from Bass to Conway assures us that Pete will be the one to finish the letter and, more broadly, that he will be to Sam Stryker as Col. Sam Conway was to John Stryker. The letter explains that "I want you to be like me in some things but not like me in others," thus reprising the ambivalent catechism that enjoins the boy to solicitude for his mother even as it in effect urges him to follow his heart to the nearest Marine Corps recruiting station. There follows another wave of self-reproach and resignation: "When you grow older and get to know more about me, you'll see that I've been a failure in many ways. This isn't what I wanted. Things just turned out that way." Surely now, self-immolated on the altar of parental victimhood, Stryker stands absolved of all his domestic shortcomings. Call it the referent to the war, call it the attendant estrangement, call it his death itself, the letter's "This" is never what the hero wants. But Stryker's is a gracious fatalism: "things just turned out that way." The last of the letter reads "If there was only more time, I . . ." "I guess, he never finished it," Thomas resumes in his own voice. Conway takes the letter from Thomas and resolutely declares, "I'll finish it for him." No doubt he will, but Stryker's was never a mere letter: it is a deed of transfer, with Pete Conway as both legatee and executor. Once finished, the letter shall proclaim both the fulfillment of the heroic legacy and its continuity into the generations to come. Thus, Pete Conway fulfills the testament even as he bequeaths it. And thus, the heroic filiations of American mythology in *Sands of Iwo Jima* suggest an assured and uncontested inheritance: as Stryker stood for Pete Conway's heroic father (Sam), so now Pete Conway stands for the heroic Stryker, himself (Pete Conway) both father and model to Stryker's ten-year-old son Sam.

As Conway is putting Stryker's letter away, there is an abrupt cut to the flag raising. The hoisting of the flag, however, does not appear onscreen simply because someone in Stryker's squad looks up at the top of Mount Suribachi and happens to witness the event as if through an eyeline match. The five marines have been kneeling around Stryker's body, which faces up, in the foreground. But they are so consumed with dismay and sorrow that they fail at first to see the flag go up. The first image of the flag raising in *Sands of Iwo Jima* appears as a comforting reiteration of the familiar image in the Joe Rosenthal photograph. Six marines plant the flag on Mount Suribachi in accordance with the decrees of history and the demands of verisimilitude. Moreover, the moment provides the crucial piece of authenticating history to the film; that is, the cinematic action pretends to release the motion arrested in the photograph. If myth becomes indistinguishable from history, however, it is not because myth attains to historical clarity but because it so successfully fudges and falsifies any source of possible distinction between them, distinctions of not only, for example, temporal order, narrative direction, or significance in relation to the entire battle but also ideological motive so that what is presented as a pure distillation of patriotic fervor and resolve serves also to bury the tragic truths of the Battle for Iwo Jima.

In a drum-roll overture to the Marine Corp hymn, the soundtrack matches the moment when the flag raisers have just secured flag to pole. Then, with the flag already at the angle shown in the photograph, the flag raisers hold the famous pose. There is a cut to the men of Stryker's squad. "There she goes," Thomas says softly, and then each man, in close-up, looks up from Stryker's body to the top of Mount Suribachi. Now, in the eyeline match back up to the flag raising, the six men atop the volcano still hold the pose in the photograph, perhaps casting the five marines below (Stryker makes up the matching six) as witnesses to the eternal moment, since in effect they are looking upon the very instant that Joe Rosenthal captured. The five survivors of Stryker's squad, who had until now knelt around the fallen Stryker, now reverently stand up, their eyes fixed on the event at the top. At last the men up on Mount Suribachi straighten the flagstaff, and we are reassured that the arrested motion of the photograph, which might have suggested an ongoing and uncertain struggle, has now come to uncontested and undoubted triumph. Also, as the flag raising reproduces the facelessness of the six men, the tight individual close-ups of the men below invite the projection of their faces onto the blank ones above.

In this way, *Sands of Iwo Jima* develops the basic narrative of historical co-optation, the cultural double-dealing, and the self-subversion central to the Suribachi imaginary. The film presumes to be raising only the one flag, using the *first flag* while the men strike the pose of the second flag raisers. Upon this opacity *Sands of Iwo Jima* begets another obfuscation: the projection of the close-ups of Stryker's squad onto the indistinct faces of the flag raisers suggests that the iconic image of the flag raising is merely an instance, one of many, of America's heroic sublime.[84]

After the flag raising is completed, we see more close-ups of Stryker's men. The last of these, appropriately enough, is Conway's. Over the opening strains of the Marine Corps hymn, he casts his eyes downward. The eyeline match is on the prostrate Stryker, who now lies implausibly *face down*; the name "John M. Stryker" is stenciled on the back of his shirt, and the quarter-size entry hole of the fatal bullet is just inches under the first name and trickles the slenderest thread of blood. Conway snarls his call to action after Stryker's familiar manner: "All right! Saddle up! Let's get back in the war!" The men turn away from Stryker's body, though not without a backward glance, and then walk resolutely into the thick billowing smoke of battle that doubles unmistakably for clouds of heroic accession.

In a narrative so concerned with patronymics and appellatives, the one name at the end, "John M. Stryker" on the back of the man's shirt, now contains them all; it stands for the resolution of conflicts between not only the generations but also what is historical merely and what is enduringly mythic. Indeed, *Sands of Iwo Jima* seems all too aware of what might appear to the goof-obsessed as a continuity blunder but is in fact a trope, though no doubt clumsily executed, for establishing the importance of the name. In the next-to-last cut from the flag raising, the men, still kneeling around Stryker's body, had risen to their feet as they maintained their gaze on Mount Suribachi's summit. In this shot Stryker lies face-up, and as the camera tilts up with the men as they stand, he disappears from the lower frame. The men continue to look up and away to the top of Suribachi, and there is one last cutaway to the flag, which now flies upright. The film then cuts to the close-ups of the men. The last of these is a close-up of Conway, who suddenly looks down, and then we marvel to see, in the match cut, that Stryker is now lying face-down, allowing us to see the name on the back of the shirt as well as the spot where the bullet hit. The "goof" may lie in the disparity between the two shots of the dead Stryker, but it is mitigated by the deliberateness with which the second of the two shots urges a nation to reflect and remember, to aspire and emulate. In the name is the inspiration itself, for we see the name not on the shredded uniform of a battle-mangled body such as those of the historical thousands strewn all over the island but instead as if invested with lapidary dignity, the man himself his own serene and solemn memorial.

But if Stryker has been enshrined as the essence of American heroism, it is because John Wayne himself has attained his primal and preemptive cultural apotheosis. The legacy is Wayne. His cultural power, however sourced in and nurtured by the Suribachi imaginary, enables him at once to embody and transcend it. He embodies it, yet not as its personification merely or as a dramatic composite of this or that other iteration of it but instead as its own essential stuff, so that the Suribachi imaginary—*even* the Suribachi imaginary—now stands as an attribute to this heroic essence. The Battle of Iwo Jima itself has become only a moment in the enduring struggle to preserve a heroic legacy. Virtually indifferent hereafter to the historical moment, Wayne's mythic being rides out of the western landscape into world wars and guerrilla wars alike, himself the nation—"John Wayne, American"—as inscribed on the Congressional Gold Medal struck only a few days before his death. And yet, his heroic being itself substantiated the anxieties of the time, hearkened vigilantly, restlessly, to the footfalls of the myriad disruptive demons of America's great and abiding disquiet. At the end of "the year of shocks," the triumphant and triumphalist ending of *Sands of Iwo Jima*, which might have seemed a continual and unequivocal affirmation of a glorious national destiny, came instead to portend a harried flight from the galling American worry over murky ancestries and murkier destinies and over the dubious battles ahead and the requisite manliness to not only win them but also consecrate them in the national mythology.

## CHAPTER 3

# His "Children Rawly Left"

## John Wayne's "Boys" and the Vietnam Generation

> But if the cause be not good, the king himself hath a heavy reckoning to make when all those legs and arms and heads, chopped off in a battle, shall join together at the latter day and cry all, "We died at such a place," some swearing, some crying for a surgeon, some upon their wives left poor behind them, . . . some upon their children rawly left.
>
> —William Shakespeare, *Henry V*

> A l'époque de l'Armistice et de la reddition sans condition du IIIe Reich et du Japon, dans tous les milieux américains, on s'exclame, «Comment aurions-nous pu gagner la guerre sans John Wayne?»
>
> —Eric Leguèbe, *John Wayne, l'homme et le mythe*

### "Forging" Boys into Men: The Trailer for *Sands of Iwo Jima*

The title *Sands of Iwo Jima* bursts suddenly on the screen and briefly blocks out the standard with the seal of the US Marine Corps, which had appeared onscreen only an instant before. On the soundtrack, a lusty rendition of the Marine Corps hymn already blends with the two superimposed images to recall Americans to themes of heroic sacrifice and national glory in the battle now more than five years in the past. Wearing a

Marine Corps combat uniform, John Wayne emerges in a circle-open shot followed by the credits for his supporting cast, not only John Agar, Adele Mara, and Forrest Tucker but also "The Gallant United States Marines!" Over this title, there are newsreel shots of marines in various sorts of basic training exercises. "These are your boys," a voice-over now declares, "who John Wayne as Sergeant Stryker forged into fighting men." A new close-up of Wayne appears, and the voice-over tells us that he (Wayne as Stryker) is barking orders at these "men who said he was as hard-hearted as steel." The recruits tumble and charge, thrust bayonets at dummies, and jump from high platforms into the water below. Before the end of the trailer, Wayne will appear a second time, again in close-up, accompanied by another adulatory avowal: "His Greatest Performance!" "His Biggest Picture!"

With chapter 2 as context, this chapter develops in part out of two simple questions implicit in the voice-over's reference to "your boys," namely who is the "you" being addressed and who (and whose) are the "boys"? It seems unlikely that the voice-over would be addressing the parents of the "boys"—these *men*—many of them just recently home from the war. Perhaps the voice-over summons the younger brothers of the veterans, those who had just missed out on World War II. In *Retreat, Hell!* (Lewis, 1952), for example, Jimmy McDermit (Russ Tamblyn) was too young for World War II. He comes from a family of marines, and he looks at Korea as his opportunity to claim his heroic inheritance. Moreover, both *Retreat, Hell!* and another movie of the Korean War, *The Bridges at Toko-Ri* (Robson, 1954), introduce their protagonists as veterans of World War II. Both protagonists leave behind the fine middle-class lives they had secured after World War II. They are hardly "boys."

Perhaps the voice-over in the trailer is exhorting the veterans of World War II to entrust their own boys to John Wayne. Surely, however, the combat veterans of that war had already become "men" in ways that neither the trailer's voice-over nor Wayne could have imagined. Their "manhood" answered to not only their triumph but also the sustained and chastening nightmare solitude of the terrors that haunted them long after their return from the war. Besides, many who fought in World War II knew that Wayne had ducked military service: "The word *hero*, to me," writes William Manchester in his memoir of World War II, "is redolent of . . . John Wayne being booed in a Hawaiian hospital by an audience of wounded Marines from Iwo Jima and Okinawa, men who had had macho acts, in the phrase of the day, up their asses to their armpits."[1] Echoing Manchester, Kenneth D. Rose notes that "the Hollywood war that Wayne was fighting especially rankled combat veterans because Wayne's characters never exhibited any traces of combat's most common denominator: fear. American servicemen who were polled during the war overwhelmingly agreed that combat never became less frightening, and more than 20 percent of the men in one division reported that fear had made them lose control of their bowels during combat."[2] Randy Roberts and James S. Olson acknowledge that Wayne "was not so popular with the soldiers and sailors who were fighting the war."[3] They recount the story told by director Edward Ludwig during the filming of *The Fighting Seabees* (1944), with location scenes in the South Pacific. "'There was a saloon,' Ludwig recalls, 'near our location frequented by servicemen and every time Wayne would go in there, some guy would pick up a fight with him.'" The servicemen knew that Wayne was "'play-acting that he was in the military service for his country.'" It is unlikely, then, that many World War II veterans would have thought of themselves as the "boys" that Wayne had "forged into fighting men."

By the equivocal alchemy of the movies, Wayne had acquired the biography that he had failed to earn in wartime. The cultural encouragement to imitate Wayne would take on a weighty role in the daily lives of the boys, but many—too many—of the veterans who might have most effectively forewarned them of war's horrors returned home only to lapse into that familiar, nearly collusive and all but universal *silence*, into that troubled and reticent sotto voce that would fall mute well before the tale of horrors suffered and survived. It would be up to John Wayne to drill the new generation of boys, and Iwo Jima—the historical battle now co-opted by what we called in chapter 2 "the Suribachi imaginary"—would serve as a template of all the battles they would fight "for years to come."

The notorious silence of World War II veterans became complicit with Hollywood's falsifications of war. Perhaps nowhere in the literature of the Vietnam War is there a more telling example of this generational lapse than in the last stateside fantasy of Tobias Wolff's splendid memoir of the Vietnam War, *In Pharaoh's Army* (1994). Even in the hour just before they are to board the bus to the airport (thence to Vietnam), the young recruit somehow still believes that "until now nothing had seemed irrevocable.

I had persisted in the unconscious faith that no matter what I did, . . . I would be excused from taking this last step."[4] Wolff then appeals to all the fathers of the World War II generation:

> Nothing could stop [the recruits' induction]. Except . . . what? . . . Hijackers. A gang of hijackers in front of a barricade, wielding shotguns and pitchforks and clubs, shining bright lights into the [bus] driver's eyes. The driver stops. They come up the steps and down the aisle, flashing their beams from face to face until they find the ones they're after. They call our names, and then we know who it is behind the blinding lights. It's our fathers. Our fathers, come to take us home.
>
> Crazy.
>
> But not as crazy as what they actually did, which was let us go.[5]

Some two decades after *Sands of Iwo Jima*, Kurt Vonnegut visited a buddy from World War II, Bernard V. O'Hare, who was to help Vonnegut write a book about their experiences during the war. Early during the visit, Vonnegut notices that Bernard's wife, Mary, can barely hide her anger, and though he feels certain that he is the object of that anger, he remains for a good while at a loss to tell what he has done to earn it. Eventually she reveals the source of her hostility. "'You were just *babies* then! . . . You were just babies in the war—like the ones upstairs! . . . But you're not going to write it that way, are you.' This wasn't a question. It was an accusation."[6] Vonnegut meekly replies that he does not yet know how he will write the novel. "'Well, *I* know,'" Mary responds. "You'll pretend you were men instead of babies, and you'll be played in the movies by Frank Sinatra and John Wayne or some of those other glamorous, war-loving, dirty old men. And war will look just wonderful, so we'll have a lot more of them. And they'll be fought by babies like the babies upstairs." Duly chastened, Vonnegut tenders a promise: if he finishes the novel, he tells Mary, "'I give you my word of honor: there won't be a part for Frank Sinatra or John Wayne.'"[7] Word of honor or no, in 1969 when the resulting novel, *Slaughterhouse-Five*, was published, the babies had already followed Wayne to Vietnam, many of them believing, at first, that war looked "just wonderful."

## Now Playing at the Royal

*The Last Picture Show* (Bogdanovich, 1971) evokes a post–World War II Texas small town, Anarene, gasping out its last days, dying of not only socioeconomic despondency and historical irrelevance but also moral and spiritual inanition. On its last day before closing forever, the Royal Theater, owned by Sam the Lion (Ben Johnson), shows Howard Hawks's *Red River* (1948), starring John Wayne as the irascible Texas cattle baron Thomas Dunson. (The titles of two other Westerns—*Wagon Master* [Ford, 1950] and *Winchester '73* [Anthony Mann, 1950]—also appear on the Royal's marquee, but John Wayne is absent from both of them.) Of war movies, however, there has been but one title up on the marquee: *Sands of Iwo Jima.* Over the years, the "boys" had come to the Royal to neither see nor witness, to neither worship nor testify, and not only to "make out." No, they came to be blessed, anointed. But Anarene's moral torpor and social miasma of betrayal and lies and infidelities instantiate an America (it is late 1951, and the Korean War rages on) living in the fast-fading bloom and bedimmed radiance of its World War II victory, a nation now content to look backward, via the Old West and the latest war, that it may project its past into a future, a future perforce conceived not of hope but of anxiety and even despair. "There is simply no way in this town to touch life and glow," wrote Roger Ebert of *The Last Picture Show.*[8] So, in the end, when Duane Jackson (Jeff Bridges) leaves Anarene to fight in Korea, *The Last Picture Show* offers us a view of the fraught and tortuous way to the heroic myth after World War II: animated by a mythic past pressed to do the moral office at which the older generation has failed, the young American—this one "boy" of John Wayne's—goes forth to make his impossible future.

When Marine Corps recruiters came to Ron Kovic's high school, they summoned up images from the young man's mythic sources. "It was like all the movies and all the books and all the dreams of becoming a hero come true. I watched them and listened as they stood in front of all the young boys, looking almost like statues and not like real men at all."[9] Then, the heroes become in-the-flesh demigods who have stepped out of the movie screen. "As I shook their hands and stared up into their eyes, I couldn't help but feel I was shaking hands with John Wayne and Audie Murphy. They told us that day that the Marine Corps built men's body, mind, and spirit. And that we could serve our country like the young president [Kennedy] had asked us to do."[10] Kovic evokes the ecstasy that overcame the boys whenever they beheld the heroic sacrifices in movie versions of Bataan, the Bulge, and Iwo Jima. And Wayne's heroism was but a distillation of the heroism that they knew to be *their* birthright. This war now in Vietnam, wherever on Earth that might be, was *their* war, a war surely like their fathers' own. Loyal and guiltless witnesses that they were, what could they have foreseen of betrayal and deception, of the unredeemed Loss and tragedy that came to identify their generation?

Throughout much of *Go Tell the Spartans* (Post, 1978), set in Vietnam in 1964—the year before the first battalions of US marines landed in Da Nang—a maverick officer, Maj. Asa Barker (Burt Lancaster) is puzzled not so much by the boldness of a mere draftee, Corporal Courcey (Craig Wasson), as by the inspiration behind that boldness. Finally, it hits Barker: Courcey thinks that Vietnam is World War II. Barker says, "You know what you are Courcey? You're a tourist. Too bad we couldn't have shown you a better war, like hitting the beach at Anzio, or smashing through to Bastogne with Patton. That was a tour worth the money. This one? This one's a sucker's tour, going nowhere, just round and round in circles." The children had kept "faith" with their fathers, had honored their fathers' "flags," yet they would have no "Good War." They would waste their dreams of glory on "a sucker's tour."

## The "Cause" and the "Fight"

On the day before he is to ship out to Vietnam, Lt. Robert E. Lee "Bob" Hodges Jr., the protagonist of James Webb's *Fields of Fire* (1978), communes devoutly with the three sources of his decision to join the Marine Corps: his father's sacrifice in World War II, the generations of Hodges citizen-warriors reaching back before the American Revolution, and Hollywood war movies of World War II and Korea. The collective sway of these influences, Hodges believes, forms "a continuum, a litany. Pride. Courage. Fear. An inherited right to violence. And the pride accumulated, even as the reasons themselves became more amorphous."[11] When still a small boy, Hodges discovers a footlocker that had belonged to his father, who died before Hodges was born. "There before him . . . lay the remains of [Hodges's] real father."[12] These shards and oddments—the uniforms, the ribbons and medals, the letters home, and the one dreaded letter still in its US Army envelope—drive Hodges's innocent eagerness for his own war.

The second source of Hodges's heroic legacy is his paternal grandmother. Every Sunday at lunch, she delights him with thrilling accounts of the Hodgeses' exploits. "We always been out here," she intones, "since the first days when we took the wilderness, all the low blue mountains from Cherokee and Saponi and Tutelo. Those were some fights, what I mean, when it was just a man and his family against them Indians."[13] She is her grandson's epic muse, delighting him with tales of his clan's deeds: "[General Lee himself] told them [the Hodgeses] they were God's bravest creatures, that they'd earned a glory spot in heaven."[14] Hodges's genealogy underwrites the mystic bond, the unbroken "continuum." Moreover, the ancestors relieve him of obligations to political, ideological, and even patriotic motives, for "it was the fight that mattered," as Hodges insists, "not the cause."[15]

Hodges's response to the heroes of Hollywood war movies forms the third source of the continuum—of the heroic continuity—through which he claims his inheritance. "And the movies. They were their own communion. If John Wayne wasn't God then he was at least a prophet. Hodges and a half-dozen friends would walk the five miles into Hillsville on Saturday afternoons and sit in awe through *The Sands of Iwo Jima* [*sic*], *The Bridges at Toko-Ri, The Guns of Navarone, Anzio, The Battle of the Bulge*, and dozens others. It was all there on the screen."[16] Only the first of these titles (*Sands of Iwo Jima*) stars John Wayne, but in Hodges's imagination, the unmentioned protagonists in the other four movies (respectively, William Holden, Gregory Peck, Robert Mitchum, and Henry Fonda), prominent though they all were in their time, are but minor stars reflecting Wayne's self-sourced, resplendent magnificence. Thus, rather than casting suspicion on Hodges's movie memory, the passage above offers one more attestation of Wayne's vast influence on the Vietnam generation. The father whom Hodges knows mostly by means of trinkets, baubles, and the narratives of the harridan grandmother lives in the heroic person of John Wayne. Indeed, like the heroic Hodgeses dating back to pre-Revolution days, Wayne's single and abiding character fought in virtually all of America's wars from the French and Indian War to World War II and then the Vietnam War. Wayne was his own heroic genealogy.

In the infamous May 1971 interview in *Playboy* (an interview controversial enough that its rediscovery in 2019 resulted in calls for renaming the Orange County, California, airport), Wayne claimed that at an American Legion convention, none other than Gen. Douglas MacArthur anointed him as something quite like the deity he is for young Hodges: "'You represent the American Serviceman," Wayne says MacArthur told him, "better than the American Serviceman himself.'"[17] As Richard Slotkin notes, MacArthur's statement "suggests that Wayne's mythic figure is not merely a representation but a valid substitute for and even an improvement on the real thing."[18] And as I noted in chapter 2, Congress ordered that a Congressional Gold Medal be struck in Wayne's honor. On the recommendation of Wayne's friend Maureen O'Hara, it read "John Wayne, American."[19] Wayne's death in June 1979 did not diminish his preeminence in American culture. In 1980, President Jimmy Carter posthumously awarded Wayne the Presidential Medal. Who, then, could blame John Wayne's boys for their faith in this exceptional American when heroic generals, veterans organizations, the US Congress, and the president himself could so ingratiatingly rhapsodize over him?

Following the heroic trail to his generation's war, Hodges goes to Vietnam believing the place to be an ancestral battleground. He is one with the many whose experience would find representation in the account of "a former marine from Texas" who, as Robert Jay Lifton reports, "brought to Vietnam what he considered a heritage of honor transmitted over the generations and going all the way back to the Alamo: 'I remembered the stories my grandfather used to tell me about it. . . . So I thought that . . . like the Alamo was a special moment for people way back and World War II was my father's moment, Vietnam was my moment. . . . When I got there I kissed the earth because I considered it sacred ground.'"[20] But in Vietnam, the young men's sacrifice, as genuine and heartfelt if not more so than their fathers', still failed to authenticate America's claim to a special heroic destiny. Let Webb's Hodges protest that he was in the war for the fight only, not for the cause, but such an insistence immediately discloses a poignant irony, namely that the combat soldier driven to Vietnam by Wayne's movie heroics relived the American past only by converting it to or confusing it with mythology. History repeats itself not because it is forgotten but because it is misremembered. As a representative of his generation, Hodges—young Hodges, at least—embraces the spirit of the mythic warrior who never lost a war, but in casting Wayne as a proper incarnation of such a mythic warrior, Hodges also embraces the "warrior" who never fought in a war.

And heroism was wholly contingent upon decisive and uncontested victory. Hodges may fight only for the fight's sake, but that is likely because, as an American nurtured in John Wayne's sort of "history," he expects to win. The heroic inheritance demanded victory—victory if not always in a given battle then certainly in the war—before proceeding to the soldier's full investiture as hero. By contrast, losing precludes heroism, thwarts inclusion in the mythic lists. As for martyrdom and righteous sacrifice in a defeat—as in *The Alamo*, where Wayne's Davy Crockett dies in battle—these are only provisional states. Promotion to heroic status awaits the instant of final victory *in the war.* Thus, Crockett's martyrdom at the Alamo undergoes elevation to heroic status not so much by how he fought or died there but by the Texan victory in the War for Texas Independence at San Jacinto on April 21, 1836, some six weeks after the Alamo.

Not unlike Webb's Hodges, Pvt. James Vincent ("Cherry") Chellini, the young protagonist of John M. Del Vecchio's novel *The 13th Valley*, embraces the idea of a heroic continuum. Inspired (also like Hodges) by a sense of kinship with the heroes of World War II, Chellini, upon first arriving in Vietnam, "imagined himself as a part of the liberating armies coming into France or Belgium in the old World War II movies."[21] Eventually, however, we learn that his division's mythic bond with World War II is as strong as with Hollywood war movies. Del Vecchio pointedly reminds us that the 101st Airborne Division, the "Screaming Eagles," carried with it to Vietnam the fighting spirit it had taken a generation earlier to World War II. "The division ethos was purposefully directed and developed from the style, zeal and *esprit de corps* of the airborne of World War II. . . . The 101st had stormed through Europe at Eagle's Nest and Berchesgadten, and Zon, had endured the Battle of the Bulge at Bastogne with General Anthony C. McAuliffe's famous 'Nuts' reply to German demands for surrender, had jumped into Normandy on D-Day. In Vietnam the firebases were named after World War II locales and slogans: Veghel, Bastogne, Eagle's Nest, Ripcord, Airborne, Checkmate, Rendezvous and Destiny."[22] The achievements of the 101st in World War II became the stuff of myth. The unit itself—and therefore the legacy that its victories conferred—made heroes of its men in Vietnam. So, then, Chellini's 101st Airborne Division will reenact the glories of yore through its own unique achievements.

In the "Author's Note" to the 1998 edition of *The 13th Valley*, Del Vecchio describes the process that brought him to understand the Vietnam War as an inexhaustible source of America's finest virtues. Echoing the clarion call of President John F. Kennedy in his inaugural address, Del Vecchio writes, "Indeed, the more I read, the more I researched, and the more veterans I spoke with, the more I realized how nearly universal were the values and positive behaviors Americans exhibited in Southeast Asia, how closely we participants believed in the altruistic ideals—to bear any burden . . . to defend freedom—under which we went to war."[23] The pith of this testimony, above, is already present in Del Vecchio's dedication: "To the vast majority of Americans who served honorably, heroically, in the most moral war this nation has ever engaged, I wish you peace, prosperity, happiness, and vindication."

Yet, some of Del Vecchio's own characters express a more cynical view of what makes a war right. Here is the seasoned soldier Daniel Egan enlightening Chellini on war's "essence":

> "War," Egan said forming his lips into a trumpet and sensuously blowing the word at Cherry. "They send you to the far corners of the earth. You hear the blasts of artillery and bombs. You get weapons, helicopters. You can call all heaven down, all hell up, with your radio. War. It's wonderful. It don't make a gnat's ass difference who the enemy is. Every man, once in his life, should go to WAR." . . .
>
> Cherry hesitated, then muttered, "Yeah, but is it right?"
>
> "Winning makes it right," Egan snarled.[24]

First you win, and only then are your soldiers heroes; heroism itself is among the "spoils" of victory. But if you lose, your war becomes unjustifiable and a source of national humiliation.

Would the claim in *Fields of Fire* that Vietnam was made right by the fight itself or *The 13th Valley*'s claim that Vietnam was the "most moral" of American wars have been at all necessary if America had *won* in Vietnam? Do they not, these declarations, in themselves attest the Loss? Do they not confirm the historical impossibility of the Vietnam War as a link in the heroic continuum? Do they not invoke and validate the rupture? Indeed, America's Vietnam narratives presuppose the rupture, and the rupture is their foundational and irreducible theme. Thus, it is not the assessment of victory or defeat but rather the abiding historical tragedy of Vietnam that resists the demands to cast the American soldier as a hero. To insist, accordingly, that heroic continuity persisted without interruption in Vietnam is tantamount to denying the soldier something far more commensurate with his humanity, namely the soul-searing benediction of the tragedy that became, in the end, the distinguishing mark of his presence in his very own historical moment. Not, then, the stigma of shame for the Loss, *nor* the censure of the American generations, nor the specious apologies for a war fought for the fight's sole sake but rather tragedy immemorial and horrific—tragedy, one wants to say, *un-American ennobles* the Vietnam soldier precisely because he fought and lost. The Loss defines these soldiers. The rupture, before which they stood resistant and helpless witnesses, bore with it the myth's own disavowal of them, its repudiation of their war. Who, then, will dare demand, as if bereft of all empathy, that they be mere mythic heroes when they are in fact so fearfully intimate with all-chastening tragedy?

Yet, America refused to see, to acknowledge, the children abandoned by John Wayne. Unable to call them heroes and being stone blind to their tragic humanity, an outraged American mythology hit upon a way to account for the Loss: *the myth would separate the soldier from the war.* It is a demand sourced in both pro- and antiwar texts, since both ideological postures take the soldier's victimhood for granted. We find a particularly vehement version of that demand in Robert Jay Lifton's *Home from the War*. "We need to make [a] sharp distinction between the nobility and bravery of individual men in facing death or saving comrades, and the dreadful, filthy, unnecessary war they were asked to fight."[25] Similarly, though with the veteran's, not the psychiatrist's, perspective, John M. Del Vecchio's *The 13th Valley* states that "errors, corruption, and/or stupidity do not tarnish ideals—only those who perpetuate the immoral or incompetent act."[26] Both declarations, it is worth noting, appear in editions published more than a decade after the original publication, thus reflecting the national guilt—now to be charged to a faithless nation—over the opprobrium so eagerly heaped upon Vietnam veterans *during* the war.

But the impulse to separate the soldier from the war was alive and well during the war, concentrating its passionate intensity on which powers to blame for the impending loss. The urge to separate the soldier from the war was meant to salvage not the soldier's courage or his integrity or his battered humanity but rather the heroic legacy and the myth of heroic continuity. The myth was simply more important than the soldier.

In 1970, many Americans still refused to believe that victory in Vietnam was out of reach, and the years of war had not made the definition of victory any clearer. For such Americans, the Nixon-Kissinger idea of "peace with honor" foretokened an unacceptable outcome. Nixon and Kissinger's invective and the denunciation fell persistently on a murky and diffused yet somehow potent conspiracy devoted to denying America's Vietnam soldiers their destined due of victory. The documentary *No Substitute for Victory* (Keen, 1970), in reality a prowar philippic hosted by John Wayne, provides the following message over its title: "In appreciation to all those who have given their time and experience recording these facts of history in the best interests of America—thank you."[27] Appearing in his sumptuously appointed office, Wayne asks, "What kind of a war is this that we're not supposed to win?" Wayne's question is only ironically rhetorical, for it betrays its own anxiety. Indeed, the gravity itself of Wayne's question is clear in his having to ask it at all as well as in the implied awareness that to have to ask the question is already to have broken with "history."

Toward the end of *No Substitute for Victory*, we hear from Peter Stark, a member of the US Special Forces who invokes both the mythic archetypes of America's Revolution and the paranoid style in the form of a Viet Cong (VC) invasion of America. As Stark speaks, Barry Sadler's hugely popular anthem "Ballad of the Green Berets" plays softly in the background:

> The choice made for us nearly two hundred years ago by our Founding Fathers is now up for review in Vietnam and everywhere else, in the Mekong Delta and in the halls of the Congress of the United States of America. . . . We will never surrender to communism because we know what it is. There will be no Viet Cong in the United States of America. We will fight. We know that there is a possibility that we may not triumph, but it is not inevitable that the enemy triumph, if he is opposed. . . . We should win in Vietnam. We can win in Vietnam.

America "should win in Vietnam," because two hundred years of winning have so closely identified the nation's wars with victory that to lose now would amount to nothing less than the nation's very undoing. In unintended deference to this paranoia, Stark entertains the "possibility that we may not triumph"; he considers, that is, the otherwise unthinkable eventuality: the prospect of an irreparable breach of faith with the centuries-old covenant of unchallenged privilege and divine favor. And the focus of the blame for the impending catastrophe falls upon a simple yet charged designation dear to the paranoid style, the indefinite *they*. Hence, in *First Blood* (Kotcheff, 1982), as Rambo (Sylvester Stallone) says to his handler Colonel Trautman (Richard Crenna) by way of self-vindication, "*They* drew first blood, not me!" And again later Rambo says, "Who are *they* to protest me?" And according to Sgt. Barnes (Tom Berenger) in *Platoon* (Stone, 1986), "*they* want to fight their war with one hand tied around their balls."

These paranoid jeremiads—the *they* implies Rambo's isolated *me*—expose the soldier's estrangement from communities both military and civilian. Consider the following checklist, drawn from important movies of the Vietnam War, illustrating the isolation of the Vietnam soldier. In *Coming Home* and *Born on the Fourth of July*, the disabled veterans are pointedly isolated, as if quarantined or, perhaps more painful, virtually incarcerated, in a rehab center. In both *First Blood* and *Rambo: First Blood Part II*, John Rambo is the very image of isolation, alone, cold, hungry, and embittered, in the northwest woods and again in the sequel, crying out his piteous entreaty for respect and honor from *they*. In the opening sequence of *Apocalypse Now*, Captain Benjamin Willard (Martin Sheen) all but surrenders to that familiar Vietnam veteran's lament, that he doesn't belong back home anymore than he does in Vietnam. At the end, Willard assassinates Col. Walter E. Kurtz (Marlon Brando) not in blind obedience to his military orders but instead to relieve at last the pain of the most broken and anguished character in any Hollywood Vietnam movie. *Platoon*'s own lost soul, Sergeant Barnes, badly wounded and alone in a small clearing in the jungle, waits for Private Taylor (Charlie Sheen) to kill him and extinguish at last his mad rage. Or consider the last time we see *Platoon*'s Sergeant Elias (Willem Dafoe), himself (like his nemesis Barnes) forlorn and badly wounded, surrounded by the enemy, and at last falling to his knees even as he strikes a last pose that evokes the crucified Christ, forsaken therefore if not by God the Father then by the helicopter point-of-view shot rising remorselessly to isolate him further and then abandon him. Or take the devastating loneliness of *Full Metal Jacket*'s Private Leonard Lawrence, cruelly nicknamed Private Gomer Pyle (Vincent D'Onofrio), alone at night amid the row of spotless "heads," his M-14 locked and loaded, lying in wait for his tormentor Sergeant Hartman (Lee Ermey) so that he may avenge the obloquy and the humiliation and the brutalizing. After he kills Hartman, Lawrence blows his own brains out. At least as acutely isolated as Lawrence, *The Deer Hunter*'s Nick (Christopher Walken) escapes his Viet Cong captors only to become a lost soul in the vast and depraved "wilderness" of Saigon in the last days of South Vietnam. Or, to sum it all up by returning to Captain Willard, this time only moments before he kills Kurtz, he says in voice-over, "*They* were going to make me a major for this, and I wasn't even in their fucking army anymore."

In Vietnam, the American soldier could make a sacrifice as heroic as the ones he had imagined his ancestors had made and still find himself somehow unjustified. He could only hope that in Del Vecchio's terms, "error," "corruption," and "stupidity" in the management of the war—the stuff of loss—would never quite drown out his bitter avowals of devoted sacrifice, his woeful if righteous claims that he was in fact a patriot, and that—but for the war's outcome—he had faithfully complied with the terms of his patrimony. In Vietnam, the uninterrupted continuum of triumph tacitly affirmed by the myth becomes instead the remorseless persistence of tragedy. The myth itself seems not only a historical prod with which to goad the ever-eager innocents but also a perverse denial of the irremediable tragedy of all wars. Tragedy, universal and age-old, makes the American myth of heroic continuity merely local and, in the end, utterly unexceptional.

## "Seventeen Years of War Movies"

Paul Fussell calls our attention to the influence of movie images on the generation destined to fight battles much different from those in the Somme or the Argonne Forest. "If one's perception of the Second War naturally takes the form of one's response to cinema," then, Fussell claims, "one's perception of the Vietnam War equates that experience with the films of the Second War."[28] Michael Herr makes a similar claim about "kids who got wiped out by seventeen years of war movies before coming to Vietnam to get wiped out for good. You don't know what a media freak is until you've seen the way a few of those grunts would run around during a fight when they knew that there was a television crew nearby; they were actually making war movies in their heads, doing little guts-and-glory Leatherneck tap dances under fire, getting their pimples shot off for the networks."[29] In the first decade after World War II, Hollywood presented the "boys" with deeds of valor—what could they have known of the limits of verisimilitude?—that lured them into asserting their heroic birthright. How else but on Hollywood's warrants of authenticity were they to nurture their expectations of life in actual combat? In 1955, Audie Murphy played himself in *To Hell and Back* in which, presumably, he reenacted his wartime exploits with unsparing exactness. Who would not want to be such a hero in their own war? Sustained for decades by the dream factory, the myth awaited a time when the young would ignore the last difference between movie combat and actual combat. Their clutch at authenticity was the loss of their innocence, their stab at heroism their tragedy. "In the early 1960s," Fred Turner notes:

> John Wayne served as an intermediary between private lives and national myths. Through him, individual citizens gained access to the immense emotional treasure-house of American right and might. Wayne's "willingness to use violence" impelled prepubescent boys to play cowboys and Indians and to attack each other with chrome-plated mock revolvers. In the political realm it prompted their parents to support the use of violence overseas. Having seen that justice flowed in John Wayne's wake in the movies, many Americans assumed that justice must likewise naturally flow in the wake of American interventions abroad. American power was a sign of America's moral superiority over other nations[,] and as they watched John Wayne, Americans—particularly young male Americans—could feel that power in themselves.[30]

Yet, Wayne is also, of all the mythic influences, the one whom the erstwhile "boys" came to blame for their betrayal in Vietnam. It is "all too true," the critic and playwright Eric Bentley argued in 1972, "that the concerted efforts of antiwar propagandists have failed to prevent, let alone stop, a single war. John Wayne, on the other hand, an explicit champion of pugnacity and an implicit instigator of aggression, might claim to have got wars started. Along with the statesmen of the *Pentagon Papers*, he is one of 'the people who brought you Vietnam.'"[31] Young Philip Caputo, for one, imagined the reality of combat by imagining himself as John Wayne at war. "The country was at peace then, but the early sixties were years of almost constant tension and crisis; if a conflict did break out, the Marines would be certain to fight in it and I could be there with them. Actually there. Not watching it on a movie or TV screen, not reading about it in a book, but there, living out a fantasy. Already I saw myself charging up some distant beachhead, like John Wayne in *Sands of Iwo Jima*, and then coming home a suntanned warrior with medals on my chest."[32] If the young Caputo would have known of Wayne's actual combat experience, would he instead, in imitation of Wayne, have stayed at home? In Vietnam, Michael Herr wrote in 1977, "all the mythic tracks intersected, from the lowest John Wayne wetdream to the most aggravated soldier-poet fantasy."[33] If Vietnam had served as the intersection of America's "mythic tracks," then Wayne had crossed them all, bestridden them, a colossus culturally authorized to embody national fantasies doubling as national hopes that in time transformed into national tragedies.

"Without warning," reports the narrator, Joker, in a passage in Gustav Hasford's *The Short-Timers* (the source novel for Stanley Kubrick's *Full Metal Jacket*), "the New Guy charges for the clearing. He fires blind. He lopes along with the fluid grace of a meat eater, a predator attacking. . . . The New Guy wants warm blood to drink. The New Guy wants human flesh to tear apart and devour. The New Guy's eyes are red; the New Guy's eyes glow in the shadow world around us. . . . He fires blind. The New Guy doesn't know what the hell he's doing. He thinks he's John Wayne. He hasn't been born yet."[34] The New Guy doesn't know what he's doing *because* he is imitating John Wayne (and Wayne, who skipped the war, cannot know what he's doing). To be "born" is to know—it is the innocence lost in and to the tragic knowing—that, as Animal Mother tells Joker later, Vietnam "ain't no Hollywood movie."[35]

The references to John Wayne took on a much different tone when the men returned from Vietnam. A US marine of the Third Reconnaissance

Battalion, Frank Matthews, told Christian Appy how he "learned that thinking of the war as a movie could be dangerous":

> Once in the middle of a firefight I decided to pull a John Wayne stunt. I saw a VC wide open, but it was just too easy [to shoot and kill him]. So I hollered at him first so he'd see me. Then I took off toward this log, jumped over, wanting to pop up shooting on the other side. But I broke my arm trying to pull that stunt. I wrote a letter to John Wayne telling him there was no damn way that stunt could work 'cause I broke my wrist trying it. I never did get an answer, but I sure wrote him.[36]

Fred Turner aptly generalizes Matthews's complaint against Wayne, the disillusion that would unavoidably manifest all the signs of injury in consequence of a fundamental breach of trust. "Even as their parents settled into their armchairs and read about 'Wagon-Train GIs' driving off 'Red-men,' combat infantrymen were discovering that Vietnam might not bear any resemblance to the Old West. As Americans, they had been raised on the faith that if they went to battle, they would, like John Wayne, acquire a muscular masculinity. War would 'make them men,' grant them hard bodies and the ability to control them, to make choices, to be in charge of their destinies. Yet, when they actually arrived in combat, soldiers found that they often had little control over their fates."[37]

The American soldier's experience in Vietnam revealed a betrayal of almost conspiratorial proportions, the betrayal by the same culture that had so dazzled him, that had winked and connived to numb him with a pander's lie proffered as a credo. The very purpose and mission that the mythic hero had seemed to embody and that they themselves—believing the seeming—had sought to embody was so hopelessly absent in Vietnam that the absence itself already accounted for the greater part of the betrayal.

## "Horrid King Besmear'd"

In time, the accumulated invectives against John Wayne doubled as denunciations of the Loss itself. For instance, at the very beginning of

Malcolm Clarke's disturbing and moving documentary *Soldiers in Hiding* (1984), a former door gunner with the 101st Airborne, identified simply as "Fred," remarks, "Nobody's John Wayne over there." Now hiding (one is never sure from whom or what) in the woods of Washington state—and so in the kind of setting where the hero of *The Deer Hunter* (as we shall see in chapter 5) makes his peace with the wilderness and where John Rambo, in *First Blood*, lets loose his warrior's rage on self-satisfied middle America—Fred attests the absence of Wayne in the alien "over there." Defined more by the rupture than by the historical war in general, the Vietnam generation revised the mystique of John Wayne through something like Ron Kovic's indignant imprecation: "I gave my dead dick for John Wayne. . . . Nobody ever told me I was going to come back from this war without a penis."[38]

And yet, if John Wayne had somehow failed Ronnie and "Fred" and countless others like them, had they not themselves failed John Wayne? Perhaps it was in consequence of this presumed failure—replicated innumerable times—that America exacted so severe a retribution on the wayward children of John Wayne. The Vietnam soldier's bitterness, then, however intense, had become its only possible alternative to Wayne, and the need to renounce or censure or revile Wayne became only another way of expressing that bitterness. And so, Wayne turned against the "boys" whom he had tried to no avail to "forge" into men. "I feel compelled to bring up the fact," he shamelessly told *Playboy*, "that under the guise of doing good, these kids are causing a hell of a lot of irreparable damage, and they're starting something they're not gonna be able to finish. Every bit of rampant anarchy has provoked a little more from somebody else. And when they start shooting policemen, the time has come to start knocking them off, as far as I'm concerned." The alarmed interviewer asked, "What do you mean by 'knocking them off'?" Wayne replied, "I'd throw 'em in the can if I could. But if they try to kill you, I'd sure as hell shoot back."[39] The "kids," generationally considered, became the father's chief enemy. The *Playboy* interview appeared only one day after the first anniversary of the shootings at Kent State University on May 4, 1970. Some "kids" had been indeed "knocked off."

The testimony of Vietnam veterans validates the condition that came to be known as the "John Wayne Syndrome." "The double-edged quality of the Wayne icon," writes Richard Slotkin,

> appears in the complex of war-related stress disorders identified by Vietnam veterans and their doctors as "John Wayne Syndrome." The common feature of the syndrome was the soldier's internalization of an ideal of superhuman military bravery, skill, and invulnerability to guilt and grief, which is identified at some point with "John Wayne." The identification is . . . with Wayne as a figure of speech, signifying the supposed perfection of soldierly masculinity. Since that ideal is, in fact, impossible to live up to, "John Wayne Syndrome" often took the form of excessive guilt or shame for feelings of guilt or grief.[40]

Jonathan Shay's idea of the soldier's "fiduciary assumption" shows some significant affinities with Slotkin's description, especially since it too concerns a soldier's response to authority. Shay's term describes the soldier's implicit trust in "the vast and distant military and civilian structure that provides a modern soldier with his orders, arms, ammunition, food, water, information, training, and fire support."[41] Such a structure, Shay explains, "is ultimately a moral structure, a *fiduciary*, a trustee holding the life and safety of that soldier. The need for an intact moral world increases with every added coil of a soldier's mortal dependency on others." Considered, accordingly, as a specific cultural construction of Shay's "fiduciary assumption," the John Wayne Syndrome helps explain the soldier's sense of betrayal in Vietnam. In the eyes of the children, John Wayne—because of both his onscreen actions and the resulting cultural influence—is the principal "fiduciary," the incorruptible guarantor of heroic identity. The Loss undermines the soldiers' trust in Wayne. Theirs, in consequence, is the rage, the Achillean *mēnis*, directed at the "betrayal of what's right," which constitutes "an essential part of any combat trauma that leads to lifelong psychological injury. Veterans can usually recover from horror, fear, and grief once they return to civilian life, so long as 'what's right' has not also been violated."[42] American soldiers in Vietnam had an implied right to insist on the legitimacy of their mythic heroes. The logic, if such it is, of this right implied the fidelity of the soldier in due return for the authenticity of the hero's deed, onscreen or on the battlefield. Therefore, the heroic deed had to be repeatable. Otherwise, there could be no transfer of the heroic legacy. When Frank Matthews writes to Wayne to tell him that his onscreen stunts in World War II movies do not work in Vietnam, he in effect scolds the patriarch for being a fraud, appearing thereby to have set himself free of his authority. But has Matthews set himself free? He also—in both the botched attempt to enact the hero's deed and the writing itself of the letter—confesses to an inadequacy, thus implicitly confirming Wayne's deftness. Nonetheless, each interpretation of such a grievance discloses the soldier's sense of betrayal: Matthews complains of a lack of correspondence between history and myth. Somewhere in his apparent carping about Hollywood goofs and gaffes, there is also, chiefly perhaps, a plaintive lament about the interruption of the myth's continuity. There has been a rupture.

Perhaps Wayne came to act as a jealous patriarch, goading his children into the very thing that he himself had avoided. During World War II, Garry Wills remarks, Wayne

> was making it clear that if single-minded careerism would get him there, he was bound to make it. This cost him the chance to serve his country at its time of greatest unity against worldwide foes. Some in Hollywood never forgave Wayne for that. Part of John Ford never forgave him. A few even claim that Wayne did not forgive himself—that the compensatory superpatriotism of later years, when he urged the country on to wars in Korea and Vietnam, was a form of expiation. If so, it was not enough. This is a man who called on other generations to sacrifice their lives, and called them "soft" if they refused.[43]

The patriarch charges the children with his own sins, and they, in their pain, enact his penance. Culturally, mythically, Wayne becomes Milton's vision in *Paradise Lost* of Moloch in Hell:

> horrid King besmear'd with blood
> Of human sacrifice, and parents tears,
> Though for the noyse of Drums and Timbrels loud
> Thir childrens cries unheard, that past through fire
> To his grim Idol.[44]

Well might those who did fight rail against Wayne, as did Henry IV of France against his absent friend. "Hang yourself, brave Crillon! we fought at Arques, and you were not there."[45]

## "Happy Childhoods" and Vietnam

In Hasford's *The Short-Timers*, a US marine in Hué, Crazy Earl, achieves a tragic martyrdom by the manner of his death. Joker (Hasford's narrator) and the rest of the squad "stand over Craze as Cowboy says, 'Craze did a John Wayne. He finally went berserk. Shot BB's at a gook machine gun. The BB's bounced off the gook gunners. You should have seen it. Craze was laughing like a happy little kid.'"[46] Perhaps it was some such scene that compelled Michael Herr to declare for all time that "Vietnam was what we had instead of happy childhoods."[47] Crazy Earl's America had raised him to believe in the eminently replicable reality of its mythic acts. In Vietnam, he had attested his faith by enacting it with the preferred magical firearm of his childhood, a BB gun. And why not, since he had been told that it was just like that of his heroes' Winchester rifle? The manic moments just before Crazy Earl's death reveal the consequence of the same obsessive faith that drives the eternally endearing innocent, Ralphie Parker (Peter Billingsley), in *A Christmas Story* (Clark, 1983). Like Crazy Earl, Ralphie is faithful to the magical power of (as he breathlessly describes it to Santa at the shopping mall) "an official Red Ryder carbine action two-hundred shot range model air rifle with a compass in the stock and this thing that tells time." Now imagine Ralphie in Vietnam, where he easily enough swaps places with Crazy Earl. And why not? Why should Ralphie's BB gun, "Old Blue," be any less magical than Natty Bumppo's "Killdeer" or Davy Crockett's "Betsy"? In Vietnam, this old American trope of the named rifle would await its ironic iteration in *Full Metal Jacket* when Leonard Lawrence—"Private Pyle"—kills his drill instructor and then himself with an M-14 he had earlier named "Charlene."

Imagine, then, the soldiers' heightened sense of betrayal when they saw what their M-16 did to the enemy. Lifton tells us of a soldier's "reaction to witnessing the bodily disintegration of" a VC "guerrilla he himself shot from about thirty feet when in combat. 'I was surprised by how much damage my weapon did,' was what he said to me, his pained tone conveying his horror and awe of being (as well as *firing*) an instrument [capable] of such sudden and grotesque annihilation."[48] And Philip Caputo shares a horrific "in-country" epiphany arrived at through an almost pornographic encounter with human anatomy and physiology under fire: "And the mutilation caused by modern weapons came as a shock. . . . We were sickened by the torn flesh, the viscera and splattered brains. The horror lay in the recognition that the body, which is supposed to be the earthly home of an immortal soul, which people spend so much time feeding, conditioning, and beautifying, is in fact only a fragile case stuffed full of disgusting matter. Even the brain, the wondrous, complex organ that generates the power of thought and speech, is nothing more than a lump of slick, gray tissue."[49]

In Vietnam War nonfiction, few horrors approximate the one reported by Ron Kovic in *Born on the Fourth of July.* On a night patrol, the marines in Kovic's unit see "little figures moving back and forth" against the dim lights of a Vietnamese village.[50] Once an illumination round lights up the village, the marines begin firing indiscriminately. Finally the firing ceases, and the marines reach the village, where Molina, another marine,

> turned the beam of his flashlight into the hut." "Oh God," he said. "Oh Jesus Christ." He started to cry. "We just shot up a bunch of kids!"
>
> The floor of the small hut was covered with them, screaming and thrashing their arms back and forth, lying in pools of blood, crying wildly, screaming again and again. They were shot in the face, in the chest, in the legs, moaning and crying. . . .
>
> There was an old man in the corner with his head blown off from his eyes up, his brains hanging out of his head like jelly. He [Kovic] kept looking at the strange sight, he had never seen anything like it before. A small boy next to the old man was still alive, although he had been shot many times. He was crying softly, lying in a large pool of blood. His small foot had been shot almost completely off and seemed to be hanging by a thread.[51]

Thus, the Vietnam narrative burst open and spilled over what the World War II movie, supervised by the Hays Code and fronted by John Wayne and the myth of heroic continuity, had kept tightly and ever so respectably shut.

## Indian Fighters from the Sky

The Western, World War II, and the Vietnam War converged, if briefly, in *The Green Berets* (Wayne and Kellogg, 1968). As others have already noted, the name of the Wayne character in *The Green Berets*, Col. Mike Kirby, harks back to his character in *Fort Apache*, Captain Kirby York, as well as to the third movie in the cavalry trilogy, *Rio Grande*, where the Wayne character's surname takes on a final "e," Yorke.[52] And the name reappears in the World War II piece *Flying Leathernecks* (Ray, 1951), where Wayne plays Maj. Daniel Xavier Kirby. Wayne is thus a genealogy unto himself, a single (though hardly evolving) line of descent stretching over almost a century of American wars. Moreover, this simple if glaringly factitious connection of wars by way of a recurrent name allowed the filmmakers to present a Vietnam War movie as a seamless extension of the myth of heroic continuity.

This convergence of subgenres was further sustained and no doubt to an extent inspired by the mystique of the Green Berets—the US Special Forces—as promoted by President Kennedy's well-documented fascination with counterinsurgency and his concomitant appeals to a "New Frontier."[53] (Enhancing the mystique was the enormously popular Barry Sadler song, "The Ballad of the Green Berets.")[54] As John Hellmann notes, "The Peace Corps, the Alliance for Progress, the domestic emphasis on physical fitness, the 'get-the-country-moving-again' economic policies, the support for black civil rights, the space program, the 'can-do' cabinet team—every aspect of the New Frontier evoked the ideal found in [William J. Lederer and Eugene Burdick's 1958 novel] *The Ugly American*, the ideal central to the American mythic heritage: that America could preserve the rewards of grace only by a disregard for them in pursuit of its errand."[55]

This New Frontier fervor explains the irresistible urge of Kennedy's advisers to cast the Special Forces in the mold of the American Indian fighter. In an essay titled "Internal War: The New Communist Tactic," Roger Hilsman, Kennedy's director of intelligence and research in the State Department, expressed dismay at the resistance of the American military to learn from counterinsurgency measures in earlier wars, specifically in the Philippines and Malaya as well as in France's doomed effort to recolonize Vietnam after World War II. Hilsman, however, especially deplored the military's neglect of lessons learned from America's own Indian Wars:

> In my judgment, it is nonsense to think that regular forces trained for conventional war can handle jungle guerrillas adequately. Yet in spite of some very hard lessons—Magsaysay in the Philippines, the British in Malaya, and the French in Indochina and Algeria—we have been slow to learn. . . .
>
> . . . Have we forgotten that we were the ones who had to teach the British regulars "Indian fighting" back when we were still colonies? Have we forgotten that we taught the British regulars another kind of lesson in "Indian fighting" during our own revolution?[56]

But this call to remembrance involves an appeal to "myth," not to history. It is myth, not history, that insists on continuity, as Hilsman does.

The volume containing the Hilsman essay includes a contribution by Walt W. Rostow, the Kennedy-appointed chair of the State Department's Policy and Planning Council, perhaps the most ardent hawk in Kennedy's circle of civilian advisers. One of the group that David Halberstam dubbed "the best and the brightest," Rostow coined the phrase "new frontier." In his contribution, titled "Guerrilla Warfare in Underdeveloped Areas," he declares, "There is no rule or parable in the Communist [guerrilla] texts that was not known at an earlier time in history. The operation of [Francis] Marion's men in relation to the Battle of Cowpens in the American Revolution was, for example, governed by rules that Mao merely echoes."[57] The frontier exists—or more accurately, is invoked—as the mythic space where the hero enacts a stable, reciprocal, and reiterative deed of conquest. The heroic frontier myth would forever underwrite the victory to follow from the tried-and-true strategy of the Indian fighter in the primal wilderness.

And now in *The Green Berets*, John Wayne, however stout, starched, and stiff, still trailed in his wake these powers that had come to constitute, identify, and sustain the mythic wilderness acumen in evidence throughout his three decades of fighting Indians (and Japanese) on the movie screen. He would bring to Vietnam a counterinsurgency wisdom acquired in the cinematic versions of the Indian Wars dating back to his Breck Coleman in *The Big Trail* (Walsh, 1930), almost a decade before Ringo in *Stagecoach* (Ford, 1939), and thence via the cavalry trilogy and others, including John Farrow's *Hondo* (1953) and the unapologetic racist Ethan Edwards in *The Searchers* (Ford, 1956). And a decade later all this mastery, though mellowed by age and failing health, figured as well among the many burdensome things that Col. Mike Kirby carries to Vietnam.

## John Wayne's "Boys" in *The Green Berets*

Well before John Wayne's "boys" would assume their various personae in Hollywood movies of the Vietnam War, they were generationally represented by one character in *The Green Berets*: Sergeant Petersen, played by Jim Hutton. During the first half of the 1960s, Hutton became a familiar presence though hardly a heroic one. Born in 1934, he was, to be sure, older than the initiates seeking sexual and social guidance from movies such as *Where the Boys Are* (Levin, 1960), *The Honeymoon Machine* (Thorpe, 1961), *Bachelor in Paradise* (Arnold, 1961), and *The Horizontal Lieutenant* (Thorpe, 1962). But his boyish looks and lanky 6'5'' frame evoked the gawky adolescents of the day, those "boys" given more to entitled ease than to dreams of glory or anxieties of legacy.

*The Green Berets* seeks to influence (or perhaps merely discredit) two groups: the antiwar element and the "liberal" press. (Half a year before the July 4, 1968, premiere of *The Green Berets*, CBS's Walter Cronkite had declared that the United States in Vietnam was "mired in stalemate.")[58] In *The Green Berets*, both Petersen and the cynical journalist George Beckworth (David Janssen) have to be won over to Wayne's version of the Vietnam War, Beckworth so that he may tell the war's story aright and Petersen so as to become a righteous warrior doomed to die his gruesome scapegoat's sacrifice for his generation's sins. Beckworth's and Petersen's stories share a crucial trope: a thoroughly stereotyped Vietnamese child proves central to the requisite ideological transformation. If Beckworth's epiphany requires the ghastly death of the Montagnard girl that he befriended earlier, Petersen's illumination demands the sacrifice of his own life in defense of the orphan Vietnamese boy "Hamchunk" (Craig Jue). After his epiphany, Beckworth will write the "truth" about Vietnam, John Wayne's truth, no doubt. But when all seems settled in the Americans' favor, Petersen insists on "taking point," surely deeming himself capable of doing so after all the nasty fighting. Instead, he will be dragged helplessly, implacably by a hidden rope and end up skewered upside down on a gigantic punji trap (figures 3.1 and 3.2).

Petersen's grisly end may well enough illustrate the unimaginable enormities of the VC as *The Green Berets* would have us see them, but the sudden shock of his death cannot dispel the suspicion that this way of dying manifests Wayne's bitter remonstrances against the younger generation of Americans. The moment, then, serves less as an indictment of the evil VC than as Wayne's judgment and denunciation, with his own cruel reckoning amounting to the abandonment of the very generation upon which he was to transfer the heroic legacy.

Beckworth's conversion following the death of the little girl he had been caring for seems the result of a cruel punishment—a ghoulish I-told-you-so that Kirby serves up—for Beckworth's cynicism about the war. But *The Green Berets* disowns Petersen. Where Beckworth seems now, at the end, prepared to report the "truth," Petersen has failed to earn the promised inheritance. Indeed, Petersen invites comparison with Frank Matthews, the soldier-witness in Christian Appy's *Working-Class War* who imitated a Wayne stunt and got a broken arm for his troubles. So too, then, only much more severe, is Petersen's penalty, a hideous sight meant as object-lesson, namely the testimony, posthumous of course, that there is only one American hero, that that hero is his own legacy, and that he abides through all the American wars. It is the simple, impenitent catechism that demonstrates Wayne's deep disdain for the "soft" generation.

## The Return of the Child-Other

A mascot in the most degrading sense, Hamchunk embodies the sentiment of imperialist wardship. When we first see him, he is stretching a trip wire across a muddy path. Petersen, the victim, falls face-first in the mud (an overdetermined foreshadowing of the mode of his death). Moments later, after Petersen arrives at the forward camp ("Dodge City"), the sergeant leading him to his new quarters introduces him to Hamchunk. "He's become a permanent fixture around here," the sergeant explains. "He's an orphan. Lived most of his life with missionaries . . . until they were assassinated. Maybe you could use an interpreter. The missionaries taught him English." Petersen is already balking at the idea of an emotional attachment to the boy. But the boy asserts himself: "You numbah one." (*The Green Beret*'s crudely offensive orientalism insists that

Hamchunk turn the last syllable of Petersen's name into the Japanese honorific *san*, hence Peter-san.) Then, looking up at the towering Petersen, Hamchunk adds, "I choose you."

**Petersen:** I don't want to be chosen.
**Sergeant:** I don't think you have much choice.
**Petersen:** Choice, Mr. Hobson? I haven't had a choice since I was selected for this outfit.
**Hamchunk:** You get used to me. You funny.

The sergeant "remembers" Hamchunk's story, thereby muting the child's voice and appropriating, perhaps all but erasing, the child's own memory. The sergeant also claims that Hamchunk speaks English, but his account of the child, besides usurping Hamchunk's own story, limits the boy's speech to the leavings ever allotted the Other: clichés, mispronunciations, mangled inflections, and truant verbs, all of which merely reminds us that he has nothing of consequence to say.

Later in his new quarters, Petersen is ready to turn in for the night when Hamchunk appears before him. Petersen soon asks the boy where he sleeps. "Anywhere," replies Hamchunk. Unmoved, Petersen climbs into the upper bunk, but the boy remains standing, quietly insistent, irresistibly cute. So, Petersen relents: the boy climbs up on the bunk and disappears behind him. The camera stays with the shot until we see the little arm of the boy appear from behind Petersen in a hug. The moment initiates Hamchunk's crudely allegorical role: tiny Vietnam depends utterly on the condescending stewardship of the gigantic America represented by the 6'5" Petersen. Hamchunk's disappearance behind Petersen suggests not only the diminished presence of the Vietnamese in the American-driven narrative but also the attempt to cast the prosecution of the war itself as for all intents and purposes an exclusively American concern. That the camera shows only the boy's tiny arm around his "father" reeks of the age-old imperial delusion that casts the infantilized Other as a devoted subordinate, as with Miguel in *The Real Glory*, an inferior in whose inchoate and derivative humanity the "father" never vests so much love as he does forbearance. In the bunk, Hamchunk reaches out tenderly to hug Petersen, but Petersen is, here at least, unresponsive. The impulse to connect is wholly the child's; the man seems unmoved, or at best resigned to endure his "white man's burden." Suddenly, though, *The Green Berets* produces a radically transformed Petersen, patriotic, courageous, and able, a man with a purpose. This new Petersen emerges fully formed in consequence of his new relationship with Hamchunk, perhaps. But the patriotism and the courage and the newfound purpose are all imperial abstractions, and they circumscribe Hamchunk utterly, defining him even as they overwhelm him, damning him to everlasting otherness.

When Kirby leads the squad that ventures into the Montagnard village to bring the natives to the safety of Dodge City, Petersen is part of the squad. Indeed, he leads the squad. But when he reaches the edge of a clearing, Kirby, though trailing the entire group, shouts "Freeze!" It is difficult to see how Kirby could have detected a trip wire lying ahead of Petersen and the rest of the squad when he had just now fallen in behind them. But no matter, this is John Wayne, he of the bespoke stunts: he pulls carefully at the trip wire, and suddenly a punji trap fastened to a bent branch swings out horizontally and impales on the tree next to Petersen. In his first mission as a Green Beret, Petersen proves to be merely green. As he fell for Hamchunk's trip wire earlier, so would he have fallen for the punji trap had it not been for Kirby's timely intervention. The old hero proves more alert, more cunning, even more nimble than the much younger Petersen.

Sobered by the enemy's massacre of the Montagnard villagers, Petersen becomes a leader. Only moments after the village scenes, Petersen is already coming into Dodge City from a reconnaissance patrol in the "bush." As the only American in the group, he has assumed the role of the white Indian fighter—Slotkin's "man who knows Indians"—who leads a band of natives against their own. He is now, or would be, the heroic type of Green Beret in Robin Moore's source text, Bernie Arklin, for example, who presumably tells Moore "the story of his life as a revered chief of the hard-fighting . . . Meo tribesmen of Laos."[59] More important, Petersen seems to be on his way to becoming John Wayne.

Once back in Dodge City, Petersen makes a grim report: the VC is building "lots of caskets and ladders." A moment later, he explains to Beckworth that "when Charlie [i.e., the VC] knows he's got a nice box to be buried in, he's just as brave as hell. . . . They throw the ladders across the [barbed] wire to get at us, and later they use them for litters." "By 'later on,'" Beckworth asks, "you mean, when everybody's dead?" "Everybody," Petersen replies, "women, children, everybody." Suddenly, Petersen has become an expert in guerrilla warfare. At the end of this sequence, Hamchunk proudly carries the M-16 belonging to his giant of a guardian. Dwarfed by the rifle, the tiny would-be warrior becomes the clownish sidekick cherished by the imperial narrative—proud, presumptuous, and ridiculous—good mostly to elicit a derisive chuckle or a driblet of condescension.

Inevitably, the enemy launches an assault on Dodge City. The fight grows desperate, and the massacre imminent. Behind a breastwork within the fort, Petersen, busy but calm, mans a mortar. (Kirby meanwhile is flying back to Dodge City from a meeting to plan the abduction of a high-ranking general of the North Vietnamese Army, but his helicopter is shot down, and the survivors, including Kirby, have to fight their way into the fort.) In Kirby's absence, Petersen commands. But then, an enemy shell explodes nearby and kills Hamchunk's dog. Petersen realizes that Hamchunk is not in his assigned foxhole and goes off to find him. By the time he does, the boy has finished burying the dog. Petersen's condolences elicit, perhaps even exact, the boy's compliant admission of absolute dependence on the white American. "He was all you had, wasn't he? You don't have anybody else in the whole world, do you?" The boy, disarmingly if predictably, replies, "Except you." Petersen picks the boy up and totes him under his arm as one would a small farm animal to the slaughter or a toddler in midtantrum—America's version of the "white man's burden" as *tableau vivant.*

## The Last Lost "Boy"

The fall of Dodge City now inevitable, Petersen delivers Hamchunk to one of the evacuation helicopters headed for Da Nang. Petersen instructs the pilot, "Take care of that kid, no matter what happens." Cut to the fallen fort, where the victorious enemy pillage, plunder, and desecrate the bodies of the dead, all of it in the familiarly fiendish tumult of Hollywood Indians plundering fort or cabin or wagon train. Then, they run their flag up the pole. Even as the Americans and the Vietnamese civilians are in full retreat, however, Kirby calls in an air strike from "Puff the Magic Dragon" (outfitted with three "miniguns," each capable of firing four thousand rounds per minute). "Puff" mows down every last one of the enemy.

The narrative now turns to the kidnapping of Phan Son Ti (William Olds), a North Vietnamese general. Dispensing with any effort to connect the events in Dodge City with the ones in Da Nang, *The Green Berets* instead puts on display the high-tech way of abducting and extracting a hostage: a large airplane outfitted with two prongs on its nose snares the balloon to which Phan Son Ti is tethered and hoists him up into its bowels.[60] We never see or hear from the general again. On the way back to the fort, Kirby orders Petersen to "take the rear," but Petersen demurs: he has fought bravely in the raid on the general's mansion and deserves to take point. "Sir," he remonstrates, "could I have a choice just for the hell of it?" "Yeah," Kirby snarls, "you can have a choice just for the hell of it."

**Petersen:** I'll take the point.
**Kirby:** I said you can have a choice.
**Petersen:** Yes, sir, that's why I'm taking the point.

Petersen dashes off to take his place at the head of the squad, and Kirby, beaming a proud smile, takes the rear. The exchange—that is, both the dialogue and the switch of places in the squad—suggests that the long-deferred transfer of a heroic legacy in Vietnam has come at last: the aged hero of the Western and World War II yields both place and authority to the young soldier. But suddenly Petersen finds himself unaccountably tied by the ankles and dragged helplessly, swiftly, inexorably toward the huge punji trap that has just as suddenly emerged from the brush (figure 3.1). Facing out and upside down, Petersen dies a horrific death, impaled as one crucified in the manner of Mantegna's St. Sebastian (all abristle with arrows) and of St. Peter, who as tradition holds was nailed to a cross and upended (figure 3.2).

One Green Beret's curse against the VC doubles as meager eulogy for Petersen. And now Kirby reclaims his old rightful place at point. Kirby, who ostensibly came to the "critical area" only for a brief period before being "snow[ed] under with paperwork," must now, though old and tired, step once more into his accustomed role if only by the dubious means of reassuming Wayne's timelessly heroic persona. Wayne usurps Petersen's inheritance by placing his own persistent persona at

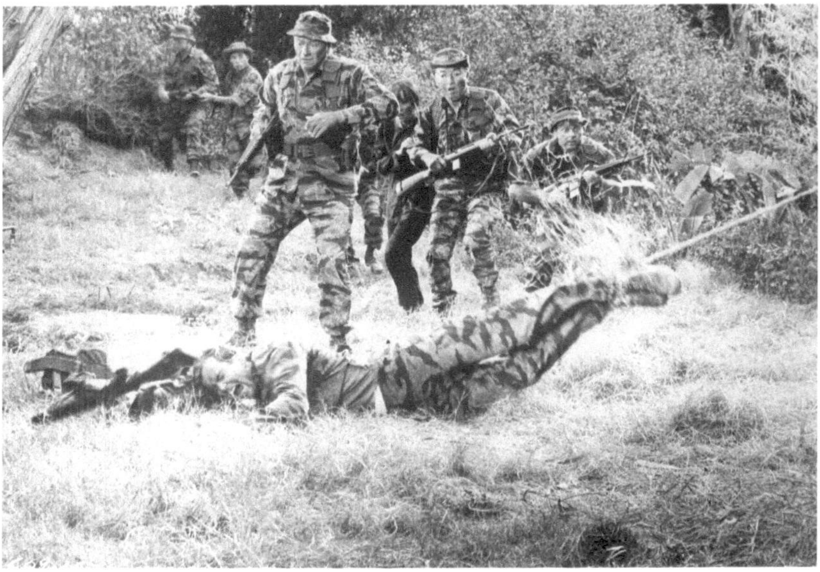

Figure 3.1. *The Green Berets*. Sergeant Petersen (Jim Hutton) caught in trap. Watching in horror are Colonel Kirby (John Wayne) and Colonel Cai (Jack Soo).

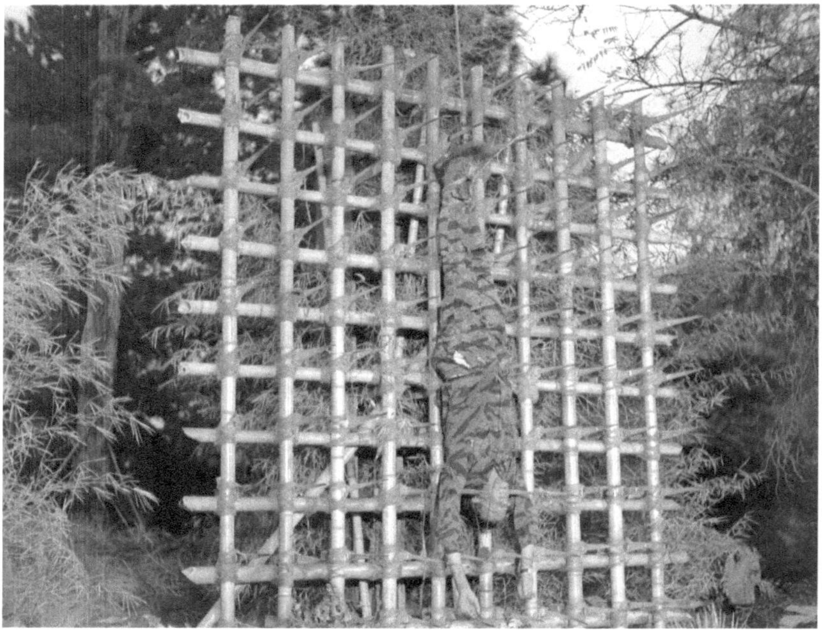

Figure 3.2. *The Green Berets*. Sergeant Petersen (Jim Hutton) impaled.

the head of a historically and culturally different war. Indeed, Wayne/Kirby would erase the Vietnam War itself. By replacing the young hero with the old hero—or, better yet, with the hero of old—*The Green Berets* unsuspectingly narrates its own ironic version of the rupture. This rupture is readily evident in the contrast between *The Green Berets* and *Sands of Iwo Jima.* In *Sands of Iwo Jima*, Pete Conway promises to finish the letter on Stryker's behalf and orders the squad to "saddle up" and "get back in the war." The line of succession extended back to "the Conways" and thence, unbroken, to their successors, affirming the triumph of the myth of heroic continuity over the anxiety of legacy. In *The Green Berets*, however, the Stryker counterpart, Colonel Kirby, cannot die: there is no Conway to take up the struggle, not so much because Petersen proves unworthy of such a legacy as because this war itself—this war that is ever Other to the myth of heroic continuity—always and already undermines the heroic legacy. Kirby's age alone, his evident weariness, reflects the myth's own exhaustion in Vietnam even as it bares an impenitent obduracy, Kirby's and Wayne's both. Thus, Wayne's stubborn persistence becomes the meager measure of continuity, to be known not by thematic sameness but instead by the reactionary response to the difference, a reaction, unfulfilled, that glaringly exposes the anxiety that was to be dispelled.

After the rest of the squad leaves the frame, Kirby picks up Petersen's rucksack on which his Special Forces beret is pinned. Petersen, impaled, attests to the revocation of a legacy for an entire generation. And what more glaring testimony of the convulsive recision of the legacy than the inexcusably—one might well say vindictively—lurid spectacle of American youth so rancorously denied its patrimony? Is it, however, that Petersen has been found to be not so much careless as unworthy of his heroic legacy? Is there something in the time and manner of his dying, something not only in the way of penance for an unheeded warning or of forfeiture on account of a failed diligence but instead something like an adjudication that revokes the new generation's inheritance? Has Kirby—has Wayne—"forged" the "boys" not into heroes but instead into sacrificial victims? Has Kirby thus meted out punishment (a "soft" generation thrown at so many hard and sharp bamboo spikes) for the high crime not of opposing the war but of *not having a "good war" to fight*? More important, perhaps, how does *The Green Berets* respond to the threatened break in the great unbroken line of heroic continuity? What vision is it able to produce to reassure a beleaguered nation that the torch had indeed been passed to a new generation?

Now on the tarmac in Da Nang, Beckworth, on his way to join the green berets in the bush, points Hamchunk to the landing strip where he expects Petersen to arrive and tells the boy to "take care of yourself." Hamchunk is left alone. To witness the puny child's bewilderment in the immensity of Da Nang—as if assailed by planes, jeeps, tanks, front-end loaders, and Hueys—is to see at once that the one thing the boy cannot do is take care of himself. Soon he is darting from one Huey to the other calling out for his "Peter-san." Frantic now, Hamchunk runs to the last Huey only to be told that Petersen is not there either. In tears, Hamchunk runs to the seashore and faces the setting sun. Kirby now enters the frame:

**Kirby:** You always knew it could happen, didn't you?
**Hamchunk:** But I didn't want it to.
**Kirby:** None of us did.
**Hamchunk** [*only now turning to face Kirby*]: Was my Peter-san brave?
**Kirby** [*kneeling, facing Hamchunk*]: He was very brave. Are you going to be?
**Hamchunk:** I'll try.
**Kirby:** I know you will. [*Placing Petersen's beret on Hamchunk's head.*] And I'm sure that your Peter-san would want you to have that.
**Hamchunk:** What will happen to me now?
**Kirby:** You let me worry about that, Green Beret. You're what this is all about.

Even before Kirby finishes delivering these lines, the film's last, a cut shows man and child at the extreme left of the Panavision screen. Kirby takes Hamchunk by the hand, and they walk slowly screen right along the beach. On the far right side of the screen, the sun is sinking.

In Hollywood's Vietnam imaginary, the Vietnamese exist only as the object of America's ideological gaze. The helpless orphan, nameless but for a crude, offensive epithet, allegorizes the disdain and the racism inherent even in America's professions of sacrifice for the freedom of a people it always and already considers unworthy of such blessings or such sacrifices. The boy's pidgin English, his dependence, and his diminutive form itself are much of what there is of Vietnam in *The Green Berets.* And Kirby's last words confirm the child's status as a mere allegory of Vietnam. Thus, Hamchunk's allegorical identity reveals both a *non-Vietnam*—for the child personifies neither history nor culture nor even a personal memory of Vietnam, so that he is only Vietnam as *lack*, as *absence*—even as he in fact allegorizes the American cultural moment that wills only its own definition of Vietnam. Next to the hero of heroes stands the bantam boy, his smallness derided by the outsize beret, so that the token of gallantry and mastery becomes instead the image of abject dependence. Not equals, not even allies, the Hamchunks of the world enter the frame of the imperial gaze having already surrendered culture, history, and even language to the harsh prerequisites, namely that they serve only and indefinitely as America's wards and that by their equivocal embrace of the old platitudes as much as by their slavish reliance on American military power, they shall have no nobler purpose than the continual acclamation of America's exceptional magnificence. If Hamchunk is indeed what Vietnam itself "is all about," then here, at this moment when Vietnam stands in the presence and shadow of the greatest of all American heroes, it can do no better than to avow and proclaim the hero's power and prerogative.

In the absence of a younger hero, Wayne succeeds himself. He is still his own legacy, preempting, eliding, and annulling the heroic patrimony of the Vietnam generation. He abides; he is his own continuing line of descent, principle and avatar of the heroic, and thus immortal. He becomes metagenerational. As if connected to the Kirby York(e) of the Indian frontier and to the Kirby of World War II, this Kirby in Vietnam emerges as America's foremost cultural vampire, coursing through time and history, devouring an increasingly attenuated legacy, and nurturing only the anxiety over it. Petersen, by contrast, is the failed heir, one more bungler of the "John Wayne thing" in Vietnam. Petersen's disaster at point makes a mockery of the idea that he could have succeeded Kirby. If Kirby could spot a trip wire ahead while walking behind the squad, why could Petersen not spot one right in front of him? And yet, if Petersen is no more than his generation's martyr, can we not still insist that Wayne failed to forge his "boys" into "fighting men" as Sergeant Stryker was supposed to do twenty years earlier? Petersen's miscarriage of the heroic deed instantiates the whole misbegotten brood born of the "John Wayne wet dream" even as it also evidences the pronouncement of the veteran, "Fred," in *Soldiers in Hiding*, that "there's no John Wayne over there"—none, that is, except John Wayne himself, the revenant forever haunting the heroic inheritance.

## "Facing West"—Again

Of all the clumsy production gaffs and technical goofs in *The Green Berets*, none seems to have evoked greater popular scorn than that peculiar Da Nang "sunset" in the South China Sea as Hamchunk and Kirby walk along the beach in the final shot. Rather than join the chorus of detractors, however, we might briefly consider the moment in the serviceable light of Coleridge's "willing suspension of disbelief" if only to see whether that sunset might elicit something other and more productive than a howl of derision. Say, then, not that *The Green Berets* failed to create a Vietnamese sunset when it sank the sun in the ocean and not behind mountains or trees or buildings, and say only that it was much too caught up in its prowar messaging to have been reasonably concerned with geographical verisimilitude. Besides, if all things Vietnamese are here met with condescension, indifference, or contempt, why not Vietnamese geography as well? (What else was the 1954 Geneva Convention's partition of Vietnam at the 17th parallel but a historic instance of the imperial disdain for the geographies of national identity?) Would that general attitude, that slant, not expose America's unexamined arrogance respecting even such eternal things as where the sun sets in what part of the globe?

Still, the botched citation points to a mythic geography. Kirby/Wayne, now more than half a decade after Kennedy's death and almost a century after Whitman's visionary poem "Facing West from California's Shores" (minus the parenthetical doubt expressed in its concluding couplet), once again faces West. Standing in California, the continent's edge, Kirby also stands at that timeless point where Mrs. Collingwood, herself facing west, lost sight of the men but not of the flags, lost sight of a heroic generation but not of the heroic genealogy, of the men, then, but not of their legacy. There, at that impossibly unhistorical point, York-Stryker-Kirby, all of these characters and personae consolidated in the transcendent, transgenerational Wayne, would again and always remain "John Wayne, American," fulfilling a legacy revoked for all others, flouting the trust whereby he was to forge boys into men, and presiding over the annulment of history while yet undoing the very myth that he embodied.

# PART II

# CHAPTER 4

# The Heroic Imperative, the Lost War, and the Rupture

> I now knew my early impressions had been based not on reality but on a boyhood diet of war movies and blood-and-guts novels.
>
> —Philip Caputo, *A Rumor of War*

> Eyes open, be alert—old imperatives, old movies It all swirls together, clichés mixing with your own emotions, and in the end you can't tell one from another.
>
> —Tim O'Brien, *The Things They Carried*

## The Heroic Imperative

They went over there in unknowing affirmation of their innocence, and so they carried, as if all things else had not been burden enough, an unwavering belief in the unyielding historical foundations of America's heroic narrative. What tale could such a myth narrate but that of an exceptional history? Each generation had claimed its own moment in America's timeline, and now that they had grown up into young manhood, the relentless menace of a great oncoming convulsion, like nothing even their fathers had known, urged them to take their place in the muster rolls of the American new order of the ages. They believed that they knew the stakes, and they accounted themselves worthy and declared themselves ready. Their worshipful growing up had charted their steady initiation into the lore and arcana of the heroic myth, much of it (entirely too much of it) Hollywood-wrought. They knew intimately the gods of their movie theater pantheon, and they knew the needful tools, the requisite rites, and the authenticating gestures. "I grew out of one war and into another," Tim O'Brien writes. "I was bred with the haste and dispatch and careless muscle-flexing of a nation giving bridle to its own good fortune and success. I was fed by the spoils of 1945 victory."[1] Hollywood Westerns and war movies substantiated the testimony of history, the noonday history that confirmed the special and splendid destiny. Moreover, such a revelation strengthened their faith in an incontestable tenet of the mythic history, that is, their war dispensed with justification. Right and might were theirs already, no less a part of their inheritance than their commitment to the fight. All else was but the breathless wait for their moment, as in the scene that follows the US Marine Corps recruiter's presentation at Ron Kovic's high school in *Born on the Fourth of July* (Stone, 1989). Six young men, including Kovic (Tom Cruise), sit around a table at the ice cream parlor. As the camera dollies in from a medium long shot of the group, Steve Boyer (Jerry Levine) reports that according to his older brother, "there's going to be a war in." But he falters and has to ask the other boys, "What is it?" Two or three of them offer the name of the place: Vietnam. "And he said," Boyer continues, "that the marines will be the first in, and it ain't gonna last long." Then Kovic announces his decision: "So if we don't sign up soon, we're gonna miss it. I've already decided. I'm going in. I'm not waiting. I'm going in now." Over the skeptical mumbles of some of the other boys, Kovic adds, "Our dads got to go to WW II. This is our chance to do something, be part of history, guys." They were strangely blessed, these innocents tragically bereft of the needful foresight to tell myth from history.

The myth of heroic continuity begot, nurtured, and defined *the heroic imperative*, namely the urgent obligation to enact, perhaps even to surpass, the heroic deeds of the fathers. The heroic imperative designates a generation's ideal of unquestioned duty to the nation and thus fully and richly complies with President John F. Kennedy's exhortation to "ask what you can do for your country." Four basic assumptions sustained the heroic imperative:

*The national war narrative itself guarantees an American victory.* All of America's past wars were unequivocal triumphs because each one had been driven by a pellucid moral vision. And future wars would reliably unfold their own convergence with America's higher destiny.

*The heroic imperative transcends, even as it essentializes, "mere" civic obligation.* The urgent call to "ask what you can do for your country" was in itself already the unequivocal affirmation of the nation's heroic legacy.

*America's war chronicles confirmed the American people's exceptional character.* Accordingly, the generations were to inherit and in time profess a faith in a special privileged history.

*Heroism presupposed victory.* The nation's defeats—at the Little Bighorn in 1876, aboard the Battleship *Maine* in 1898, and at Pearl Harbor in 1941—were in reality tests of the national resolve, and the martyrs of our worst debacles could resolutely await the certain and redemptive victories to come at Wounded Knee, the San Juan Heights and Kettle Hill, and Iwo Jima and Okinawa, tragedies all transmuted into heroic glory.

So charmed (or ensnared) by the heroic imperative, the young never could have imagined theirs as a *counterlegacy*, an inheritance shaped by their tragedy, a despised legacy, then, that left them despairing of atonement and reconciliation.

## "The One Great Power" and the "Reference Point"

However acute the nation's Cold War anxieties, however zealously professed the allegations of conspiracies in high places, and however shrill and importunate the omens of imminent apocalypse, losing a war remained unthinkable in the afterglow of victory in Europe and Japan. "When the Second World War was over," wistfully recalls Clark Clifford, President Lyndon Johnson's second (and last) secretary of defense, "we were the one great power in the world. The Soviets had a substantial military machine, but they could not touch us in power. . . . In addition to feeling a sense of responsibility, we also began to feel the sense of a world power—that possibly we could control the future of the world."[2] Convinced of its exemption from the common fate of past empires,

America would make it known that its devastating military power served a perfect justice.

Even so, these blessings were daily threatened by events that plagued America's sense of global mission. And so, as if to assuage the anxiety, the nation turned to its heroic myth and its greatest achievement, still so fresh in America's (and the world's) memory. In the Canadian-made documentary *Vietnam: The Ten Thousand Day War* (1980), Max Cleland, a decorated veteran who lost both legs and an arm in Vietnam, notes ruefully that America "became hostile and in many ways alien to the Vietnam veteran. There was never really that homecoming." Cleland's assertions in this scene clash harshly with the certitude and aplomb permeating the scene that follows it, which includes familiar images of American post–World War II jubilation, especially those of a victory parade in New York City, the endless columns of GIs marching to the adulation of multitudes. The actor Richard Basehart, in voice-over, intones, "Times Square, 1945: a celebration of victory in World War II. It is the reference point for the GIs that go to Vietnam." Then, he provides the basic historical context of the heroic imperative. "After two world wars and Korea, America's patriotism is unquestioned. [*CUT. Vietnam-generation GIs marching on parade ground, training on Hueys, etc.*] Now a new generation goes to war with the same sense of duty. Most go with a simple creed—a belief that, when America calls, that call must be answered. The slogan was 'my country right or wrong.'"[3] The cut from Cleland's lament takes us back to the giddy days following the end of World War II but well before Vietnam. Here in this celebration, the young generation had a model for its own homecoming. A nation just as grateful and no less appreciative would welcome them back from Vietnam.

Yet no Vietnam veterans came home to anything even faintly resembling such celebrations. The Vietnam veteran's homecoming—"*that* homecoming," in Cleland's wistful expression—had long since become a forlorn hope. American "society" became "hostile" to the Vietnam soldier not because of the drugs, the shamming, or the fragging, or even because of the documented atrocities but instead because the Vietnam soldier failed to win a war, a war in which the very definition of winning had eluded even "the best and the brightest." Never mind the young soldiers' condition as victims, the betrayal of their patriotic enthusiasm, or the dashed dreams of heroism. They were easy marks easily made to bear the full brunt of the Loss. So, there would be no national rejoicing; America could muster nothing nobler than mere relief, signaled by their homecoming, that that vicious war was over. And peace? Peace, for now, meant hardly more than weariness endured. In Denis Johnson's *Tree of Smoke*, William "Skip" Sands, the central character, once "a spy for history's greatest nation," is now, after the war, writing a farewell letter to a long-lost love: "There was once a war in Asia that had among its tragedies the fact that it followed World War II, a modern war that had somehow managed to retain or revive some of the glories and romances of earlier wars. This Asian war however failed to give any romances outside of hellish myths."[4]

And America remained steadfast in its refusal to separate the hero from the Loss. "Because I'm a loser, according to their standard," bitterly complains Jack McCloskey, a Vietnam veteran, "they want nothing to do with me. I think when I was wounded in Vietnam my blood ran just as heavily and my pain was just as heavy as my father's and [that of] other fathers of Vietnam veterans."[5] Let an impenitent Gen. William C. Westmoreland in 1980 or for that matter a conciliatory President Barack Obama three decades later assure us that the United States never lost a major battle in Vietnam.[6] "'You know,' said Col. Harry G. Summers to a North Vietnamese counterpart after the war, 'you never defeated us on the battlefield.' To which the officer replied, 'That may be so, but it is also irrelevant.'"[7] And let the precise cultural historian assure us that no one in America ever spit on the soldiers returning from Vietnam.[8] Even so, Vice Adm. James Stockdale, who suffered the tortures of his North Vietnamese captors for almost eight years, affirmed upon his return that "'the pain and the loneliness [of imprisonment] were shallow complaints compared to finding yourself stripped of all entitlement to reputation, love or honor at home.'"[9]

## Amplifying the Rupture

The rupture designates a break with the narrative of America's privileged destiny. Each American war won had constituted at once a discrete point and its extension through the national timeline; each triumph linked past and future in confident and coherent affirmation of a blessed teleology. Nonetheless, we must not dismiss the possibility that the narrative of uninterrupted American exceptionalism gained acceptance, even currency, because of the Loss. Accordingly, Vietnam becomes a source of difference: it introduces discrepancy, divergence, conflict, and resistance, thus at once and paradoxically isolating the Loss from the myth and perhaps casting it as the exception that affirmed the continuity associated with victory. In this way, the rupture itself, though surely in its ironic mode, loomed ominously over strategies to "restore" continuity. The rupture promoted tendentious redefinitions of victory so that, for instance, America never lost a battle in Vietnam—an evasion put forth as proof. America demanded new face-saving definitions of mission and victory and called for separating the soldier from the war in all wars to come.

Chiefly, however, the rupture indicated a lapse not only as the tragic outcome of the heroic imperative but, worse, as a decline, a backsliding. The war evinced America's fall from grace, and the nation, though often in denial, grudgingly learned that it was not exempt from the fate of empires, thus an ironic version of continuity. As such, Vietnam exposed American exceptionalism as old-fashioned imperial vanity and arrogance. And in the singular failure of the war to reconsecrate (or perhaps merely to resanitize) the heroic myth, there was now abundant evidence of the vapid presumptions that had so long seemed to sustain the national narrative in a state of perpetual exaltation. Perhaps, then, America's decisive victories, those that had fed the myth, had also presaged the Loss, somewhat after the remorseless unfolding of events that, as with Oedipus, cast the hero himself as the criminal. And so, as in many such tales, someone had to be scapegoated even if, in the end, those doing the blaming would become the ones to blame. Samuel Hynes holds that Vietnam is of all America's wars the one

> that can teach us most. . . . But for the people of the United States, the Vietnam War is more than a lesson in political unwisdom. It lingers in American minds like the memory of an illness, a kind of fever that weakened the country until its people were divided and its cause was lost. That fever is in the narratives Americans have written about the war, and it makes their soldiers' tale different from the tales of other modern wars—not simply because the United States lost, though that had not happened before, but because in the loss there was humiliation and bitterness and the burden of complicity in a nation's moral failure.[10]

As a once-expected victory might have affirmed heroic continuity, now losing placarded the soldier's betrayal of the heroic legacy. Oliver Stone's *Platoon* (1986) offers an especially fatalistic expression of the rupture in a brief yet too candid exchange between Pvt. Chris Taylor (Charlie Sheen) and Sergeant Elias (Willem Dafoe). The dialogue follows a savage fist-fight between Elias and Sergeant Barnes (Tom Berenger) shortly after Barnes kills a Vietnamese woman in cold blood.

**Chris:** Barnes has got it in for you, don't he?
**Elias** [*charitably*]: Barnes believes in what he's doing.
**Chris:** And you, do you believe?
**Elias:** In '65, yes. Now, . . . no. What happened today's just the beginning. We're gonna lose this war.
**Chris** [*incredulous*]: Come on! You really think so? *Us?*
**Elias:** We've been kicking other people's asses for so long, I figure it's time we got our own asses kicked.

The myth of uninterrupted and everlasting American invincibility, it turned out, was but the long and patient rehearsal for the tragic fall. In time, the American narrative of the Vietnam War came to invoke *honor* as a cover for the Loss. America had never before known peace but as the fruits of victory. Now, though, there would be peace, as President Richard Nixon promised, and it would be "peace with honor." Nixon's "silent majority" displayed posters and signboards clamoring for "Home with Honor" implying, surely despite their own earnestness, that honor was the mere scourings of the victory that should have been.

The rupture is a consequence of a historically compelled and guided reflection on the Loss. The heroic imperative, by contrast, not only dispenses with but altogether precludes justification, apology. To the heroic imperative, reliance on ideology is at best a derivative, a dilution, of the fight in relation to which the *cause*, as in Webb's *Fields of Fire* (see chapter 3), is mostly irrelevant. For the new generation, the upheavals of the 1960s (from Berlin and Cuba in 1961 to the convulsions of 1968), the almost daily emergencies of a morbidly extravagant decade, blazoned the coming of the "boys'" heroic time, charted their path to glory. Thereafter, the narratives of the Loss would reflect the great national dismay over the outcome of the war, over the outcome itself, that is, without regard to or as a consequence of the waste or the tragedy or the too soon ceded moral high ground. The narratives of the Loss revealed the vast extent to which merely winning had guided America's primal animus, first against Vietnam itself and then against the returning veterans.

America came to acknowledge the Loss but only, and no doubt paradoxically, that it might so revive the heroic mythic. The rupture itself became the means of reaffirming the myth of heroic continuity. We would see this paradoxical appeal to the Loss in the historical fudges that drive the first two Rambo movies. A certain *they* did not let *us* win. To expose this treasonous cabal meant that in some way America could get to "win this time," as Rambo hopes in *Rambo: First Blood Part II.* We would also see the same chicanery in Ronald Reagan's characterization of the war as a "noble cause." But in a much more insidious way, the Loss could be reintegrated into the myth by casting it as the requisite reflection on all our wars before Vietnam, all of which shared the one common outcome: an American victory. As foil or contrast to such success, the Loss made clear the glory that had been, and in moments of historical reflection we would be careful to interject "except for Vietnam." We must wonder whether it was not the regret and the pain and the shame of the Loss that eventually drove Americans to the adoration of the World War II veteran.

## Notes and Conjectures Concerning the Rupture

The four centuries of American development have chronicled uprisings and massacres enough, crises, crucibles, and catastrophes aplenty, and a surfeit of tragic defeats in battle and the collective mourning that followed from, say, Tidewater Virginia in 1622 to the Little Big Horn in 1876, Pearl Harbor in 1941, and Bataan in 1942. But every uprising had been quelled, every crisis mollified, every defeat avenged, and every tragedy, if not quite justified (there had been so much wasted and outraged life) then at least reconciled with the auguries of unending American greatness. So, then, every war was won. And every win made it increasingly clear that Americans could, in both fact and faith, expect nothing but victories, however "dubious" the battles or equivocal the "cessations of hostilities." Thus, as long as America continued to win wars, the heroic myth and its continuity might have all seemed little more than a supplementary point of national bluster. What need was there, after all, of a hard look back, of anything like an unbiased—or, in the old Arnoldian sense, disinterested—interrogation of both myth and history? Sometimes myth is only the incurious person's history.

But then at the height of America's pride, the Loss swept remorselessly over the nation's historical complacency—over the easy shibboleths and the comfortable canting—to leave behind mostly a bewildering havoc of doubt and anxiety about America's existential identity. The Loss, in short, enforced an acknowledgment of the rupture. And no wheedling or coaxing would restore the fusty bond with an exceptional destiny. The heroic legacy had come to an end. Among those who lived in the time immediately after the Vietnam War, who could forget that for two or three years toy firearms were not to be seen on the shelves of suburban toy stores? Was there in this sudden absence a naive, perhaps even despairing hope that the absence of toy guns would keep American children from future wars? Or was this bumbler's tactic a part of the general drive to forget Vietnam? Was this to be, then, the first American generation denied the nurturance of their own heroic imperative, the quickening agency inherent in their anguished awareness of their historical moment? And if the veterans of the Vietnam War bore the full burden of the Loss, did this mean that the Loss would be their children's inheritance?

If oblivion was to be achieved by so shallow an expedient as the disappearance of toy guns, how much more effective would be the call by prominent Americans of the time, President Gerald Ford himself and Secretary of State Henry Kissinger, to put the Vietnam War "behind" us? A grave and stilted argot was suddenly let loose to characterize the war's aftermath—"normalization," "conciliation," "cooperation," the graceless piousness of the *-tion* words made respectable, if no less devious, by the recurrence of Gallicisms such as *détente* and *rapprochement*. And the jargon failed to obscure or even soft-pedal the Loss or mitigate the disorienting, estranging feeling of a great tragedy unjustified or make clear that the actual role of such noble-sounding words was in fact to promote a national oblivion so to discourage—and deny the need for—a national soul-searching. Perhaps the Loss could be mitigated, winning and losing redefined, the myth itself revived, out of a feigned amnesia. It is certain that a number of Vietnam War movies—for instance, the first two Rambo movies and *Uncommon Valor* (Kotcheff, 1983)—could presume, if only by invoking the arrogance that had gone the way of the myth itself, to reverse the course of history by willfully ignoring it. But all the aspersions and vilifications, the reproaching and the stigmatizing, could only confirm the irrevocable fact of the rupture.

Was it only here, then—the Loss, irrevocable in 1975, casting its remorseless shadow on the Bicentennial in 1976—that the continuity of American invincibility acquired, one might say, an urgent nostalgia? In time, such a necessary delusion could pronounce the Vietnam War "a noble cause," as President Reagan did, acting more like a medieval apothecary leeching or bleeding the Loss from the soldier than as a leader committed to binding the nation's wounds. So, too, it seemed all of a sudden vital to declare—postwar, mind you, when the information could hardly be news—that the United States had never lost a battle in Vietnam, as President Obama (among others before him) did in other conflicts. What would the Loss be without such exalted fudging? The Loss would otherwise return in visions of divine rebuke and of the nagging suspicion that the old exalted promise, which is to say the heroic inheritance itself, had been a delusion all along and that the glories of the past, including those presumed revelations of high destiny, merely concealed the lies spun out of ghastly entanglements and sordid motives and outraged power. The denials, the delusions, and the urge to overleap the rupture formed, accordingly, one side of the contrast that arose as a sort of national emergency from the Loss. The Loss itself, stark and stubborn, would supply the other side of the contrast, the side that triggered the consciousness of a faded glory and bared the shrill, wearisome vanity of exceptionalism.

Ironically, the Loss lent a great urgency to the continuity of the myth, invoking it not so much as an incentive to win but as a reminder that ours was not to lose any more wars. (Recall the half-frantic hope that the war in Iraq would not turn into "another Vietnam.") In its function as a contrast, the Loss, at once and paradoxically, extends continuity, for it marks the historical moment to be transcended, the myth to be recovered. Who will deny the young their own go at the heroic legacy? Their historical burden began to take shape in the instant of the Loss. Their inheritance was not victory but rather the goad to "win this time," as Rambo says. It thus becomes at once necessary and impossible to deny Vietnam (the Loss) by invoking it ("this time"). In the very act whereby the Loss may extend the continuity of the myth, it reels the myth back in. After the Loss, it is more clear than ever that the heroic imperative is in fact the anxiety of legacy uplifted into the sublime. So soon after the Loss, how could America be expected to resist the tsunami of patriotic and military nostalgia that swept the nation whenever henceforth it would recall World War II?

Hollywood Vietnam War movies identify the rupture as the tragic outcome ironically arising from the protagonist's innocent and ardent desire to earn his place in the chronicles of the heroic myth. He is vigilant, he is prepared, he is patriotic, and he revels in his ancestry, genealogical propinquity be damned if need be. It is the legacy itself that impels him to join the honored generations. Moreover, all the petty afflictions of his personal life—and even at times his vital hometown attachments—often resolve themselves in or yield earnestly to the allures and assurances of the myth. And all American wars seem to him the same, namely an impassioned clutch at redemptive glory. Perhaps no protagonist seems more qualified for heroism than Col. Walter E. Kurtz (Marlon Brando) in *Apocalypse Now* (Coppola, 1979). We learn, for example, that Kurtz is third-generation West Point, scion of general command officers who distinguished themselves in the two world wars. Not even the commanders in Nah Trang, who send Captain Willard (Martin Sheen) to assassinate Kurtz, can resist praising the colonel (however hypocritically) for the great American that he was (and might have been) before suffering his irrevocable abjection in Vietnam's heart of darkness. Beyond such intimations of glory, however, there is only the hard, if at times gradual, fall. Willard, who gives us the highlights of Kurtz's dossier in voice-over, identifies the moment when Kurtz, who might well be the army's "glass of fashion and mold of form," began the irreversible backsliding that would end in utter perdition: "in 1964," he says, Kurtz "returned from a tour with Advisory Command in Vietnam, and things started to slip. His report to the Joint Chiefs of Staff and Lyndon Johnson was restricted. Seems they didn't dig what he had to tell them." Kurtz has glimpsed the end of the myth in Vietnam. As we will see in chapter 6, he embodies the rupture, and his doing so acquires its highest, most poignantly tragic iteration of the rupture if only because the promise of unmatched glory had until recently seemed so assuredly fulfilled.

At times, the narrative of the rupture opens with a full-formed protagonist, an American in readiness to carry out the old wilderness mission of his ancestors, his skills in the woods not so much learned as inherited.

One such example is Sergeant Meserve (Sean Penn) in *Casualties of War* (1989), Brian De Palma's unrelenting tale of atrocity and depravity in Vietnam's wilderness based on the article (and subsequent book) by Daniel Lang. Though tasked with leading a squad on a long-distance reconnaissance patrol, Meserve takes it upon himself to recast the mission. Seeking to avenge a buddy slain in a previous engagement, he leads his men through a hamlet, and there he abducts a young woman (played by Thuy Thu Le), dragging her through the jungle and to her doom. Here is the American narrative of "Indian" captivity turned on its head. All but one of the squad members (Eriksson, played by Michael J. Fox) rape the girl, and eventually they all, except Eriksson, become complicit in her murder. *Casualties of War* claims no vital stake in the emergence of the rupture. The rupture, rather, seems as if to lie in wait for Meserve, his complete moral breakdown enveloping him wholly from the start. The rupture reveals unbidden secrets. If Meserve's turn to the wilderness forges a link with the ancient mastery of the white man over the Indians and the beasts, does it not also connect him to the record of evil in what Hawthorne in "Young Goodman Brown" calls "the unconverted wilderness"?[11] Is he not, as the Wicked One explains to Goodman Brown, a living reminder that "the fiend in his own shape is less hideous, than when he rages in the breast of man"?[12] Meserve's mythic skills were acquired in the home of America's raging heart, which is the howling wilderness, New England's or Vietnam's. Meserve is Robert Montgomery Bird's demonic "Nick of the Woods," the daytime humble Quaker whose uncanny stealth and cunning in the night sustain his secret, insatiable revenge against the Indians and turns him into a "savage" or, more in keeping with the nomenclature of the time, a "renegade." The wilderness, for the likes of Meserve and his fellow American demons, was at once a prod to satiate unimaginably depraved desires and a miscreant's hideout where they could at least hope against hope to avoid the gaze of divine censure.

In the first half of *The Deer Hunter* (Cimino, 1978), the American wilderness, both in itself and in its stark contrast with the steel mill town (Clairton, Pennsylvania), functions as the felicitous home of the American hero. That is, the wilderness is not only the source of his training for the war to come but also the site that, as it were, enlists his reverence and guides his chaste and righteous responses to nature in general and deer hunting in particular. (I address *The Deer Hunter* in greater detail in chapter 5.) The protagonist of *The Deer Hunter*, Michael Vronsky (Robert De Niro), appears first not in the sublime woods but in a hellish steel mill while wearing a hazmat suit as he tests the temperature of a reheating furnace with a pyrometer. Soon, however, Michael doffs the hazmat suit and metamorphoses into an American hunter able to read celestial signs and wonders auguring a propitious hunt. Not long after, he will make an impassioned argument for the proper and humane way to kill a deer, thus appealing to the doctrine, in evidence throughout Fenimore Cooper's *Leatherstocking Tales*, of "one shot." "A deer," Michael insists, "has to be taken with one shot." More creed than craft, more piety than sport, as is fit and proper for a descendant of Natty Bumppo and Faulkner's Ike McCaslin, Michael's hunter's ethos is clearly sourced in and instantiated by the lore and traditions of American wilderness skills and thus by the same mastery required to defeat the Indian in the wilderness or the Viet Cong in South Vietnam. Thus, Michael's mythical ancestry harks back to the earliest hunter-warriors of the American forests—to John Smith and John Underhill and John Mason, dating back to the century and a half before Daniel Boone and Simon Kenton—and owes at least as much to Fenimore Cooper's Hawkeye. And this heritage, referenced and alluded to throughout the long initial Clairton, Pennsylvania, portion of *The Deer Hunter*, seems to not only set the preconditions for an American victory in Vietnam but also guarantee the continuity of American heroism and righteousness beyond Vietnam. Already before the rupture, Michael's wilderness skills seem to guarantee his triumphant return to Clairton. And relying on this same expert hunter's mastery, he presumes to guarantee the rescue and return—mind and body intact (since neither suicide nor dismemberment figure explicitly in the myth)—of his two buddies from Clairton, Nick (Christopher Walken) and Steven (John Savage), both of whom fight alongside Michael. And yet, everything that follows thereafter—in two long episodes in Vietnam as well as in post-Vietnam Clairton—only humiliates these expectations, declares them mere threadbare certitudes that beget only despair and grief and tragedy. If *The Deer Hunter* remorselessly narrates the undoing of Michael's wilderness virtues, it is perhaps because it also—and inseparably from the agency of the protagonist—narrates the end of the heroic myth and thus names the rupture as the settled, inexpugnable precondition of future American war narratives.

The list that follows emerges as an inventory of ideas present in and derived from specific narratives of the Vietnam War, that is, in and from narratives of the rupture. Meant primarily as a reference source, the list obeys no strict hierarchy (the items are numberless) with respect to the rupture, though some entries may well appear more basic—and certainly more useful—than others, especially when brought into relation with particular tropes and themes. Overlap is unavoidable, though it is possible to detect some progression from the stubbornly factual to the frankly speculative. But no item should command more than a merely descriptive status, serviceable therefore as a guide through the fate of the heroic myth in narratives of the Vietnam War. As a whole, then, the list at once evinces and encourages thought not only about these movies but from them as well.

- The rupture emerges with the Loss and is coeval and copresent with the Loss (rather than its derivative or aftereffect). This twin birth, so to call it, indicates a *reciprocal naming* of the rupture by the Loss and of the Loss by the rupture.
- The rupture is coextensive with the Loss, each referencing the other and thus influencing the shape of post-Vietnam American war narratives.
- The narratives of the rupture incite and interrogate American narratives of wars both before and after the Vietnam War.
- Before the rupture, the heroic myth had implicitly claimed a stable, ontological status; its presumed exemption from history and time—from what the tradition refers to as "the World," "Time," or "mutability"—had lent to the heroic legacy its aspect of exclusive and unshared privilege, the double blessing of being at once *underived* and *originary*.
- The rupture carries thematic value.
- The rupture is not an intrusion in the narrative and instead *drives* the narrative.
- The rupture is a force of revision, at once transforming the American war genre and contributing to reassessments of the myth of heroic continuity as a given in American war stories.
- The Loss and the rupture are not, however, indistinctly the same, fungible.

- The Loss instantiates the historical (and in some respects historic) outcome of the Vietnam War; the rupture corroborates the myth, avouches it, even as it reveals the myth in its new—which is to say its *ironic*—mode.
- The rupture neither cancels outright nor supplants the myth, neither revoking nor nullifying it, let alone eradicating it. Indeed, the rupture, however paradoxically, *binds the Loss to the myth.* The rupture both reclaims the myth and subverts it, hence a transformed myth, namely a myth that admits not so much of epistemic falsification as of irony and tragedy and thus of analysis and critique. The rupture, then, drags the myth into narration, thus denying it the uncritical ontological status of "continuity" in the ooze and sludge of undifferentiated time.
- The rupture therefore resists characterization as a void, as some sort of narrative black hole swallowing even oblivion itself. The rupture is not a lacuna, a gap, for these imply disconnection when in fact the rupture (instantiating the Loss) reveals the myth in its new condition as source and index, if not quite of tragedy then of abject victimhood wrought of a great betrayal.
- The rupture reminds us of the myth's origin not in an unprecedented and all-redemptive *novus ordo seclorum* supervised by the "Eye of Providence" but rather in the unappeasable "heart of darkness" that dwells (yet?) in America's "howling wilderness."
- The rupture, doubtless ironically, binds America's heroic myth to a different, more comprehensive "continuity," connecting it to human memory itself and therefore to a "continuity" indifferent to protestations of national privilege and exception. *The rupture binds the American war narrative to the universal tragic at the heart of all war stories.*
- The rupture resists and all but confounds any historically complacent or ideologically tendentious avowals of the myth's enduring integrity.
- The rupture purges the myth of its claims of cultural hegemony, of its presumptions of narrative self-determination, of its status as a higher, teleological or millenarian history, of the tragic ironies inherent in its self-profession as the preeminent source of American (that is, white Christian) values. It reminds us,

as Charlie Marlowe notes in Conrad's *Heart of Darkness*, that empire's "strength is just an accident arising from the weakness of others."[13]

- The rupture itself provides the myth with the means of isolating the Loss as an aberration, with the possibility even of *denying* the Loss. But the rupture casts sufficient doubt on the myth of heroic continuity to suggest that the myth may well have attained its specific cultural and even historical appeal *after* the Loss.
- The rupture thus teaches the futility of eliciting or evoking the myth as if it had never suffered upheaval: any effort to wedge the myth into the post-Loss present and enlist it as a force for national rebirth is already an encounter with the rupture in the form of history's stern and subversive demurrals.
- The Loss yields no regenerative "again." The "again" always and already argues its own status as a hopeless delusion or as arrant pandering and flimflammery. As the poet Clint Smith might put it, "there is / no solace in rearranging language to make a different word / tell the same lie."[14]
- The rupture makes possible the liberation of the hero from both triumph and Loss but does not exempt him from time or tragedy.
- There may be critical possibilities to be profitably pursued by treating the rupture as a momentous event marking the end of a phase in the development of the United States. In its role as a historical limit, the rupture offers a parallel to the end of the "first phase," as Frederick Jackson Turner called it, of American growth (as implied by the demographics laid out in "Extra Census Bulletin, No. 2").[15]

## Nothing, Waste, Betrayal

W. D. Ehrhart was in the thick of the Tet Offensive of 1968. The marines of his unit had been trying to wrest the ancient capital city of Hué from the well-entrenched North Vietnamese Army. Ehrhart's thirteen-month tour of duty is almost up, and it already includes the full portion and more of war's horrors and heartaches: the killing of unarmed Vietnamese civilians, the dreaded if unsurprising "Dear John" letter, the death of fellow marines from his unit, and, if much less common, the devastating news that a beautiful Danish woman with whom he had enjoyed a blissful R&R in Hong Kong has been found dead; she was raped, slashed about the face, and tortured with lighted cigarettes before she was murdered. Though Ehrhart is near the end of his tour, it is only in Hué that he experiences anything like the large-scale war that he had once imagined he would fight someday. At first, Ehrhart writes, "the whole thing was like the war movies I'd watched with intense delight as a boy. Men shouted and ran and crawled around on their elbows and knees with their rifles cradled in their arms; weapons barked and stuttered; smoke and debris erupted in fiery columns; whole slabs of buildings crumbled and collapsed to the street."[16] Here was combat as athletic contest, as rite of passage, as imminent heroic achievement, all as in the movies that had delighted him. But Ehrhart's gloss on this "movie" moment in Hué turns to the agony and the revulsion that soon break the spell of the mythic spectacle. "The screams were real," he reminds us, "and when men fell down they didn't get up, and the sticky substance splattering against your leg was somebody's intestines." Still, he remarks, it was a good thing that for once the enemy "was willing to stand his ground and fight it out until one side or the other won." For Ehrhart, Vietnam had heretofore demeaned the heroic imperative. It had been a war of "stumbling around in the boondocks finding nothing—or worse than nothing: those maddening mines and snipers; of searching hooches and calling somebody's lunch Vietcong supplies; of beating up old men and women; of cowering down helplessly in the darkness as mud and mortar rounds fell out of the sky; of swinging away at an enemy without substance or form or being." And although he admits that he was "scared utterly witless," he also tells us that the Battle for Hué gave him "the greatest adrenalin high" he had ever experienced.

But even in the midst of his combat-induced euphoria, Ehrhart fights against not only an enemy made visible at last but also an American narrative that could cozen a young man into complete surrender to a specious mythology. The passage below expresses the helpless if righteous rage against all that seems to lead to this one moment of combat in extremis, this unabating turmoil of the soul where fury, fear, seduction, betrayal, and bitterness mix indistinctly. "And I fought back passionately," Ehrhart writes.

> I fought back at the mud of Con Thien, and the burning sand of Hoi An, and the alien blank faces in the marketplace at Dien Ban; at the Pentagon generals, and the Congress of the United States, and the *New York Times*; at the Iron Butterfly, and the draft-card burners, and the Daughters of the American Revolution; at the murderer of Dorrit von Hellemond, and the son-of-a-bitch who had taken Jenny flying in his private airplane; at the teachers who had taught me that America always had God on our side and always wore white hats and always won; at the Memorial Day parades and the daily Pledge of Allegiance and the constant rumors of peace talks and the constant absence of peace; at the movies of John Wayne and Audie Murphy, and the solemn statements of Dean Rusk and Robert McNamara; at the ghosts of [fallen comrades] Roddenbery and Maloney and Rowe and Basinski and Calloway and Aymes and Falcone and Stemkowski; at [bullies from school days] Jerry Dougherty and Lloyd Drescher and Jimmy Whitson; at freedom and democracy and communism and the monumental stupidity with which I had delivered myself into the hands of the nightmare; at the small [Vietnamese] boy with the terrible grenade in his hand, cocked and ready to be delivered into my lap. . . . I had no idea—had not the slightest inkling—what I was fighting for or against.[17]

Such is the horror that often emerges in narratives of the rupture. Ehrhart's catharsis—this brilliant burst of a penetrating yet forbidding wisdom wrought of rage and regret—takes the form of a *nothing* where victory should have been. The compounding surfeit of this inventory of fears and wrongs and rancors validates the soldier's assessment of his Vietnam experience as a nothing. The unsparing inclusiveness of his repudiating, exorcising litany somehow leaves a ghastly and disconcerting void as the sum total of his Vietnam experience: the historical rupture as moral abyss.

The rupture took the form of a chastening insight into the life and meaning of America's myths, and what had once seemed the solid footing of noble causes and unshakeable principles gave ground and became the quagmire from which history taunted and mocked the heroic imperative. Hence, Ron Kovic's poignantly personal version of the rupture as he lies badly wounded in the battlefield: "I didn't think about praying, all

I could feel was cheated. All I could feel was the worthlessness of dying right here in this place at this moment for nothing."[18] Or consider the insight of Robert Mason, a helicopter pilot during the war. "Nothing that I saw convinced me that we were doing the right thing in Vietnam. I even harbored a sympathy for the enemy, which made me feel guilty. . . . In the air, I did my job the best I knew how. I flew, as did all the pilots, into hot LZs because in the middle of the confusion the hazy principles over which the war was fought disappeared."[19] A generation that had shaped its most cherished identity by embracing the heroic myth now found itself defined by the resultant "nothingness" of the rupture, where "hazy principles" vanish altogether.

At the very end of *Born on the Fourth of July*, Ron Kovic gives us a page or so of nostalgia in the form of a generation's cultural touchstones on the eve of Vietnam: baseball, basketball, hoola-hoops and ping-pong, boy scouts and *National Geographic*, Mickey Mantle, his best girl, and Del Shannon's "Runaway."[20] But Kovic's experience in Vietnam and after, during a harrowing struggle with his wounds, made it evident that a moral wilderness had forever overwhelmed the noontide bliss of the American backyard. Even before the end of the war, America could count on the combat soldier to invoke his own common encounter with this nothing, this residual void that defined the war. As a decorated commander of a Swift Boat, LTJG John Kerry brought the Vietnam soldier's dismay into national prominence when he testified before Congress in late April 1971. Testifying before a committee headed by Senator J. William Fulbright of Arkansas, Kerry addressed the "feelings" that veterans brought back from Vietnam. "The country," he warned (indeed prophesied), "doesn't know it yet, but it has created a monster, a monster in the form of millions of men who have been taught to deal and to trade in violence, and who are given the chance to die for the biggest nothing in history; men who have returned with a sense of anger and a sense of betrayal which no one has yet grasped."[21]

In the aftermath of the climactic battle in John Del Vecchio's *The 13th Valley*, three troopers lie dead. When the helicopters come for the many others wounded, these three dead men have to be left behind because the company has come under heavy fire. At the roll call for the battalion's dead, Cherry, disruptive even throughout the religious service, realizes that no one has called out the names of the three dead soldiers. Lieutenant

Thomaston, sitting next to him, tells him that the army has classified the three as missing in action. Here, Cherry invokes the nihilist mantra of the soldier in Vietnam—"Fuck it. Don't mean . . ."—but just before he actually utters the last word, Thomaston interrupts him: "'Don't say it, Soldier.'"[22] Here, nothing—its meaning eloquently underscored by the prohibition against its utterance—becomes a cynical recognition of the causes of the war's tragedy, namely the absence of a clearly defined and resolutely commanded and unfalteringly obeyed purpose. That Lieutenant Thomaston keeps Cherry from saying the last word, however, hardly spares the three fallen soldiers from Cherry's nihilistic judgment. Indeed, the *not* saying it, the self-conscious silence itself, already speaks it.

There had been tragedy aplenty in Vietnam, as there had been in every other American war, but only Vietnam seemed to make it well-nigh impossible to reconcile the calamitous losses with the values that America might have once meant to defend and uphold there. In the resulting absurdity of his condition, the soldier saw a nothing that he could somehow, and no doubt paradoxically, endow with a wealth of meaning. Nothing was not to be the all of the war's meaning, but nothing, surely, was a great deal of it. The Loss provoked the heroic myth's spiteful reckoning, the complicit, embittered, and, not least, hollow nostalgia by which it scourged and drove off the insistence on America's often shameful conduct in the Vietnam War. Thus, America's post-Vietnam response to the rupture turned to the heroic legacy as a way of ignoring the historical, cultural, and, yes, moral implications of the Loss. But in this very condemnation, the reaction to the Loss forced Vietnam into a place of its own in the long line of wars won, but only as a cautionary tale, an enduring if despised foil. America invoked the heroic myth as an instrument of judgment, and the myth presumed to damn and disavow a whole generation while failing to concede its own complicity in the Loss. As if reiterating these unacknowledged ironies, America's post-Vietnam anxieties concerning the nation's conduct in future wars took shape out of the nothing that the American combat soldier had so intimately known in Vietnam. And the sententious abjurations of the American soldier and of the general conduct of the war became in themselves a way, however ironic or circuitous, of revalidating the myth's continuity. The mad drive for reinvoking and later restoring continuity would contribute to the implicit demand for more wars, any war so long as it was not "another Vietnam." Any war would enable America to exorcise the demons of Vietnam, as George H. W. Bush may have thought he did when he exulted over his Gulf War victory.

In the irrepressibly sardonic American lexicon of the Vietnam War, waste—both noun and verb—functions as a correlative of nothing. The venerable *Oxford English Dictionary* recognizes the peculiar Vietnam War–engendered locution of "waste" in an apposite example from 1971: "[4] c. To beat up, kill, murder (someone); to devastate a place, to kill its inhabitants. *slang* (orig. and chiefly *U.S.*)," as in "1971 *Guardian* 2 Apr. 12/2 The intention to 'waste' My Lai (s.v. 'waste')." "Waste" identifies the senselessness of the sacrifices that, in other American wars—in wars won—would be accounted "noble" and "heroic." It is because of this senselessness that "waste" inevitably names the Loss. Late in *A Rumor of War*, Philip Caputo tries to "do a bit of proselytizing among the clerks in the HqCo office" by declaring that the war is "unwinnable." He argues that the war "was being fought for a bunch of corrupt politicians in Saigon. Every American life lost was a life wasted." When a lance corporal argues that "'if we pulled out now, then all our efforts up to now would have been in vain,'" Caputo counters, "'In other words, because we've already wasted thousands of lives, we should waste a few thousand more.'"[23] This darkly ironic realization comes to Caputo while at work as a "casualty reporting officer." He had known Walter Levy from their days at Quantico, and now he learns from a field report that Levy, though already wounded in action, was still trying to help a fallen corpsman when he (Levy) was killed by a sniper. Caputo dutifully takes down the relevant information, including the address of Levy's next of kin. "That would be his parents in New York City. What would it be like when they answered the bell and saw a man in uniform standing in the doorway? Would they know instinctively why they had come? What would he say? How do you tell parents that all the years they had spent raising and educating their son were for nothing? Wasted. In that war, soldier's slang for death was 'wasted.' So-and-so was wasted. It was a good word."[24] Waste becomes the manifest form of the Vietnam soldier's nothing; it invests *nothing* with dismay, with shock, with rage, with that raw horror triggered by the startling, bewildering encounters that howl revulsion and resentment at principle and purpose.

## "Redeeming Negations": Sisyphus at Dong Ap Bia

Hollywood never admitted its own betrayal of the Vietnam soldier, never acknowledged the silence and the darkness of its indifference. But when at last it seemed safe to make movies of the Vietnam War, it was all but inevitable that betrayal would become a recurring trope in virtually all of them. John Irvin's *Hamburger Hill* (1987) enables a first look at this elemental trope. Betrayal in *Hamburger Hill* acquires its significance as the soldier's recognition of the war's meaninglessness, its nothing, as in the repeated phrase "It don't mean nothin'." *Hamburger Hill* dramatizes the attempts during May 11–20, 1969, of Lt. Col. Weldon Honeycutt's Third Battalion of the 187th Infantry Regiment (Rakkasans) of the 101st Airborne Division to take the North Vietnamese redoubt atop Dong Ap Bia (or Ap Bia Mountain, known in US Army maps as Hill 937 and sardonically named "Hamburger Hill" by Americans).[25] When the battle was over, young Americans had once again been afforded ample opportunity to see what it was like to be "given the chance to die for the biggest nothing in history," as John Kerry had defined the US effort in Vietnam. On June 5, only two weeks after the Americans had taken the mountaintop at great cost, Maj. Gen. John M. Wright, who had assumed command of the division soon after the battle, "ordered the position on the mountain abandoned."[26]

Even before the battle's end, "Hamburger Hill" came to exemplify the American public's indignation with the prosecution of the war. The name became a metaphor for the absurdity of the war and expressed the anguish of a nation that could not confirm its mythic best in the same flint-hearted commanders that the heroic myth might have once exalted. The nation, however, could hardly have fathomed the folly of this mission as intensely as did the soldiers themselves, prodded to bleed for that mountain. Baffled by a remorseless lack of fidelity, the soldier of *Hamburger Hill* discovers that his "inability to understand becomes the existence that illuminates everything,"[27] as Albert Camus puts it in *The Myth of Sisyphus*, for "the absurd is born of confrontation between the human need and the unreasonable silence of the world."[28] In our case, the "human need" is the heroic imperative in Vietnam: it seeks fulfillment, justification. And "the unreasonable silence of the world" corresponds to the heroic myth's betrayal of the soldier, a betrayal that in the end may as well be sourced in the indifference of the presiding gods. Accordingly, the rupture "is that divorce between the mind that desires and the world that disappoints, [the] nostalgia for unity, this fragmented universe and the contradiction that binds them together."[29]

Psychologist Jonathan Shay's encounters with Vietnam veterans allowed him to conclude that their stock of phrases—such as "Don't mean nothin'" and "Fuck it"—constituted "the Vietnam combat soldier's mantras, spread out to engulf everything valued or wanted, every person, loyalty, and commitment."[30] The nihilistic wisdom, the disconcerting insight wrought of the betrayal, grew clamorous and in time even eloquent in its condemnation of the myth by means of an ironic denial—a denial that nevertheless affirms outrage, protest, and defiance. At the site of the rupture lay not merely a break with the myth but also an *unsettling* of it, not only its discontinuity but also its abrogation. Nothing, then, becomes the soldier's version of Camus's "redeeming negation."[31]

The young soldiers in *Hamburger Hill* are yet more of John Wayne's forsaken "boys," sacrificed to the insentient gods of the mountain. They die at haphazard, and the ones who survive affirm no higher purpose or principle. The death of McDaniel (Don James), one of several African American paratroopers, sparks the rage of Spfc. "Doc" Johnson (Courtney B. Vance). Johnson, who is Black, blames the white superior officer, Sgt. Adam Frantz (Dylan McDermott), for assigning "point" to McDaniel, who was only a few days "short." Johnson and Frantz are about to go at each other when a private known only as Motown (Michael Boatman) steps between them. Spinning Johnson around to face him, Motown says, "It don't mean nothin', man. It don't mean nothin'." At first Johnson seems confused, but then Motown gives him a hand-slap that begins the change of the stark denial into an assertive, rhythmic refrain: "It don't mean nothin', not a thing, man. It don't mean nothin'," all to the rhythm of hand-slaps, on and on, mantric in its effect. Then Private Washburn (Don Cheadle) joins in, and the three Black paratroopers continue the chant until Johnson calms down completely.

The phrase itself—but more important, perhaps, the incantatory repetition of it—bares the soldier's anguish even as it consoles him in his heartache, rescues him from his own despairing sense of futility, of abandonment, of isolation. "The absurd world," Camus writes, "more than others derives its nobility from that abject birth. In certain situations, replying 'nothing' when asked what one is thinking about may be pretense in a man. . . . But if that reply is sincere, if it symbolizes *that odd state of soul in which the void becomes eloquent* [emphasis mine], in which the chain of daily gestures is broken, in which the heart vainly seeks the link that will connect it again, then it is as it were the first sign of absurdity."[32] The soldier's chant delivers him from the absurdity that provoked it. He lives in beginnings, for "living is keeping the absurd alive."[33] His nothing is the insistent avowal that proclaims—out of dismay and grief, out of denial and disbelief and defiance—his new beginning, his distinct existence, his presence at the leading edge of the rupture. All past reason and purpose, past even the hope for vindication that he now knows to have been an illusion, the soldier fashions his very being out of the incomprehension mirrored in the mountain's—and so in the war's—blank indifference. His nothing becomes the source of his exceptional self, apart, authentic, transgressive, no less American than the America that, as he learned in Vietnam, had never really been.

Another prominent character in *Hamburger Hill*, Sgt. Dennis Worcester (Steven Weber) has served several tours in Vietnam, and in his jeremiad, which I cite at length below, he seeks to explain the Vietnam soldier's deep-seated sense of betrayal. So remorseless—and so intensely felt—is the cant of "peace and love" back home that Worcester accounts Vietnam itself a refuge from "the World." As the men rest in a small clearing, 2nd Lt. Terry Eden (Tegan West), the genre's classically callow lieutenant, comes over to Worcester's side. Eden has received a "Dear John" letter, but the rejection only sharpens his ache for home, so he wants to know why Worcester keeps "coming back" to Vietnam. The "world," Worcester says, is "overrated," his bitterness spilling over into outright bigotry:

> Well, you're right about everybody loving everybody back there, sir. They tattoo it to their foreheads, and they wear little buttons on their flower shirts, you know. Yeah, they love everybody back there—cats, dogs, niggers, spics, kikes, wops, micks, greaseballs. Yeah, they're real fond of Luke the Gook back home, if y'all can believe that. They got a button for him too, yeah. They love everybody but you. I was medevacked after Dak To. *There* was a hill! And we were met at Oakland by pretty little things, you know what I mean? I mean, they had hair down below their asses, you know.

> And they had bags full of [*PAUSE, choking with anger*] dog shit. Well, don't mean nothin'. I'm back from the Nam, man. Nothin' is ever gonna bother me again. I get home: wife is sitting cross-legged on the floor, kids is running around barefoot, there's a hair-head taking a leak in the john. "Sorry about that," I said. That don't mean nothin', either. I go down to Polly's for a beer: Old Man Finnegan is doing shooters; they policed [*sic*] his boy in the Ia Drang Valley, sent him home in a rubber bag with "Members Missing" stamped on it. That don't mean nothin'. It don't mean nothin', except [*PAUSE, incredulous*] he keeps getting phone calls from these kids, college kids, saying how glad they was that his boy was killed in Vietnam, Republic of, by the heroic People's Army that's sitting right on top of this fucking hill. That's why I'm here.

The homeland had become enemy territory, and Americans at home were the enemy's second front. When "Johnny" came "marching home," he was actually returning to Vietnam—to "Indian Country"— for another tour of duty.

## Killing John Wayne and Making a "War Face"

Before Vietnam, Hollywood presented history and myth as a single national narrative. Myth was but history dramatized, and history unfolded a heroic destiny. But Hollywood may well have accomplished a good deal more than it intended by mere rote application of tropes for simultaneously embellishing and sanitizing war; for Hollywood promoted a process of reciprocal authorization, shaping history even as it itself took shape out of America's faith in the historicity of the myth. By contrast, the Vietnam War, even from the start, intimated a significant divergence from the myth. The old narrative of American triumphalism had so far endorsed and empowered the myth of heroic continuity. After the war, however, the convergence of history and myth could make clear only the subversive irony that Vietnam alone had introduced into America's war narratives.

One palpable form of that irony was the "killing" of John Wayne in Hollywood's Vietnam War. By the late 1970s, when Hollywood deemed it safe to make movies of the war, the raging fires of national division had begun to die down. As it sought to narrate a new American war story, Hollywood would again turn to the old myths and mythic tropes but only so that it might set the context for undoing them. Hollywood revived the myth and the mythic hero in order to kill them. Michael Cimino did this in *The Deer Hunter* (1978), and Francis Coppola did it in *Apocalypse Now* (1979). Stanley Kubrick was late with his offering, but his *Full Metal Jacket* (1986) proved no less instructive than the earlier explorations of the ironies at the heart of the Loss.

The fresh-shorn US marine recruits stand at attention in front of their bunks while the senior drill instructor, Gunnery Sergeant Hartman (Lee Ermey) paces to and fro before them, his face, by turns, mere inches from that of each recruit down the line, as he regales each one with bespoke slurs. While Hartman taunts and demeans Private Brown (Peter Edmund), an African American recruit whom he summarily renames Private Snowball, there is a cut to the row of recruits far across the barracks, leaving Hartman far in the background. In an unmistakably John Wayne voice, the recruit in the foreground, surnamed Davis (Matthew Modine), speaks as if addressing Hartman: "Is that you, John Wayne? Is this me?" Hartman, indignant, tries frantically to identify the offending recruit. The gunnery sergeant accosts a recruit, whom he soon names Cowboy (Arliss Howard), and begins to choke him, but now Davis (still standing at attention) confesses: "Sir, I said it, sir!" Immediately, Hartman dubs him Joker and then sends him to his knees with a vicious uppercut. When Joker staggers back up to his feet, Hartman asks demandingly, "Private Joker, why did you join my beloved Corps?"

**Joker:** Sir, to kill, sir!
**Hartman:** So you're a killer!
**Joker:** Sir, yes, sir!
**Hartman:** Let me see your war face!
**Joker** [*confused*]: Sir?
**Hartman:** You got a war face? Aaaaagh! That's a war face. Now let me see your war face!
**Joker** [*grimacing, producing a weaker, shorter yell than Hartman's*]: Aaagh!
**Hartman:** Bullshit! You didn't convince me. Let me see your real war face.

Joker tries a louder yell, squinching and snarling, but Hartman shouts, "You don't scare me. Work on it!" Having heard Hartman berate Snowball and Cowboy, Joker may well have wondered if he was in the presence of a John Wayne avatar ("Is that you, John Wayne?"), perhaps of Stryker himself in *Sands of Iwo Jima.* Joker then follows his first question with one seeming to express the singular privilege of being in the avatar's presence ("Is this me?"). But, of course, these questions of Joker's are nothing if not deeply cynical. Joker, who lives by artful equivocation, shapes his slippery identity by subtle contraventions of the heroic myth. In a memorable scene, Joker and other marines stand beside one of the mass graves where the enemy has buried thousands of South Vietnamese civilians, some of them alive, as history tells us. A "Pogue" Colonel (a starched rear-echelon incompetent played by Bruce Boa) commands Joker to explain how he can "write 'Born to Kill' on [his] helmet *and* . . . wear a peace button" on his flack jacket. "I think," Joker fudges, "I was trying to suggest something about the duality of man, sir—the Jungian thing, sir." Befuddled, the colonel demands, "Whose side are you on, son?" Joker replies with a masterstroke of evasion, "Our side, sir." The colonel is perfectly satisfied with Joker's answer.

In *Full Metal Jacket*, the absence of John Wayne in all but name (an absence all the more deeply felt in the character of the Wayne wannabe, Hartman) promotes an enlightening and ironic trope for the rupture—specifically, the recurrent, predictable, and invariably violent death of all the characters who presume to lead the platoon in combat (thus perhaps recalling Petersen's death at point in *The Green Berets*). Hartman, the ersatz Wayne, is not shot by the enemy, as Stryker is in *Sands of Iwo Jima*, but instead by the sorely abused Pvt. Leonard Lawrence, whom Hartman derisively calls Private Pyle after the inept marine played by Jim Nabors in the TV series *Gomer Pyle, USMC* (1964–1969). (Joker consistently calls him Leonard, as I will hereafter.) In the murder of Hartman, *Full Metal Jacket* declares itself already a different war movie, so that Hartman's death inevitably alludes to "fragging," the practice, especially prevalent late in the war, of murdering officers whose aggressiveness imperiled a unit. Indeed, *Full Metal Jacket* affirms Vietnam's difference—the rupture, then—by insisting on the death of any marine who, officially or not, assumes a position of leadership in combat. In short, if you lead you die. And in this Vietnam you cannot die but ingloriously, with none of the verve or vaunt of the old movie heroes. Ingloriously and ironically, Hartman's greatest bootcamp "success"—the gifted sharpshooter who suddenly emerges from Leonard's abject bumbling—murders him.

Three others besides Hartman assume leadership of the squad only to die a short time thereafter. And while dying is hardly in itself noteworthy in a war movie, here it becomes a way of reminding us of the "children rawly left," of Hartman's failure—and by implication John Wayne's own—to "forge the boys" into men. Not surprisingly, each foredoomed leader identifies himself with pursuits traditionally associated with American manhood—the Marine Corps, of course, but also college football and the American West. The first of these is Cowboy's platoon commander, Lt. Walter J. Schinoski (Ed O'Ross), whose men call him "Mr. Touchdown" because he "played a little ball for Notre Dame." Among the ruins in the outskirts of Hué, Mr. Touchdown walks behind one of three tanks and well ahead of the squad (perhaps in a harebrained football play formation) when suddenly the tanks are hit by a mortar barrage. All the men hit the ground for cover except Touchdown, who continues to stand for a few seconds before he staggers and falls, more as if tackled than shot dead.

Almost immediately thereafter, Crazy Earl (Kieron Jecchinis) assumes command of the squad, and suddenly the zany necrophiliac (we first meet him as he poses for photos next to his "Bro," a fully uniformed and very dead North Vietnamese Army soldier, played, so to speak, by Duc Hu Ta) becomes a confident and determined squad leader. But later, while the squad is again on patrol through the ruins of Hué, Crazy Earl spots a large pink stuffed rabbit in the rubble. He reaches for it, it explodes, and he dies instantly. When Cowboy reports Crazy Earl's death on the walkie-talkie, "Murphy" (Stanley Kubrick, uncredited), the voice on the other end, replies, "You're senior NCO, Cowboy, you're in charge." Cowboy's promotion is a death sentence and bears all the authority of directorial fiat. Never a confident leader, Cowboy sends Eightball (Dorian Harewood) to find a way out of the deadly sniper's field of vision, but the sniper (Ngoc Le) spots Eightball and badly wounds him. While Eightball writhes in agony out in the open, Doc Jay (John Stafford), disobeying Cowboy's order to stay back, rushes to Eightball's rescue, and the sniper shoots him dead. On the verge of panic, Cowboy and his men, including Joker, follow the thuggish Animal Mother (Adam Baldwin) to the

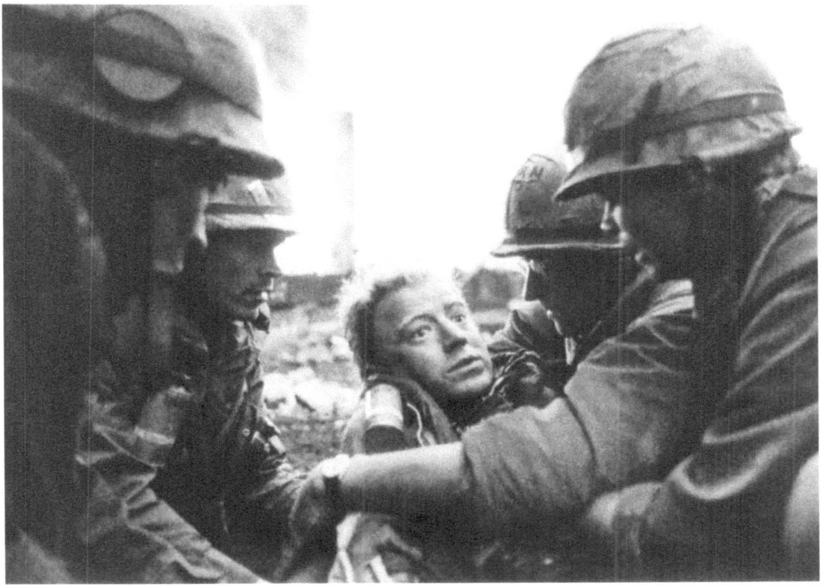

Figure 4.1. *Full Metal Jacket.* Death of Private Cowboy (Arliss Howard).

relative safety of a ruined building. Cowboy tries to contact "Murphy" again, and as he unaccountably stands up to talk on the radio, there is a cut to the sniper's point of view. Cowboy's back is exposed to her line of sight; he is hit and dies in Joker's arms (figure 4.1).

At the other end of radio communication, "Murphy's" silence may as well amount to godlike indifference. In an earlier scene, Cowboy had told a documentary camera that "when we're in Hué, it's like a war, what I thought a war was supposed to be: there's the enemy, kill them." With enemy troops in fixed positions in the city, Hué during the 1968 Tet Offensive evoked the war that Cowboy had grown up watching at the movies. Also in the same interview Cowboy had complained, "I hate Vietnam. There's not one horse in this country. There's something basically wrong with that." In his childhood, Cowboy could never have a war in a place and time that would scorn and baffle an American boy's dream of reenacting the essential American myth. At his last he came to know Vietnam only as the absence of horses, cowboys, and John Wayne.

All out of leaders, the remaining members of the squad move stealthily through yet another bombed-out building. Each marine goes off in

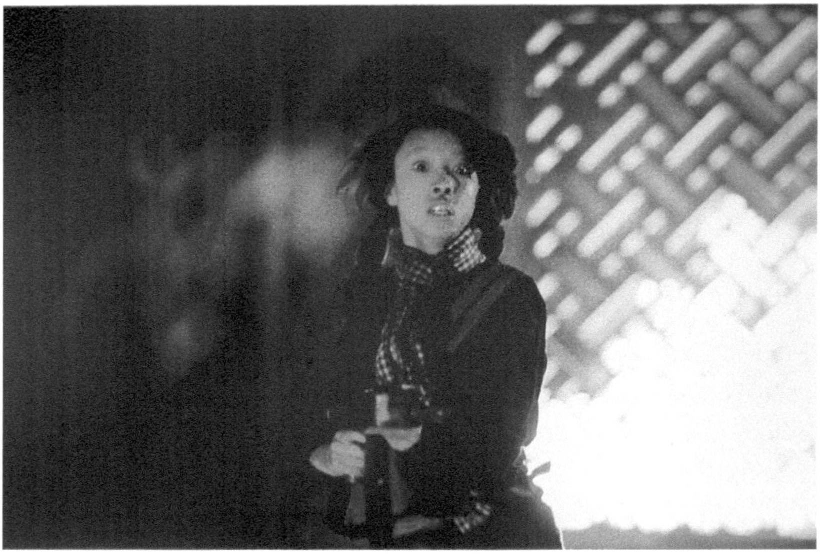

Figure 4.2. *Full Metal Jacket.* Viet Cong sniper (Ngoc Le).

a separate direction. Joker comes up behind the sniper. From behind a column he takes careful aim with his M-16, but when he pulls the trigger, the rifle jams. The sniper, responding to the clicking noise of the malfunctioning rifle, whirls around (only now do we see that the sniper is a teenage girl) and fires her AK-47 from the hip at Joker (figure 4.2).

As Joker fumbles with his service pistol, someone outside the frame shoots the sniper, and she falls, badly wounded. Rafterman has saved Joker's life. Soon we see a tableau of the squad members standing more or less menacingly over the agonizing sniper, a depraved rape fantasy to haunt them the rest of their days. The sniper, however, though bleeding and breathing heavily and rapidly (the mordant "climax") remains until her last moment a resistant, retributive force—Nemesis as the ghastly spectacle of supplicating agony, execrating these marines' "erect-nipple wet dreams of Mary Jane Rottencrotch and the Great Homecoming Fuck Fantasy" (as Joker says in voice-over, recalling his own adolescence).

Animal Mother tries to assert command of the squad. But Joker, eyes locked on the sniper's own, refuses to leave her "for the mother-loving rats," as Animal Mother wants to do (not least perhaps because he lacks the courage and the compassion to administer the coup de grâce). "I'm

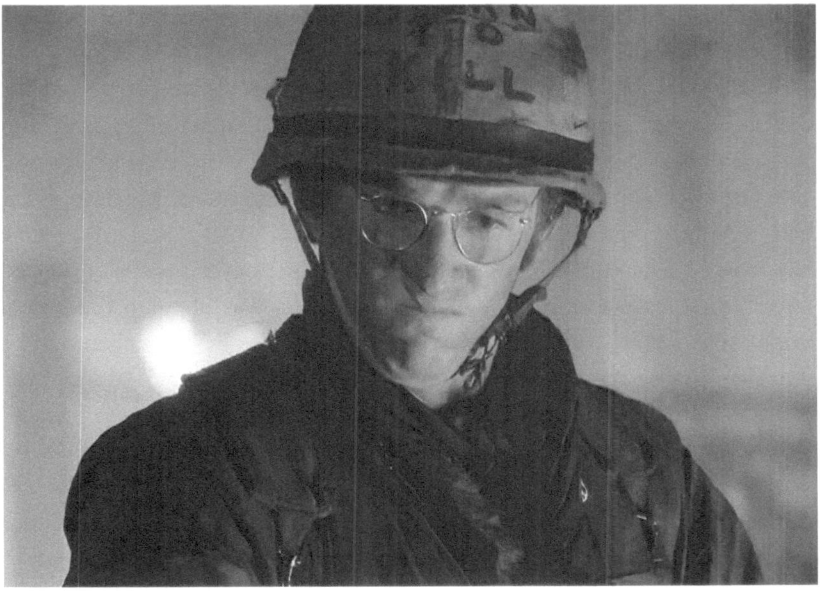

Figure 4.3. *Full Metal Jacket.* Joker (Matthew Modine) and his ironic "war face."

not trying to run this squad," Joker wisely says. "I'm just saying we can't leave her like this." Suddenly the sniper, who seems to have been praying in Vietnamese, says softly, breathlessly, mantra-like in English, "Shoot me. Shoot me. Shoot me." Animal Mother taunts Joker to "waste her," thus making it clear once more that he, Animal Mother, is all brag and bluster and no compassion.

A close-up now shows the sudden transformation in Joker's face. He looks down at the sniper with eyes wide open, service pistol aimed at her (again the mockery of coitus). He purses his lips and pushes a corner of his mouth up almost to the base of his nose. His brow furrows and frowns, and his chin pushes up and pulses against his lips. He blinks only when the shot goes off, hence Joker's "war face" (figure 4.3).[34]

Here, now, before he shoots the sniper, we can see an anger at having to shuck off the protective mask of adolescent cynicism and equivocation, a rage, then, at having to comply with his own elemental and unfiltered humanity. This, though, is very much Joker's own war face, not Hartman's or Wayne's. And Joker's war face registers not menace or empty self-importance but instead the powerlessness to suppress the disabling abjection, the despairing protest against the visceral insistences of both terror and conscience.

In the fatal shot itself, Joker finds—from within the absurdity and the darkness—the compassion to put an end to the sniper's suffering, but not even this act of mercy can be simple enough, clean enough, to save him from the demons that he shall tussle with the rest of his days. Joker had joined the Marine Corps, he told Hartman, "to kill," and kill he now has, one on one, looking straight into the sniper's eyes, in a way that he never could have foreseen when he thought he was obeying the heroic imperative. Much earlier, summoning yet again the slick cynicism that he relies on for protection from Vietnam's horrors, Joker had wisecracked before a documentary camera: "I wanted to see exotic Vietnam, the jewel of Southeast Asia. I wanted to meet interesting and stimulating people of an ancient culture and kill them. I wanted to be the first kid on my block to get a confirmed kill." He had offered, in effect, a digest of the ambivalence arising from and nurtured by the innocent faith that the heroic myth could reconcile divergent expressions and iterations into a coherent vision of American might and right, to reconcile, say, the Marine Corps with the Peace Corps, the Special Forces' A-team with its B-team, the anxiety of legacy with the heroic imperative, and winning "hearts and minds" with "bombing them back to the stone age" or, in Joker's own universe, the peace sign button with "Born to Kill" written on his helmet cover. So, Joker gets his "confirmed kill" when he shoots the sniper, but in dumb conformity with the war's own tragic ironies, he kills for mercy's sake.

All five marines remain standing, transfixed, over the dead sniper. Rafterman, in his awkward adolescent stupefaction, expresses admiration for what he takes to be Joker's cold-blooded courage and tries to giggle away his shock with a joke that no one laughs at. Donlon (Gary Landon Mills), himself seeking solace in mindless hero worship, mutters approvingly, "Hard core, man; fucking hard core." The camera remains on Joker and his war face. By holding steady on Joker's war face, the camera reveals not a hero but rather a youth torn by the cruel and unexpected realization of his once-innocent desire to kill—innocent, I say, because his America, having assured him that he would never fight but for right, also thereby assured him that he would forever enjoy an exemption from unending remorse.

Silhouetted against the harsh glow of Hué's smoldering fires, scores of marines tramp onward. There is no semblance of a formation. No one leads. Joker's voice-over, resonant and confident, reemerges. Summoning up the old cynicism, he seems to claim his heroic birthright, his rendezvous with destiny: "We have nailed our names in the pages of history enough for today. We hump down to the Perfume River to set in for the night." The voice inhabits another temporality than that of the visual action. Its tone, if not also its content, would like us to think that all that we have just witnessed onscreen is worthy of inscription in the "pages of history." So boldly enunciated, the claim that the marines have made history is more appropriate to the myth; for if Joker's "pages-of-history" account is to be taken "mythically," then his is but a war lie, and that lie would deny the anguish in the guilt-reflecting war face. Moreover, Joker's pages-of-history metaphor alludes to *continuity*, suggesting that what the marines have only now seen and done is part of an unbroken whole: history and myth indistinct from each other as if this one, too, was one more of America's "good wars."

In "good wars," however, the deadly sniper—say, the sniper who shoots Stryker in *Sands of Iwo Jima*—is never a young virgin-warrior peering desperately into the American soldier's soul and begging him to shoot her. If what we have just witnessed is indeed history, it is so only because it is not, indistinctly, myth, because that historical moment, that one page of history, undermines whole ages of myth. Joker's war face expresses his scorn for the heroic myth, and his claim to have earned a spot in history only signals the recurrence of his earlier cynical responses to the obscene absurdity of the Vietnam War. His cynicism also belies the tone of the claim, the boast in it, and even the metaphorical form of it and underscores the difference between the "good" American wars and America's Vietnam, between the myth of heroic continuity and the rupture. It is horror, not heroism, that abides, and Joker's war face becomes the stamp and sign of the soldier's true inheritance, no matter the war.

Even as the men, still in long shot, continue their formless march, we begin to hear the strains of a familiar tune, not the Marine Corps hymn, as at the end of *Sands of Iwo Jima*, but instead the "Mickey Mouse March." We first hear the chorus, spelling the hero's name: "M-I-C-K-E-Y M-O-U-S-E." The marines sing a verse that seems never to have been part of the original song, "We play fair and we work hard and we're in harmony," as if propitiating the blameless leader of innocent days while affirming their own moral fitness and soldierly readiness as club members in good standing.[35] Already in their early days as marines, the adjectival "Mickey Mouse" had come to designate the insignificant, even the contemptible, as when Hartman, discovering Leonard, Cowboy, and Joker in the "head," demands to know "What is this Mickey Mouse shit?" Surely, however, these marines in Hué invoke a time before lapse and loss, a time before the Vietnam inferno where they nonetheless, if still incongruously and sardonically, break into song. Such memories, summoned up in such a place and time, mark the pervasive despair that provokes their nostalgia even while subverting it. And in truth, theirs had been all along, even in their childhood, if not a false innocence then at least a tenuous, compromised innocence relentlessly stalked by the heavy shadow of doomsday in duck-and-cover-drills, backyard bunkers, Big Brother paranoia scenarios, and the surfeit of mushroom-cloud nightmares and "we-will-bury-you" Nikita Khrushchev assurances. Their innocence had been rather like a fantasy, yet they remained faithful apprentices despite the sorcerer's sore absence from Vietnam.

As the men continue their march, Joker appears in a medium shot. In the foreground, he lopes on abreast of Rafterman and Animal Mother. The scores of marines still sing enthusiastically, even imitating Mickey's falsetto in the chorus. In midsong, however, Joker's voice-over reemerges. "My thoughts drift back to erect-nipple wet dreams about Mary Jane Rottencrotch and the Great Homecoming Fuck Fantasy. I am so happy that I am alive, in one piece, and short. I'm in a world of shit, yes. But I am alive. And I am not afraid."[36] There is a liberating irreverence in Joker's voice-over intrusion into the hymn, as invocations of the leader recede before the would-be celebrants of the Great Homecoming Fuck Fantasy. And if we did not take the "Mickey Mouse March" ironically before—if we naively thought (or if they themselves did) that the leader of the club could guide the blood-soaked marines to a redemptive affirmation of their innocence—we do now. Yet, there is a way in which the ironic mustering of Mickey Mouse connects with Joker's voice-over. The voice-over takes us through the narrative of an *American generation*, from childhood fantasies to adolescent sexual desire leading only to yet another fantasy (the Great Homecoming Fuck Fantasy), this one leading to a generational war adventure culminating not in tragedy but rather in heroic adulthood. Only here, in Vietnam, the "fuck fantasy" is transformed into the "wasting" of the sniper, into the "confirmed kill" that finds fulfillment only in the puerile testimony of Donlon and Rafterman. And the narrative of the generation comes to its Vietnam chapter as if the war were over. "I am so happy that I am alive," says Joker. And he is "short," that is, he has only a few days left in his tour. He also knows, however, that he will not soon overcome the demons of Vietnam: Hartman's sadism, Leonard's suicide, the mass grave outside Hué, Cowboy's death, the sniper begging to be shot, and the shot itself. And indeed, to the extent at least that the voice-over might be "outside" the action—and thus follows after it—we do know that Joker's condition persisted after Vietnam. So, he is indeed, as he says, "in a world of shit." Hartman had used that same phrase as part of a threat to wayward recruits. In the suicide scene, Joker himself had pleaded with Leonard to put the loaded rifle away because they would both be "in a world of shit," but (in a refulgent revelation of pure truth) Leonard replied, "I *am* in a world of shit." So, now that we hear Joker echo Leonard, we know his anguish to be no less than Leonard's own.

Joker lives, however, and he is not afraid. What is it that he does not fear? The judgment of the heroic myth, perhaps in the form of guilt for the rupture and the Loss, of the guilt for feeling guilty? All of this and more, surely. Yet, Joker also affirms his triumph over the insidious cozenage of the heroic imperative. His ironic voice lays bare the perversities into which the heroic myth led a generation. He becomes his own leader, attesting his individual humanity as itself the source of freedom from all heroes and heroic myths. In his acknowledged anguish—to have silenced it would have amounted to yet another war lie—he asserts his hope for a generational identity free from the smothering constraints of the heroic imperative.

## CHAPTER 5

# Two Narratives of the Rupture

## The *Deer Hunter* and *Coming Home*

We really won over there, huh, Mike? We won?
—Emcee/Grocer, *The Deer Hunter*

That *The Deer Hunter* won best picture at the 51st annual Academy Awards tonight was almost incidental to the fact that John Wayne presented the award.
—Aljean Harmetz, *New York Times*

You go back home and everything you wished was different is still the same and everything you wished was the same is different.
—Cormac McCarthy, *Cities of the Plain*

### "Last time to be John Wayne"?

It is late on Academy Awards night, April 9, 1979, and time to hand out the evening's last Oscar, for best picture. Johnny Carson, the master of ceremonies, introduces comedian Bob Hope, who, in a video from the previous year's awards ceremony, had sent best wishes to John Wayne, who was at the time recovering from cancer treatment in a Boston hospital. But tonight Wayne will announce the winner. The instant Carson utters the mythic name, the glitterati are on their feet, applauding enthusiastically.[1] Wayne appears atop one of two wide staircases winding down to center stage. With lissome and lively steps, he hastens down and saunters to the podium. "Despite the obvious fact that he was dying," writes Scott Eyman, "the [audience's] love seemed to energize him."[2] But now as Wayne takes his place behind the podium, he seems so gaunt and drawn as to almost baffle recognition. Randy Roberts and James S. Olson note that "there was an audible gasp from the crowd,"[3] and Eyman reports that producer Howard W. Koch worried about Wayne: "'He looked like death.'"[4] And surely many in the TV audience must have registered a similar dismay. Perhaps they had last seen Wayne as the cancer-ridden John Bernard Books in *The Shootist* (Siegel, 1976), but Books would have seemed positively blooming next to the specter now before them. Still, Wayne knew his place in his public's heart. The ovation, he tells the audience, is "just about the only medicine a fellow really needs," and he adds that both he and "Oscar," though "a little weather-beaten, . . . plan to be around for a whole lot longer."[5] Wayne died a little over two months later on June 11, 1979.

On this night before Wayne appeared onstage, the Oscar for best actress had gone to Jane Fonda for *Coming Home* (Ashby, 1978). Fonda, of all people, had somehow become culturally respectable in the eyes of established Hollywood. A decade or so earlier, however, American conservatives had nicknamed her "Hanoi Jane" for her antiwar activism. But Wayne—of all people—had forgiven her.[6] And now the great American hero was about to announce that *The Deer Hunter*, "a film [he] despised because of its negative portrayal of the Vietnam War," had won the award for best film.[7] Irony and all, however, no one could ignore just how gracious Wayne was to the filmmakers including director Michael Cimino, who went up to receive the award. Even here as Wayne steps aside in dignified acceptance of the triumph of his ideological foes, he characteristically, if unselfconsciously, strikes the graceful pose that so charmed Garry Wills, the contrapposto, as seen in the figures of David by Donatello (ca. 1440) and Michelangelo (1504–1507).[8] As the Oscar winners step up to the microphone and mouth the obligatory platitudes, we focus instead on Wayne, thumbs lightly in his vest pockets, as if the poise and grace of Brett Coleman in *The Big Trail* (Walsh, 1930) or of Ringo in *Stagecoach* (Ford, 1939) had briefly inspirited the ravaged body.

Perhaps Wayne "despised" *The Deer Hunter* because it confronted him, as if by proxy, with the undoing of his own heroic image. After all, *The Deer Hunter*, as we will see in the next section of this chapter, produces a Special Forces Vietnam veteran so completely distraught by his war trauma as to singlehandedly unstring the heroic mystique that Wayne's *Green Berets* tried to fob off as the true American military conduct in Vietnam. We may also wonder, however, if a particular reference in *The Deer Hunter* could have triggered or perhaps exacerbated Wayne's aversion. Following the roisterous reception celebrating the wedding of Steven (John Savage) and Angela (Rutanya Alda), five friends drive up to the mountains surrounding their steel mill town, the mostly fictional Clairton, Pennsylvania, where the stateside action of *The Deer Hunter* unfolds. Three of these five, Steven, Michael (Robert De Niro), and Nick (Christopher Walken) will ship out to Vietnam the very next day. Although they are already at the site of the hunt, Stanley (John Cazale)—crude, malicious, abusive Stanley—still wears his tuxedo, bowtie and all. Incongruously, he also wears a cossack cap with a red reflector on its front. Stanley announces that he forgot his hunting boots and asks Michael for his spares. Even before Michael says no, Stanley produces a blued snub-nosed revolver and begins to wave it around recklessly. None of the friends seem much more than amused by his antics, but Michael remains adamant. "Every time he comes up here," he says to the other three, "he's got no knife, he's got no jacket, he's got no pants, he's got no boots. All he's got is that stupid gun he carries around like John Wayne." Now addressing Stanley directly, Michael adds, "That ain't gonna help you." This, the first of two hunting sequences in *The Deer Hunter*, goes on for a good while longer, and I will return to it later in this chapter. For now, I attend only to Michael's reference to Stanley as John Wayne so as to introduce *The Deer Hunter* as a narrative of the rupture.

In the spring of 1979, even as Wayne yet clung to life, it was possible to scorn him with a simile at the other end of which was not only the most contemptible American character in *The Deer Hunter* but also the eminent actor John Cazale, who died of lung cancer soon after completing all his scenes for *The Deer Hunter* more than a year before Wayne's own death.[9] How, then, could Cazale's Stanley be "like John Wayne"? What mirror could Cazale's Stanley have held up to John Wayne that could cause Wayne to hate the movie to whose producers he now handed the Oscar? *The Deer Hunter* declared itself a different movie of the Vietnam War, one without the clumsy pieties of *The Green Berets* a decade earlier. The difference that so nettled Wayne, that made it impossible for him and his generation to recognize their war and their war movies in *The Deer Hunter*, went far to stake out and illuminate the differences between World War II and Vietnam, between victory and the Loss. The differences themselves already identified the rupture, the break, perhaps irreparable, in the continuity of the heroic myth.

*The Deer Hunter* readily subverts our understanding of America's heroic myth because it so deftly invokes the genre that had made John Wayne America's preeminent hero: the Western. As John Hellmann has observed, "the western formula affords Cimino the strengths of the central national myth in dealing with Vietnam as a collective American trauma. At the same time, *The Deer Hunter* achieves more than a perpetuation of past myth by its understanding of the essence of the myth and its critical examination of it."[10]

*The Deer Hunter* unfolds as a critique of the Western's pervasive presence in the Vietnam War. In this way, the film narrates the clash of myth and history in the context of the myth of heroic continuity. As Hellmann asserts, "Vietnam functions in the film as a mirror image of America, a dark landscape turning upside-down the benign landscape of Cimino's mythic Alleghenies."[11] This "inversion" of the American myth, a rough equivalent of the rupture, implicitly demanded something very like a reckoning, a coming to terms at last with that wayward and willful disregard for American history, an impulse and a practice long so vital to the myth. Hollywood had dared to narrate—perhaps to celebrate—the end of the myth of heroic continuity, and on Academy Awards night 1979, neither the dazzle and the glamour nor the good wishes or even the collective gasp itself could veil the broader irony, namely that a dying John Wayne made his last public appearance to hand Hollywood's highest honor to a movie that implicitly, if unmistakably, narrated the undoing of his heroic persona.

## A Different Green Beret

Another scene might have also rankled Wayne. The wedding reception sequence is well under way when a US Special Forces sergeant (Paul D'Amato) appears in the veterans hall. Framed by a low interior archway, the sergeant stands in medium shot, virtually alone, screen left. On a nearby table, the gaudy papier-mâché bells improbably toll the arrival that no one notices. As we shall soon see, the sergeant hails from Vietnam's heart of darkness, perhaps an only survivor of torture or of a fierce firefight, and serves as a Melvillean Ishmael already foretelling, in terse and cryptic language, the end of America's heroic myth. As the sergeant makes his way to the bar, there is a cut to Michael and Linda (Meryl Streep). They stand side by side, facing the back bar, at one end of the bar. Unnoticed by Michael and barely so by Linda, the sergeant appears in the background, walks just behind them, and takes his place at the opposite end of the bar. Now Nick enters the bar, and Linda, the guilty thing surprised, runs to him but soon returns to the dance hall, while Nick stays with Michael at the bar. Soon Steven joins them, and now, all three of them, long since thoroughly soused, face the back bar. Steven is first to notice the sergeant. "Hey! Green Beret!" he yells. Alone at his end of the bar, the sergeant, unresponsive, stares straight ahead. In the reaction-shot close-up we see the sergeant's "thousand-yard stare," eyes without life, without "speculation," like those of Banquo's ghost. Michael, also delighted to see the Green Beret, then stands him a drink, but the sergeant still makes no acknowledgment and holds his sphinx-like stare into nothing. Undeterred, Michael holds up his glass and shouts at him "*Nastrovia!*" The sergeant swivels in his barstool. His eyes, framed by heavy eyebrows and deep, dark circles, lend a phantasmal cast to his face (figure 5.1).

The sergeant then turns, silent still, facing the back bar. Trying to get past Steven to get closer to the sergeant, Michael says, "We're going over there." The three friends fairly mob the sergeant: Nick to his left, Michael to his right, and Steven in the background. Michael taps the sergeant on the shoulder and repeats, "We're going over there." The sergeant lifts his shot glass as if for a toast and simply, clearly, and quite unexpectedly says,

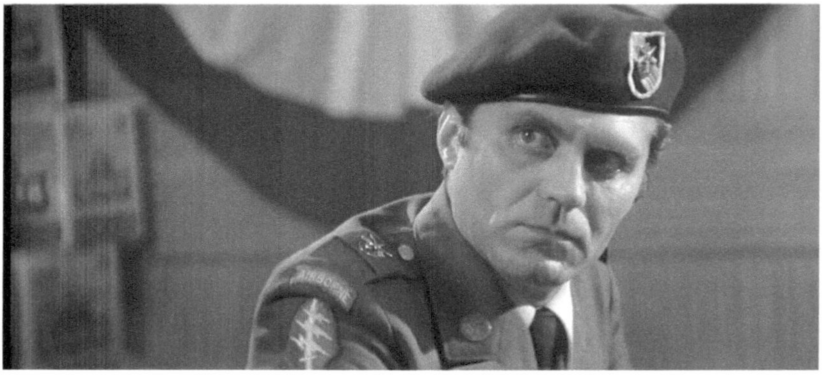

Figure 5.1. *The Deer Hunter*. The "Other" Green Beret (Paul D'Amato).

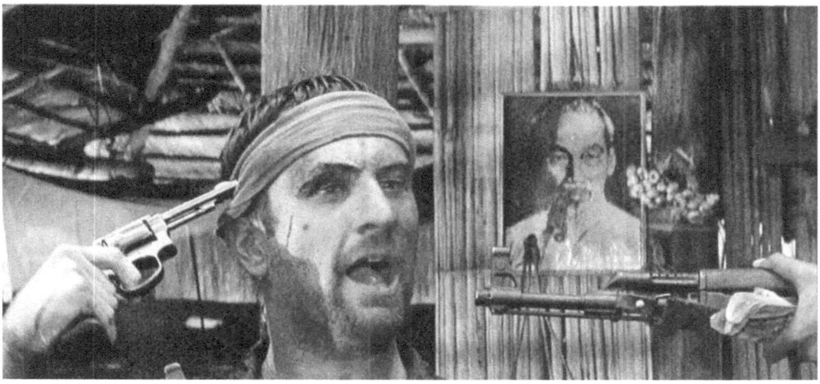

Figure 5.2. *The Deer Hunter*. Michael (Robert De Niro) "plays" Russian roulette.

"Fuck it!" Michael tries to blunt the discomfiting response to the toast: "Well, what's it like over there? Can you tell us anything?" But his "Fuck it!" is in fact the sergeant's "anything" that he can tell them. It is his apt version of "*Don't mean nothin'.*"[12] The sergeant again lifts his glass and again repeats the anathema, "Fuck it!" Now back at the other end of the bar, Michael mocks the sergeant. "Hey," he calls out, "fuck it!" provoking the laughter of his two friends. The reaction shot of the sergeant shows him once again in close-up, only now he gives the four friends the slightest of smiles, dismissal and damnation both.

At first, the three friends see pure John Wayne-ness in the sergeant—nothing of the darkness that suffuses his face—and their eventual mockery of him as the scene comes to a close establishes their blindness, a blindness perhaps willful, meant to blunt the dread so palpably arising from the impassive figure before them. The sergeant's alienated presence foreshadows Michael's own alteration into something very much like this unquiet and indrawn disposition (figure 5.2). Only after Michael's first return from Vietnam do we discover that he, alone of the three, belongs to the Special Forces. He wears a uniform remarkably similar to the sergeant's, down to the flash on his beret. The uniform that might have once identified him as a mythic type instead binds him to the tormented sergeant and thus helps foreshadow his own undoing as mythic hero. And Nick too shall develop his own affinities with the sergeant. Already in captivity but especially in the final Russian roulette scene in Saigon, Nick has the sergeant's hollowed-eyed zombie look, the visage and vision of the lost soul, the "thousand-yard" stare.

## "One Shot"

As both deer hunter and Green Beret, Michael seems to unequivocally embody America's heroic type. At least potentially, he also embodies the hero's presumed ubiquity: the unwearied force, diffused throughout history yet undiminished by time, of a mythic hero arising to confront his generation's trial of heroic manhood. Michael retains a hold, be it ever so attenuated a hold, on this American type but only until the deadly shot in the last Russian roulette game, the shot that kills Nick and severs Michael even from the little that remains of America's heroic type. This is the shot that at once announces and establishes the rupture and ushers Michael into an unsettling postmythic America.

Just before the wedding ceremony we see in detail the interior of Michael and Nick's home, a converted trailer on the outskirts of town. The walls are appointed with all the identifying tokens of latter-day frontierism: mounted deer heads, hunting rifles, and perhaps most significant, an official photograph of the New Frontiersman himself, John F. Kennedy. Here, Nick initiates his first important exchange with Michael:

**Nick:** For Christ's sake, Mike, Steven is getting married in a couple of hours. I don't know what the hell we're doing talking about hunting a last time before the army. The whole thing, it's crazy.

**Michael:** I'll tell you one thing. If I found out my life had to end up in the mountains, it'd be all right. But it has to be in your mind.

**Nick:** What? "One shot"?

**Michael:** Two is pussy.

**Nick:** I don't think about "one shot" that much anymore, Mike.

**Michael:** You have to think about "one shot." "One shot" is what it's all about. A deer has to be taken with one shot. I try to tell people that, but they don't listen.

With no small measure of anxiety mixed in with his cultural type's traditional fervor, Michael advocates for the chief tenet of the hunt, "one shot," an advocacy that enjoys a long and illustrious career in American culture. "To me," Natty Bumppo catechizes in *The Pioneers*, "the flesh is sweeter, where the creater has some chance for its life; for that reason, I always use a single ball, . . . for, when a body knows how to shoot, one piece of lead is enough for all, except hard-lived animals."[13] Michael too reveres the woods, and like Natty's own, his hunter's ethic addresses an even higher, transcendent principle, the hunter's mystical bond with a hallowed American tradition, a bond moreover that readily converts his hunting skills into the mastery necessary for success in war, especially guerrilla war. And yet this ethos is already from the outset subverted and rendered false by the very setting wherein Michael would most zealously affirm it: the Vietnam War.

We first meet the "deer hunter" not in the wilderness but instead as he stands on the edge of a huge cauldron of bubbling iron ore. He wears a fire-protective suit and dips a pyrometer into the liquid ore. Soon, though, his shift is over, and he emerges from the hellish steel mill into the early morning light already clad in the clothes he will wear to the hunt. As Steven will later be first to notice the zombie Green Beret at the bar, so here he is first to notice the unusual images in the sky. But it is Michael who knows what they are. Looking up, he exclaims, "Holy shit! You know what that is? Those are sundogs!" They are, Michael explains, "a blessing on the hunter sent by the Great Wolf to his children. . . . That's an omen, you know that? You know that we could have one great fucking hunting trip tonight?" Careless of the scientific explanation for this phenomenon of refracted light and ice crystals, Michael nonetheless knows the signs, the lore, the auguries, and the benevolent spirits themselves. And he knows the Indian (or at least the "Indian thing"), which presumably identifies him as a "man who knows Indians" and therefore gives him an advantage in Vietnam's "Indian Country."

Having already seen Michael in the steel mill, however, we sense that he invokes the mystique of the hunt as a form of spiritual solace that protects him against the encroachment of industry into an already diminished wilderness. Yet, Michael earns his living in the very world that threatens the wilderness, and more pertinently, his job at the mill contributes indirectly to the very war that shall forever undo his frontier America illusions. Besides, Michael has to drive a long way to the hunt, and he drives, of all vehicles, a 1959 Cadillac Coupe DeVille, its overall length and its exaggerated tailfins but two of the damning emblems of America's industrial hubris concentrated in the one production. Moreover, the mountain country strains to replicate a primal site. Wide asphalt roads lead to the mountains, and the friends own a comfortable cabin there. *The Deer Hunter* thus makes it well-nigh impossible to identify a natural American site of spiritual regeneration. Instead, the film transforms a vestigial American wilderness into the howling jungles of alien, demon-teeming Vietnam, there to expose the heroic myth to a sort of cultural stress test it cannot hope to survive. Yet, the Vietnamese wilderness—the lush and forbidding jungle that we see in, say, *Apocalypse Now, Platoon*, and *Rambo: First Blood Part II*—is almost entirely absent in *The Deer Hunter*. The one brief firefight takes place on open ground, with helicopters overhead, and later the three friends' escape from their Vietnamese tormentors depends in large measure on the adventitious appearance of Huey helicopters rather than on any wilderness wisdom of Michael's. Indeed, most of the Vietnam scenes take place in a chaotic and depraved Saigon, its corrupt Virgilian guide the unctuous Old World deceiver, Julien. And the two different Russian roulette hells, one in the jungle and one in Saigon, mock the American "errand into the wilderness." Besides, Clairton is no city upon a hill. In Clairton, Linda's drunken father punches her in the face, and at the wedding reception, the oafish Axel (Chuck Aspegren) forcibly hoists his girlfriend (Mady Kaplan) on his shoulder and carries her to a coat closet, saying to her, "Do you want to fuck or fight?" Here also Stanley delivers a vicious punch to his girlfriend's jaw because the bandleader/emcee/grocer (Joe Grifasi) groped her while dancing with her. (He punches the girlfriend, not the offending man.)

Clairton's sordid underside reappears toward the end of the wedding reception sequence. Just outside the veterans hall, Steven shares his "life's one true secret" with Nick: he "never really did it with Angela," which means that he is not and knows that he cannot be the father of the baby that Angela is carrying. At the end of the reception outside the hall, Stanley whispers something vile in Michael's ear, most likely revealing that Nick is the father of Angela's baby and thus undermining Michael's close friendship with both Nick and Steven. Dismayed, Michael begins to walk away from Stanley, who holds him back by the sleeve of his tuxedo jacket. But Michael squirms out of it and then leaps on the hood of the Cadillac, jumps off on the other side, and sets off at a dead run, doffing the rest of his tuxedo and every other last stitch of clothing as he goes. Steven, with Angela beside him, follows in the Cadillac. Nick, Axel, and

John (George Dzundza) run after him, but these last two soon drop off. Finally, Michael collapses on an outdoor basketball court not far from his and Nick's trailer. Nick arrives before any of the others, covers his friend's nakedness, and stands over him. Then, over a cut to a close-up of Nick, Michael asks, "Hey, Nick. You think we'll ever come back?"

> **Nick:** From Nam?
> **Michael** [*offscreen*]: Yeah.
> **Nick:** You know something? The whole thing, it's right here. I love this fucking place. I know that sounds crazy, but if anything happens, Mike, don't leave, don't leave me over there. . . . Just don't leave me. You gotta promise me that, Mike.
> **Michael:** Hey . . .
> **Nick:** No, man, you got, you gotta promise, definitely.
> **Michael:** Hey, Nicky. You got it, pal.

Is it innocence that explains Michael's readiness to endorse this covenant with Nick, or is it hubris? An idle question, since their shared perdition at the end makes motive and impetus and heroic inheritance itself all but insignificant.

## A Compromised Celibacy

As embodiment of the American hunter-warrior type, Michael should well be celibate, as Natty Bumppo is and as is William Faulkner's Ike McCaslin. Also like Natty, Ike is not only accomplished in the hunt but also exalted by it. And Ike too begins not old merely—like Natty—but ageless: "Isaac McCaslin," reads the opening sentence of *Go Down, Moses*, "'Uncle Ike,' past seventy and nearer eighty than he ever corroborated anymore, a widower now and uncle to half a county and father to no one."[14] Uncle Ike, then, remains to the last "husband but no father, unwidowered but without a wife."[15] Ever as they are for Natty, so too for Ike "the woods would be his mistress and his wife."[16] And so too is the celibacy of Ethan Edwards (John Wayne) in John Ford's *The Searchers.* Ethan appears fully formed out of the desert, a Confederate renegade in the service of two lost causes: the South's and that of his own solitary struggle against his abiding yet impermissible desire for Martha, his sister-in-law.

Not unlike these mythic forebears' own, Michael's celibacy is bedeviled by the pressures of the world against the myth. In another scene from the first hunting sequence, Michael (he has already denied Stanley the extra pair of boots) sits on the hood of the Cadillac, legs over the side, rifle across his lap. Michael holds up a rifle cartridge and asks, "Stanley, you see this? This is this! It ain't something else. This is this!" Cryptic as these assertions may appear at first (and they remain so to Stanley), they nonetheless suggest Michael's understanding of the moment and its purpose: the hunt is the hunt, and a rifle cartridge is a rifle cartridge. If you come to the hunt in your tuxedo and without boots and with only a snub-nosed revolver instead of a deer rifle, then you are woefully unprepared. More important, however, you scorn the hunt and its solemn rituals; you slander the very same gods whose signs (the sundogs) had earlier vouchsafed good hunting. But Stanley just turns his own impudence into an assault on Michael's manliness. However perversely Stanley tries to retaliate, his coarse, homophobic response to Michael's catechism introduces celibacy as an essential trope in the story of the wilderness hero:

> I fixed you up a million times. [*Appealing to the others.*] I fixed him up a million times. I don't know how many times I must have fixed him up with girls. And nothing ever happens. Zero. Hey, you know your trouble, Mike, huh? Nobody ever knows what the fuck you're talking about. Huh? [*Mockingly.*] "This is this." What the hell's that supposed to mean, "This is this"? I mean, is that some faggot-sounding bullshit or is that some faggot-sounding [Nick *interrupts him*: "Shut up, Stan, will you? Hey, man, you're out of line." Michael adds: "Watch out with that gun, Stan, watch out with that gun." Stanley, *undeterred, resumes.*] There's times—do you know what I think? There's times I swear I think you're a fucking faggot.

No less than Natty Bumppo's love for Mabel Dunham in *The Pathfinder* or than Ethan Edward's for Martha, Michael's celibacy is deeply compromised by his own proscribed desires. At the wedding reception, he reveals his attraction to Linda, and Linda, though she will soon accept Nick's proposal of marriage, is hardly indifferent to Michael's awkward feints and advances. In the vexed consummation of his love for Linda following his first return from Vietnam (where Nick still languishes), Michael shall relinquish all claims to the heroic status, betraying not only his friend but also his own mythic type, betraying him as Nick himself did Steven.

Racked by alienation and remorse, Michael avoids his coming-home party in the trailer and asks his cabbie to take him to a motel. Once there, he paces about restlessly or else sits on the luggage rack in a Rodinesque pose, not so much thinking or questioning, it seems, as grieving. Later in the same scene he squats in a corner of the room, his back against the wall, as if making himself small or buckling under the weight of his guilt. His face registers the great dismay, the burden of betrayal not only with Linda but also of the promise he made to Nick at the basketball court. At dawn, spying from afar, Michael watches the disappointed guests file out, but when he enters the trailer, Linda is still there. At first in this scene, everything is about Nick: Linda "was hoping" that Michael had brought Nick with him, she has been knitting a sweater for Nick, and so on. But eventually Linda asks Michael, "What about your wounds?" "There's nothing," he replies. "Just the usual complications, that's all." "We heard . . . ," Linda starts to say, but Michael interrupts her. "No, that's not true. A lot of guys go through it." Why the hedging, the failure to name the wound? What did "they" hear? Could this—whatever it may or may not be—have its source in Stanley's perverse rumormongering? Is Michael in his own awkward way reassuring her that he is sexually capable? Is he so? Certainly, *The Deer Hunter* delays the consummation scene enough to cast suspicion about the site, sort, and effect of Michael's "wound." His trauma in Vietnam—sourced not only in the Russian roulette ordeal during his captivity but also in his failure to rescue Nick—means that what he implicitly took to be the essential American experience, including his deep devotion to living it, was all along a delusion, a trifle made tragic by the vanity that once presumed to sustain it. And now, as his restiveness in this scene suggests, he has no sense of who he is.

Back at the trailer, Michael packs up some of his belongings to take back to the motel. When Linda proposes that they "go to bed [to] comfort each other," Michael replies only that he feels "a lot of distance" and rushes out to his Cadillac. But Linda runs after him and gets in the car with him. At the motel, she comes out of the bathroom with only a towel wrapped around her. Michael lies in bed over the bedcovers, still in his

Special Forces uniform, his eyes closed. Though Linda gets in the bed, Michael remains immobile and unmoved. Even when Linda gets under the covers and timidly lays her head on his shoulder, Michael remains as if benumbed, vacant, empty. His eyes stay shut until the scene's end. In this tableau of tormented and besieged celibacy, the hero's uniform, as if it were his medieval knight's armor, shields him from the allures of the beloved, from his own dark desires, from the unrelenting oncoming of guilt to rack his dark hunter-warrior's soul.

## The Second Hunting Sequence

Almost immediately after the four friends—Axel, John, Stanley, and Michael—arrive at the cabin in the mountains, we see Michael alone, rifle in hand. He is walking on an outcrop, his image reflected on the surface of a tarn below. Ethereal choral voices accompany him as he strides these remnants of America's empyrean heights. Suddenly the mythic buck appears before Michael, who quickly frames it in his rifle's sight. The buck turns and faces him squarely, and Michael holds his aim on it. But suddenly he points the rifle upward and fires into the air. Above the roar of the falls below, he says, "Okay!" He comes down a bit from the crest, sits on a boulder, and shouts "Okay," and "Okay" reverberates through the mountains, a refrain perhaps that acknowledges the end of his mythic illusions. Much earlier—untold ages earlier, it seems—Michael had imagined that it would be "all right" if he found out that his "life had to end up in the mountains." Now, however, he has entered America's postmythic phase, and perhaps even against his will, he has been reborn in the spaces of the rupture.

Somehow, the end of the "one-shot" ethos up in the mountains makes possible the consummation of Michael and Linda's love (so that the last of one sort of venery marks the beginning of the other sort). But before this consummation, Michael has a crucial office to perform: the due chastening of Stanley. With Michael still away in the mountains, Stanley, profane as ever, shoots twice at a buck that he has chased into a tarn; he then wades in the water and grabs the struggling animal by the antlers. Axel and John, still drunk after their own earlier pursuit of a deer, laugh uproariously at Stanley's impious drolleries. Back at the cabin, Stanley produces a nickel-plated version of the snub-nosed revolver that he brandished about in the first hunting sequence. Axel asks Stanley what the gun is for, and Stanley replies, "In case." Axel gratuitously insults Stanley's girlfriend, and Stanley responds as if deeply wronged. "You say that one more time!" he yells while pointing the gun at Axel. "Say it! Say it!" Here Michael enters the cabin, comes up behind Stanley, and takes the gun from him. Stanley cries out, "What the hell was that for? What'd you think it was, loaded?" Michael (reenacting the traumatic experience in the jungle Russian roulette episode) breaks open the revolver's cylinder, closes it, and shoves the muzzle against Stanley's head. Michael then points the gun toward the ceiling and pulls the trigger. The gun goes off. He then breaks open the cylinder again, and the remaining live cartridges spill out. With a deliberateness that recalls his Viet Cong (VC) tormentor's own, Michael now loads one live round, spins the cylinder, flips it locked, and brings the muzzle up against Stanley's forehead. "How do you feel now, huh?" he asks. "Huh, big shot?" Michael pulls the trigger, and the gun dry-fires. He looks defiantly at Axel and John, storms out of the cabin, and flings the nickel-plated gun into the tarn.

The helpless, suffocating terror that Michael, Nick, and Steven suffered during their captivity now becomes Stanley's own. But if the moment condignly unmans Stanley, it also functions as Michael's desperate effort to reverse the roles of victim and victimizer. Michael becomes the torturer, and Stanley becomes the victim. In an inversion of the Russian roulette game with the VC captors, Stanley assumes the part of the despised American, the part that was de facto Michael's own during his captivity, the role, that is, of the invading American whom the Vietnamese enemy views as boorish, selfish, abusive, and without convictions, thus America as a nation of Stanleys. Moreover, the humiliation of Stanley highlights Michael's impulse to silence his own clear understanding that the heroic legacy stands utterly discredited. By visiting the demons of Vietnam on Stanley, Michael unwittingly declares the loss of his own heroic identity. He heaves the nickel-plated revolver away not only in disdain of Stanley's hatefulness but also as if by doing so he, Michael, can erase the unabating fear, forget the enduring degradation. Michael's rage, and indeed even his renunciation moments earlier in the presence of the mythic deer, evoke the Green Beret sergeant at the veterans hall and his pithy repudiation of the mythic typology: Michael's "Okay!" reverberates as the sergeant's "Fuck it!"

As a result of his uneasy peace with the mythic buck and of the ensuing confrontation with Stanley, Michael is now humanized out of all mythic pretense. And his humanity, however much he may disavow it, releases him from his embattled celibacy. The scene following the friends' subdued return to Clairton from the second hunting trip finds Michael waiting for Linda outside the supermarket where she works. When she finally comes out, they drive to the trailer. The first interior shot shows Michael, bare-chested, under the bedcovers. Linda comes out of the bathroom and joins him in bed, and they make love at last. Yet, the scene is hardly sultry. Michael simply turns on his side to kiss Linda. This is all the camera allows us to see, and at least in the dramatic sense, it is quite anticlimactic. In the next shot, Michael is looking out the bedroom window at the basketball court where Nick pleaded with Michael not to leave him behind in Vietnam. In his unrelieved remorse for the consummation of his desire for Linda, Michael turns to the site—the still-accusing site—where he made the promise that he has yet to fulfill.

Before returning to Saigon to rescue Nick, Michael visits the veterans hospital to see Steven, who lost both legs in the fall from the helicopter during the attempted escape from VC captivity. Early in this scene, Michael learns from Steven that Nick is alive. Steven pulls open the nightstand drawer and says of the contents (all $100 bills), "This comes every month from Saigon. I don't understand. I don't understand. That place is gonna fall any day now." Michael realizes immediately that Nick is the source of the money and that this is guilt money for Nick's betrayal of Steven.[17]

## One (More) Shot

At the Saigon gambling den, where we last see Nick, his vacant look readily gives him away as a lost soul. His thousand-yard stare (recalling the Green Beret sergeant's own) and the track marks running the length of his forearm confirm his despair. Much earlier, however, following the escape from VC captivity, Nick was already a shriveled soul, aimless even in the Saigon hospital where he is surrounded by reminders of trauma and tragedy. At the hospital, Nick sits sideways on the second-story balustrade and stares down at rows upon rows of body bags and stacks of metal caskets in the courtyard below. He then takes a photo of Linda out of his wallet but puts it back furtively as the doctor approaches. "Are you Nikonar [*sic:* the name is Nikanor] Chevotarevich?" asks the doctor. Nick remains silent, his gaze fixed on the grim scene below. The ensuing exchange with the doctor only resigns us to the implacable grip of Nick's trauma on his dark soul:

> **Doctor:** Can you understand me, Nikonar? [*Nick turns and looks at him vacantly.*] Are you Chevotarevich? [*Nick nods yes.*] Are you sure?
> **Nick:** Yes.
> **Doctor:** "Chevotarevich," is that a Russian name?
> **Nick:** No, it's American.
> **Doctor:** All right, let me see your name tag. Is this yours?

Nick nods offscreen and replies, "It's his." The reverse angle shot shows a soldier with arms amputated to the elbows, his stumps tethered to some pulley system. He is the physical counterpart of Nick's spiritual ruin. Then the doctor asks Nick if he remembers his parents' birthdays. So oppressive and smothering is Nick's agony that he weeps silently, piteously, opening his mouth as if to speak but emitting instead the low, plaintive wail of a soul already beyond all reclamation.

In much this state, Nick now tries to telephone Linda in Clairton. But once he has the operator on the line, he abruptly says, "Never mind. Nothing. Nothing. No. Never mind." He is already a Vietnam undead with his own iteration of the "don't mean nothin'" mantra, unable to return home, dolefully disconnected from the place he once professed to love. And now there follow in quick succession two telling instances of confused identity, both of them illuminating the ways Nick's trauma enforces his alienation. In the first of these, he prowls the neon-lit streets of Saigon and sees a Green Beret in the crowd. Believing that he sees Michael, Nick yells after him, but the man he finally catches up with is not Michael. The moment only reinforces Michael's absence, and thus the broken promise of rescue and deliverance tendered as it seemed ages ago on the basketball court. In the other instance of confused identity, Nick wanders into a strip joint, where a Vietnamese prostitute entices him to go upstairs with her. The prostitute wants to be called by any name he wishes, and Nick emotionlessly says "Linda." This "Linda," however, has a baby in a crib in her bedroom. Thus, as Nick tries to re-create Clairton in Saigon, he encounters not only the othered version of his Linda but also the child whose presence alone recalls his paternity of Angela's baby so that "Linda" is Angela, and in his guilty soul he now has to confront both the abandonment of Angela and the betrayal of Steven. Shocked by the demons of havoc and remorse that suddenly arise as if from the infant's presence and already beset by the distressing images in the hospital and by the harrowing ordeal of Russian roulette torture, Nick bolts from the place. The interrupted sex with "Linda" corresponds to, just as it cruelly mocks, his failure to connect with Linda on the phone.

Wandering erratically in a dark and deserted Saigon alley, Nick hears a pistol shot, followed by faint voices in the distance and then a second shot. He now notices a sporty convertible parked in front of a building where the second-floor lights are on. There are two dead bodies in white off to the right of the car. Julien (Pierre Segui), the artful wheedler and blood pander, sits in the convertible. "You seem disturbed," he says in an unctuous Maurice Chevalier accent. Nodding toward the dead bodies, Julien asks Nick if he has ever seen this sort of spectacle before. "Up north," Nick responds. Sensing his opportunity to exploit Nick, Julien steps out of the car and, tugging at Nick's sleeve, leads him inside.

In the gambling den, Nick stands near the table where two players are ready for a game of Russian roulette. He looks on intently but calmly, betraying nothing of the terror that gripped him when his torturers forced him to play against Michael. Suddenly we see Michael in the audience, in civilian clothes. But Michael has yet to notice Nick, who now abruptly walks up to the first player (whose gun has dry-fired) to grab his revolver. Nick presses the muzzle of the revolver to the other player's temple and pulls the trigger. Again the gun dry-fires. So ironically empowered by the gun that terrified him during his captivity, Nick in effect changes places with his VC tormentors, much as Michael did when he held the gun to Stanley's head. After Nick dry-fires at the second player, the gallery erupts in outrage. Only now does Michael notice Nick and shouts to him. But Nick, unnoticing, puts the gun to his own head and dry-fires. As Nick turns to leave, Michael tries to make his way through the crowd to get to him. By the time Michael finally makes it out of the building, however, Nick is sitting beside Julien in the convertible. Michael runs after the car, shouting after Nick, who turns around in his seat and sees Michael but turns his back to him as the car speeds away. Before the car disappears into the night, Nick tosses a wad of dollar bills in the air. Michael continues to trot after the car, but frenzied pedestrians scramble for the money and block his way.

In the climactic scene, Michael will confront not only hell's own Russian roulette champion, Nick, but also the embodied repudiation and the cynical yet condign mockery of the American myth of the hunter-warrior. Nick now personifies the ruined form of the "one shot" mystique. The American hunter's "one shot" ethos reaps its most ironic iteration, which is to say its condition as a trope of the rupture, in the last Russian roulette scene. It is set in the last days of South Vietnam, in late April 1975, in Cholon, Saigon's Chinatown district. Michael arrives in Saigon in a Huey helicopter carrying military personnel to help with the evacuation of Americans. He is wearing a US Army Ranger combat uniform and a green beret. In scenes intercut with actual newsreel clips of the turmoil, Michael hops on the back of a military jeep that speeds out of the US embassy and heads in a direction opposite the South Vietnamese throng desperate for sanctuary. After more shots of the general panic, Michael, now in a white civilian suit, appears in a nighttime Saigon scene. He looks for Nick in bars and brothels, roaming through the wastescape of Saigon's last days. At last Michael finds Julien and bribes him to gain access to the gambling den. While a game of Russian roulette goes on in the pit, Michael confronts Nick backstage.

**Michael** [*to a vacant Nick*]: Hey, Nick. Are you all right? Nick, it's me. Nick, hey! Hey! What are you doing? Nick, what are you doing? Nicholas, what is the matter? . . . Do you know it's me? It's Mike. Tell me, "It's Mike." Tell me, "It's Mike."

**Nick** [*mechanically*]: It's Mike. . . .

**Michael:** Mike. Mike who? Mike who? Mike who?

**Nick:** Mike who? I don't know.

**Michael:** Nicholas, I came 12,000 miles back here to get you. . . . What's the matter with you? Don't you recognize me, huh? [*Slaps him in the face.*] Don't you recognize me, huh? [*Shaking him.*] Huh? Nicky, I love you. You're my friend. What are you doing?

Then Nick spits in Michael's face. As Nick begins to walk away, however, Michael grabs him by his shirt and slams him against a wall. "How could you fucking do this to me?" he implores. Nick again walks away from him and toward the impatient crowd. Michael bribes Julien for a place across the table from Nick.

It seems consistent with Nick's irredeemable otherness that except for parroting Michael's questions, Nick says nothing in response to his entreaties. The attempt to deliver Nick from this latter-day sort of "Indian" captivity belies Michael's own desperate if only implicit plea for two contradictory yet related results. First, that Nick forgive him for loving (and having made love to) Linda, and second, that Nick reaffirm his trust in Michael and in Michael's heroic status to deliver him from this current captivity. In other words, Nick, though deeply wounded, would reaffirm the heroic status of one in whom he can now confirm at best only a common humanity, especially since Michael has earlier confronted and confirmed, in his very soul, the deceit and the emptiness of the heroic myth in and by which he once presumed to live, hence Michael's "*Tell me*, 'It's Mike'"and "Do you know it's *me?*" and "Mike, Mike *who?*" and "Nicky, *I* love you. You're *my* friend." Nick's unresponsiveness means only that Michael's self-representations lie beyond advocacy: the "deer hunter" made his uneasy accommodation with the trophy buck, the avenger subjected Stanley to the terror that he himself suffered at the hands of the VC, and the "friend" made love with Linda. And now here, in this last confrontation with Nick, Michael, all out of roles and identities and types, fails utterly to live up to the promise he made to Nick on the basketball court. Addled, lost, and angry, Nick yet voices the undoing of the mythic hero: "'Mike *who? I don't know.*" The spittle in Michael's face merely adds contempt to the failed endorsement.

Impassive before Michael's attempt to reclaim him by recalling the trees and the mountains, Nick, the revolver already to his head, just says, "One shot." If he seems to acknowledge Michael and reaffirm the past, it is only to mock Michael's hunter-warrior obsessions. But Michael takes Nick's taunt not only for a sign of Nick's awakening from his stupor but also as a recognition amounting to Michael's own validation. The shot that kills Nick an instant later mercilessly denounces the broken promise; it signals the righteous renunciation of the heroic legacy, the tragedy of the heroic myth itself in the instant of the rupture. Nick had pleaded "if anything happens, Mike, don't leave, don't leave me over there. . . . You gotta promise me that, Mike." And Michael, compelled as much by a touching loyalty as by an unselfconscious hubris, assured him "You got it," assured him, then, as if the promise were already fulfilled in the entreaty itself. And that same pride of Michael's expresses a scorn for history, since "history," from the mythic perspective, is but the enduring and undiminished presence of "American exceptionalism" in all of the nation's critical moments, history in the form of the chronicles, by turns suasive and consolatory, in which *was* shall ever be *is*. Michael's promise to Nick held an implicit scorn for that other history, the resistant and subversive history, history in the form of narratives that confute the certitudes of the myth, that disclose the ruthless ironies that make of heroic continuity not an illusion merely but also an obstinate agent in the tragedies of America's Vietnam. "I just don't like no surprises," Michael had told Nick. The climax of *The Deer Hunter* produces Michael's tragic bargain with the "surprises" of an unacknowledged history. But history unfolds in stony indifference, even if Michael's American hubris was no more than native innocence.

At the memorial dinner for Nick at John's place, Michael and Linda avoid each other's gaze but when their eyes meet at last, Linda dashes off to the kitchen. The only talk in the scene means only to puncture the silence of an overwhelming sorrow. But if there is a great sadness here, so also is there shame and inevitably guilt, failed promises and betrayals as palpable as the grief itself. Michael again wears his Special Forces uniform, but the uniform—as it did the zombie sergeant at the bar—now brands him as witness to the Loss and not as a hero. Michael is living testimony of the rupture, just as the nation itself—here represented by all the mourners—stands helpless before tragedy's adamant and austere demand for humanity and humility.

John, who moments earlier sobbed quietly, now softly, as if only to himself, begins to sing "God Bless America." He makes his way back to the table bearing a pan of scrambled eggs, an offering to the forlorn, heartsore communicants. Linda joins him in song, and soon enough nearly everyone else at the table joins in. But this is no jaunty, exultant

Kate Smith rendition of the Irving Berlin song; it is, rather, the prayer of a lost and broken nation.[18] Only at the end of the song do Michael and Linda make eye contact, and they exchange smiles. Michael raises his beer glass in a toast to Nick, and the rest of the friends toast "to Nick." How different, how much more subdued, gloomy, and sorrowful is this toast than the boisterous "*Nostrovia!*" that a drunken Michael hurled at the Green Beret sergeant. A freeze frame follows. There is at best an unspoken assent between Michael and Linda. Their memory of Nick shall bind them each to the other alike in love and in guilt, in both affirmation and betrayal. But any subsequent reaffirmation of America's heroic myth seems unlikely, impossible really. It is now easy to imagine Michael saying, as Nick did much earlier, "I don't think about 'one shot' that much anymore," though he well might do so in the nightmares that are sure to come. As the group sang "God Bless America" we remember perhaps that humble sign far in the background of the second shot of *The Deer Hunter:* "Welcome to Clairton, City of Prayer." But just what does Clairton pray for? The mourners' doleful appeal for God's blessing on the nation suggests that Clairton now turns to prayer not in praise of a divinity that reaffirms the heroic myth but rather in urgent and plaintive appeal for an impossible end to the implacable memory of the Loss.

## *Coming Home*: Broken Vows, Broken Nation

Hollywood's post–*Green Berets* ventures into the Vietnam War had produced, now a full decade later in 1978, two major narratives of the rupture—*The Deer Hunter* and *Coming Home* (Ashby)—two stories about the sort of homecoming that Hollywood had never quite considered, certainly not developed, until it at last came to its narratives of Vietnam. To be sure, the homecoming in *The Best Years of Our Lives* (Wyler, 1946) addresses the problems of the return for both the World War II veteran and his loved ones: the pain and strain of alcoholism and of amputation (alluding to sexual dysfunction), of marital infidelity and divorce, of fearful flashbacks. But the consecration of marriage in the concluding scene unequivocally proclaims the greatness of the mythic folk: the union of Homer Parrish (Harold Russell) and Wilma Cameron (Cathy O'Donnell) sanctifies the prewar marriage of Al (Frederic March) and Milly (Myrna

Loy) Stephenson even as it blesses the future union of Fred Derry (Dana Andrews) and Peggy Stephenson (Teresa Wright). Family—and by easy enough association the white, Christian, American family—thus joyously reaffirmed is the direct narrative outcome of victory in World War II. The closing tableau denies—perhaps dispels—the protraction of the different forms of trauma that the narrative itself has so unsparingly documented. The war is over, and so too is the readjustment to peacetime. The mythic America abides, everlastingly young, nurtured and nourished by its heroic legacy. Alien nations shall temper their wonted contumacy and bend to our providentially chartered course, and America's memorial days shall hold history and tragedy everlastingly in abeyance.

In *The Best Years of Our Lives*, Marie Derry (Virginia Mayo), Fred's wife, is not only unfaithful but also odiously self-centered and thus thoroughly ill-suited for the exalted America just emerging from the great victory. In *Coming Home*, by contrast, Sally Hyde (Jane Fonda), though unfaithful to her husband Bob (Bruce Dern), suffers little overt recrimination from anyone else besides the hapless Bob. At least at first, Sally is a kind of unruffled, cheery ingenue, an officer's accoutrement, like his uniform or his medals. Sally is, as it were, late to the late 1960s. Frumpy only to the extent that Jane Fonda can be so, Sally waits for Bob as if in a state of fatuous earnestness. But by the end of *Coming Home* she will have almost innocently exposed the demons that haunt both Bob and her lover, Luke Martin (Jon Voight). Bob's torment leads to suicide, while Luke's pain takes the shape of an overwhelmingly bitter resentment for the war. Infidelity, divorce, and suicide evince the rupture in the home front version of Hollywood's Vietnam War. Indeed, ever since *Coming Home*, virtually all narratives of the return isolate veterans from the fraught social order to which they return.[19] In many movies, Vietnam veterans return not to wistful solace or even easeful, lotus eaters' oblivion but instead to a nation that blames and condemns them for the failure of its own mythologies.

At his homecoming party, Sally's friend Vi (Penelope Milford) prods Bob to tell how he was shot in the leg. "There's nothing to tell," Bob replies. "I'm a fucking hero. They're going to give me a medal. That's the story of my leg." Laughing nervously, he adds, "Nothing to it, is there?" Sally notices the tension, however, and awkwardly tries to end it: "Well, great." But Bob snaps, "It *isn't* great!" He confesses that he accidentally shot himself in the calf, and the two women burst into unrestrained laughter. Moments later Bob shouts, "It was a goddamned accident!" And Sally asks, "Why are they decorating you?" Bob's story is neither epic nor tragic. In honor, then, of neither courage nor pain but as if in jeering evidence of the war's relentless subversion of American military heroism, Bob is to receive a medal for shooting himself accidentally. And it seems as if everyone but Bob himself—his wife and her lover, the wife's friend, a too-cynical Marine Corps, and an America all too eager to forget—is in on the joke.

Not long after the party, Bob is summoned to the offices of Marine Corps G-2 (Intelligence) not to be awarded his medal but instead to learn that two FBI agents have been monitoring Luke's antiwar activities. The agents have compromising photos of Sally and Luke. In the next scene, Bob finds Luke poolside at a club where he teaches swimming. Restrained, almost resigned, Bob says, "I told Sally I was going to do this. You have a right to know about the surveillance. They were watching the house. They've got pictures. They've got tapes. . . . That's all I have to say. The rest is up to Sally, I guess." (The Chambers Brothers' "Time Has Come Today" has been playing in the background both before and during the brief exchange between Bob and Luke by the swimming pool. As that scene closes, the song almost overwhelms the soundtrack, beginning, ominously, at "Now the time has come.")

Once Bob gets home, however, he heads to his garage and loads a stripped-down Chinese AK-47 assault rifle. He enters the house and confronts Sally. He can barely restrain his rage not only at Sally's infidelity but also at the confusion wrought by the war:

> **Bob:** If it's over with us, it's over!
> **Sally:** Well, what are you saying, that you're not even going to make the effort [to preserve the marriage]?
> **Bob** [*enraged, stretches the "is" into a great wail of pain and rage*]: What I'm saying iiis! I do not belong in this house, and they're saying that I don't belong over there!

The affliction that Bob howls out extends far beyond the disappointed hope of a return to a happy home. His torment is the nation's own, and the nation—the indistinct "they" that Bob reviles and that less than a decade earlier would have included Jane Fonda herself—in its own disabling shock over the break with its mythic past, tenders neither succor nor hope but instead casts its own aggrieved amazement against him so that he alone—so that each veteran alone—shall bear the full burden of the Loss.

"I have no home. I have no home," the Chambers Brothers lamented in "Time Has Come Today" (1967) only moments earlier on the soundtrack. No home here, with Sally; no home "over there" in Vietnam; no site of heroic deeds, no hallowed battleground or grave to remind us of his/their sacrifice or even to beckon across oceans and decades so that he, the old soldier, may in time revisit and remember and reconcile. And they—those who revile the soldier in the nation's own streets no less than those who lead them ever short of victory—repudiate Bob. It is decreed that he and his generation shall have no Omaha Beach, no Mount Suribachi. Why, then, should they have a Times Square? A mere medal for a bumbler's accident will have to do, and even then the decoration shall do far more to remind him of his shame than to bind him to heroic generations.

While Luke, in his wheelchair, hurriedly makes his way to Bob and Sally's, Bob, his fury all but exhausted, declares, "I want to be your husband. I just don't deserve to be your husband. I don't deserve the fucking medal they're gonna give me tomorrow, either. How can they give you a medal for a war they don't even want you to fight?" So, once again, *they*—and indeed, who else, in the final, dismal assessment, and throughout the unappeasable disbelief—who else indeed but *they?* At once responsible for and baffled by the collapse of its own values, America's heroic myth cannot mitigate Bob's desolation; it can only mask it with medals and ribbons pinned on splendid starched uniforms. Certainly Bob learns just enough from his homecoming to disdain these mockeries of heroism. Having discarded them, however, he then learns this much more, as his suicide makes clear, namely that his ultimate sacrifice for nation and legacy is to disappear, to self-erase, as he indeed does, naked and forsaken, in the vast Pacific, there not only to drown his outraged shame but, more important, to symbolically deliver the nation from any bitter thought or sentiment about him, about his war, and about the Loss.

Later in the same scene we learn just how deep and dark Bob's despair is and, moreover, the extent to which his despair expresses the pain of many like him. Bob still holds on to the AK-47, but he no longer threatens Sally or Luke. "Look at me. My hand. I was shaking, and I'm sorry.

I'm fucked. [*Sets the rifle down and slumps in a chair; Sally kneels before him. Luke grabs the rifle and ejects the magazine.*] I just wanted to be a hero, that's all. I just want to be a fucking hero. One day in my life, one moment. I want to go out a hero. That way I would've done something that was mine, that *I've* done." Bob is indeed "fucked," ruined, cuckolded by wife, disavowed by nation. The close-ups of each of the three characters, especially in the context of Bob's understanding of his own failure to be a hero, makes the emptying of the AK-47 magazine—by his rival for Sally's love—an easy if perhaps superfluous yet certainly cruel metaphor for his unmanning. He wanted to be a hero, to be worthy of his legacy. And that dream is now as lost as the war itself was even well before its end. And unlike other veterans in other movies—Willard in *Apocalypse Now*, Joker in *Full Metal Jacket*—Bob finds no ironic mode, avails himself of no cynical gesture or pronouncement for his disillusionment. And the absurd—the consolatory *nothing* of the soldiers in *Hamburger Hill* (see chapter 4)—is not now an option for living but only a pitiless goad to suicide.

Bob goes through with the medal ceremony, but the presiding officer makes no mention at all of the "action" that earns Bob the medal. In the very next scene Bob, alone at a desolate beach, doffs every last stitch of his Marine Corps dress blues, hanging each item of clothing carefully on the side of the lifeguard outlook post. As he strips off his uniform, he also removes his wedding band. His marriage to his wife and his marriage to the Marine Corps seem as dual facets of the one failed myth: the betrayal by one institution corroborates the betrayal by the other—the Marine Corps' *semper fidelis* and the wife's false promise of enduring fidelity—even as each one ceases to function as the returning soldier's refuge from the other. He has "no home," not with Sally, not with the Marine Corps, not in America. Suicide is Bob's tragic nightmare way "to go out a hero," his doing something "that was mine." Bob is a hero only in the ironic feat that spares America a reckoning with the end of its dearest myth.

Bob's nakedness declares his fatal liberation from the institution that, as he once believed, certified his manhood. His nakedness is not unlike Michael Vronsky's in *The Deer Hunter*, for Bob too casts off the outward show, the marks and tokens of institutional claims on the individual. But if Michael doffs his tuxedo in a gesture of revulsion at social entanglements and deceptions, he implicitly does so in favor of such public identity as is to be had in the garb of the deer hunter or in the uniform of the Special Forces. More important, Michael has someone to cover his nakedness, and Nick's simple ministration strengthens, if only for a while, the bond of brotherhood with Nick. Bob, however, has no one to cover his nakedness unless it be the sea itself. His is a triple wretchedness: no uniform to validate his aspirations to the heroic, no pity from his wife, no gratitude from the nation, which is what the medal really signifies. His is the unbearable understanding that *abandonment itself defines him*, that this forsaking, this immitigable rupture, is alone the measure of his generational identity, and that his American soldier's legacy is in the end only so much grief and rage and heartache to be swallowed up by a sea as indifferent as history itself.

As Bob strips on the lonely beach, the action crosscuts with Luke's antiwar address to the high school class as well as with Sally and Vi's drive in the Speedster to buy steaks for the planned cookout. In this shot of Sally, we see perhaps the self-subverting effort of post-Vietnam America to put the war out of memory by a willful, if telling, surrender to vapid suburban rituals. Luke's speech—though very much indeed a speech, that is, a heavy-laden, embittered, antiwar philippic, especially offered in counterpoint to the Marine Corps recruiter who precedes him—retraces America's way to the Vietnam quagmire. And the intercut scene, in which we see Bob remove a uniform much like the recruiter's own, easily confutes the rest of the Marine Corps' claim. No doubt we chafe at the recruiter's pitch but also at Luke's self-satisfied antiwar message. The legacy of Vietnam, in which the heroic yields to irony, could not have a more befitting representative than the body of the disabled veteran.

So, Luke's speech recounts the allures of the myth of heroic continuity as well as the role of the movies in promoting the great seduction. (The transcription below brackets the cuts to Bob at the beach and to Sally and Vi in the Speedster. It also retains Luke's repeated use of the interjectional and plaintive "man.")

> You know, you want to be a part of it, patriotic, go out and get your licks in for the U.S. of A. And when you get over there, it's a totally different situation. I mean, you grow up real quick. Because all you're seeing is a lot of death. [*First chords of Tim Buckley's ballad "Once I Was"; CUT: Bob in uniform at the deserted beach, walking to*

> *lifeguard station. Begins to remove his uniform. CUT.*] And I know some of you guys have looked at uniformed men and you remember all the films and you're going to think about the glory of other wars and think about some vague patriotic feeling and go off and fight this turkey, too. [*CUT: Bob still undressing. CUT: pan, long shot of Sally and Vi in the Speedster. CUT: Bob in his undershorts, taking off his T-shirt and hanging it. CUT: Luke.*] And I'm telling you it ain't like it's in the movies. That's all I want to tell you, because I didn't have a choice. When I was your age, all I got was some guy standing up like that, man, and giving me a lot of bullshit, man, which I caught. I was really in good shape then, man. I was captain of the football team. And I wanted to be a war hero, man. I wanted to go out and kill for my country. [*CUT: Bob, seen through the scaffolding of the lifeguard lookout and between parts of the uniform, the medals on the coat facing us; he removes his wedding band and places it somewhere in the uniform. Now completely naked, his back to the camera, he dashes off and dives in. CUT: Luke, as before.*] And now I'm here to tell you that I have killed for my country, or whatever. And I don't feel good about it. Because there's not enough reason, man, to feel a person die in your hands or to see your best buddy get blown away. I'm here to tell you, it's a lousy thing, man. I don't see any reason for it. And there's a lot of shit that I did over there [*chokes up*] that I find fucking hard to live with. And I don't want to see people like you, man, coming back and having to face the rest of your lives with that kind of shit. It's as simple as that. I don't feel sorry for myself. I'm a lot fucking smarter now than when I went. And I'm just telling you there's a choice to be made here.

Luke implicitly declares his bond of victimhood with Bob. Both men are casualties of the same mythology. In its very earnestness, Luke's speech urges an ironic exegesis upon us: Bob is in the act of committing suicide while Luke inveighs against the movies as a source of America's disaster in Vietnam. Not Luke in his *ecce homo* vexation but rather Bob in his immitigable misery of soul at once illuminates and subverts Luke's admonition against war and myth. Luke may have no immediate way of knowing that Bob is committing suicide to the cadences of his jeremiad, but his lamentation, even in its prolixity, becomes ironically manifested in Bob's silent anguish on the deserted beach. Luke has seen the myth fall apart, even embodying its ruined form. And if he has done terrible things in Vietnam, he is now at least wise, however dark and damning the light of such a wisdom may be. But Bob, no less than Luke, had wanted to be a hero, and also like Luke, Bob grew up convinced that the old certitudes, the enduring sympathies, and the unquestioned values—in short, the whole glorious yet dubious career of America's heroic manhood from cradle to war monument—had once been as the warrant of his individual and generational moment in the great unbroken continuum of America's heroic myth.

Bob breaks finally, fatally, with the heroic myth, but he also enacts, no doubt unwittingly, something like the national obstinacy that would reclaim the myth at any cost even to the point of forgetting, or denying, the Loss. Surely the Loss itself, the stubborn and irrefutable historical fact of it, foredooms the reclamation, makes of it an ill-fated, impossible grasp at not only military victory but also the moral vindication and thereafter at an implausible resumption of that continuity, as if the proposed resumption itself did not always and already invoke the rupture. And yet, in the final moments of *Coming Home*, Bob, in his own puny, bereft way, reenacts the primal American impulse that is also, after Vietnam, the American death wish. First, he faces west from California's shores; then, he plunges into the ocean vastness. Surely the plunge that kills him is also a last desperate lustration, an ablution however foredoomed; but his nakedness, which evokes his hopeless protest against a great betrayal, will never wash so clean as to betoken an innocence that was never his own or his nation's. And lest all this seem too precious or rarified a thing to see in poor, wretched Bob's last moments, we do well to remember the opening scene of *Coming Home*, where actual disabled Vietnam veterans, as ruined and racked in body as Bob is in spirit and as heartbroken as the friends in the last scene of *The Deer Hunter*, gather around a pool table to wrangle indecisively, bitterly, over the bootless if yet galling question "Would you go back?"

## CHAPTER 6

# "A Kingdom Diseased Like Himself"

## *Apocalypse Now* and the Embodied Rupture

> The king who is without blemish has a flourishing kingdom, the king who is maimed has a kingdom diseased like himself.
>
> —Jessie L. Weston, *From Ritual to Romance*

> "All I can tell thee is that I have seen him act the acts of the greatest madman in the world, and heard him make observations so sensible that they efface and undo all he does."
>
> —Cervantes, *Don Quixote*

### Three Versions of the Broken Hero

Late in Francis Coppola's *Apocalypse Now* (1979), Capt. Benjamin Willard (Martin Sheen) offers a grim appraisal of Col. Walter E. Kurtz (Marlon Brando), the renegade Special Forces officer whom he has been ordered to assassinate. "He broke from them," Willard says in voice-over, "and then he broke from himself. I'd never seen a man so broken up and ripped apart."[1] In Colonel Kurtz, *Apocalypse Now* produces the embodiment of America's agonizing, self-estranging experience in Vietnam. Kurtz personifies the anger and the guilt, the hope and the disillusionment, the capacity for cruelty lurking in the very impulse toward tenderness and compassion, and the anarchic will loosed of the restraints of conscience yet persistently bound to an unrelieved remorse. But *Apocalypse Now* also produces a *voice*, Willard's, a voice that plumbs the depths of Kurtz's agony. Willard's attestation of Kurtz's brokenness amounts to his own insight into a soul that stands, in the end sacrificially, for America's torturous encounter with the moral consequences of the rupture.

Other notable Hollywood movies of the Vietnam War besides *Apocalypse Now* narrate the rupture through the conflict between two antagonists, both of them American, of roughly equal dramatic importance. So framed, the conflict fastens our attention on the ideological and moral binaries that characterized America's Vietnam years. As Richard Slotkin writes, "If the 'lesson' of the war is that we are too much like the 'dirty' enemy to be true liberators, then the 'Man Who Knows Indians'—our most effective warrior—is also an emblem of what is wrong with us. But to utterly reject the heroism of that figure is to renounce the model of historical agency that has always been at the center of our national mythology."[2] The character binary in *Casualties of War* (De Palma, 1989) consists of the cruel, depraved, and vindictive Sgt. Tony Meserve (Sean Penn) and the high-minded Eriksson (Michael J. Fox), who repeatedly tries, though in vain, to keep Meserve and the other men in the squad from brutalizing Oahn (Thuy Thu Le),[3] the young Vietnamese woman they kidnap and drag along with them in their reconnaissance mission. Prodded by Meserve, the other four men—but not Eriksson—rape Oahn and later murder her.

Back from the war and on a Metro train in San Francisco, Eriksson wakes up from a troubled dream of the four men against whom he has testified in a military court. Across the aisle, Eriksson notices a young Vietnamese American woman (also played by Thuy Thu Le), who inevitably reminds him of Oahn. When she steps off the car, Eriksson follows her to return a scarf that she has left behind. Politely thankful, she starts to walk away when Eriksson calls out to her in Vietnamese. She notices his distress and asks him, "Do I remind you of someone?" Eriksson says yes. "You had a bad dream, didn't you?" Eriksson again says yes. Over choral voices on the soundtrack, she in effect releases Eriksson from his Vietnam nightmare. "It's over now, I think," she says, then turns around and walks away. What greater dispensation America's than that the avatar of a brutalized Vietnam should so graciously anoint Eriksson, should confer upon him, out of her nation's inexhaustible reserves of pain, the blessing that renders him the living emblem of the one true—of the good, perhaps even of the reborn, innocent—America?

In Oliver Stone's *Platoon* (1986), the humane Sergeant Elias (Willem Dafoe) contests the brutal Sergeant Barnes (Tom Berenger). Together these mutual enemies shape the antithetical impulses of the protagonist/narrator, Chris Taylor (Charlie Sheen), even as Taylor himself comes to embody America's ambivalent history in Vietnam. Toward the end of *Platoon* (both Barnes and Elias are now dead), Taylor surmises that the two sergeants were vying for his soul. So, then, Taylor tends toward the cruelty associated with Barnes (for example, when he fires his M-16 to make the one-legged Vietnamese boy "dance"), yet he kills Barnes, atoning for his own abuses while releasing Barnes's soul from the grip of the war's darkest demons. Also, Taylor has been from the beginning under the tutelage of the kind Elias. After the climactic firefight, *Platoon* asks us to reconcile the polarities into a vague, smoothed-over martyrdom that shows them both to be victims of an unprincipled war. On the helicopter that whisks him away from the battlefront, Taylor reflects in voice-over, "I think now, looking back, we did not fight the enemy, we fought ourselves—and the enemy was in us. The war is over for me now, but it will always be there—the rest of my days. As I am sure Elias will be fighting with Barnes for . . . possession of my soul. There are times since [then] I have felt like the child born of those two fathers." Perhaps in 1986, America was ready to embrace this somewhat artless allegory of its Vietnam anguish. It would have been tempting after all these years to dilute and uncomplicate and disentangle. But we must hasten to expose the perversity inherent in Taylor's sweeping assessment of the causes of the Loss. Taylor arrogantly—even after the Loss, as implied in the persistence of the voice-over—denies the Vietnamese any *agency* in the historical (and historic) outcome. The force and effectiveness of the enemy—of their traditions, culture, and love of country, and of the military genius that yet failed to spare them the enormity of their sacrifice—does not figure in Taylor's reckoning. Instead, the actual, real enemy remains unacknowledged, and Taylor's (and Oliver Stone's) history of the Loss, which privileges the "enemy-within" trope, remains the suasive lie that still bedevils understanding and healing.

In *Casualties of War*, Eriksson's testimony against Meserve presumes to exorcise the one freak malignancy in the nation's soul. And even if a prosecutor tells Eriksson that Meserve and the others, though undoubtedly guilty, will not serve time in prison, their crime is effectively consigned to oblivion. (In the David Lang source account, all the names are changed for fear of recriminations against "Eriksson.") Yet, Meserve and the others—not just Oahn and Eriksson—are themselves "casualties of war," good boys all caught in infernal thralldom to this singular Southeast Asian perversion of American exceptionalism. And *Casualties of War* endeavors (if all too perfunctorily and ineffectually) to mitigate the crime by reminding us that Meserve's rage stems from the death of a buddy, Brown (Erik King).

*Platoon*, however, invests Barnes and Elias with the dualism through which it seeks to explain—at once to justify and condemn—America's Vietnam. Taylor is accordingly the son of two seemingly distinct moral legacies, yet one is no more American than the other. He can kill the "evil" Barnes (or is it that he euthanizes the badly wounded prostrated Barnes, who in effect orders him to shoot?), leaving him to molder forsworn in the alien soil. But killing Barnes hardly translates into saving Elias, who himself remains in enemy territory, martyred and remembered, but homeless nonetheless. Elias's final image—he is kneeling at the edge of a clearing, mortally wounded, blood-drenched arms stretched upward (surrendering, imploring, praying, cursing?), the swarming enemy right behind him, the Huey rising remorselessly, accentuating his smallness, confirming his doom—epitomizes the failed hero of the Vietnam War, even one so accomplished in every way as Elias, this tragic "Man Who Knows Indians" (figure 6.1).

"Those two fathers" may share the unifying narrative field of Taylor's voice-over memory, but as representations of the national discord wrought by the war, they remain each in his own antipodal realm, with altogether too much tragedy in between to allow for any hope of reconciliation even by the "child" who claims them both as his fathers.

Willard cannot "terminate Colonel Kurtz's command" without also "terminating" Kurtz himself. Kurtz embodies his own bisected "command"—atrocities and high-mindedness both insanity and clear-headedness, cruelty as well as tenderness—and none of it by degrees of descent or ascent, none of it distinguished temporally, now one, then the other, but integrally and covalently dual throughout. Kurtz is his own Vietnam War paradox, and Willard's mission to kill him comports with

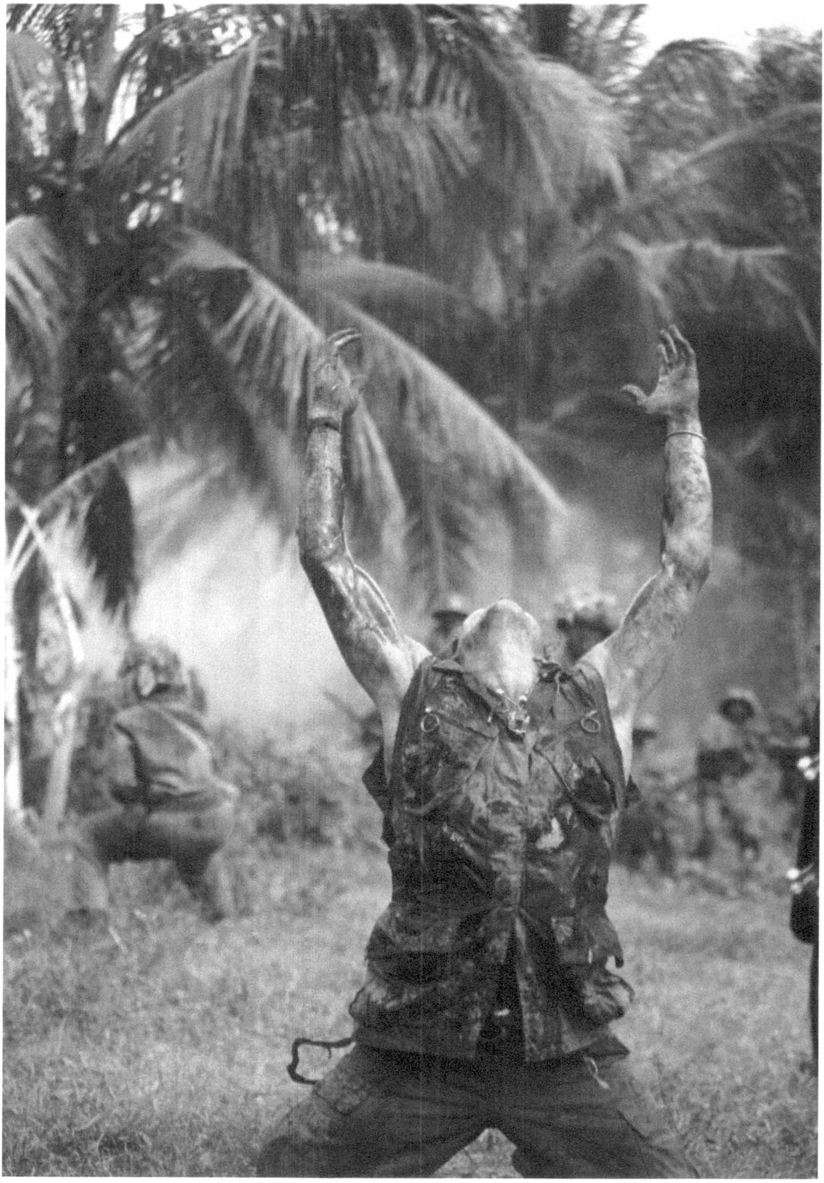

Figure 6.1. *Platoon.* Sergeant Elias (Willem Dafoe), wounded and dying, left behind on the battlefield.

the all too familiar if enduringly mystifying logic whereby it becomes necessary to destroy the village in order to save it. By the time Willard gets his mission—and even earlier, since as we learn later a mission identical to Willard's has already been ordered—there is no "good" Kurtz to be redeemed, no pre-Vietnam, enlightened Kurtz to be reclaimed from the heart of darkness. The countervailing "evil" is joined to the "good" as sinew to bone. It is hardly relevant, then, as General Corman (G. D. Spradlin) puts it to Willard, that Kurtz "was a good man, . . . a humanitarian man, a man of wit and humor" (all of it pointedly in the past tense), who has only now become one more American whose "dark side" has overcome "what Lincoln called 'the better angels of our nature.'"

Viet Thanh Nguyen writes that Willard "continues his fateful cruise up the river to confront . . . the white man [Kurtz] who has become king of the savages and who must be killed because he has shown that the white man is no different than the savages. . . . This ethical recognition of the white man's inhumanity gives *Apocalypse Now* its kick as well as its controversy. Enduring works of memory like this movie will force audiences to confront the simultaneity of inhumanity and humanity, rather than just one or the other."[4] Missing from this lucid and instructive précis is an overt challenge to the assumption that Willard acts in accordance with an *ethic* and that his "ethical recognition" enables his insight into Kurtz's dark soul. But there is never an ethic for Willard to appeal to, not unless the putative ethic can both and at once reference a "recognition" of its own collapse while remaining somehow impossibly unaltered by its own moral irrelevance. Vietnam, in *Apocalypse Now*, is the site where ethics die. With the Nung River as conduit, Vietnam binds Willard to Kurtz "like a main circuit cable plugged straight into Kurtz," as Willard himself puts it. Here "Vietnam" is neither nation (politically divided or not) nor battleground (military or ideological). It is instead the narrative space made possible by the apocalyptic abyss, by the apocalyptic "now" of not only the movie's title but also the ironic welcome sign that reads "Apocalypse Now" painted in red on a rock at the entrance of Kurtz's nightmare world, as if alluding to the ominous warning in Dante's *Inferno*, Canto III: "Abandon all hope, ye who enter here." The rupture attests to, even as it narrates, the ethical instability of the heroic myth. One might therefore say with Willard's archetype, Charlie Marlow in Conrad's *Heart of Darkness*, that out there "principles won't do" and that what is required instead is "one's own inborn strength,"[5] a strength that you attain not by appeals to codes of conduct but instead by "your power of devotion, not to yourself, but to an obscure, back-breaking business."[6] Willard's "devotion" to his assassin's mission, which is nothing less than the elimination of the one man who might have won the war, brings about the end of the myth of heroic continuity. And this ironic devotion empowers the voice, Kurtz's, that proclaims even as it laments "the horror!" Willard's fidelity to Kurtz, then, marks the end of myth and legacy and heroism. And perhaps it also signals the end of "America," for this end, this apocalypse now, unveils the horror that lurked all along in even the most exultant moments of America's mythic narrative.

Consider the pamphlet that Kurtz entrusts to Willard shortly before the assassination. It is, presumably, a lucid, humane exposition titled "The Role of Democratic Force in the Underdeveloped World," yet at the bottom of the final page he scribbles a postscript in direst red ink: "Drop the Bomb, exterminate them all." This is America's generosity punctuated by darkest rage, gall gushing onto grace, and the one man vying with both as they both vie for him. And yet it is more, for these "opposites" are not merely expressions of a garden-variety dualism. In *Apocalypse Now* these opposites become versions of each other, the actual and the potential contending continually for affirmation, for justification. The rupture, thus embodied, conjoins its binaries, though it does not thereby reconcile them each to the other.

## A Gory Sort of Empathy

Acting not in fulfillment of his official mission to "terminate" Kurtz's "command" but rather in obedience to his own humanity, Willard at last releases Kurtz from his moral anguish when he hacks Kurtz to pieces with a machete. As if in keeping with the paradoxes that define both the narrative and the war itself, Willard performs an act of undoubted loyalty. His empathy—his capacity, as Lear puts it, "to feel what wretches feel"—is first evident in his early voice-over declarations and finds its climax in the brutal deed itself. Yet, for all its raw brutality, the assassination also completes the unfolding paradox at the other end of which lies the fellow-feeling that binds Willard to Kurtz. In their mutual alienation from dysfunctional institutions and fractured myths, both characters acquire existential validation.

As a Huey helicopter ferries him to Com-Sec Intelligence in Nha Trang, Willard, in voice-over, mentions Kurtz for the first time. "It was no accident," Willard says, "that I got to be the caretaker of Colonel Walter E. Kurtz's memory, any more than being back in Saigon was an accident. There is no way to tell his story without telling my own. And if his story is really a confession, then so is mine." Thus begins Willard's narration of Kurtz's condition as embodiment of the rupture. But Willard himself is a moral casualty of the war, as aware of its dehumanizing force as of his own helplessness to resist it. "Willard's narrative in the film," writes Margo Norris, "is his confession, . . . and with it he looks into the heart of his own darkness, ranging from his military assassinations . . . to his savage murder of Kurtz, from his barely concealed racism toward Clean and Chief to his icy dispatch of the wounded Vietnamese woman [in the sampan massacre scene]."[7] The entire first scene—opening with a fade-in to a tropical jungle and ending with the desperate (if meaningfully mute) cries of a stark naked, stone drunk Willard—reveals the true source of his aptness for the mission, for Willard bears already the full weight of the war's absurdity, of the narrative that locates the corruption of America's heroic virtues in the hero's devotion to their fulfillment.

We hear the movie's first words—"This is the end," from the song by The Doors—over the exploding jungle. This is the reactive verbal burst in response to the napalm inferno that moments earlier devoured a coconut palm forest in the distance. The song's first line produces a disorienting mix of genesis and apocalypse. Principally, however, it signals the forthcoming illumination of an overwhelming moral darkness.[8] This "end" at the beginning announces the historical break with a previous order, locates an apocalypse now, at the beginning. Also, this proffered end-at-the-beginning anticipates the nature and purpose of Willard's mission: to kill, to end, to "terminate." He must end Kurtz's "command," of course, but he must also begin at the end, here, now, because all the heroic virtues and even the national delusions about them have already come to an end, hence Willard's assault against himself in the opening scene. He bears the "wilderness of pain" that The Doors sing about later in the opening song. In that wilderness awaits not a fully formed and distinct savage Other but rather a self that is both one and many, familiar yet strange, assailant and victim both. And never along the way to accomplishing his mission will Willard entertain the illusion of eventual healing or a hope for that other desperate American fantasy after Vietnam: closure.

The first event in *Apocalypse Now* produces a metaphorical vision of America's historical Vietnam War. We witness a barbaric rage—calculated yet purposeless, at once earnest and wanton—against the natural world. Moments later, Willard appears as a screen-wide upside-down head, image and sign seen again in the severed heads that litter Kurtz's camp; in the decapitation of Chef (Frederic Forrest); in the recurrent presentation of Kurtz himself as an amber-hued shaven head moving slowly in and out of the darkness; and finally, in the close-up of Willard as he emerges from the river, ready to assassinate Kurtz.

The first close-up of Willard takes up only the left half of the wide screen, while various other images are by turns superimposed on it: smoke, thick and black from the burning jungle; helicopters crisscrossing the screen; and the reappearance of the ceiling fan, its blades seeming to rotate to the slowed-down sound of helicopter rotor blades. The tangle of images and sounds denies us, for example, the relative position of Willard's head as well as any basic certainty about both exterior and interior worlds, to say nothing of any distinction about the war in the jungle and the one in Willard's soul. The self-destructive anguish that Willard is about to enact in the hotel room does not so much parallel as it internalizes the rage invoked in the initial napalming of the jungle. He too appears before us as one "so broken up and ripped apart."

Now Willard's face, still upside down, becomes suffused with orange light from the firestorm in the jungle. Willard, recall, wakes up in the same scene in Saigon. That his face comes to be bathed in the light from the napalmed jungle far away suggests, in its very implausibility, the extent to which the opening shots dispense with simple assumptions of geography and place common in other movies of the Vietnam War. And now as if to foil an easy realism, there appears screen right the stone head of an East Asian idol, perhaps after the fashion of a Buddha from Angkor Wat. In much the same spatial relation to Willard, the stone idol will reappear at the end, as Willard and Lance (Sam Bottoms) glide away upriver on the PBR (patrol boat, riverine). Now Willard's head rotates slowly counterclockwise (thus implicitly against convention) and comes to an upright position. With open eyes for the first time, he comes to the window and takes in the cityscape before him. "Saigon," he then says in voice-over. "Shit, I'm still only in Saigon. Every time, I think I'm gonna wake up back in the jungle. When I was home after my first tour, it was worse. I'd wake up, and there'd be nothing. I hardly said a word to my wife until I said yes to a divorce. When I was here I wanted to be there. When I was there all I could think of was getting back into the jungle." Willard may not be able to deliver the pithy pronouncements, record and report the meaningful (if cryptic) dreams, or articulate the complex moral insights by means of which Kurtz shall yet elucidate the collapse of America's heroic myth. Nonetheless, Willard emerges from the chaos and rage of the opening sequence with a voice, a voice, to be sure, straining already under the great burden of the rupture but still empowered to narrate his own brokenness, like Kurtz's own: "Everyone gets everything he wants. I wanted a mission, and, for my sins, they gave me one. Brought it up to me like room service." Willard exposes the sanctimoniousness of the commanders' "mission" even as he affirms his own all-too-ironic fidelity to Kurtz: "There is no way to tell his story without telling my own." In the ruin of the American soul in Vietnam, this fidelity, however paradoxical, is the last pure American virtue. But while fidelity may answer to Willard's version of the mission, it does not thereby create a new hero or rehabilitate the old one. Willard, then, declares his loyalty to the broken form of the hero. At the same time, however, his loyalty never harbors a hope for the restoration of the heroic legacy, let alone of the hero himself, hence his reflection as he steals toward Kurtz's temple to fulfill his mission: "Everybody wanted me to do it, him most of all. I felt like he was up there, waiting for me to take the pain away." Faithfully undertaken and fulfilled, then, Willard's mission extends far beyond simply killing Kurtz. Willard's mission is to bring about America's release from the ruined myth of heroic continuity and into history, however tragic that history may be.

Willard's pain takes the form of a restlessness with no fixed origin, a kind of desperate and unstructured disquiet, a "waiting for a mission." Soon his restlessness intensifies, and we see him in his olive-drab undershorts standing in front of the cheval mirror. "Every minute I stay in this room I get weaker. . . . Each time I looked around, the walls moved in a little tighter." He briefly preens himself in the mirror, gently combing his hair back with his fingers: a discomfited, now-chastened narcissist, type and cast of the nation that mistook its vanity for the high privilege of exceptionalism.

Willard now assumes, though unsteadily, different karate poses in front of the mirror (The Doors' frenetic staccato, "fuck, fuck, fuck, . . ." plays on the soundtrack.) His face now daubed with camouflage paint, his hair slicked back, he tries more karate moves. We are looking at his reflection in the mirror when he begins to cry in anguish (though still without a soundtrack). Then he whirls around suddenly and bolo-punches the mirror, smashing it. He summersaults across the bed (smearing the bed sheets with the blood from his lacerated hand) and lands, facing us, sitting on the floor on the other side of the bed. Standing—and, as we soon see, fully naked—he looks quizzically at his bloody hand and runs it over his face, still crying in torment, accompanied by The Doors' frenetic, climaxing "yeah, yeah, yeah." Willard guzzles his Martell out of the bottle and then totters about, consumed by a pain the depths of which only his unvoiced howls can fully express. He sits down on the floor, his back against the bed. With his head thrown back in an expression of overwhelming agony—his Munchian wail of silent, existential wretchedness—he covers his nakedness with the bloodied sheet. Willard's deadly empathy toward Kurtz begins already as an assault on himself.

## "Them"; or, the Anxiety of Legacy, Redux

On his way to join the PBR crew and pick up Kurtz's trail, Willard puzzles over his orders to terminate Kurtz's command "with extreme prejudice." "How many people had I already killed? There were those six that I knew about for sure, close enough to blow their last breath in my face. But this time it was an American, and an officer. That wasn't supposed to make any difference to me, but it did." The commanders know that Willard is an assassin in the Special Forces. Why else would they have summoned him? Yet, they would have him kill Kurtz because, as Colonel Lucas (Harrison Ford) explains in the same scene, "Kurtz had ordered the execution of some Vietnamese intelligence agents, men he believed were double agents."[9] Historically, at least, the commanders' reason for the assassination is specious, since Americans in Vietnam tended to cast all Vietnamese indifferently as potential enemies. Consider a brief report from Jonathan Schell. "In preparation for some of their ground operations," the marines would airdrop "Pamphlet No. 44–65" on a village.

"'The Marines are here to help you,' the pamphlet read. 'Do not run from them! If you run, they may mistake you for a Vietcong and shoot at you.'"[10] The filmmakers of *Full Metal Jacket* were only reporting the news when they had a helicopter door gunner (Tim Colceri) explain why he shot at all the Vietnamese below: "Anyone who runs is a VC. Anyone who stands still is a well-disciplined VC." On a much larger scale, the Phoenix Program—"a special program to capture or kill the cadres of the clandestine Viet Cong Government,"[11] in Neil Sheehan's definition—attempted to "pacify" the South Vietnamese countryside by implementing what might not unjustly be called genocide. Hence Willard, his six murders but a paltry fraction of the prodigal whole, aptly remarks, "Shit, charging a man with murder in this place was like handing out speeding tickets at the Indy 500."

But Kurtz, Willard is all too aware, is "an American, and an officer," and killing him is all too different. "What do you call it," Kurtz rails on the tape the commanders play for Willard in Nha Trang, "when the assassins accuse the assassin?" Much later, as Willard steals into Kurtz's temple to carry out the assassination, Kurtz is reading into his tape recorder, pondering yet another moral paradox. "We train young men to drop fire on people, but their commanders won't allow them to write 'fuck' on their airplanes because it's obscene!" In the formulation of its war strategy—indeed, in the enactment of its presumed mythic entitlement—America presupposes above all else the generic otherness of the Vietnamese and then allows that otherness to stand as the measure of their humanity. Here is American hubris run rampant, the cultural vanity—if not the heroic myth's virulent racism here denuded of the old New Frontier platitudes—that would punish the use of a single scrawled word yet revel deliriously, frenziedly, in the carnage below.

As we shall see, Kurtz's break "from himself"—his resistance, however foredoomed, to his own anguished depravity—narrates the story of the delusional, narcissistic America that he himself had come to represent in the time before the Loss. Of course, Willard's reflection on Kurtz's break "from them" implicitly includes every officer in the narrative—most memorably the narrative's own anti-Kurtz—Lt. Col. Bill Kilgore (Robert Duvall), who is also a John Wayne avatar (his call code is "Big Duke 6"). In its most basic and immediate reference, however, this "them" from whom Kurtz "broke" refers to his wife and son. In the midst of the moral squalor everywhere evident in Kurtz's compound, the two photographs next to his cot, one of the son, one of the wife, express a sort of last faint hope that he may yet step back from the edge of the abyss. He tells Willard that his son "might not understand what I've tried to be" and pleads with him that "if I were to be killed, Willard, I would want someone to go to my home and tell my son everything—everything I did, everything you saw—because there is nothing that I detest more than the stench of lies. And if you understand me, Willard, you will do this for me."

Outside Kurtz's temple, the natives already chant and dance in preparation for the ritual sacrifice of the tethered water buffalo. And Willard prepares to slaughter Kurtz. The native leader repeatedly and in measured, ceremonial rhythm brings down his machete on the water buffalo's hump, eventually, through repeated blows to the same spot, almost severing the head of the piteously helpless beast as its front legs buckle at last. And Willard, already in Kurt's den, begins to hack and hew at him with a machete of his own. The justly famous feat of intercutting between the slaughter of the buffalo and the assassination of Kurtz immediately transfers the sacrificial function of the buffalo to Kurtz. The bloody sacrifice confronts us with the real if unacknowledged reason why the commanders want Kurtz terminated—not because he has ordered the assassination of a double agent or even because he has come to preside over the moral abomination in his sector of Vietnam but instead because America needs a sacrifice to the gods of the heroic myth.

As efficient a killer of communists as Kurtz may have become, his success (if such it is) all but *demands* such depravity, such utter and undoubtedly self-conscious surrender to the malevolence rampant in his compound. But here we need to acknowledge rather than, like the commanders, condemn, for Kurtz is in fact winning the war or at the very least knows how to win the war, as he himself tells us. Moreover, out there in the heart of darkness—not contesting the darkness but embracing it—Walter Kurtz in a way fulfills the terms and conditions of his heroic inheritance. And who is to say that America's other wars—all our victories—did not themselves produce such unrestrained slaughter? If slaughter be the measure of success, as well it may have been in, say, Dresden and Hiroshima, why should Kurtz's abominations not place him proudly in line to claim his heroic inheritance? Except that Kurtz, as he himself knows too well, is fighting a war already lost. The real difference between the horrors of Dresden and of Kurtz's camp hinges on whether victory can be made to justify the abomination. In the flush of victory in World War II, where were the voices that today rue and lament Dresden and Hiroshima? The heroic myth did much work to hide its horrors in the folds of triumph. And therein lies Kurtz's dilemma as well as that of the commanders and America's own. In a war defined by cruel paradoxes, Kurtz is both and at once a stain on the heroic legacy and its fulfillment. And for the commanders, it seems, it is preferable to extinguish forever the heroic legacy—or to look back upon it not hopefully but wistfully—than to acknowledge the evil at its core.

According to the commanders (in the plenitude of their hypocrisy), Kurtz is the myth's accursed, its apostate, hence Willard's "errand-boy" mission: altogether impossibly, he is to perform a kind of resection, an extirpation of the cankerous Kurtz that yet leaves a sound and viable myth, a myth uncontaminated by contingency or by history. But they do not see that Kurtz fails (and falls) because America itself has already done so, because American values, as ostensibly sustained by the heroic myth, prove to have been always and already "hollow at the core" (to cite Joseph Conrad's source narrative). Yet, this American failure should hardly suggest that Vietnam was to America but an empty space in which to enact a foredoomed Loss. It is Vietnam itself—namely the nation and its people, the place and time, their history and its own historicizing agency—that chiefly exposes the lie of America's exceptionalist boast. For all of its reliance on irony and paradox and uncertainty, *Apocalypse Now* leaves no doubt concerning the agency of Vietnam and the Vietnamese in the Loss. For evidence, one need appeal only to Kurtz's anecdote of how the VC "hacked off" the little arms of the children that his Green Berets had hours earlier inoculated for polio. The event, as we will see later in more detail, produces Kurtz's transfigurative insight, a vision far-reaching enough to include the war and the enemy as well as an ironic view of American myth and of the dark soul lurking beneath it. And in the face of Kurtz's refulgent vision—it hit him, he says, "like a diamond bullet"—of the heart of darkness, the commanders can only prevaricate.

General Corman simultaneously invokes and denies the anxiety of legacy. Kurtz, he of the brilliant dossier, has now unaccountably failed to live up to his birthright. But Kurtz's sins—the sins for which he is to atone by acquiescing to his own assassination—are first sins "of the people."

Willard, like the biblical Aaron, "shall make an atonement for the holy place because of the uncleanness of the children of Israel, and because of their transgressions in all their sins" (Lev. 16:15–16). Thus, Corman casts Kurtz as the scapegoat. Or, in James George Frazer's formulation in *The Golden Bough* (a well-thumbed copy lies on Kurtz's night table), the commanders transfer the people's sins "to a god who is afterward slain."[12] Kurtz alone bears the stigma of the heroic myth's primal flaw. In the enactment of his mythic role, of his "errand into the wilderness," the American hero often becomes what he most hates: the enemy himself, the savage Other. But Kurtz comes to know and to accept that the savage Other in fact springs from within the American soul. He comes to understand that his own atrocities against the Vietnamese enemy do not merely mimic an alien force but arise out of circumstances propitious to the uprising of demons no less autochthonous than the heroic myth itself claims to be. Kurtz knows that the self-loathing inherent in the American soul, that it may be borne at all, requires a full transfer of its moral burden onto the Other. The heroic myth always contained and inevitably even logically demanded its own undoing.

## Kurt's Dossier and the Commanders' Narrative

The commanders in Nha Trang, though careful to lavish their highest praise on Walter E. Kurtz, also order his assassination. The hero of assured glory lives in the dossier that they hand Willard. "At first," says Willard in voice-over, perplexed by the apparent gap between the man's achievements and the order to kill him, "I thought they'd handed me the wrong dossier. I couldn't believe they wanted this man dead. Third-generation West Point, top of his class. Korea, Airborne, about a thousand decorations." Aboard the PBR already on the way to Kurtz's jungle retreat, Willard reads the dossier:

> 1946: Graduates West Point; second in Class; third-generation appointee. Completes Basic Training, Advanced Infantry Training, Fort Gordon, Georgia.
>
> 1948: Assigned, West Berlin, U.S. Sector Command, G-1 (Plans) Promoted 1st Lt.

1950: Masters [*sic*] Degree, Harvard University, History: (Thesis: The Phillipines [*sic*] Insurrection: American Foreign Policy in Southeast Asia, 1898–1905)
1951: Assigned General Staff, U.S. Command, Seoul, Korea. Tours combat zones, Division-Evaluation Team. Requests transfer to Intelligence; returned U.S. for special training, Ft. Holabird and Washington.[13]

The dossier chronicles the deeds of America's mythic hero in his full glory. The myth, the dossier would have it, is real; it lives in the man. The first entry, from 1946, places Kurtz at the very onset of America's unrivaled power, right after World War II. Moreover, the same entry reveals that Kurtz is a "third-generation appointee" to West Point: his is the birthright, the deed to the living tradition. The year 1948 notes an early landmark in a career destined for greatness: Kurtz is posted to Berlin, the first hotspot of the Cold War. Two years later in 1950, his master's thesis takes him back to the Philippines and so to America's first transpacific imperial venture (and to the site where *Apocalypse Now* was filmed). He then fights in Korea, the first great war of the foretold Armageddon.

Before Willard reads Kurt's dossier, however, he listens to Kurtz on the tape recorder in the commanders' office trailer in Nha Trang. The voice on the tape supplies a subversive context for the heroic covenant implicit in the dossier; it alerts Willard to a consciousness whose sheer extravagance of perception anticipates the moral pitfalls and entanglements along the paths of glory. "I watched a snail crawling on the edge of a straight razor. That's my dream. It's my nightmare. Crawling, slithering, along the edge of a straight razor, and surviving." Even this early, when the commanders, themselves listening, react with little more than grimaces and raised eyebrows, Willard begins to fathom the depths of Kurtz's formidable predicament and thus of his anguish. "I'd heard his voice on the tape," he says in voice-over, "and it really put the hook in me, but I couldn't connect up that voice with this man." In the disturbingly real allure of this disembodied voice, we find an early version of Willard's essential assessment of Kurtz much later: "he broke from them, and then he broke from himself." The rupture references no mere provisional aberration in the life of the hero or of the heroic myth. It is, as embodied in Kurtz, source, shape, and disposition of the pain and the grief that defines and overwhelms hero and nation both. "But we must kill them," Kurtz continues on the tape. "We must incinerate them. Pig after pig. Cow after cow. Village after village. Army after army." Who else's golden boy broods so, dreams so, rages so? Yet, America's urge to fulfill the heroic legacy already produces—perhaps because it already *contains*—the compulsion to wage genocidal war. The voice that issues these raging directives for the extermination of the Vietnamese belongs, unequivocally yet paradoxically, to the noble-looking Green Beret pictured in the black-and-white close-up of Kurtz that Willard sees in Nha Trang. In Vietnam, as Nick Turse notes with a rhetorical force that seems to echo Kurtz's rant, "the indiscriminate killing of South Vietnamese noncombatants—the endless slaughter that wiped out civilians day after day, month after month, year after year throughout the Vietnam War—was neither accidental nor unforeseeable."[14]

As if tracking America's own inexorable way to the Loss, the dossier comes to the fateful year 1964. It is the year of the Tonkin Gulf Resolution, which President Lyndon Johnson invoked to justify ordering American ground troops to South Vietnam. In 1964 Kurtz, Willard's voice-over tells us, "returned [to the United States] from a tour with Advisory Command in Vietnam, and things started to slip. His report to the Joint Chiefs of Staff and Lyndon Johnson was restricted. Seems they didn't dig what he had to tell them." Over the images of still more confidential documents, Willard resumes his voice-over gloss on the dossier: "During the next three months he made three requests for transfer to Airborne training, Fort Benning, Georgia, and was finally accepted. Airborne? He was thirty-eight years old! Why the fuck would he do that?" Kurtz's demurral awakens the suspicions of those who claim guardianship of the heroic myth. If Kurtz, to judge from the dossier, has so far sauntered smartly on the bright path of America's heroic legacy, he now unexpectedly veers far from it and enters, alone, a moral wilderness.

Chef and Willard's encounter with the tiger in the tropical jungle illuminates the dangers, as much to soul and mind as to life and limb, of Kurtz's transformation in Vietnam. Chef, a New Orleans saucier, ventures along with Willard into the jungle in search of mangoes, but as he parts the foliage for a way through, he sees a tiger staring at him from a few feet away. Still in a panic even though he is now safe back in the boat, Chef yells out "Chief, you were right! Never get out of the boat!" and repeats this practical mantra several times. Willard's ensuing reflection, in voice-over, riffs on that mantra. "Never get out of the boat," Willard repeats.

> Absolutely, goddamned right. Unless you were going all the way. Kurtz got off the boat. He split from the whole fucking program. How did that happen? What did he see here that first tour? Thirty-eight fucking years old. If you joined the Green Berets, there was no way you'd get above colonel. Kurtz knew what he was giving up. The more I read and began to understand, the more I admired him. . . . He had to apply three times and he put up with a ton of shit, but when he threatened to resign, they gave it to him. The next youngest guy in his class was half his age. They must have thought he was some far-out old man, humping it over that course. . . . A tough mutherfucker. He finished it. He could have gone for general, but he went for himself instead.

Only much later do we fully understand why Kurtz "got off the boat." For now, however, both the dossier and Willard's gloss suffice as leads to Kurtz's "breaking point."

Having played the tape for Willard, Corman fills the ensuing awkward silence with a wistful reminiscence about Kurtz. "Walt Kurtz was one of the most outstanding officers this country's ever produced. He was brilliant. He was outstanding in every way. And he was a good man, too. [*Ruefully, looking fondly at the photograph of Kurtz.*] A humanitarian man. A man of wit and humor. He joined the Special Forces, and after that, his ideas, methods, became unsound. Unsound." Corman's reminiscence (scrupulous in its use of the past tense) serves his deadly purpose. That Kurtz has adopted "unsound" methods means specifically that, on no higher authority than his own, he has "crossed over into Cambodia with this Montagnard army of his that worship the man like a god and follow every order, however ridiculous" (as Colonel Lucas bitterly puts it). But Kurtz's crossing into Cambodia resonates with one of the darker chapters of the Vietnam War. At about the same time of the historical setting of *Apocalypse Now*, President Richard Nixon, with the knowledge of only a few of his top advisers (including National Security Advisor Henry Kissinger) and a handful of congressmen, approved Operation Menu, the secret bombing of Cambodia, which ran from

March 18, 1969, to May 26, 1970.[15] One would think therefore that the commanders might come to see Kurtz's foray across the border as no more than an advance action or a long-term reconnaissance mission in support of Operation Menu.

Instead, Corman offers Willard this further development: "Well, I have some other shocking news to tell you. Colonel Kurtz was about to be arrested for murder." More perhaps than the sanctimony implicit in the word "shocking," Corman's use of the passive voice alerts us to the nimble cant of institutional equivocation and outright deceit. Kurtz is right to ask, as he does in the tape, "What do you call it when the assassins accuse the assassin?" No moral posturing can disguise the glibness that condemns in Kurtz what it demands of Willard. Can termination—the word itself a craven dodge of their murderous criminality—really convince the commanders that they themselves, yet somehow not Kurtz, are innocent of aggravated murder? It is no wonder that Willard is perplexed when Corman announces that Kurtz "was about to be arrested for murder": "I don't follow, sir. Murdered who?" But the commanders seem indifferent to Willard's puzzlement. Having told him that Kurtz "was about to be arrested for murder" (but not mentioning that they had already sent a Lieutenant Colby and his squad on an identical mission), Corman eases into an account of Kurtz's fall. Corman sucks his teeth nervously and avoids looking Willard in the eye:

> Well, you see, Willard, in this war things get confused out there. Power, ideals, the old morality, and practical military necessity. But out there with these natives, it must be a temptation to be God. Because there's a conflict in every human heart between the rational and the irrational, between good and evil. And good does *not* always triumph. Sometimes, the dark side overcomes what Lincoln called "the better angels of our nature." Every man has got a breaking point. You and I have them. Walt Kurtz has reached his. And, very obviously, he has gone insane.

Corman seems to understand Kurtz, to see Kurtz as the fallen soul out of primordial humanity. But if Corman "understands," why does he—how can he—want Kurtz dead? Should such a man as Kurtz, until so recently "a good man, a humanitarian man," not be pitied instead? Or is it that Kurtz is now so hopelessly lost to the myth that gave him his identity that to have him alive in a land, however remote, somehow poses an existential threat to the myth and therefore to the very foundations of American identity? (Here then, Kurtz compels both pity and fear, as Aristotle prescribed for all tragic heroes.) Or is it that the commanders take Kurtz's "break" as his scorn for the myth? Such questions suggest that the anxiety of legacy drives the mission that the commanders entrust to Willard. As they see it, the assassination suppresses or at least mitigates the anxiety of legacy. And yet, to terminate Kurtz means also and at the same time a surrender to that anxiety. The anxiety that compels the termination becomes evident in the termination itself. The anxiety is already the undeniable fall into the abyss of the rupture.

That the narrative structure of *Apocalypse Now* sustains such an appraisal of the commanders' challenge to Willard's and Kurtz's narratives becomes compellingly clear in Willard's long voice-over reflection following the USO/Playboy Bunny sequence. As the PBR continues its journey toward Kurtz, Willard once more takes up the dossier, but now his voice-over is intercut with echoes of statements made earlier by Corman and Lucas:

> **Willard:** Late summer/early autumn, 1968. Kurtz's patrols in the highlands [are] coming under frequent ambush. The [Special Forces] camp started falling apart. [*CUT to black-and-white photos: two children burned to death; Montagnard warrior standing by a Huey; bare-topped Montagnard woman, crying. DISSOLVE. Folder; tab reads "IVORY IV" and under it "TOP SECRET"; pouch inside the folder, in red letters "CLASSIFIED," slow TILT over photo ID's of four Vietnamese double agents.*] *Willard, resuming.* November. Kurtz orders assassination of three Vietnamese men and one woman. Two of the men were colonels in the South Vietnamese Army. [*CUT. War Office pouch with photo of Kurtz, in uniform.*] Enemy activity in his old sector dropped off to nothing. I guess he must have hit the right four people.
>
> **General Corman** [*as voice over extreme close-up of Willard*]: He joined the Special Forces, and after that his, uh . . . [*Voice trails off.*]

**Willard:** The Army tried one last time to bring him back into the fold.

**Corman** [*continuing, over Willard's voice*]: methods became . . .

**Willard:** And if he had pulled over, it all would have been forgotten.

**Corman** [*continuing*]: unsound.

**Willard:** But he kept going.

**Lucas** [*over close-up of a pointer and map*]: Now he's crossed over into Cambodia . . .

**Willard:** And he kept winning it his way.

**Lucas** [*continuing, as above*]: . . . with that Montagnard army of his who . . .

**Willard:** And they called me in.

**Lucas** [*continuing*]: . . . worship the man like a god and follow every order, however ridiculous.

The voices from Nha Trang trail off, but Willard continues. "They lost him," he says. "He was gone."

In a way, however, the commanders' rebuke of Kurtz continues in the form of photographs included in the dossier: a dead North Vietnamese soldier, battlefield ruins, Kurtz standing before battlefield memorials, two American soldiers flanking a blindfolded VC suspect. "The VC knew his name by now," Willard comments, "and they were scared of him." Kurtz, the noble soldier of the spotless dossier, has become the American shadow warrior, mystical, preternatural, cruel, and deadly. This Kurtz is a precursor of John Rambo, especially in the second installment, *Rambo: First Blood Part II*, when the hero returns to Vietnam, an army of one, ready "to win this time" what half a million Americans could not win in decades.

And Willard himself has a precursor of sorts. Living now in Kurtz's camp, Lieutenant Colby (Scott Glenn) and his men, sent earlier on a mission similar to Willard's, have themselves become renegades. Theirs is the apostasy that lends ironic validation to the heroic myth, that presents it and confirms it in the only form that it can take in Vietnam: as America's fall from grace. Bedecked in face paint and enemy scalps, they evince the otherness that corrupts the myth even as it reveals its inevitable configuration and its fated consequence. And Kurtz, we do not doubt, knows all this better than the commanders—knows it and grieves it and embodies it. Hence "the horror!" Willard shall dispense a mercy where the commanders, by the same means, would but meanly terminate with extreme prejudice.

## The Rupture and the Uses of "Insanity"

Once General Corman ends his wistful meditation on the presumed causes of Kurtz's dereliction, he tenders his judgment: Kurtz has "very obviously . . . gone insane." The diagnosis (that is, the sham clinical assessment) startles Willard, who does a double take and only haltingly stutters his agreement. "Yes, sir. Very much so, sir. Obviously insane." But Corman's diagnosis, even if based on Kurtz's disturbing recordings and on the equally troubling reports from the field, tells us little about Kurtz, especially since it invokes "insanity" to justify the assassination. In fact, as we shall see, the "obvious" diagnosis mostly masks the commanders' desperate and foredoomed effort to salvage what might be left of the heroic myth. But by declaring Kurtz insane, they instead expose their own predicament, namely their own anxiety of legacy. The diagnosis, moreover, is designed not for healing but for oblivion. As the opening scene (Willard's destructive binge in the Saigon hotel room) comes to a close, so does The Doors' song, whose last line asserts that "all the children are insane." Such a context, however limited, already vitiates the authority of the commanders' diagnosis: if all the children are insane, what makes Kurtz's madness special? Still, references to "insanity," both general and particular, recur throughout the narrative. Indeed, Kurtz himself shall level countercharges of insanity at the commanders.

Late in the narrative, Willard exposes the speciousness of the commanders' rationale for the assassination. Following Chief Phillip's death, Willard at last reveals his mission to the two remaining crew members, Chef and Lance. "There's a Green Beret colonel up there who's gone insane, and I'm supposed to kill him." Here at least, the post hoc, ergo propter hoc fallacy (via the "and") becomes one more Vietnam-inspired paradox. Even so, when Willard first confronts Kurtz's ruined camp, he appeals to insanity as a signifier of the unspeakable. "Everything I saw told me that Kurtz had gone insane. The place was full of bodies—North

Vietnamese, Viet Cong, Cambodians." The place also includes severed heads strewn about (and eventually Chef's own head, which Kurtz drops in the lap of the caged and horrified Willard) and indeed much earlier, as the PBR nears the camp, a crucifixion. But "insanity," invoked in such a context, indicates only its own interpretive insufficiency in the face of the dissolute and depraved state of Kurtz's camp. Even Chef exposes the uselessness of insanity as a descriptor of the enormity. "This colonel guy, he's wacko, man," he says, but then he corrects himself. "He's worse than crazy. He's evil!" Perhaps "evil" too fails to explain this scene so dismally teeming with such ghastly sights, but at least it casts Kurtz's "horror" in moral and not merely psychological terms.

Long before he faces Kurtz, Willard learns to respect him. "The more I read and began to understand," he says while reading the dossier, "the more I admired him." But in his first personal encounter with Kurtz, when Willard's understanding has yet to crystallize, he speaks for the commanders so that his assessment of Kurtz seems wholly theirs and thus validates Kurtz's initial assessment that he, Willard, is only an "errand boy sent by grocery clerks to collect a bill":

**Willard:** I was sent on a classified mission, sir.
**Kurtz:** It's no longer classified, is it? What did they tell you?
**Willard:** They told me that you had gone totally insane and that your methods were unsound.

The agency behind the diagnosis reappears. It is the dehumanized, institutional, careerist "they," or as Kurtz depicts them earlier, "the assassins that accuse the assassin." In other words, the diagnosis of insanity reveals their own corrupt motives. Moments before his first interview with Kurtz, Willard surveys this lowest circle of America's Vietnam hell but lacks the words to describe it, so he determines that "everything" he sees tells him that "Kurtz has gone insane." But Willard's aperçu suggests a break from the commanders, for here insanity names, albeit inadequately, the abomination inhabiting the heart of the heroic myth. Hence Kurtz's own dark eloquence, unintelligible to Willard at this point, when he calls his condition not insanity but rather *horror* and when horror, as we see in the desolation and depravity of the place, describes not only the state of his soul but also the condition of the war.

Horror discredits America's claim to providential grace. And once the Loss historicizes the myth, horror reveals its abiding presence at the core of America's other imperial wars. Implacable as time, horror recasts the heroic myth as a source of the very savagery once held to characterize America's enemies.

"Confinement," Michel Foucault writes, "is explained, or at least justified, by the desire to avoid scandal."[16] The "scandal," as far as Willard's mission might be said to express it, is that in the midst of the devastation and the atrocities, the American renegade should yet insist on his heroic due, not despite but because of his moral waywardness. "There are aspects of evil," Foucault goes on to explain, "that have such a power of contagion, such a force of scandal that any publicity multiplies them infinitely. Only oblivion can suppress them."[17] Scandalized, or pretending to be so—"He's out there operating without any decent restraint," Colonel Lucas complains—the commanders spin their tale of an insane Kurtz, intending thereby to consign him to oblivion. "You understand, Captain," Lucas then admonishes, "that this mission does not exist, nor will it ever exist." Eventually, however, Willard stands in defiance of the commanders not only because he gives us a much more human and humane—yet no less evil—Kurtz but also because his voice-over so obviously transcends, in both form and content, the commanders' mandated termination. Indeed, the end of Kurtz fails to suppress the echoes of that inauspicious if all too resonant whisper, inexorable as the PBR's wake, that follows Willard back to America: "the horror! the horror!" (figure 6.2).

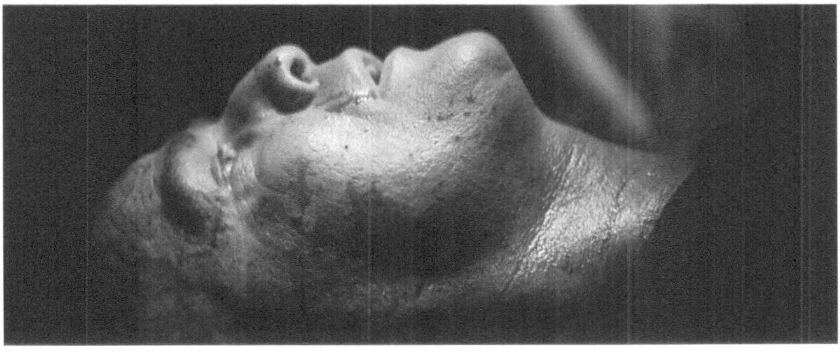

Figure 6.2. *Apocalypse Now*. Col. Walter E. Kurtz (Marlon Brando) in his last moments whispers "The horror! The horror!"

As the requisite for oblivion, the termination of Kurtz would reassign the heroic myth to a time before the rupture, to the last instant, extended indefinitely, when Walter E. Kurtz will be again the "brilliant, humanitarian man." Only after the termination can Kurtz somehow reclaim the fateful moment when "things started to slip," the time before the scandalous nightmares and the genocidal deeds, the time therefore before the rupture exposed the heroic myth itself as the source of the horror. Surely Kurtz's camp reveals atrocities hardly different, for sheer heinousness, from those that the VC cadres committed against the children of the village where the Special Forces, as Kurtz eventually relates, inoculated them for polio. But that similarity reveals not Kurtz's surrender to the methods and ideologies of the enemy, an apostasy, but rather the stunning recognition—"like a diamond bullet," as he puts it—of the ineradicable inherence of the rupture in the myth. The rupture is not, accordingly, at the "end" of the myth; it is not the myth's consequence, a separate, contingent occurrence from which it is yet possible to protect and preserve the myth. Rather, *the rupture abides in the myth*. The myth, even in its diminished form, may disclaim Vietnam on the basis of the Loss, and since all of America's other imperial wars were chronicled and attested victories, then they erased all possible distinction between myth and history. Before Vietnam, then, American history was a privileged affair, mythic in the ancient, foundational sense. Nonetheless, the rupture, though seeming to originate with Vietnam, reveals itself in the form of a palimpsest of the mythic narrative. Vietnam, the rupture, is always and already there, especially in the Vietnam meant to be excluded from the line of inheritance. Indeed, Vietnam becomes the reference point continually compelling, affirming, and inscribing the inescapably historical character of the heroic myth.

And so, America's Vietnam War passes into history and, baring (and bearing) the stigma of the Loss, comes at last to occupy its unwelcome spot in the line of America's wars. But in this arrangement, the rupture refers American history to the tragic course of earlier narratives—narratives of worlds from which America, since its beginnings, had invoked only for the sake of declaring its independence from them. Of course, in his condition as embodiment of the moral ruin that undergirds civilization's "sweetness and light," Kurtz becomes one with Conrad's prototype, Mr. Kurtz, the "universal genius" presiding over "the great demoralisation of the land." Yet, Walter Kurtz also mirrors Macbeth, the "peerless kinsman" who soon enough finds himself "in blood / Stepped in so far, that should I wade no more, / Returning were as tedious as go o'er." Moreover, Kurtz invites comparison with Sophocles's Ajax, the once-formidable warrior now cheated, dishonored, and cozened, bewailing his humiliation while torturing and mutilating the hapless beasts he takes for enemies. Kurtz is Achilles (as in *Achilles in Vietnam*, Jonathan Shay's great book on war trauma), his rage mollified at last by Priam's plea but only after he has effectively, except for the craven Paris, wiped out the Trojan lists. And perhaps Kurtz is the fallen Adam himself—the embodiment of the deeded perfection now everlastingly rebuked, his birthright forfeited and surrendered to history. "What Vietnam did to America via television," notes Lawrence Wright in CNN's series *The Sixties*, "was introduce us to a new kind of America, one that was not pure, one that committed the same kinds of atrocities that are always committed in war, but we had never allowed ourselves to see them."[18]

Indeed. But it was not television alone that revealed this other America and its connections to other epochs. In a span of some four centuries, from Mistick Fort (1637) to Sand Creek (1864), Wounded Knee (1890), Bud Dajo (1906), Bud Bagsak (1913), and My Lai (1968) and thence, lest we believe it all consigned to a past that cannot possibly return, to the Kandahar massacre in 2012, history itself shows both that America was enduringly capable of committing "the same kinds of atrocities" as other nations had committed earlier and that it promoted—by implied appeals to the heroic myth itself—a stultifying indifference to deeper meanings that might have amplified the genocidal thrust of those events. In Kurtz's Vietnam, the fable of American heroism—the myth of an entitlement held, however implicitly, to have been granted in perpetuity to America alone and proclaimed as the earthly deliverance from history and tragedy—becomes instead the narrative empowered to humanize a nation if only for its sins.

## "The Smell of Victory," Judgment, and the Heroic Legacy

Well into the river voyage, the men on the PBR spot a sampan and prepare to board it (over Willard's objections, since he wants to keep moving Kurtz-ward). Chief Phillips (Albert Hall) orders Chef aboard the sampan to search its cargo. Chef, terrified, glances at the contents from the safety of the PBR, but Phillips remains adamant, so Chef boards the sampan and rummages and scours erratically, just to show Phillips that there are no weapons on board. But as Chef moves toward an upturned yellow can lying against the port side, a young Vietnamese woman runs to stop him. Immediately Mr. Clean (Larry Fishburne) opens up with his M-60. Lance sprays the sampan with his M-16, as does Chef from the sampan's deck. The slaughter done, the Americans find a puppy under the yellow can. The young woman, badly wounded, begins to stir, and the men of the PBR, suddenly moved to pity, discuss taking her "to some friendlies." But Willard will not be delayed. Without further argument, he stands on the PBR's gunwale, pistol in his grip, and orders Chef out of the way. Even as Chief Phillips begins to cite "the book" on proper evacuation procedure for civilian casualties, Willard dispassionately, almost serenely, fires one shot, killing the woman instantly. He calmly says to Chief, "I told you not to stop. Now, let's go."

Early in the long Kilgore episode, which precedes the sampan massacre scene, a young Vietnamese woman runs toward a Huey as if for protection among the Americans, but instead she tosses in a grenade she had been hiding in her straw hat. It is no doubt some such deception that Chef feared when Phillips ordered him aboard the sampan. Where fear mingles freely and indistinctly with hatred, Robert Jay Lifton notes, Americans in Vietnam "could momentarily create the illusion that, in rounding up and killing small children, old people, and women from the villages, they had finally gotten the enemy to stand up and fight. That is the kind of illusion that took shape at My Lai and that can take shape in an atrocity-producing situation. It was not just My Lai; it was Vietnam."[19] Willard's summary execution of the wounded young woman casts the sampan massacre scene as more than an allusion to My Lai and other American atrocities in Vietnam. Taking his cue from Chief Phillip's feckless effort to transport the wounded woman to a hospital, Willard muses (in voice-over), "It was a way we had over here of living with ourselves. We'd cut them in half with a machine gun and give them a Band-Aid. It was a lie, and the more I saw of them the more I hated lies. Those boys [the PBR crew] were never going to look at me the same way again, but I felt like I knew one or two things about Kurtz that weren't in the dossier." This meditation anticipates Kurtz's story of another atrocity, one committed by the North Vietnamese and the VC against children whom Kurtz's Special Forces had only hours earlier inoculated against polio. The end of the anecdote is proverbial about the Loss: "Because it's judgment that defeats us," Kurtz says. Even in isolation from that episode (which I discuss further below), in relation to which it stands as a dread summation of America's Vietnam War, Kurtz's dark dictum reaffirms Willard's scorn for America's perfunctory, if not indeed hypocritical, compassion toward the Vietnamese. "Judgment," as Kurtz invokes it, both presupposes and manifests scruples, qualms, and conscience, all of it measured against and in accordance with an overarching ethic, a corpus of principles, say. But ethics and principles—laws, then—are wholly absent in Kurtz's Vietnam. So, the meaning of "judgment" here better approximates the anticipation of remorse than it does the incurred guilt following the dark deed. In war, judgment is the enemy of action.

Colonel Bill Kilgore may resemble a mythic American hero but mostly because he so unselfconsciously exposes the heroic myth to its own inherent and therefore subversive horrors. In his grotesque excesses, Kilgore may show some kinship with Kurtz. But Kilgore knows nothing of doubt, of judgment, and in this way he functions instead as Kurtz's foil. "He was one of those guys," Willard remarks at a beach party that Kilgore has all but dragged him and the PBR crew to, "that had that weird light around him. You just knew he wasn't going to get so much as a scratch here." In his last scene (in the 1979 release), Kilgore expresses his heartfelt regret that "someday this war's going to end." In this respect, Kilgore offers a stark contrast to Kurtz, whose dying pronouncement "The horror! The horror!" attests to the collapse of the myth under the weight of doubt and guilt, of judgment. In the original release of *Apocalypse Now*, the Kilgore episode is framed by massacres. Before we meet Kilgore (in early drafts of the screenplay he was named, even more coarsely, "Kharnage") we know him for the indiscriminate devastation that his unit visits on the Vietnamese. An Operation Arc Light raid—B-52 Stratofortress bombing missions that ran consecutively for eight years, each sortie carrying thirty tons of explosives[20]—precedes our first encounter with Kilgore's Air Cavalry. The helicopters that appear on the far side of the river, ready to join the fight (whether they are needed or not), belong to the unit that is to escort the PBR to the mouth of the Nung River. "It was the Air Cav, First of the Ninth," Willard says looking at it through binoculars. He also notices that "they were supposed to be waiting for us another thirty kilometers ahead." "Well!" he scoffs. "Airmobile. Those boys just couldn't stay put." The first cut from the long shots of the helicopters (we are still in the first of two villages that suffer imminent destruction) shows Kilgore's handiwork up close: in the chaos on the ground, a GI tends to a Vietnamese mother and her badly burned baby. Now, again in voice-over, Willard tells us that the 1st of the 9th "had cashed in its horses for choppers and gone tear-assing around Nam looking for the shit. They'd given Charlie a few surprises in their time here. What they were mopping up now hadn't even happened yet an hour ago." Kilgore operates with heedless audacity. It is no coincidence that he wears a cavalry hat and even has spurs on his cavalry boots, that he has a bugler play the cavalry charge before going into battle, or that his radio name is Big Duke Six. He has fashioned himself after not only the cavalry officers of the Indian Western but also "Duke" Wayne and is in Vietnam to fight "Indians," with helicopters as his cavalry.

Moreover, Kilgore represents America's disordered and easily distracted conscience in Vietnam, as in the "death cards" scene following the assault on the first village. Kilgore has been placing Air Cavalry-themed playing cards on dead VC cadres. "There isn't one worth a jack in the whole bunch," he says of the dead or wounded Vietnamese. But suddenly his attention shifts to a wounded enemy soldier lying face-up on the ground, holding his entrails in with a pot lid. So Kilgore, moved by the man's grit, shares the water from his canteen with him. But he absentmindedly pulls the canteen away the moment a trooper announces that Lance Johnson, the famous California surfer, is in their midst. Moments earlier, a trooper shouts into his bullhorn a proclamation—in English no less—of American compassion, a message utterly outrageous in this scene of widespread Vietnamese agony. "We will not hurt or harm you," the trooper blares. "We are here to help you. We are here to extend a welcome hand." As if such an outrageous incongruity were not cruel enough, a subsequent announcement later in the same scene doubles the irony: "We have a body count. Repeat. We have a body count." And to underscore the preposterousness of the whole sequence, a priest in camouflage celebrates mass in the midst of the ongoing devastation. Elsewhere in the village, a water buffalo flies tethered to a helicopter. Kilgore's Vietnam War is a veritable midway of American-made wonders, all of them featuring the variously slaughtered Vietnamese.

In Kilgore's world, surfing answers almost as much to mission as body count does. A mere "goofy foot" by his own admission, Kilgore stands in infantile awe of Lance's "nose-riding" and "cut-backs." Kilgore's war seems but a day job, and he will replicate middle-American suburban rituals with the same determination that he makes war. He likes "to finish operations early" and relax in the evenings. If you are Airmobile, then yours is an easy commute between the slaughter and the early-evening relaxation. Appropriately, memorably, Willard comments, "Kilgore had had a pretty good day for himself. They choppered in the T-bones and the beer and turned the LZ into a beach party. The more they tried to make it just like home, the more they made everybody miss it." Moments later, Willard approaches Kilgore with a map and shows him two possible sites where Kilgore's 1st Squadron, 9th Cavalry, 1st Cavalry Division—the 1/9—can escort the PBR. Kilgore tells him that one of the villages "is kind of hairy. . . . They have some pretty heavy ordnance." But when Kilgore asks Mike from San Diego (Kerry Rossall) whether he knows anything about Vin Drin Dop, Mike says, "That's a fantastic peak." Kilgore is as if transfixed by Mike's description of the surfing in that beach. Alas, Vin Drin Dop is "Charlie's point," Mike says. But Kilgore is so charmed by the possibility of a "six-foot peak" that he will have his helicopters "pick [the PBR] up and put it down like a baby, right where you want it." Mike, fearful still, objects: "It's Charlie's point." But Kilgore responds, "Charlie don't surf!" Surfing becomes a metaphor for America's insubstantial and untenable claim to moral ascendancy in Vietnam. In Kilgore's war, America's cultural (and military) vanity takes the form of the genocidal assault on Vin Drin Dop for the sake of surfing "tube city." So much for hearts and minds.

In noiseless flight accompanied only by choral voices on the soundtrack, the distant helicopters make their way to Vin Drin Dop. Soon, however, they begin to blast Wagner to "scare the hell out of the slopes," as Kilgore explains earlier. An abrupt cut presents Vin Drin Dop, silent, peaceful, the women tending their gardens. A young teacher in a white ao dai leads the schoolchildren (all in their neat uniforms) from the tile-roofed schoolhouse to the spotless village square. (These shots function as the Vietnam War's version of the peaceful Indian village just before the cavalry's assault, the sort of surprise attack one can see in John Ford's *The Searchers* and in Ralph Nelson's 1970 rendition of the 1864 Sand

Creek Massacre, *Soldier Blue.*) Already the villagers are running along a bridge, some arming themselves with their cached weapons. In the cut that follows, the helicopters begin firing on the village, and the reverse shot shows villagers in a panic, helpless before the onslaught. Even as the slaughter continues, Kilgore's Huey flies over the beach, and with exuberance Kilgore asks Lance, "What do you think?" Lance, believing that Kilgore refers to the devastation below, replies, "Wow! It's really exciting, man!" Kilgore quickly corrects him: "No, no! The *waves!*" Moments later, Kilgore notes in frustration that the tide doesn't come in for another six hours. When Willard, exasperated, challenges him at last—"Goddamn it! Don't you think it's a little risky for R&R?"—Kilgore, vexed yet still determined, replies, "If I say it's safe to surf this beach, Captain, it's safe to surf this beach!" When he strips to the waist, we think he is going to join the reluctant surfers, but instead he reaches for the radio transmitter and calls for the bombing of the treeline. "Bomb them into the Stone Age, son," Kilgore orders, recalling the infamous remark attributed to Gen. Curtis LeMay.

Seemingly out of nowhere, the F-5 jets swoop down and drop their loads of napalm. As it did in the first image of the narrative, the jungle explodes in an all-devouring extravagance of flames and black smoke. And now Kilgore, surrounded by "that weird light" that told you "he wasn't going to get so much as a scratch" in the war and standing up straight while all the others still cower, asks, "Do you smell that?" He gazes serenely into the distance and, as if in a trance, answers his own question. "Napalm, son. Nothing else in the world smells like that." Relaxed, crouching by the edge of Willard and Lance's foxhole, Kilgore continues his napalm rapture. "I love the smell of napalm in the morning. You know, one time we had a hill bombed for twelve hours, and when it was all over, I walked up. We didn't find one of them, not one stinking dink body. But the smell, you know, that gasoline smell—the whole hill smelled like [*pregnant pause*] victory" (figure 6.3). Now back in medium shot (Willard is once again in the frame), Kilgore says with heartfelt sadness, "Someday this war's going to end."

Kilgore's is the way to American victory in Vietnam, victory by way of genocide, of the scorched-earth strategy that leaves "not one stinking" enemy body behind, that (as Calgacus claims in Tacitus's *Agricola*) makes a desert and calls it peace, the kind of war that not only kills the enemy

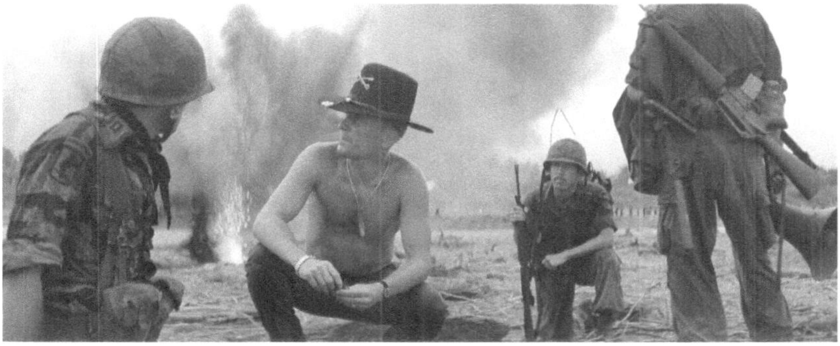

Figure 6.3. *Apocalypse Now*. Lt. Col. Bill Kilgore (Robert Duvall) in his reverie about "the smell of napalm in the morning."

but also causes them to disappear. Several times in the latter stages of the Kilgore episode, late in the beach party scene, we see far in the background a line of twenty or so Vietnamese prisoners moving along the shoreline. The summoned napalm strike consumes them so that again, as when Kilgore went up the bombed-out hill and didn't find even one body, so too now the Vietnamese prisoners in the background simply vanish. Butchery for the sake of surfing may provide a plain enough example of the "banality of evil," but it also portends the Loss. Kilgore's is the way to America's moral ruin.

"'Someday this war's going to end,'" Willard says in voice-over, repeating Kilgore's lament as the PBR finally leaves the 1/9 behind. "If that's how Kilgore fought the war, I began to wonder what they really had against Kurtz." Why indeed do the commanders abet Kilgore and condemn Kurtz? Not long after the Kilgore episode, Willard (in voice-over) reads an intercepted letter in which Kurtz explains to his son the actions that led the commanders to accuse him of murder: "In a war there are many moments for compassion and tender action. There are many moments for ruthless action, what is often called ruthless, but may in many circumstances be only clarity, seeing clearly what there is to be done, and doing it—directly, quickly, awake, looking at it." "Ruthless" here refers to the stark, utterly reckless, wholly unmediated fury of the mortal encounter, the desperate lethal intimacy in which the victims, as Willard himself knows, are "close enough to blow their last breath in my face." By contrast, Kilgore's indifference toward Vietnamese life seems to answer to the requirements of not only military efficiency but also extravagant, which is to say genocidal kill ratios. "Death from Above" is neatly painted on the nose of Kilgore's helicopter. But Kilgore's way of killing from afar spares him a cheek-by-jowl encounter with the enemy such as Willard's. The truth is, however, that Kilgore lacks even a trace of the reflective humanity that we see in Kurtz and in Willard. Indeed, it is this lack that makes Kilgore adept at genocide. It is impossible to imagine him in any but this particular iteration. If he does reflect on war, it is only to lament the day the war ends.

Freed at last from the tiger cage, Willard, exhausted, malarial, lolls listlessly close to Kurtz's cot. Suddenly, Kurtz speaks out of the darkness. "I've seen the horrors, horrors that you've seen." A shadow merely, he now stands over Willard. "But you have no right to call me a murderer," Kurtz says. "You have a right to kill me. You have a right to do that, but you have no right to judge me. It's impossible for words to describe what is necessary to those who do not know what horror means. Horror. Horror has a face. And you must make a friend of horror. Horror and moral terror are your friends. If they are not, then they are enemies to be feared. They are truly enemies."

And now Kurtz summons the image—stark, appalling, abominable—from the depths of a fiendish deed:

> I remember when I was with Special Forces—it seems a thousand centuries ago. We went into a camp to inoculate some children. We'd left the camp after we had inoculated the children for polio. And this old man came running after us, and he was crying. He couldn't say. We went back there, and they had come and hacked off every inoculated arm. There they were in a pile, a pile of little arms. And I remember: I, I, I cried, I wept like some grandmother. I wanted to tear my teeth out. I didn't know what I wanted to do. And I want to remember it. I never want to forget it. I never want to forget.

But now Kurtz pivots toward his realization, unsettling and unexpected yet also transformative, of the meaning of the ghastly scene, namely his unapologetic embrace of the sense behind this enormity:

> And then I realized, like I was shot . . . with a diamond bullet right through my forehead, and I thought, "My God! The *genius* of that! The genius! The *will* to do that—perfect, genuine, complete, crystalline, pure!" And then I realized they were stronger than we because they could stand it. These were not monsters. These were men, trained cadres—these men who fought with their hearts, who have families, who have children, who are filled with love. But they have the strength, the *strength* to do that. If I had ten divisions of those men, then our troubles here would be over very quickly. You have to have men who are moral and, at the same time, who are able to utilize their primordial instincts to kill without feeling, without passion, without judgment—without judgment. Because it's judgment that defeats us.

The encounter introduces Kurtz to a fidelity so inviolate ("perfect, genuine, complete, crystalline, pure") that only blood, pain, and ruthlessness—absolute sacrifice, then—can properly express it. Such fidelity, however paradoxical, strained, or seemingly perverse, implicitly rejects indecision and aversion and thus doubt and guilt, perhaps even irony. Certainly it repudiates the modern American anxieties that Kurtz subsumes under "judgment," the "judgment that defeats us." A group of America's best ventures into a village presuming to instantiate the grand moral gesture of American exceptionalism, that is, winning hearts and minds by disinterestedly lavishing upon the benighted the happy consequence of American know-how. Yet, no sooner do they leave the village than the enemy reclaims the scene and then fiercely confutes, indeed *excises*, this self-congratulatory, patriarchal benevolence. Surely somewhere in this horrific calculus the enemy demonstrates, to recall Walter Benjamin's famous axiom, that "there is no document of civilization which is not at the same time a document of barbarism."[21] The American syringe induces the VC machete. (Here, then, is an apt if discomfiting scorn for Canavan's arrogant claim, in *The Real Glory*, that Edward Jenner's invention of vaccination will live forever.) In this heinous deed, Kurtz insists, these men revealed a humanity beyond the ken of America's "timid, lying morality." Thus, despite the enormity of their deed—indeed, because of it—Kurtz will have Willard believe that these cadres are "filled with love."

Kurtz's refusal to condemn the enemy as well as his ability to see in the pitiless deed itself *their*—the enemy's own—hope for victory arise from his realization that such cruelty inheres in America's heroic myth itself. The savage Other, he now understands, inhabits no "exterior," is nothing like the distant, aberrant exotic. Accordingly, Kurtz sees the rupture as belonging to and, indeed, originating in the heroic myth itself, thus betokening the end of the myth even as it declares the historical impossibility of its regeneration. These men, these cadres, rising before Kurtz out of the spectacle of pitiless brutality will win the war. In the image of the pile of little arms, in this vision that blazons in innocent blood the purifying excision of America's viral invasion of Vietnam, Kurtz sees the enemy's radical rejection of not only Western medicine but also the moral claims of a nation as efficient in preventing dread diseases as in engulfing a foreign land in flames. Vaccinating a few children for polio while bombing their country to utter ruin is here of a piece with the American habit of cutting "them in half with a machine gun" and giving them a "Band-Aid."

Kurtz may dream of ending America's "troubles" in Vietnam "very quickly." Yet, that same impracticable dream together with its own secret desire to annul history, further exposes the ironies within the heroic myth, for the myth would seek not only acquittal but also vindication, would demand the dissolution of the nauseating ambiguity, the indecision and the second-guessing, the self-serving paradoxes, the outright lies, and the unspeakable atrocities, and, most of all, the resultant and ceaseless guilt. Kurtz's doomed yearning for release from guilt would likewise produce a myth free of history's adjudications. Thus only would the heroic myth abide, with hardly a thought to the possibility that such brutality never really originated in an Other—in one always and already considered distant, beyond the pale, one who could be pointed to and segregated, to be then vilified and exterminated—but instead in one that had ever been America's own, intimately, inseparably, aboriginally, the very soul and center of the heroic myth. The Loss in Vietnam meant that American savagery would not thereafter lie swaddled in folds of national glory or tucked away all but unremarked in a dark precinct of the City upon a Hill. Savagery, not insanity, became the true scandal. Savagery was the legacy.

Kurtz's "horror" incorporates not only American atrocities in Vietnam but also the realization that America's heroic myth served as a cover for the savagery abiding in the American soul. The continuity of the heroic myth, which America had long learned to trust as the predictable reaffirmation of its exceptional legacy, became instead the periodic eruption of violence out of a core of those boisterously proclaimed principles and ideals that the myth had enduringly claimed to defend. And now at last Willard, emerging stealthily from the river, is ready to carry out the assassination. "Everybody wanted me to do it," he says, "him [Kurtz] most of all. I felt like he was up there, waiting for me to take the pain away. . . . Even the jungle wanted him dead, and that's who he really took his orders from, anyway." In an ecstasy of empathy—perhaps the supreme paradox in a narrative and a war built on paradoxes—Willard butchers Kurtz. Willard is the executioner, the enforcer on this day of reckoning and rupture, this apocalypse, now, for hero and myth alike. Kurtz's passivity before Willard's wild slashing hastens his own end and the myth's end as well.

Following the assassination, Willard rifles through Kurtz's modest belongings and comes upon an urgent message, in heavy red pencil, scrawled by an intemperate hand across one of the neatly typed pages of the report titled "The Role of Democratic Force in the Underdeveloped World." The words in red pencil give pithy expression to the full sense of the horror in their one desperate directive, even graphically depicting the trajectory to ground zero:

> Drop
> the
> BomB
> EXTERMINATE
> Them ALL!

The "Them ALL" of the scribble includes many more living creatures than those referenced much earlier by the recorded voice that urged genocide: "We must incinerate them. . . . Village after village. Army after army." The "Them ALL" is unsparingly inclusive, implicitly lumping Vietnamese and Americans indiscriminately in a vision of the end time. The narrative that was to affirm Kurtz's exceptional status now denies him even the ancient blessings, those old immunities and exemptions that the capricious gods vouchsafed to the old heroes who survive the terrors of hubris only to live out their days in an accursed wisdom.

Shirtless, besmeared with Kurtz's blood and still bedaubed with camouflage face paint, Willard appears atop the long staircase of Kurtz's temple. In his right hand Willard carries the machete, in his left Kurtz's papers. The natives gathered around the stairway kneel before him perhaps in gratitude for their deliverance, perhaps in submission to the new deity. Willard comes down a few steps and throws down the machete and then joins the throng. The myth of heroic continuity had always depended on "regeneration through violence" for its very being, but the ritual killing of Kurtz negates even the possibility of a resumption of, let alone the regeneration of, hero or myth. Still, Willard carries Kurtz's papers—the "story," as he told us much earlier, that is "really a confession"—with the quondam epic now turned jeremiad. Kurtz's papers document the dark complacencies of imperial policy, the lies that await their apocalyptic end, the righteously self-destructive rage clamoring for a reckoning. But the papers, including the red-ink scrawl, do not yet reflect the full range of a vision that can so tenderly yearn for a son's understanding while proclaiming the inescapable, all-pervasive "horror." Thus, horror identifies not only the genocidal desire but also the astonished realization that America's dearest convictions could have so unaccountably and yet so decidedly resulted in the moral darkness of the Vietnam War.

Persistent, importunate, the voice of "Almighty" (the code name for the planned bombing of Kurtz's camp) crackles repeatedly over the PBR's radio, demanding a decision from Willard. But Willard turns the radio off, affirming this one last time that his mission was never the commanders' own and, more so, implicitly spurning the Kilgore solution, that is, the devastation that leaves "not one stinking" body in its aftermath. Also, Willard implicitly repudiates the nuclear option called for by the red-pencil scrawl. The devil's bargain whereby America became a military "Almighty" stands now discredited, exposing its presumption that military might begets moral right.

With Willard at the wheel (and only the catatonic Lance for its crew), the PBR backs away from the dock, and almost at once a superimposed stone idol appears, taking up the rightmost third of the screen, sharing the narrative space with a close-up of Willard, and reminding us of its much earlier appearance when Willard let loose his demons in the hotel room in Saigon. Does the idol escort or usher the two Americans out of Vietnam? Does it mock the heroic myth, just as it might have once mocked France's *grande mission civilisatrice* after Dien Bien Phu in 1954? Faint and whispered, as if echoing his dying words moments earlier, Kurtz's utterance "The horror! The horror!" appears, resonant, on the soundtrack. Disembodied, reverberant, portentous, it reechoes itself, evoking the centuries of accumulated horrors, each piled on the other as if marking each replication of a primal sin. The utterance echoes beyond the man's mortal days, becoming the measure of America's heroic type and of the myth itself—a judgment of them, a curse upon them—the last words to gainsay first prerogatives. For an instant, the idol and the close-up of Willard are almost precisely superimposed. As Willard moves his head, his image dissolves into darkness, but the idol, now shrouded in a greenish smoke, remains onscreen one moment more. The disappearance of the last American in the presence of the indigenous idol becomes a correlative of the severed inoculated arms: Vietnam eradicates America as a ruinous virus. America's heroic myth, now demystified, passes into history as Vietnam's own horror. And the idol, alone onscreen, reclaims the land, the culture, and the history, indeed the victory. Long before this last moment, Willard noted that the crew of the PBR "weren't looking for anything more than a way home." "Trouble is," he added, "I had been back there, and I knew that it just didn't exist anymore." If there is now no America back home, how can there be one in Vietnam? On their way to Kurtz, Willard witnessed Americans—Kilgore and the surfers, say, or the libidinous louts at the USO show, the commanders at Nha Trang, or perhaps even the PBR crew with its genocidal tendencies against the native people—Americans all desperately trying to make Vietnam "just like home" and dismally failing at it the harder they tried.

The enemy's defiant suspension of judgment unveils his "strength," the "will" (or so Kurtz), but it also shields his unrepentant cruelty, keeps it from spilling over into its own horror. This calculated rejection of compassion will ensure the victory of the North Vietnamese and the VC if only because the opposite of that rejection, a "judgment" that would produce the sort of compassion evident in the inoculating mission, is certain to "defeat us." But if we are to take the ghastly carnage of Kurtz's camp as evidence of his own attempt to suspend or circumvent judgment, then "the horror" originates in the failed attempt to act "without judgment." To say therefore that America lost the war because it judged is at least to suggest that America, however bereft of purpose, nonetheless reaped a new humanity from its tragic experience in Vietnam. Such meager harvests seldom win wars; and in Vietnam, no less than in the mythic continuum, winning was ever all.

In the American centuries before the Vietnam War, the heroic myth populated the national narrative with tales that confidently assumed the mythic origins of American history. But this assumption, amounting to an article of faith, came to suggest America's inherent distrust of its own humanity—the nation's better angels maligned as its manifest weakness—hence, perhaps, the travesties of empathy in *Apocalypse Now*, the embarrassed and embarrassing gestures of stunted compassion yielding to outright cruelty: a water canteen yanked away from a dying man holding his guts in with a pot lid, "Band-Aids" for those cut in half with machine guns, and vaccines that fail to protect the children from unspeakable ruthlessness. But as long as the myth could be upheld, what were such halfway measures and botched gestures compared to actually winning in Vietnam? In an ecstasy of triumph, who would care to suggest that *winning itself* accounts for—even as it exposes—the scandalous brutality at the core of the heroic myth?

The rupture, perhaps because it marks and describes America's fall "into" history and tragedy, engendered a reactionary impulse to restore the heroic myth. In this view, the rupture was not Loss—that is, a clean break with the continuity of the heroic myth and its triumphs—but rather mere disruption, something easily enough mended, seamlessly stitched, perhaps by invading Grenada (Ronald Reagan) or by burying the "ghosts of Vietnam . . . beneath the sands of the Arabian desert,"[22] as President George H. W. Bush declared in the immediate aftermath of the Persian Gulf War. In this view of the war, the rupture is but a cautionary tale: this Vietnam, it tells itself, this unheroic, helpless, self-commiserating confessional of a tragic war, is what happens when we defer to "judgment."

Perhaps some such plot twist on the rupture loomed already before the broken nation on March 30, 1971, when Lt. William Calley, the chief criminal at My Lai (March 16, 1968), addressed the military tribunal that had a day earlier found him guilty of mass murder. "If I have committed a crime," he said, "the only crime I've committed is in judgment of my values. Apparently I valued my troops' lives more than I did that of the enemy."[23] Calley invoked "judgment" not as a source of moral suasion but instead as a means to a feckless—and clearly unrepentant—stab at self-exoneration. Moreover, My Lai, as he would have it, was just one more battle against an enemy, not a raging orgy of atrocities directed against women, children, and old people. His "values," then, in his narrative bore no relation to the massacre, since the assault that most of us called a massacre was in fact meant to save the lives of his men even as they raped and pillaged and burned and killed. And only now had he learned, as one surprised, that the indiscriminate slaughter of women, children, and old people was not, as he had judged, a virtue to invoke in his own defense.

Soon enough the time would come when Vietnam might be counted among America's victories, for it is certain that Ronald Reagan had such a thing in mind when he recast the Loss as a "noble cause"—if America's had not quite been a military victory, it had certainly been a moral one. Not surprisingly, then, the rupture became the way back to the myth's continuity. When John Rambo asks, "Do we get to win this time?" the "time" inevitably unfolds *after* the Vietnam War, thus after history, then myth again, as if history had never been. So, then, might our leaders have asked themselves before Kuwait in 1991, before Afghanistan in 2001, and before Iraq in 2003, "Do we get to win this time?" Still, the longing to revitalize the myth would inevitably recall history from oblivion not only in the memory and presence of the Loss but also in the very determination to forget it. Here, then, in this dilemma lurks already the damning evidence of an anxiety, the anxiety of a legacy in the end shaped by both the historical Loss and the continued presence of America's heart of darkness beating wildly against the substance and being of its dearest myth.

# CHAPTER 7

# After John Wayne

## Mythic Legacies, Clint Eastwood, and the Paths to *American Sniper*

"I say, young gentleman, may Providence bless your undertaking, which is altogether for good; and remember, that to outwit the knaves it is lawful to practice things, that may not be naturally the gift of a white skin."
—James Fenimore Cooper, *The Last of the Mohicans*

"Eye, sartain—finger, lightening—aim, death."
—James Fenimore Cooper, *The Deerslayer*

### *Oscar Presents: The War Movies and John Wayne*

On November 27, 1977, ABC TV preempted its regular 9:00 P.M. program, the *Sunday Night Movie*, for a two-hour special titled *Oscar Presents: The War Movies and John Wayne.*[1] Now in 1977, while the miasma of the Loss still hung noisomely over the nation, John Wayne, hosting the show, sought to memorialize the good old wars and the good old movies about them.

As if heralding the different war films soon to come, however, Hollywood had released Robert Aldrich's *Twilight's Last Gleaming* two months before Wayne's special. The protagonist, a rogue US Air Force general named Lawrence Dell (Burt Lancaster), breaks out of prison, gains access to nine siloed Titan nuclear missiles, and threatens to start World War III if the president does not release documents in which the Pentagon admits that there is no hope of winning the Vietnam War, and yet, in spite of the dismal consensus, still decides that the war must be continued in order to prove American resolve to the Soviet Union. Less than three months after the special, Hollywood released *The Boys from Company C* (Furie) and *Coming Home* (Ashby), both in February 1978. Conscious or not of these impending releases, the Thanksgiving special seemed to prepare the nation to resist movies certain to be much different from those that Hollywood had churned out throughout the decades since World War II and even earlier, such as *The Real Glory.*

*The War Movies* (to abridge the special's title) presents many clips from films starring John Wayne and as many perhaps from other movies. But for the notable exception of the clips in a segment hosted by Jeff Bridges (discussed below), all the clips, we can rest assured, carry the imprimatur of Wayne and the Academy of Motion Pictures Arts and Sciences. The clips, all of them from fictional narratives, are intended to show us actual (or, at the insistence of the presenters, "true" or "real") American men and women at war and in wartime. Most of the clips are of World War II narratives, and Wayne and all but one of the other presenters proffer unabashedly nostalgic versions of America—almost exclusively *white* America—at war.

Wayne "hosts" the show, but his very presence, the product of half a century of heroic roles, proclaims him the undisputed hero of the special. More important, Wayne serves as the program's "historian," appropriating history's narrative authority in order to authenticate and promote the premised realities of these mythic narratives. The special's uncritically held assumption—namely that these movies, these myths, are for all intents and purposes uncontested deeds and events of lived historical experiences—at once exposes and subverts the inversion of roles whereby Wayne, who did not serve in the military, now empowers his mythic persona as the source of historical authority. Accordingly, he becomes a correlative of the show's own unblushing arrogation of a "history" that is sourced in myth.

Looking about as tuckered out as his own J. B. Books in *The Shootist,* Wayne stands in the boiler room of a battleship. But this boiler room teems implausibly with old 5,000-watt light fixtures from a movie set. Thus, cinema's visual economy readily reaffirms the vital links given already in the show's title: the war, the movies, John Wayne. Wayne quickly informs us that Hollywood made some 1,700 movies during the years of World War II. Some of them, he explains, were intended to help

Americans forget about the war for a while, but "others," he continues, now announcing his role as historian, "showed us what it was really like, what it was all about." Hollywood, so the bold purport, had in fact *documented* America's struggle even while *dramatizing* it.

Each of the program's segments (bracketed by commercial breaks) stakes out a broad topic. Following Wayne's introduction, Walter Matthau presents a segment on wartime humor. It includes clips from, for instance, Abbott and Costello in *Buck Privates* (Lubin, 1941) as well as the rousing last scene of *This Is the Army* (Curtiz, 1943), featuring the Irving Berlin number "This Time" (choreographed by the character played by Ronald Reagan). A subsequent segment, presented by the actress Brenda Vaccaro, addresses romantic entanglements during the war.

Slightly more than half an hour into the show, Wayne introduces Louise Fletcher, who was still basking in the glow of her Oscar for her Nurse Ratched in *One Flew over the Cuckoo's Nest* (Forman, 1975). Reminding us of the American nurses trapped in Bataan at the time of the Japanese invasion of the Philippines, Fletcher notes that "this was a woman's war too." Yet, not ten minutes later she tells us that the darkest days of the war "called for heroes, and one man, perhaps more than any other, became Hollywood's symbol of the rough, tough, fearless fighting man, as American as the Rocky Mountains: John Wayne." The old Wayne mendacity was on again. The cultural icon was the battlefield hero. Fletcher's introduction cuts to the scene from *Back to Bataan* (Dmytryk, 1945) in which Wayne, as Col. Joseph Madden, receives news of the American surrender on April 9, 1942. There follows right away the first shot of John Stryker in *Sands of Iwo Jima*, the young marines in the mess tent wondering aloud where their new drill sergeant is, and Stryker parting a tent flap and announcing, "He's here." Thus, *The War Movies* takes us in a trice from the calamitous news of MacArthur's retreat and Gen. Jonathan Wainwright's surrender at Bataan to victory on Iwo Jima three years later. So cloyingly unctuous is Fletcher's segment on the matter of Wayne's heroism that it prompts an intervention from Wayne himself. At the close of the segment, Wayne returns and in a wry, self-deprecating tone says, "I was brave." Not even Wayne himself could gloss over the sham, even if his ironic interjection fell far short of acknowledging—let alone apologizing for—not only his failure to serve but also the lies that long veiled the failure.

## *The War Movies* and . . . Jeff Bridges?

These World War II movies, according to Wayne, will "bring back a lot of memories for a lot of us" but will also "let our children know what it was like to be alive then." He thus calls to mind the good war that the "children"—John Wayne's "boys," as in the trailer for *Sands of Iwo Jima*—missed out on, the war they had lacked in their own recently ended and lost war. And now American memory, co-opted by this recrudescence of unapologetic nostalgia posing as history, would in effect deny that the Vietnam War had ever even been. Still, Oscar included (if on sufferance) the perspective of a representative "boy," a delegate for the disinherited. Well into the program's second hour, Jeff Bridges, even then a celebrity baby boomer, introduces a segment of his own. Bridges links two Hollywood generations: his own and his father Lloyd's. But the Loss that came to characterize the son's war precluded his presence in the program's triumphalist segments and thus set him apart from the unblushing self-regard saturating the other segments.

Bearded and in faded jeans—surely an interloper hippie—Bridges in effect introduces a schism of sorts within the Hollywood World War II canon. *Home of the Brave* (Robson, 1949), released in the same year as *Sands of Iwo Jima*, addresses racism in the US military. Here Private Finch, Lloyd Bridges's character, continually defends the squad's only Black man, Pvt. Peter Moss (James Edwards), against the racist slurs of a squad mate, T. J. Everett (Steve Brodie). Even Finch, however, comes within one syllable of the full measure of obloquy. "You yellow-bellied nig . . . ," he snaps at Moss in a particularly tense scene before catching himself.[2] Even now in 1977, Wayne "was unhappy about the inclusion of a scene" from *Home of the Brave* "because it did not reflect what he thought of as the reality of the American fighting man."[3] Bridge's inclusion of Billy Wilder's World War II prisoner-of-war story *Stalag 17* (1953) might have vexed Wayne on personal grounds as well. The film opens with the voice-over of Cookie (Gil Stratton Jr.), a prisoner of war and a sort of sidekick to the protagonist, Sgt. J. J. Sefton (William Holden). "I don't know about you," Cookie begins, "but it always makes me sore when I see those war pictures, all about flying leathernecks and submarine patrols and frogmen and guerrillas in the Philippines." Cookie's grievances readily identify contemporary Wayne war movies beginning, in his list, with *The Flying Leathernecks* (Ray, 1951), about US Marine Corps airmen, and *Operation Pacific* (Waggner, 1951), about submarine warfare. And in *Back to Bataan*, Wayne organizes "guerrillas in the Philippines."[4] But Cookie's introduction implies as well a general rebuke to Wayne himself for his failure to serve, and his sardonic voice-over prepares us for Sefton's unsparing cynicism, directed especially at war profiteering but also at his fellow prisoners of war, whom he considers dupes of the war machine. This theme of Americans in conflict with each other during the war also appears in a clip from *The Caine Mutiny* (1954)—directed by Edward Dmytryk, who had been removed from the Hollywood blacklist only two years earlier—in which Captain Queeg (Humphrey Bogart) exhibits disturbingly erratic and patently craven behavior. *The Young Lions* (1958), also directed by Dmytryk, addresses two topics that would have been proscribed in wartime films. The film gives both voice and humanity to a German officer, Lt. Christian Diestl (Marlon Brando), and exposes anti-Semitism as a blight on the US Army itself. Four American Aryan types severely beat their own squad-mate, Pvt. Noah Ackerman (Montgomery Clift), who is Jewish. Yet, when the half-starved Diestl stumbles upon a Nazi concentration camp recently emptied of its prisoners, he refuses food from the camp's commandant, whom he knows to have participated in the extermination of Jews. Last in Jeff Bridges's segment are clips from *Mister Roberts* (Ford and Le Roy, 1955) featuring the incompetent and buffoonish skipper of the cargo tender USS *Reluctant*, Captain Morton (James Cagney). Morton's hopes for promotion depend entirely on foiling the plans of his efficient, well-liked Lt. (junior grade) Doug Roberts (Henry Fonda), who has applied for a combat assignment. Roberts eventually gets his transfer and dies in a naval battle. Morton never gets his promotion. But Wayne will have the last word before the Bridges segment is quite done. "A few movies," Wayne says, fairly scowling at the camera, "may have taken it upon themselves to find fault with the American fighting man." Wayne's balky meddling cuts, outlandishly, crassly, to the first scene of *Patton* (Schaffner, 1970), when Patton (George C. Scott), alone on a stage and with a huge American flag behind him, exhorts his armies to heroic action. *Patton* redivivus was just the thing to dispel the haze of incertitude and equivocation, the unnerving demurrals, and even the judicious cowardice in the clips of the Bridges segment.

When *The War Movies* comes out of commercial one last time, Wayne is standing between two larger-than-life-size Oscars, sentinels of sorts watching over the nation's greatest movie hero. Wayne's sign-off does not surprise. "And so, from Oscar, a salute to the movies of wartime and their indelible portrait of the best of what we were." Such "best" of America—"the best years of our lives," to invoke the title of that great war movie—was already three decades in the past. "We are grateful," Wayne concludes, "that [Hollywood war movies] were there to illuminate our heritage and enrich our lives." The end credits roll thick and fast while the invasion scenes from *Sands of Iwo Jima* play in the background. Not many of the viewers who had yet to succumb to the tryptophan torpor of the leftover turkey might have realized that *The War Movies*, even as it sought to "illuminate our heritage," had failed to mute—might have in fact intensified—the anxiety that still lurked, as ever, in the exultant chronicles of American heroism. The stubborn slog through the mush of a contrived history subsumed war's horrors under a fantasized national memory and but for rare moments presented "Oscar" himself as a false witness.

## Clint Eastwood and the Heroic Legacy

The rise of Clint Eastwood to "iconic" cultural status roughly coincides with the relative decline of John Wayne's own. Eastwood's *The Outlaw Josey Wales* (1976) was released less than two months before *The Shootist* but grossed approximately two and a half times more at the box office.[5] Even before *Josey Wales*, however, Eastwood's star had been long enough in the ascendant to all but compel Wayne to star in two lamentable urban cop movies, *McQ* (Sturges, 1974) and *Brannigan* (Hickox, 1975), both of which were clearly patterned after the first two of Eastwood's Dirty Harry Callahan stories, *Dirty Harry* (Siegel, 1971) and *Magnum Force* (Post, 1973), as well as after *Coogan's Bluff* (Siegel, 1968). No doubt Hollywood thrives on imitation, on rip-offs even, but here was the great American hero, Wayne, old, ailing, and stubbornly refusing retirement, submitting instead to these pathetic facsimiles of the upstart Eastwood. By 1968, Eastwood had established a rough sort of stardom with a well-crafted persona that entirely erased his fresh-faced Rowdy Yates of the TV series

*Rawhide* (1959–1966). Under the direction of Sergio Leone, Eastwood suddenly became the laconic and cynical Man with No Name (whatever his sobriquet may be in each movie, "Joe," "Manco," "Blondie") in Leone's so-called Dollars Trilogy: *A Fistful of Dollars* (1964; US 1967), *For a Few Dollars More* (1965; US 1967), and *The Good, the Bad, and the Ugly* (1966; US 1967). Notably absent from these three is the classic Western's affirmation of exceptional nationhood. There is little that inspires the Man with No Name to disinterested self-sacrifice on behalf of a higher national destiny or of a more equitable apportionment of the national wealth. He may not be entirely heartless, but the profit motive abets even the more gratifyingly humane outcomes of his violent interventions. Moreover, the limited moral returns that follow the climactic shootout are obscured by characterizations of the American West as the source and site of rampant corruption and greed. Besides, the hero's six-gun never seems more than merely magical, more akin to the six-gun of Western B movies that can fire seven or more shots from a six-shot pistol without reloading. Still, "magical" is not always mythic. In *The Good, the Bad, and the Ugly*, for example, the gun that makes the Man with No Name wealthy fails to create a better world or affirm a new order or identify a mythic successor. The magical gun declares that the shocking body count in the hero's wake (adding considerably to the carnage of the American Civil War, which serves as grim background throughout much of the action) serves to obscure any reemergence of national virtues.

The Man with No Name never leaves behind a heroic bequest, for unlike the hero of the classic Western, he has no identifiable heirs. The Eastwood sidekick, even when he seems to possess attributes that identify him as an heir to the heroic legacy, almost always comes to an end that denies him presence in the final scenes. When he doesn't predecease the hero—as do, for example, Lightfoot (Jeff Bridges) in *Thunderbolt and Lightfoot* (Cimino, 1974) or Jamie (Sam Bottoms) in *Josey Wales*—the Eastwood sidekick is absent from the climactic shootout, absent both as heir and witness. Thus, Chico (Reni Santoni) in *Dirty Harry* gets shot well before the last scene and cannot be present when Harry confronts "Scorpio" (Andy Robinson) the final time. Crushing remorse after his one killing compels *Unforgiven*'s Schofield Kid (Jaimz Woolvett) to renounce, indeed condemn, the violence he once glorified. These enforced absences provide an ironic commentary of their own on the tragedy that inheres in the myth. As we will see, however, the fate of the Eastwood heir will sustain a profound transformation in *Gran Torino*, a non-Western that nonetheless deftly tracks the evolution of the Eastwood protagonist with his sidekick.

Four Eastwood movies following *The Good, the Bad, and the Ugly* and *Hang 'Em High* (Post, 1968), give us a far different protagonist than the one that by now might have been referred to as a persona. In one such movie, *Paint Your Wagon* (Logan, 1969) Eastwood, implausibly enough, sings. In another, *Two Mules for Sister Sara* (Siegel, 1970), Eastwood plays a prostitute's dupe. And he is symbolically castrated by the women he seduces and betrays in a hospital for Confederate soldiers in *The Beguiled* (Siegel, 1971). And as a preening, self-adulatory disc jockey in *Play Misty for Me* (Eastwood, 1971), he finds himself stalked by a jilted, knife-wielding former sex partner. Eastwood may have sought to expand his dramatic range, but these four movies, however minor in a canon that spans five decades, play significantly against the persona that made him famous.

*The Outlaw Josey Wales* complicates Eastwood's Western persona, releasing it from both the otherworldly gunfighter and the deadly urban cop. Josey doesn't appear onscreen as a ready-made killer with the magical gun. He becomes an avenging force only because Kansas "Red Legs" wantonly raid his place, kill his son, rape and kill his wife, and burn his cabin to ashes. After the Red Legs ride away from the ruined American Eden, Josey converts his grief into a deadly dexterity with an old six-gun he recovers from the ashes of his cabin. Uniquely (so far) in the Eastwood canon, the hero's tragic past sustains his mythic skill so that the magical six-gun functions as a correlative of his unyielding rage and unabating woe. It seems fitting therefore that in the climactic confrontation with the archvillain, "Red Legs" Terrill (Bill McKinney), Josey, who at times packs as many as four pistols, runs out of ammunition for all of them. After so many scenes of massacre by means of firearms (one scene includes a Gatling gun), violence becomes suddenly primitive, up close and all too personal, when Terrill, perceiving an advantage over the disarmed Josey, comes at him with a cavalry saber. Josey, however, grabs Terrill's hand on the hilt and slowly drives the saber right through him. We are not to miss the righteousness of Josey's cause as he enforces—without a sense of irony, as it seems—the Christian rule against taking up the sword (Matt. 26:52), and we remember that the saber that kills Terrill is likely the same one with which Terrill slashed Josey across the face when the Red Legs invaded the Wales homestead.

In the last scene of *Josey Wales*, Fletcher (John Vernon), the Confederate guerrilla leader who rode with Josey but became his pursuer after the South's surrender, enters the Lost Lady saloon in the exhausted border town of Santo Rio in Texas, where Josey has made friends while training them to fight the Red Legs. Josey's friends tell Fletcher of a rumor that Josey Wales was killed in a fight with five pistoleros. Moments later when Josey walks into the Lost Lady, his friends greet him as "Mr. Wilson." But now in the bright light outside, Fletcher faces Josey, who has been wounded in the firefight that preceded his confrontation with Terrill. Fletcher notices the blood dripping onto Josey's boot. Himself weary of the pursuit and of this absurd protraction of the Civil War, Fletcher pretends not to recognize Josey, addressing him as Mr. Wilson. He will keep chasing Josey Wales, he tells Josey, and then adds, "I think I'll try to tell him that the war is over. What do you say, Mr. Wilson?" Responding to his new identity, Josey replies, "I reckon so. I guess we all died a little in that damned war." And then he rides away. If Josey Wales is "dead, all right," then perhaps *The Outlaw Josey Wales* has compellingly narrated—forcibly if but allusively—a way out of the bitter divisions, not unlike those of the Civil War, spawned by the Vietnam War, at the time America's most recent "damned war."

*Josey Wales* gave us a hero whose humanity released the Eastwood persona from the cynical, grasping protagonist of the earlier heroic roles, especially in the Spaghetti Westerns. Josey suffers loss, Josey cries, Josey bleeds. There was to be, however, no undeviating progression away from the ethereal hero. Between the two last Harry Callahan movies—*Sudden Impact* (Eastwood, 1983) and *The Dead Pool* (Van Horn, 1988), both featuring a far more vulnerable Harry than the one of the earlier Dirty Harry movies—Eastwood's otherworldly gunfighter returned to the Western. In *Pale Rider* (1985), he plays "Preacher" and appears in the world of violent strife as an answer to the urgent prayer of the adolescent Megan Wheeler (Sydney Penny). In the opening sequence, a dozen or so duster-clad thugs employed by Coy LaHood (Richard Dysart), the iron-hearted owner of an environmentally catastrophic hydraulic gold mining operation, ride out of nowhere against a community of small-time placer miners, destroying much of their camp and wantonly killing a cow as well as Megan's pet terrier, Lindsay. Megan goes alone into the woods to bury her dog, and she plaintively recites Psalm 23, now and then interspersing it, glossing it, with brief, innocent pleas that punctuate her pain, her fears, and her hopes. A cut now shows lowering gray skies and distant mist-shrouded mountains, and out of this mist and to the accompaniment of the thunder, a lone rider on a pale horse approaches at a steady trot. Preacher's is already the needful otherworldliness that by its very presence identifies an evil so pervasive and so powerful that it can be defeated only by an avenging angel with a magical gun. The six scarred-over bullet wounds in Preacher's bare back, which we see much later, present him as something like a resurrected stigmatic even while they confirm a violent past. (He is not, however, so incorporeal a presence that he fails to provoke the concupiscence of both Megan and her mother Sarah, played by Carrie Snodgress.)

As the conflict with LaHood intensifies, Preacher rides to a Wells Fargo Express office and exchanges his preacher's collar for the two six-guns and a cartridge belt in a safety deposit box. In familiar Eastwood fashion, Preacher (with some help from Hull Barret, Sarah's husband and Megan's stepfather, played by Michael Moriarty) razes LaHood's mining operation, lobbing sticks of dynamite that all but eradicate the outrage against nature. Then he rides to town alone to confront Stockburn (John Russell), who leads LaHood's enforcers and the other dozen or so thugs. The lesser villains duly dispatched, Preacher now faces off against Stockburn in the dusty street. The outcome of the shootout will make it clear that it was Stockburn who put the six shots in Preacher's back. Preacher, reloading as he walks toward Stockburn, calmly approaches to within two or three feet of him. Stockburn is stunned, unable to draw his pistol, to run, to plead for his life before the unrelenting approach of the avenging revenant. "You!" he finally exclaims, and his recognition of this implacable ethereal force is his doom. Preacher empties his six shots into Stockburn. The camera testifies to the moral exactitude of Preacher's avenging deed by making sure that we see the six shots exiting from Stockburn's back. Once again on his pale horse, the pale rider trots back to the mountains from whence he came.

Throughout its first half or so, *Unforgiven* (Eastwood, 1992) pointedly, even obsessively repudiates the ready-made pugnacity of the Eastwood persona. William Munny's compulsive reassurances to any and all listeners—"I ain't like that anymore"—place him assuredly in a postmythic moment. Reformed by domesticity, Will has left behind his evil ways and has tried his inexpert hand at farming, a Jeffersonian yeoman farmer manqué. Here, the classic Western's agrarian ideal has become a foul, full-blown Augean squalor of maze-like fences enclosing only swine ordure, rotten slop, and "fevered" hogs. In this enervating chaos, moreover, the Western's faithful wife—she of the soft suasions and long-suffering resignation in classic Westerns—is already dead when the story begins: dead, that is, though abidingly present as something of a horn-mad harpy, enforcing Will's temperance from beyond the grave. Claudia "cured" him, Will attests, of his "evil ways," but to judge from the first time we see him, the "cure" has condemned him to hog hell, Claudia as Circe, then, minus the allure if not quite without the mischief. Will may have done enough penance for his previous sins, back when he was "a man of notoriously vicious and intemperate disposition" (as the opening roll-title puts it), but his acknowledged if unintended complicity in Ned's violent death reawakens the primal, demonic rage in him.

Ned Logan (Morgan Freeman), once Will's partner in outlawry, has become a modestly successful farmer. Nonetheless, he follows Will and the Schofield Kid to Big Whiskey, Wyoming, for a third of the $1,000 reward offered by the prostitutes of Greely's Saloon to whoever kills the two young cowboys who disfigured Delilah Fitzgerald (Anna Thomson) after she mildly mocked one of them. Following the murders of the two guilty cowboys, Sheriff Little Bill Daggett (Gene Hackman) flogs Ned, a Black man, to death. Will, stunned by the news of Ned's death, resolves to avenge him and to atone for luring him away from home and hearth.

Undoubtedly, Will's vengeance acknowledges, however tacitly, his personal complicity in the historical sins of slavery and lynch law. Still, the sought-after redress and the hoped-for absolution require, ironically, Will's relapse; they demand, that is, the reemergence of the unrivaled hero of myth and magical guns. At Greely's, Will cuts down half a dozen men—and first Greely himself, though he is unarmed—with a six-gun he only now comes into possession of (the Kid's relinquished Smith and Wesson Schofield model). And Will calmly administers the coup de grâce to Little Bill who, though gut-shot and dying and all too guilty, says that he doesn't deserve such a death. "Deserve's got nothing to do with it," Will responds before shooting. Then, unscathed and unrepentant, he rides out of Big Whiskey in heavy rain and thunder. Old Glory, still waving after the recent Fourth of July celebration, appears prominently on the right third of the screen, seeming to bless Will's and America's own wild justice. Justice is then Will's, perhaps, but so too is the unabating remorse that shall hound him the rest of his days even if Claudia's ghost has run out of remonstrances and even if the end scroll-up tells us that Will has long since left the revolting pigpens of Hodgeman County and was last seen in San Francisco, "where it was rumored he prospered in dry goods."

## *Gran Torino* and the Paths to *American Sniper*

*Gran Torino* (Eastwood, 2008) attempts to decouple inheritance from violence, thus releasing the young heir from the cark and curse of the heroic imperative and its attendant anxieties. The heirloom is not a six-gun but rather a mint-condition 1972 Gran Torino Sport Fastback. Free and unconstrained at the end, the young heir, Thao Vang Lor (Bee Vang), drives his Gran Torino easefully along Lake St. Clair. To be sure, violence, especially and most disturbingly rape and torture, figures here as prominently as it does in *Josey Wales* and no less graphically than in *Unforgiven.* But the Eastwood hero in *Gran Torino* brings about the deliverance of Thao and his sister Sue (Ahney Her) by explicitly, in fact ritualistically, abjuring gun violence. This repudiation of violence is possible in part because Walt Kowalski (Eastwood) dramatizes his own death, staging it as a pointedly countergeneric "shootout," one he knows he cannot survive, the way earlier Eastwood heroes did. But Walt's dying—that is, the method of it, as distinct from the mere resultant death—guarantees the arrest for murder of the Hmong gangbangers who terrorize his neighborhood (they rape Sue and torture Thao). Moreover, Walt's sacrifice thwarts Thao's willful turn to gun violence, since the young man seeks to avenge Sue's rape by arming himself against the goons.

Walt Kowalski, an irascible, bigoted, and terminally ill widower with a strong dislike for every member of his family, receives an unsought benediction in the love of Thao and Sue and in his own for them. Thao and Sue, with their extended family of three generations, some of whom fought alongside the United States in Vietnam,[6] have moved in next door to Walt, and Walt's virulent racism, unabating throughout the six decades since he fought in Korea, compels him to look upon the siblings and their family as just more Asians to revile. Walt killed many communist Koreans—"we used to stack fucks like you five feet high in Korea, use you for sandbags," he snarls at one of the Hmong thugs—and he earned a Silver Star for heroic if unspecified actions. But as we learn later, he cannot shake the dark memory of one Korean soldier, an unarmed youth he shot in the face. This soldier, Walt confesses to Thao, was "some poor kid that wanted to just give up," adding that the youth was "just like you." Since that time, moreover, Walt has also endured some sixty years of unshakable remorse for that one killing: "not a day goes by that I don't think about it," he confesses to Thao. And now, as the action builds toward the climactic shootout, the guilt and the racism of six decades become as if foreshortened, urgently clamoring for a last grasp at atonement. And that atonement is impossible without the denunciation, in action more than words, of the heroic legacy.

In several scenes throughout but especially in the climactic shootout, Walt performs a vital yet unmistakably ironic gesture: he mimics a "pistol" with his index finger (the barrel) and thumb (the hammer). The mock pistol necessarily references the Eastwood persona's oneness with the magical six-gun, but now it chiefly destabilizes and subverts its claims to otherworldly powers. The mock pistol diminishes the power and authority of the heroic myth by a dissimulation of the indispensable generic act. In the climactic shootout, Walt faces six gangbangers alone at night (he comes to their lair where some stand on the porch and others post themselves at windows). Standing fully visible before them, he calmly fires the mock pistol at each one. By mock-shooting the gangbangers, he identifies them as latter-day Western villains, "miniature cowboys," as he derides them, thus further enhancing the generic aspect of the confrontation while undermining it. At that moment when the heroic plot calls for a shootout, the hero turns to a simulacrum of gun violence, thereby renouncing violence even as he invokes it.

After he mock-shoots each gangbanger, Walt pulls a cigarette from his jacket pocket and asks the hair-trigger tense hoodlums for a light. They stand nonplussed. "No?" he asks. "Me, I've got a light," he says and begins to mutter the Hail Mary while slowly reaching inside his jacket pocket. Before his hand comes out in full view, the hoodlums cut him down. (We see later that he was holding a Zippo lighter with an Air

Cavalry insignia.) This light of Walt's, that is, the sacrifice that safeguards his redemption,[7] atones for the cruelty of a legacy whose terms and conditions reiteratively consign the hero's heir to a violent destiny. Thus, continuity, which presumes to sustain the myth's anxious resistance to and distraught denial of history and tragedy, ipso facto condemns each new generation to the same all too foreseeable horror. Walt's narrative of transgression and atonement seeks deliverance *from the sins of the heroic myth.* If the heroic legacy always and already transfers the promise of generational glory, so now does it also transmit its own singularly perverse indifference to the life of the young. So dark, indeed, is this sin of indifference to new life that atonement for it demands a sacrificial death in which the Eastwood hero, once impossibly incorporeal (as in the Spaghetti Westerns and *Pale Rider*), becomes the flesh-and-blood martyr. This time it is his loss that produces the deliverance of the young. Only in this postheroic (dare we say post-Eastwood) America can Thao and Sue live free—ride that Gran Torino—in the now-liberated and liberating spaces of the rupture.

## *American Sniper* as Myth and as American Tragedy

Throughout most of its running time, *American Sniper* (Eastwood, 2014) seems stubbornly intent on reviving the mythic tropes to which *Gran Torino* assigns an ironic role. Nowhere in *American Sniper* is the return to mythic tropes more obvious than in the reappearance and dominant presence of the magical gun. We see the muzzle of the sniper rifle before we do the face of the sniper himself: Chris Kyle (Bradley Cooper) comes into being as an extension of the rifle. In this way, he is the latest iteration of America's frontier hero, not so much a character as a *type*. His oneness with the rifle is as Hawkeye's to "Killdeer," Daniel Boone's to "Old Tick-Licker," Davy Crockett's to "Old Betsy," and Lin McAdam's (James Stewart's) to the "one in one thousand" Winchester in *Winchester '73* (Anthony Mann, 1950). Moreover, Kyle's deadly skill evokes Natty Bumppo's "one-shot" ethos in *The Pioneers* even as it implicitly negates Michael Vronsky's fraught appeals to the "one-shot" mystique in *The Deer Hunter.* Eventually Kyle's buddies dub him "Legend," a nom de guerre that, though more wryly than reverently tendered, still identifies not only skill in marksmanship but also body count as an affirmation of the heroic inheritance.

Prone on a rooftop, sighting through his riflescope—we are still in the first three minutes of running time—Kyle, flanked by his spotter, sees an Iraqi man, a civilian, on a high balcony some two hundred yards away. The man seems agitated at the sight of a US Marine Corps convoy making its slow way in the dusty street below. Radio control gives Kyle a green light to shoot the man, who now hurriedly makes a call on a cell phone, but the man disappears, and we never see him again. Still sighting the same building through his scope, Kyle tilts down and spots a woman and a boy some eight or ten years old stepping out on the dusty street. He immediately notices that the woman's arms don't swing naturally when she walks, and he interprets this to mean that she is hiding something in the folds of her abaya. And indeed, she soon produces a Russian-made RKG-3 antitank grenade and hands it to the boy, who now becomes Kyle's target. Cut to an extreme close-up of Kyle's finger on the trigger; then to the boy, grenade in hand, running toward the marines; and finally to a close-up of Kyle taking deep breaths while tracking the boy with his riflescope. A shot rings out, but there is no match cut to the Iraqi boy, whose death seemed certain. Instead, we see a head-on shot of a white American boy in the lush autumn woods, still pointing his rifle. He has just killed his first deer. This is young Chris Kyle (Cole Konis), of about the same age as the Iraqi boy, whose fate (as that of the convoy) will remain unknown for a good while.

In its first sixty-seven seconds of running time, *American Sniper* introduces the full-formed hero, but it takes the ensuing half hour to trace, in retrospect, his mythogenesis from the initiation in the woods to bronco riding. Only a few scenes after the deer hunt, the adult Kyle and his brother Jeff (Keir O'Donnell) are watching breaking news of the near-simultaneous attacks on the US embassies in Nairobi, Kenya, and Dar es Salaam, Tanzania, on August 7, 1998. Here, then, is one more fatal provocation accruing to the national memory: Fort Sumter in 1861, Havana Harbor in 1898, Pearl Harbor in 1941, the Tonkin Gulf in 1964, and the yet to be attacks on September 11, 2001. Already the heroic imperative exacts the hero's compliance. So, the aimless small-time rodeo rider who finds his girlfriend in flagrante delicto in his own bed suddenly transforms into a paladin of righteous retribution. Kyle enlists in the US Navy and becomes a Navy SEAL. Shortly thereafter he meets Taya (Sienna Miller), courts her, begins sniper training, and has sex with her, and his marksmanship improves greatly. Now living together, Kyle and Taya watch the unfolding events of September 11 on TV. They marry, and he deploys to Iraq, America's latest "over there."

Only after all these events (as well as some others, also in the long flashback but still to be considered) in Kyle's mythogenesis have acquired their due importance in the making of the hero does the action return to Iraq, as if to pick up on the fate of the young Iraqi boy and woman and the marine convoy. The footage, though differently sequenced, is the same as in the opening shots. In other words, the flashback scenes between the end of the opening sequence and the resumption of the action in Iraq—at the end of which he kills both the boy and the woman—function to not only establish Kyle's mythic credentials but also justify the two shootings. The flashback, in other words, seeks to remove any trace of doubt, of Kurtzian "judgment that defeats us," regarding the higher purpose of Chris Kyle's and America's mission in Iraq. Despite the narrative's eagerness to avoid or, more precisely, delay irony, the long flashback to Kyle's American youth functions already as a source of irony. In the service of an ingenuous view of the heroic myth, the flashback sequence highlights the moral necessity of excusing—which is to say of rendering guiltless—Kyle's bloated body count.

"Our ROEs [rules of engagement] when the war kicked off," Kyle tells us in his autobiography, "were pretty simple: *If you see anyone from about sixteen to sixty-five and they're male, shoot 'em. Kill every male you see.* That wasn't the official language, but that was the idea."[8] (Had Kyle followed this ROE in letter and spirit, he would have had to spare both the woman and the boy.) The continuity of the heroic myth now clearly reveals—and reveals itself as—the persistence of this genocidal rancor throughout the generations. In their sham legality, the ROEs in Iraq mimic Kurtz's red-pencil scrawl, "exterminate them all." Even more relevant to Chris Kyle and *American Sniper*, the ROEs recall the war cry of Fenimore Cooper's archetypal hunter-warrior, Hawkeye, in *The Last of the Mohicans:* "Extarminate the varlets! no quarter to an accursed Mingo!"[9] The juxtaposition of the American hunting scenes with the killings in Iraq presents the idyll of the American forest as the prerequisite of—indeed the covenant with—the death dealing in Iraq's blasted cityscapes. If you mean to kill

"Indians," you must first be an accomplished deer hunter. Astonished that he has brought down the buck, young Chris drops his rifle on the grass and bounds toward his kill. But his irascible father (the perhaps fortuitously named Wayne, played by Ben Reed) stops him in his tracks: "You don't ever leave your rifle in the dirt." The neophyte learns that he is one with his rifle. "You've got a gift," says Chris's father, adding to this praise the requisite prophecy: "You're gonna make a fine hunter someday" and therefore as fine a killer.

Fenimore Cooper culled America's wilderness experience—in, for example, the already heavily mythologized Daniel Boone of John Filson's *Kentucke*—as if in search of a supple and adaptable principle that, while admitting of fictional treatment and aspiring to the condition of myth, could still justify the genocidal tendency in America's centuries-long Indian Wars. In tacit agreement with the patterns of racial and racist conflicts unfolding since the earliest colonial days, Cooper hit upon a serviceable doctrine based on long-established binaries: "red" and "white," each skin "color" corresponding to and identifying a set of "gifts." Thus, Hawkeye, who insists that he is "a man without a [racial] cross"—meaning that he is pure white—obsessively references "the gifts of my color."[10] As he commiserates with Chingachgook for the death of Uncas, Hawkeye somehow must affirm the brotherhood of universal grief by invoking the familiar terms. "The gifts of our colours," he tells the bereaved father, "may be different, but God has so placed us as to journey in the same path."[11] Much earlier, however, in the heat of the fight for the conquest of North America, the doctrine of "gifts" finds symbolic expression in the postulated inborn superiority of the white man in rifle marksmanship (the setting is Fort William Henry in the aftermath of the historic massacre). "There is one rifle," Hawkeye assures us, "which will play its part so long as flint will fire or powder burn! I leave the tomahawk and knife to such as have a natural gift to use them."[12] The gift becomes nothing less than a racial birthright, an integral part of the heroic inheritance, its transmittal critical to the continuity of the heroic myth. "For myself," Hawkeye remarks, accounting for his gift, "I conclude all the Bumppos could shoot; for I have a natural turn with a rifle, which must have been handed down from generation to generation."[13]

Out of the enduring tableau of an armed youth and his mentor in the dark woods emerges "the myth of the essential white America," as

D. H. Lawrence proclaimed in his meditation on the *Leatherstocking Tales.* "All the other stuff, the love, the democracy, the floundering into lust, is a sort of by-play. The essential American soul is hard, isolate, stoic, and a killer. It has never yet melted."[14] In Iraq, the Americans, not surprisingly, refer to the insurgents as "savages," thus naming the high stakes of the long-deferred duel with the Iraqi version of Cooper's villain Magua: the deadly sniper "Mustafa" (Sammy Sheik). Kyle kills Mustafa from an astonishing 2,100 yards away, and the feat (as myth names murder) so exalts both color and gift as to make of Kyle a national treasure. In the "Legend's" birth out of attestable history, the anointed hero atones for the Loss and reinstates the myth.

## Parable as Irony

Still in the long flashback that interrupts the shooting of the Iraqi boy, the camera closes in on tokens of young American boyhood on a shelf in the home of Kyle's parents. Prominent among these are a spent rifle case and a small New Testament Holy Bible that Chris earlier filches from the back of a church pew. Over these shots, Wayne Kyle begins his dour homily, below. But even as he speaks, the action cuts to a schoolyard where Chris's brother Jeff (Luke Sunshine) is getting much the worse of it in a fight with a bully. Soon Chris rushes into the fray and pummels the bully brutally. In the cut back to the Kyle home, Jeff's shiner becomes Wayne's "text." The Sunday dinner table parable purports to explain the motive for Chris Kyle's deeds in Iraq. More important, however, the supposed moral authority of Wayne Kyle's allegory becomes a means of justifying the shooting of the Iraqi boy and woman. "There are three types of people in this world," Wayne Kyle begins,

> sheep, wolves, and sheepdogs. Now, some people prefer to believe that evil doesn't exist in the world. And if it ever darkened their doorstep, they wouldn't know how to protect themselves. Those are the sheep. And then you've got the predators. They use violence to prey on the weak. They're the wolves. And then there are those who've been blessed with the gift of aggression [*CUT. Schoolyard fight; Chris intervenes.*] and the overpowering need to protect the

> flock. These men are the rare breed that live to confront the wolf. [*CUT. Dinner table.*] They are the sheepdogs. [*Suddenly, Wayne pulls out his belt from around his pants waist.*] Now, we're not raising any sheep in this family [*Folds belt lengthwise, slams it hard, noisily, on the table.*] And I will whup your ass if you turn into a wolf. [*Mrs. Kyle and boys visibly intimidated.*] But we protect our own. Now, if someone tries to fight you or tries to bully your little brother, you have my permission to finish it.[15]

One wonders what, precisely, Wayne might mean by "*finish* it." Should the fight with the schoolyard bully end as does the shooting of the boy and woman or of the "bully" Mustafa? Regardless of Wayne's specific meaning, "finishing" here smacks of *winning*, of a decisive and uncontestable victory. Chris Kyle was born in April 1974, one year after the last Americans returned from Vietnam and a year before the fall of Saigon (April 30, 1975). He inherits, then, the first war that America failed to "finish." Thus, Wayne Kyle's sense of what it means to finish implies an anxiety about the outcome of American wars after the Loss, an anxiety that the 1980s expressed through John Rambo's burning question: "Do we get to win this time?"

Young Chris maintains that "the guy was picking on Jeff," and Jeff assures Wayne that it was so. And Wayne asks again, "Did you finish it?" Chris nods a solemn yes, and the scene comes to a close. Such, then, is the easy, high-contrast, ingenuous morality that sustains the heroic legacy in *American Sniper*, a morality utterly resistant to the possibility that the enemies' perspectives (were they so much as permitted to articulate even one) might easily confute, perhaps even reassign, the several roles of Wayne's parable.

The heroic legacy, trailing its ancient genocidal impulses all the way to Iraq, comes to Chris Kyle in a prefigured convergence of man, mission, and myth. He is "blessed," we now know, with and by "the gift of aggression." In Iraq, accordingly, Kyle reenacts the American rage against the native on the native's own soil. "Welcome to Fallujah," says one of the superior officers in an early scene in Iraq, "the new Wild West of the old Middle East." The Iraqi "savages," this officer maintains, have been rounded up and taken away so that any remaining "savage" or "wolf" in Fallujah must be assumed (if one is permitted to extend the metaphor) to have bolted the reservation for the warpath and is therefore fair game, she-wolves and wolf pups included, to judge by the results of Kyle's "kill" on that one day.

After the Sunday dinner scene (in flashback still), the action cuts to an iconic if completely contextless shot. The camera is inside a large darkened barn, and the barn doors are wide open. In the rectangle of bright light just outside stands a white-hatted cowboy; he just stands there with his back to the camera even as the last words of Wayne Kyle's homily—"Well, then you know who you are. You know your purpose."—bleed over the shot. Once Kyle has become a Navy SEAL, he meets the true woman, Taya. In the middle of their wedding, he and the other SEALs learn that they will be deployed to Iraq. When Taya expresses grave fears, Kyle seeks to calm her. "It's all part of the plan." He might as well have said "It's all part of the legacy." Even before his first tour in Iraq, Kyle's mythic résumé—"sheepdog," hunter, cowboy, SEAL, sniper—already promotes and glorifies the grim body count to follow.

Now clutching the grenade, the Iraqi boy begins a reluctant trot toward the marine convoy. Kyle's shot hits him in the chest, and the boy falls dead, dropping the grenade. Then, the woman runs toward him, not to tend to him or mourn him but instead to retrieve the unexploded grenade and hurl it at the marines. As she begins her throw Kyle shoots her, and the grenade explodes a few yards from where she falls. No marines are hurt. But this time there is no wide-eyed astonishment, no exuberant run toward the kill, as in Kyle's preadolescence. Kyle's distress at having killed the boy presages the moment much later when, undone by the continual pull of conscience against jingoism's diminishing power to justify so much bloodshed, he calls Taya in the middle of a firefight and plaintively declares that he is "ready to come home."

In the immediate aftermath of the two killings, however, Kyle seeks not solace but rather self-vindication. Done recounting the events of the day to a colleague, he adds in reference to the Iraqi woman, "Dude, that's evil like I've never seen before." In his dinner table sermon, Wayne Kyle had scorned those who "prefer to believe that evil doesn't exist in the world." When Chris Kyle declares that the Iraqi woman was categorically evil, he remains willfully resistant to the inevitable and unforgiving ironies. What is the difference between the sniper Mustafa and the sniper Kyle if each one acts in his role as "sheepdog" to his comrades? Would Kyle the boy-hunter have turned into a boy-insurgent if it had been the United States that had been invaded by a foreign power? Would Taya take up the dropped grenade and hurl it at a column of soldiers from an occupying army? There are other subversive ironies, each no less compelling than the ones emerging from Kyle's self-identification with the terms and premises of his father's dinner table allegories. Is evil not what the Iraqi boy sees himself fighting against? How can the woman's "pure evil" be reconciled with the impossibility that Kyle's moral assessment could know aught of the history that compels her to action? Is Kyle the sniper not in a way bully to both boy and woman, "wolf" to their victimhood, himself "evil" to their "sheepdog's" cause? Is Kyle, then, a dupe of the patriotism that seeks to justify the historically unjustifiable?

The marines remain pinned down on a rooftop, the insurgents fairly swarm the building, and a blinding sandstorm looms, yet Kyle, almost in a panic, turns away from the fight, phones Taya (who can barely hear him), and tells her he is "ready to come home" (figure 7.1).

Only now, with the sandstorm full-force already upon them, does Kyle rally and covers the marines' retreat. Last man out of the building, he runs after the evacuation vehicle but is shot, and though he quickly resumes his run, the vehicle is already rolling away without him. Once he comes dimly in sight, several of the marines reach out and pull him into the vehicle, which quickly disappears in the storm. But the camera

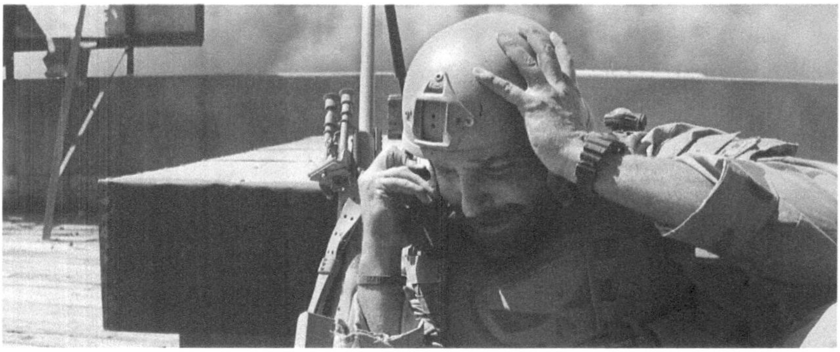

Figure 7.1. *American Sniper*. Chris Kyle (Bradley Cooper) calls wife Taya (Sienna Miller) midfirefight to tell her he is coming home.

returns to the storm, back where Kyle was shot, and it is then that we see the abandoned sniper rifle and the New Testament Holy Bible where he has dropped them. If the moment's desperate exigency amply justifies abandoning the rifle for its weight, still the image clearly evokes the scene when the young hunter dropped the rifle after he had shot his first deer. Moreover, in the context of the call to Taya, the abandoned rifle suggests Kyle's desperate renunciation of the magical firearm and thus of the very source of his identity as hero, as Legend. And what of the New Testament Holy Bible, so reverently appropriated in church and so neatly laid out among his other boyhood treasures? What becomes of the vague comfort of merely having it at hand (since we never see Kyle reading it) in a grim and alien land? Thus, the abandoned rifle and the lost Bible suggest the crisis of the heroic legacy in the Iraq War of *American Sniper.* Lost in a raging sandstorm of transcendent significance, these culturally charged symbols, jettisoned, abandoned, only half visible, become corroborative tropes of the rupture. And the overwhelming sands wear away at America's heroic myth, render it ephemeral, a thing of mere vanity undone utterly by the menacing indifference of the land itself, that weapon immemorial. The desert that censures and chastens also casts America's exalted mission as only one more failed invasion, one more historic repulse of imperial vanity, as Percy Bysshe Shelley taught in "Ozymandias": "Round the decay / Of that colossal Wreck, boundless and bare / The lone and level sands stretch far away."[16] There is no birth of a new order, no emerging heir, only sand and whirlwind and war unceasing.

Many critics and reviewers of *American Sniper* felt compelled to settle the question as to whether Chris Kyle was a "hero." "The controversy surrounding *American Sniper*," Anthony Zurcher wrote at the time of the movie's release, "has little to do with the film as an artistic effort, which has generally been praised by critics. It has everything to do with Kyle himself, the Navy Seal who served four tours of duty in Iraq killed more than 160 people there and authored the autobiographical book upon which the film is (sometimes loosely) based."[17] Was Kyle a hero for protecting his fellow Americans from deceitful, cunning, and cruel Iraqi "terrorists," or was he a trigger-happy murderer letting loose his racist rancor with impunity? Film critic Amy Nicholson, who called the movie "one of the most mendacious . . . of 2014," lamented that "*American Sniper* convinces viewers that Chris Kyle is what heroism looks like: a great guy who shoots a lot of people and doesn't think twice about it."[18] But this assessment merely describes what the American hero does, who the American hero intrinsically is, in every American war. Indeed, Nicholson's judgment stumbles on this very irony when she declares, "I kept wondering who Kyle himself had been imitating. Sylvester Stallone? John Wayne? Or the ultimate irony, Clint Eastwood himself as Dirty Harry?" In this way, Kyle himself becomes a mythic incarnation of "the essential American soul," as D. H. Lawrence described it, "hard, isolate, stoic, and a killer."

Perhaps no one raised as passionate a voice in praise of Kyle than conservative commentator, bronze medal recipient (for service in the Iraq War), and *New York Times* columnist David French. French railed against Kyle's "leftist" detractors in several pieces at the time when *American Sniper* was first in nationwide release. French's verdict was that "the movie gives America something it's lacked since the start of the war—a war hero on a truly national, cultural scale. . . . [W]ith the success of this movie, Chris Kyle has entered the pantheon of American warriors—along with Alvin C. York and Audie Murphy—giving a new generation of young boys a warrior-hero to look up to, to emulate."[19] Significantly enough, French's list of past heroes stops at World War II (with Audie Murphy). The omission of a hero from the Vietnam War implicitly acknowledges the rupture. The Loss thwarts the birth of an heir who would extend the myth into the Iraq War. What, then, was gained in the Iraq War that might have elevated Chris Kyle to the unambiguously heroic status of Alvin York or Audie Murphy? Diplomat Dennis Jett (though he confessed that he had not seen the movie before writing about it) placed Kyle's feat in the context of America's presumed motives for invading Iraq: "treating Kyle as a patriot and ignoring any other possibility allows Americans to ignore the consequences of invading a country that had no weapons of mass destruction, had nothing to do with 9/11, and had no meaningful ties to Al Qaeda."[20] Still, Jett establishes an important historical context for *American Sniper*: the infamously fudged casus belli and the war's own indeterminate outcome mar Kyle's labors, because unlike York's and Murphy's, Kyle's "kills" are not endorsed by victory. With the Loss in its more recent past, the war in Iraq sought a solid, credible, ideologically justifiable war, a war to somehow reinstitute the myth of heroic continuity, to span the gap laid bare by the Loss, a war therefore if not to redeem the Loss then one at least to make possible the conditions to forget it altogether. But the mission to forget was not accomplished anymore than the one implicitly proclaimed by President George W. Bush aboard USS *Abraham Lincoln* on May 1, 2003. Thus, Kyle's deeds lack the incontrovertible victory demanded by the heroic myth. And the myth of heroic continuity, however battered by the persistence of the Loss, remains unbendingly averse to ambiguity.

## Tropes That Bind . . . and Damn

Kyle returns stateside but not home. Sitting alone at a bar at an airport somewhere, he recalls the Melvillian isolato "living on a separate continent of his own." He recalls *The Deer Hunter*'s Michael Vronsky, the returning soldier so overcome by horror and tragedy that he hides from the friends who gather to welcome him back. Once home, however, Kyle merely sits in front of the TV staring vacantly ahead. A soundtrack plays a war's cacophony: machine guns, explosions, and even the electric hand drill, the Iraqi Butcher's preferred instrument of torture, as we saw in the early Iraq sequences. But when the camera comes around to the reverse shot, we see that the TV screen is blank. The war noises are all in Kyle's head. Later at a cookout with other families, Kyle becomes increasingly agitated by the tug-of-war between two boys and the Kyles' own pet dog. When one of the boys stumbles, the dog playfully nuzzles into his neck, but Kyle jumps to the "rescue," pulls the dog away from the boy, removes his belt, doubles it lengthwise, and raises his arm to strike the dog. Taya, horrified, stops him just in time. The moment, of course, compels comparison with the schoolyard episode when Chris came to Jeff's aid against the bully, but it also reminds us vividly of Wayne Kyle slamming his doubled-up belt on the dinner table. We realize that Chris may have become his truculent father, and we confirm the banality of the father's dinner table homily in this moment when the hero, so painfully traumatized, confuses a family mutt with a "wolf." More important, however, the scene reveals the force of the rupture in the hero's broken and betrayed soul. Consistent with the horrors of post-traumatic stress disorder, Kyle cannot distinguish between home and battlefield, between trauma-sourced hypervigilance at home and his responsibilities to the marines in the convoy, between the desire to serve his country and his complete if helpless immersion in the soldier's hell that he carries wherever he goes.

Lest Kyle's war turn into "another Vietnam" and he into another Vietnam veteran—one, that is, bearing the burden of offensive platitudes and vulgarized as the spaced-out, drug-addled, fearful yet enraged veteran—*American Sniper* turns from Kyle in his post-Iraq terrors to scenes, some little more than vignettes, that ease him back gently among the cherished images and conceits of the American West. For instance, Kyle returns from a shopping trip to find his cowboy boots neatly laid out by the side of the bed. After he looks at them fondly, the action cuts to a brief scene where he and his daughter, McKenna (Madeleine McGraw), looking over a white plank fence, gaze lovingly at a white stallion, a dead ringer for Silver himself. Kyle says to McKenna, "It's not a bad life out there, is it?" Here is the cowboy's dream reasserting its hold on Kyle again: "Just my rifle, pony, and me" out in the "purple light" of the canyon, as Dean Martin croons in *Rio Bravo.* Except for a wife, children, fences, post-traumatic stress disorder, and a mortgage and car payments, Kyle's idyll lies within easy reach. (An initiation hunting trip complements the serene and meditative scene between father, daughter, and white stallion. Because of its importance as a final look at the heroic legacy, I will turn to it only after first considering the last sequence.)

In a close-up waist-level shot of Kyle, we see an outsize rodeo belt buckle and a hand holding a nickel-plated Colt 1873 revolver, the quintessential (and for the hero de rigueur) firearm. Immediately, however, a superimposed title appears over this image: "February 2, 2013." On this date, Kyle will be murdered. History, if only in the cryptic form of a foretokened tragedy, already disrupts the regeneration of myth and hero. Still, Kyle, Colt in hand, makes his way stealthily to the kitchen, where he finds Taya. With all the seriousness of a sheriff disarming the villain, he says, "Hands in the air, little lady. . . . Now, you drop them drawers, but you drop 'em nice and easy." Taya beams at what she rightly takes to be a sign of her husband's restored mental health. "I'm so proud of you," she says, "and you're such a great father, and I'm so happy that I've got my husband back, and I also know how hard you fought to get there." But aside from a brief scene with a psychiatrist who takes him to meet disabled veterans (thus suggesting that Kyle has recovered and can serve as a model for those who have not), we see precious little of anything like a hard-fought struggle with the darkness.

Indeed, this absence of narrative markers of a mental and spiritual ordeal highlights the extent to which Kyle's rebirth relies almost entirely on well-timed association with the tropes of the classic Western, as if the comfort derived from such relics actually performs the curative, redemptive office of grace itself. As Kyle grips his Colt, Taya notices his blue jeans. "Now tell me one other thing," she says teasingly. "Did you pleat those jeans?" Embarrassed, he admits that he did, and she, playful still, responds, "Oh, you're just a regular old cowboy again." Moments later Taya asks him if he is going "to the range," and indeed he is, to his home on the (shooting) range to tender his hero's mercy to a broken man, a veteran not unlike Kyle himself whose own restoration may well depend on his getting right with the gun. The gun pervades these last moments of domestic bliss. As the last scene comes to a close, Kyle still grips the six-gun even during the last embrace, when the fist holding the gun barrel down rests, naughtily enough, on the small of Taya's back.

Seemingly facile and desultory, these tropes of the classic Western, together with Taya's testimonies and attestations, proclaim Kyle's freedom from trauma, and trauma is the force of bondage to history. What better proof, then, of his complete regeneration and of his newfound authority to bequeath the heroic birthright than the Western's trope of the scheduled shooting lesson? And what more devastatingly tragic version of the shooting lesson than this one in which the student kills the master, the Legend?

As she watches Kyle cross the threshold and greet the sorry-looking pupil standing by the pickup truck in the driveway, Taya's deep consternation (in the reverse shots) anticipates the impending tragedy. The salutary effects so recently attributed to romantic dalliances and cultural affirmations alike are shockingly interrupted, all but erased, by news of the murder of Chris Kyle and his friend Chad Littlefield on February 2, 2013, at the hands of Eddie Ray Routh at the shooting range with their own guns.[21] We see now that the entire last scene, which began with the fatal date superimposed on the belt buckle and the Peacemaker, in effect labored throughout under history's stern demurral and under the fateful judgment of the tragic disposition indwelling in the heroic legacy. Taya still watches warily, knowingly, from her front door as the screen goes black and the bleak, severe message announces Kyle's death.

And so, *American Sniper*, seemingly toward the end so intent on healing Chris Kyle by dint of association with the Western, misses or else dismisses the opportunity to see Routh as a mirror for Kyle. Routh (of course minus a Taya of his own, children, and cowboy dreams) is himself the broken soldier who wants out of the war but cannot quite come home. Accordingly, Routh's minimally historicized appearance (he is never named, and he is credited only as "Marine," played by Geoff Pilkington) determines that tragedy afflicts the myth not as a force conspiratorially imposed on it by an unspecified external source but rather as the myth's own historical consequence. Not far beyond the patriotic fervor that would reinvent the continuity of the heroic myth against the counsels and remonstrances of history lies the horror made manifest by the myth's innate capacity for tragic self-subversion, so that every cry and clamor for its affirmation bares already and always the dark desire for an American tragedy. Chris Kyle, whose questionable deeds in Iraq might have nonetheless suited the needs of Hollywood, the heroic myth, and the persistent urge to overcome the Loss became, in Eastwood's vision, a victim—an outcast—no different from the veteran of the Vietnam War. Kill as he might, there would be no victory, no atonement for the ghosts of Vietnam. And isn't there thus an inevitable self-victimization present in the blind, ahistorical faith in the restorative power of the old tropes, namely that the hero should yet again find himself undone by the very powers that made him? Once he becomes a victim of the myth, the hero himself becomes the sign of the rupture, and the heroic imperative, so innocently—dare one say so sheepishly—once obeyed, merely charts the well-trod way to tragedy.

The autumn woods are resplendent once again, and father and son again walk in them as if in all the innocence of the Creation's first day. Each one carries a rifle, however, for the boy is to be initiated into the timeless sacramental American faith in the wisdom of the wilderness and of the hunt from whence emerges the mythic hero. The father, who knows what it is to kill man, woman, or child, provides the essential lesson. "You know that it's a heck of a thing to stop a beating heart," the father says. "Yeah," Colton (Max Charles) replies, though clearly he doesn't know. The reverence for the "beating heart" will never prove so overpowering that the father will forgo the son's initiation even if he, the father, knows every inch of the path that led him from the same eternal and sublime woods to the howling desert, from that first buck long ago to that woman and that boy in the sand-blown streets, and to at least some 160 more Iraqis.[22] Thus now, though seemingly so safely away from the blood and the grief of the father, the initiate Colton Kyle will inherit not only his American manhood but also the myth's indebtedness to history, which after all amply reveals the curse in the glory, the abidingly tragic in the myth. The father's faith in the myth, evident in the reenactment itself of his own first buck, points the way to the torments that await the son. The boy's initiation into the primal ritual of American manhood may or may not result in his individual tragedy, but the parallel event in the very next scene—that is, to the other shooting lesson, to the man who is about to kill Kyle—bares already the legacy's consequences in the spectral, threatening form of Eddie Ray Routh, whose disturbed psyche attests to the power of history to dismay the exceptionalist claims of the myth. The glory and grandeur of the woods yields with disturbing ease to the brimstone torments in Routh's soul.

When Kyle, just before leaving with Routh, tells Colton "Y'all look after our women, okay? It's a big responsibility," he confirms Colton as his heir. Colton is the new "sheepdog," and even if Routh, the menace lurking in the rear seat of the pickup, is "wolf" to Colton's father, he is also, in the chaotic collapse of the preposterously puerile allegory, as much a victim as Colton's own father was. Perhaps this boy will someday aspire to become "Legend," unaware (perhaps) even through all his warrior days that the glories of the heroic legacy themselves manifest and perpetuate America's primal sins. "Regeneration through violence" had long since come to imply a younger generation's assent to the heroic imperative, its foundation in and emergence from violence. Paradoxically, violence becomes both the thing regenerated and the presumed regenerative force. Violence is not only the cause of regeneration but is also the transferred, resumptive force itself, not an attribute of the myth but rather its very substance and form. Violence is the center and source of the vaunted continuity of the heroic myth. The perpetuated deadliness is the legacy. Violence, proverbially, does not end violence and instead sustains it, fosters it, and—ever indifferent to history's dire warnings—celebrates it as a thing distinctly, persistently, and irremediably American.

# Notes

## Introduction

1. For the full text of the "Long Telegram" (February 22, 1946), see "The Charge in the Soviet Union (Kennan) to the Secretary of State," The National Security Archive, George Washington University, https://nsarchive2.gwu.edu//coldwar/documents/episode-1/kennan.htm. See also X [George F. Kennan], "The Sources of Soviet Conduct," *Foreign Affairs* 25, no. 4 (July 1, 1947): 566–82.

2. *The Vietnam War*, episode 4, "Resolve," directed by Ken Burns and Lynn Novick, written by Geoffrey C. Ward, and narrated by Peter Coyote, aired on September 20, 2017, on PBS. See also E. W. Kenworthy, "Kennan Bids U.S. 'Dig In' and Await Talks in Vietnam," *New York Times*, February 11, 1966, 1, 3.

3. Adam Serwer, "Birtherism of a Nation," *The Atlantic*, May 13, 2020, https://www.theatlantic.com/ideas/archive/2020/05/birtherism-and-trump/610978/.

4. Timothy Egan, *A Fever in the Heartland: The Ku Klux Klan's Plot to Take over America, and the Woman Who Stopped Them* (New York: Viking, 2023), xxi.

5. Nicholas Confessore, "How Tucker Carlson Stoked White Fear to Conquer Cable," *New York Times*, April 30, 2022, https://www.nytimes.com/2022/04/30/us/tucker-carlson-gop-republican-party.html.

6. Tim O'Brien, *The Things They Carried* (New York: Broadway Books, 1990), 89.

7. O'Brien, *The Things They Carried*, 90.

8. O'Brien, *The Things They Carried*, 116.

9. James Baldwin, "Down at the Cross" [1963], in *The Fire Next Time* (New York: Vintage Books, 1993), 101. Originally published in the *New Yorker* as "Letter from a Region in My Mind," November 17, 1962, 142. In the decades since the original publication of Baldwin's essay, several prominent Black writers have challenged the heroic myth in ways that echo Baldwin's own. See, for example, Adam Serwer, *The Cruelty Is the Point: The Past, Present, and Future of Trump's America* (New York: One World, 2021), esp. 38–73 and 114–129. See also Clint Smith, *How the Word Is Passed: A Reckoning with the History of Slavery across America* (New York: Little, Brown, 2021). In Colson Whitehead's novel *The Underground Railroad* (New York: Doubleday, 2016), Elijah Lander, a fictional Frederick Douglass, condemns the white myth in terms that recall Baldwin's critique in *The Fire Next Time*.

10. Carol Anderson, "Self-Defense," in *The 1619 Project: A New Origin Story*, ed. Nikole Hannah-Jones, Caitlin Roper, Ilena Silverman, and Jake Silverstein (New York: One World, 2021), 266.

11. Trymaine Lee, "Inheritance," in *The 1619 Project*, 301.

12. Viet Thanh Nguyen, *Nothing Ever Dies: Vietnam and the Memory of War* (Cambridge: Harvard University Press, 2016), 106.

13. Nguyen, *Nothing Ever Dies*, 107.

14. James Q. Whitman, *Hitler's American Model: The United States and the Making of Nazi Race Law* (Princeton, NJ: Princeton University Press, 2017), 137.

15. William Faulkner, *Absalom, Absalom!* (1936; Corrected edition: New York: Vintage International, 1990), 283.

16. Toni Morrison, "Mourning for Whiteness," *New Yorker*, November 14, 2016, https://www.newyorker.com/magazine/2016/11/21/aftermath-sixteen-writers-on-trumps-america#anchor-morrison.

17. Toni Morrison, *Beloved* (New York: Vintage Books, 2004), 236.

18. Nikole Hannah-Jones, "Democracy," in *The 1619 Project*, 12 (emphasis added).

19. Walt Whitman, "From Pent-up Aching Rivers," in *Walt Whitman: Complete Poetry and Collected Prose*, ed. Justin Kaplan (New York: Library of America, 1982), 248.

20. Christian G. Appy, *American Reckoning: The Vietnam War and Our National Identity* (New York: Viking, 2015), 144.

21. Joan Didion, "John Wayne: A Love Song" [1965], in *Slouching towards Bethlehem: Essays* (New York: Farrar, Straus and Giroux, 2008), 30.

22. Robert Frost, "The Gift Outright," in *Robert Frost: Collected Poems, Prose, and Plays*, eds. Mark Richardson and Richard Poirier (New York: Library of America, 1995), 316.

23. Appy, *American Reckoning*, 144.

24. Michael Beschloss, *Reaching for Glory: Lyndon Johnson's Secret White House Tapes: 1964–1965* (New York: Simon & Schuster, 2001), 194.

25. *The Pentagon Papers: The Defense Department History of United States Decision-making on Vietnam*, Senator Gravel Edition, 4 vols. (Boston: Beacon, 1971), 3:348–49.

26. *The Pentagon Papers*, 3:349.

27. Ronald Reagan, "Peace: Restoring the Margin of Safety," speech delivered at the Veterans of Foreign Wars Convention, Chicago, August 18, 1980, https://www.reaganlibrary.gov/archives/speech/peace-restoring-margin-safety.

28. Richard Slotkin, *Gunfighter Nation: The Myth of the Frontier in Twentieth-Century America* (New York: Atheneum, 1992), 655.

## Chapter 1

1. Frederick Jackson Turner, "The Significance of the Frontier in American History," National Humanities Center, July 12, 1893, https://nationalhumanitiescenter.org/pds/gilded/empire/text1/turner.pdf.

2. Walt Whitman, "Facing West from California's Shores," in *Walt Whitman: Complete Poetry and Collected Prose*, ed. Justin Kaplan (New York: Library of America, 1982), 266–67.

3. *Extra Census Bulletin No. 2* (Washington, DC: Department of the Interior, Census Office, April 20, 1891), 4.

4. Michael Herr, *Dispatches* (New York: Vintage International, 1991), 46.

5. Herr, *Dispatches*, 46.

6. Among the most useful commentaries are Peter Bogdanovich, *John Ford* (Berkeley: University of California Press, 1968); Ronald Davis, *Duke: The Life and Image of John Wayne* (Norman: University of Oklahoma Press, 1998); Ronald Davis, *John Ford: Hollywood's Old Master* (Norman: University of Oklahoma Press, 1997); Brian W. Dippie, *Custer's Last Stand: The Anatomy of an American Myth* (Lincoln: University of Nebraska Press, 1994); Richard Drinnon, *Facing West: The Metaphysics of Indian-Hating and Empire Building* (New York: Schocken, 1980); Scott Eyman, *Print the Legend: The Life and Times of John Ford* (New York: Simon & Schuster, 1999); Tag Gallagher, *John Ford: The Man and His Films* (Berkeley: University of California Press, 1986); Paul Andrew Hutton, "Correct in Every Detail," in *The Custer Reader*, ed. Paul Andrew Hutton, 488–524 (Lincoln: University of Nebraska Press, 1992); Joseph McBride, *Searching for John Ford: A Life* (New York: St. Martin's, 2001); Geoffrey O'Brien, "John Ford: Superstar," *Village Voice* 31, no. 42 (October 21, 1986): 41–43; Leland Poague, "'All I Can See Is the Flags': 'Fort Apache' and the Visibility of History," *Cinema Journal* 27, no. 2 (Winter 1988): 8–26; Andrew Sarris, *The John Ford Mystery* (Bloomington: Indiana University Press, 1975); and Richard Slotkin, *Gunfighter Nation: The Myth of the Frontier in Twentieth-Century America* (New York: Atheneum, 1992).

7. Walt Whitman, "Specimen Days," in *Walt Whitman: Complete Poetry and Collected Prose*, ed. Justin Kaplan (New York: Library of America, 1982), 764.

8. Walt Whitman, "From Far Dakota's Cañons (June 25, 1876)," in *Walt Whitman: Complete Poetry and Collected Prose*, ed. Justin Kaplan, 592–93 (New York: Library of America, 1982).

9. Poague, "'All I Can See Is the Flags,'" makes much of the visual possibilities of this moment.

10. All the relevant sources here use "Moro" (from Lat. *Maurus*, i.e., an inhabitant of the old Roman province of Mauritania), the Spanish exonym dating back to the Middle Ages, for Muslims, whether from northwest Africa or, centuries later, from the southern archipelago of the Philippines.

11. *Glimpses of the Louisiana Purchase Exposition and the Famous Pike* (Chicago: Laird and Lee, 1904), caption to "Philippine Village" by Louis Biederman, n.p. For a map of the fairgrounds, see *The Standard Guide of the World's Fair* (St. Louis: Blattner Brothers, 1904). See also *Official Guide to the Louisiana Purchase Exposition*, comp. M. J. Lowenstein (St. Louis: Official Guide Co., 1904), 122.

12. Quoted in Angie Debo, *Geronimo: The Man, His Time, His Place* (Norman: University of Oklahoma Press, 1976), 415.

13. Roy Harvey Pearce, *Savagism and Civilization: A Study of the Indian and the American Mind* (Berkeley: University of California Press, 1988), 53.

14. Stuart Creighton Miller, *"Benevolent Assimilation": The American Conquest of the Philippines, 1899–1903* (New Haven, CT: Yale University Press, 1982), 250–51.

15. Nick Deocampo, "Imperialist Fictions: The Filipino in the Imperialist Imaginary," in *Vestiges of War: The Philippine-American War and the Aftermath of an Imperial Dream, 1899–1999*, ed. Angela Velasco Shaw and Luis H. Francia (New York: New

York University Press, 2002), 228. *Advance of Kansas Volunteers at Caloocan* (June 5, 1899) is available at the Library of Congress, https://www.loc.gov/item/98501192.

16. *Col. Funstan Swimming the Baglag River* (September 23, 1899), Library of Congress, https://www.loc.gov/item/99407593/.

17. Deocampo, "Imperialist Fictions," 229.

18. "America's Forgotten War in the Philippines," *New York Times*, April 1, 1989, https://www.nytimes.com/1989/04/01/opinion/americas-forgotten-war-in-the-philippines.html.

19. James Q. Whitman, *Hitler's American Model: The United States and the Making of Nazi Race Law* (Princeton, NJ: Princeton University Press, 2017), 41.

20. Whitman, *Hitler's American Model*, 40.

21. John Ford's *Stagecoach* was released on February 15, 1939; see Internet Movie Database, http://www.imdb.com/title/tt0031971/releaseinfo. *The Real Glory* was released on September 15; see Internet Movie Database, http://www.imdb.com/title/tt0031842/releaseinfo. Other well-known Westerns from 1939 are *Allegheny Uprising* (Seiter), *Destry Rides Again* (Marshall), *Dodge City* (Curtiz), *Drums along the Mohawk* (Ford), *Frontier Marshal* (Dwan), *Jesse James* (King), and *Union Pacific* (DeMille). See Internet Movie Database, https://www.imdb.com/search/title/?year=1939&title_type=feature&.

22. Quoted in Miller, "*Benevolent Assimilation*," 254.

23. Jack McCallum, *Leonard Wood: Rough Rider, Surgeon, Architect of American Imperialism* (New York: New York University Press, 2005), 205.

24. Patricio Abinales, "An American Colonial State: Authority and Structure in Southern Mindanao," in *Vestiges of War*, 90.

25. Abinales, "An American Colonial State," 92.

26. An older generation of Indian fighters—among them Jacob Smith (1840–1918), Adna Chaffee (1842–1914), Arthur MacArthur (1845–1912), and J. Franklin Bell (1856–1919)—served in the suppression of the Filipino insurrection. Since *The Real Glory* deals with the war against the Moros in the southern islands of the archipelago, I focus on two notable Indian fighters of the younger generation, Pershing and Leonard Wood.

27. Donald Smythe, *Guerrilla Warrior: The Early Life of John J. Pershing* (New York: Scribner, 1973), 23.

28. Smythe, *Guerrilla Warrior*, 83–84.

29. Slotkin, *Gunfighter Nation*, 16.

30. Smythe, *Guerrilla Warrior*, 186.

31. Smythe, *Guerrilla Warrior*, 188.

32. For a clear explanation of the noncombatants' movements to and from Bagsak, see Vic Hurley, *Swish of the Kris: The Story of the Moros* (New York: E. P. Dutton, 1936), 224–30.

33. Smythe, *Guerrilla Warrior*, 202. Peter Gordon Gowing, *Mandate in Moroland: The American Government of Muslim Filipinos* (Quezon City: New Day, 1983), writes that some weeks after Bud Bagsak, John McLean (Gowing has it as "McLeod"), a quartermaster employee, told a San Francisco reporter "that 2,000 Moors had been killed, including 196 women and 340 children" (240).

34. Smythe, *Guerrilla Warrior*, 204.

35. Historians tend to cite the number of Moro dead given initially by American officials to American newspapers. That number is six hundred. However, as Gowing

notes, Bud Dajo "was simply the last, most dramatic and most publicized of a long list of military operations Wood authorized as Commanding General of the Department of Mindanao. . . . [A] quick tally of some figures which Wood himself revealed in various reports and private correspondence makes it possible to estimate *conservatively* that about 3,000 Moros were killed while the American loss was less than 70" (Gowing, *Mandate in Moroland*, 164).

36. Quoted in Jack C. Lane, *Armed Progressive: General Leonard Wood* (San Rafael, CA: Presidio, 1978), 128.

37. Miller, "*Benevolent Assimilation*," 267.

38. *The American Film Institute Catalog of Motion Pictures Produced in the United States: Feature Films, 1931–1940: Film Entries, M–Z*, ed. Patricia King Hanson (Berkeley: University of California Press, 1993), 1748–49.

39. Charles L. Clifford, *The Real Glory* (London: William Heinemann, 1937), 5.

40. Larry Swindell, *The Last Hero: A Biography of Gary Cooper* (Garden City: Doubleday, 1980), 221.

41. Cited in Swindell, *The Last Hero*, 222.

42. "The Real Glory (1939)," *American Film Institute Catalog*, https://catalog.afi.com/Catalog/moviedetails/4869.

43. Benjamin Church, "Entertaining Passages Relating to Philip's War . . . with Some Account of the Divine Providence Towards Benj. Church Esqr." in *So Dreadfull a Judgment: Puritan Responses to King Philip's War, 1676–1677*, ed. Richard Slotkin and James K. Folsom (Hanover, NH: Wesleyan University Press, 1978), 397.

44. Theodore Roosevelt, *The Winning of the West*, Vol. 2, *Louisiana and the Northwest, 1791–1807* (Lincoln: University of Nebraska Press, 1995), 26.

45. Richard Hofstadter, "The Paranoid Style in American Politics," in *The Paranoid Style in American Politics and Other Essays*, 3–40 (Cambridge: Harvard University Press, 1964).

46. The origins of the juramentado, according to Sixto Y. Orosa, "lie in the jihad, the holy war of Islam against Christians. A juramentado was a frenzy-driven religious fanatic. He expected immediate translation to Paradise if he carried out his purpose. He was prepared and purified as for entering the mosque, a priest attending him, and his scalp and eyebrows were shaved. He put on a white gown (sarong) and took an oath before the Koran. Then he set out to kill the first Christian that he met and to keep on killing till he himself was killed." Sixto Y. Orosa, *The Sulu Archipelago and Its People* (Yonkers-on-Hudson, NY: World Book, 1923), 89.

47. Gowing points out that Americans learned the strategy of intimidating the Moros with pig skins and pigs' blood from the Spaniards and that the strategy "cut down on the number of juramentados for a while" (*Mandate in Moroland*, 99). According to Thomas Fleming, John J. Pershing, serving as governor of Moro Province, intimidated a group of Moros who were reluctant to sign an agreement by ladling pig's blood from a pail and holding it under their noses. "He then drew back his arm as if to fling the blood in their faces. The visitors shrank back. Then, slowly, silently, they came forward and scratched their marks on the paper, pledging somewhat dubious allegiance to the United States of America." Thomas Fleming, "Pershing's Island War," *American Heritage*, 19: no. 5 (August 1968), https://www.americanheritage.com/pershings-island-war. Smythe, however, reports a different result with pig skins. See Smythe, *Guerrilla Warrior*, 162–63. This lore concerning Moros and porcine matters

persists. In the summer of 2017, President Donald Trump declared his admiration for Pershing because Pershing had Moros shot with bullets dipped in pig's blood. See Linda Qiu, "Study Pershing, Trump Said. But the Story Doesn't Add Up," *New York Times*, August 17, 2017, https://www.nytimes.com/2017/08/17/us/politics/trump-tweet-pershing-fact-check.html?_r=0.

48. R. L. Bullard, "Preparing Our Moros for Government," in *The World's Story: A History of the World in Story, Song, and Art*, Vol. 1, *China, Japan, and the Islands of the Pacific*, ed. Eva March Tappan (Boston: Houghton Mifflin, 1914), 555.

49. Philippines Embassy, *The Story of Our Flag, Coat of Arms, and National Anthem* (Washington, DC: US Library of Information, 1949), 3.

50. Philippines (Republic) Embassy, *The Story of Our Flag*, 2.

51. Orosa, *The Sulu Archipelago and Its People*, 56–57.

52. See *Correspondence Relating to the War with Spain Including the Insurrection in the Philippine Islands and the China Relief Expedition, April 15, 1898, to July 30*, 1902, 2 vols. (Washington, DC: US Government Printing Office, 1993), General Orders No. 66, July 4, 1902, 2:1353.

## Chapter 2

1. It now seems likely that Bradley was not in the photograph after all. The position long assigned to Bradley may have been in fact occupied by Pfc. Harold Henry Schultz. See Matthew Hansen, "New Mystery Arises from Iconic Iwo Jima Image," https://omaha.com/new-mystery-arises-from-iconic-iwo-jima-image/image_b9c97612-5c3b-11e7-b10e-a34b95d0f3b6.html.

2. And includes, perhaps, a second wave of Iwo Jima movies, almost six decades after *Sands of Iwo Jima*, Clint Eastwood's *Flags of Our Fathers* and *Letters from Iwo Jima*, both released in 2006.

3. The opening credits introduce Rene A. Gagnon, Ira H. Hayes, and John H. Bradley as "the three living survivors of the historic flag raising on Mount Suribachi." Only after these names do we read, "Historical note—The First American Flag Was Raised on Mount Suribachi by the Late Sgt. Ernest ["Boots"] I. Thomas, Jr., U.S.M.C. on the Morning of February 23, 1945."

4. Holland M. Smith and Percy Finch, *Coral and Brass* (New York: Scribner, 1949), 261. A biography of James Forrestal suggests that "the story may well be apocryphal." See Townsend Hoopes and Douglas Brinkley, *Driven Patriot: The Life and Times of James Forrestal* (New York: Knopf, 1992), 199.

5. "Marines Fight Way to Airfield on Iwo Isle," *New York Times*, February 20, 1945, late city edition.

6. Casualty figures are from George W. Garand and Truman R. Strobridge, *Western Pacific Operations: History of U.S. Marine Corps Operations in World War II*, Vol. 4 (Washington, DC: US Government Printing Office, 1971), 525.

7. "War News Summarized: Wednesday, February 21, 1945," *New York Times*, February 21, 1945, late city edition.

8. Garand and Strobridge, *Western Pacific Operations*, 537.

9. Warren Moscow, "Foe Holds on Isle: Mortars, Mines Block Men Battling toward Second Iwo Air Field," *New York Times*, February 22, 1945, late city edition.

10. Warren Moscow, "Japanese Hit Back: One of 2 Heavy Blows Believed Repulsed—Our Casualties at 5,372," *New York Times*, February 23, 1945, late city edition.

11. Moscow, "Japanese Hit Back," 6.

12. Staff Sgt. David Dempsey, Marine Corps Combat Correspondent, "Ghastly Ruin Lines Iwo Landing Beach," *New York Times*, February 23, 1945, 5.

13. Garand and Strobridge, *Western Pacific Operations*, 564 (emphasis added). For a compelling explanation of how Mount Suribachi came to fall so much earlier than the rest of the island, see Kumiko Kakehashi, *So Sad to Fall in Battle: An Account of War*, trans. Giles Murray (New York: Presidio, 2007), 68.

14. Warren Moscow, "Airfield Edge Won: Third Marine Division Fights Way to Fighter Strip on Iwo Isle," *New York Times*, February 24, 1945, late city edition.

15. Garand and Strobridge, *Western Pacific Operations*, 569.

16. By wireless to the *New York Times*, "Marines Seize Most of Iwo Airfield: One Runway Won," *New York Times*, February 26, 1945, late city edition.

17. United Press, "Forrestal Pays Tribute to Marines; He Hit Iwo Beach behind Them," *New York Times*, February 26, 1945, late city edition. The photograph of Secretary Forrestal is on page 5.

18. Figures are from Robert S. Burrell, *The Ghosts of Iwo Jima* (College Station: Texas A&M University Press, 2006), 83.

19. Warren Moscow, "U.S. Planes Use Iwo Field, Marines Push On: Americans Storm and Take Iwo Hill," *New York Times*, February 27, 1945, late city edition.

20. "3-Ply Marine Push Wins More of Iwo," *New York Times*, February 28, 1945, late city edition.

21. Seated extreme left is Ira Hayes, who helped hoist the second flag. Extreme right is Sgt. Henry "Hank" Hansen, who helped raise the first flag.

22. Jim Bishop, *FDR's Last Year: April 1944–April 1945* (New York: William Morrow, 1974), 479 (emphasis added). I note, however, that 27,000 "American lives" is an inflated number even for total American casualties on Iwo Jima. Bishop does not reveal Roosevelt's source for the figure.

23. Bishop, *FDR's Last Year*, 479.

24. Richard Wheeler, *Iwo* (Annapolis, MD: Naval Institute Press, 1980), 188.

25. James Bradley, with Ron Powers, *Flags of Our Fathers* (New York: Bantam Books, 2000), 234.

26. Bill D. Ross, *Iwo Jima: Legacy of Valor* (New York: 1st Vintage Books ed., 1986), 321 (emphasis added).

27. "4,000 Marine Dead on Iwo Indicated: Admiral Turner Says Loss Was Less Than Fifth of Japanese Killed—Operation Praised," *New York Times*, March 16, 1945.

28. Robert Trumbull, "Marines Conquer All of Iwo; 4,189 Slain, 15,308 Injured," *New York Times*, March 17, 1945, late city edition.

29. For an example of the calls to replace US Navy and US Marine Corps command in the Pacific, see the editorial "MacArthur Is Our Best Strategist," *San Francisco Examiner*, February 27, 1945.

30. In this assessment of the muddling of casualty figures in the battle, I have followed Burrell, *The Ghosts of Iwo Jima*. Historians, Burrell notes, "have overlooked the strategic decisions that sent these warriors to make such horrific sacrifices. One can honor the Marines' bravery without conflating it with their commanders' wisdom" (126).

31. Trumbull, "Marines Conquer All of Iwo."

32. Ross, *Iwo Jima*, 335.

33. Robbie Lieberman, "Communism, Peace Activism, and Civil Liberties: From the Waldorf Conference to the Peekskill Riot," *Journal of American Culture* 18, no. 3 (Fall 1995), 59–65.

34. Richard Hofstadter, "The Pseudo-Conservative Revolt—1954," in *The Paranoid Style in American Politics and Other Essays* (Cambridge: Harvard University Press, 1964), 64.

35. For a facsimile of the "Long Telegram," see "#OTD February 22, 1946 | The Long Telegram," Truman Library Institute, February 22, 2022, https://www.trumanlibraryinstitute.org/kennan/.

36. For a discussion of Kennan's views in terms of "courtship" and "seduction," see Alan Nadel, *Containment Culture: American Narratives, Postmodernism, and the Atomic Age* (Durham, NC: Duke University Press, 1995), 29–33.

37. X [George F. Kennan], "The Sources of Soviet Conduct," *Foreign Affairs* 65, no. 4 (Spring 1987): 852–68, http://www.jstor.org/stable/20043098.

38. Richard Hofstadter, "The Paranoid Style in American Politics," in *The Paranoid Style in American Politics and Other Essays* (Cambridge: Harvard University Press, 1964), 29.

39. Hofstadter, "The Paranoid Style in American Politics," 29–30.

40. Lieberman, "Communism, Peace Activism, and Civil Liberties," 59.

41. Marion Starkey, *The Devil in Massachusetts: A Modern Inquiry into the Salem Witch Trials* (New York: Knopf, 1950), vi.

42. "Cinema: New Pictures," *Time* 54 (October 17, 1949), 102 and 104.

43. Cited in Roger M. Williams, "A Rough Sunday at Peekskill," *American Heritage Magazine* 27, no. 3 (April 1976), https://www.americanheritage.com/rough-sunday-peekskill.

44. "Communists: Picnic at Peekskill," *Time* 54 (September 5, 1949), 15.

45. Cited in "Birth of a Riot?" *Newsweek* 34 (December 12, 1949), 55.

46. See Lieberman, "Communism, Peace Activism, and Civil Liberties," 61.

47. "The Peekskill Riot," *Washington Post*, August 29, 1949, 6.

48. "Communists: Picnic at Peekskill," 15.

49. "Nightmare in Peekskill," *The Nation* 169 (September 10, 1949), 243–44.

50. "Nightmare in Peekskill," 244.

51. Williams, "A Rough Sunday at Peekskill."

52. "Nightmare in Peekskill," 244.

53. Howard Fast, "Peekskill," www.trussel.com/hf/peeks2.htm. Originally appeared in *Masses and Mainstream* 4 (May 1951). The cited web page, however, erroneously provides the date as "March 1949," a time when the Peekskill Riots were still half a year away.

54. John Egerton, *Speak Now against the Day: The Generation before the Civil Rights Movement in the South* (New York: Knopf, 1994), 365.

55. James Baldwin, "Down at the Cross: Letter from a Region in My Mind," in *The Fire Next Time* (New York: Vintage, 1963), 54–55. Originally published in *The New Yorker*, November 17, 1962, as "Letter from a Region in My Mind."

56. *The Blinding of Isaac Woodard: How a Horrific Incident of Racial Violence Became a Powerful Catalyst for the Civil Rights Movement*, PBS: American Experience,

March 20, 2021, https://www.pbs.org/wgbh/americanexperience/films/blinding-isaac-wwoodard/#part01.

57. Gilbert King, *Devil in the Grove: Thurgood Marshall, the Groveland Boys, and the Dawn of a New America* (New York: HarperCollins, 2012), 35.

58. King, *Devil in the Grove*, 36.

59. King, *Devil in the Grove*, 127.

60. King, *Devil in the Grove*, 132.

61. See Amanda Holpuch, "Four Black Men Wrongly Charged with Rape Are Exonerated 72 Years Later," *New York Times*, November 22, 2021, https://www.nytimes.com/2021/11/22/us/groveland-four-exonerated-florida.html.

62. "Life Visits Audie Murphy," *Life*, 19, no. 3 (July 16, 1945): 94–97.

63. Don Graham, *No Name on the Bullet: A Biography of Audie Murphy* (New York: Viking Penguin, 1989), 2–3.

64. Quoted in Graham, *No Name on the Bullet*, 8.

65. Graham, *No Name on the Bullet*, 20–21.

66. Audie Murphy, *To Hell and Back: The Classic Memoir of World War II by America's Most Decorated Soldier* (New York: Henry Holt, 2002), 188–89.

67. Murphy, *To Hell and Back*, 243.

68. Graham, *No Name on the Bullet*, 246.

69. Graham, *No Name on the Bullet*, 247.

70. Meyer Berger, "Veteran Kills 12 in Mad Rampage on Camden Street," *New York Times*, September 6, 1949, https://timesmachine.nytimes.com/timesmachine/1949/09/07/84278658.html. Soon after the massacre, the toll was given as thirteen.

71. "Killer on a Rampage in East Camden, N.J.," *Newsweek* 34 (September 19, 1949), 21–22.

72. "12 Minutes of Murder: War Veteran Runs Amok in Camden and Kills 13 with a German Pistol," *Life* 27 (September 19, 1949), 61–62.

73. "12 Minutes of Murder," 61.

74. "Man Who Killed 13 Is Adjudged Insane," *New York Times* (October 8, 1949), https://timesmachine.nytimes.com/timesmachine/1949/10/08/issue.html.

75. Ellis M. Zacharias, "The Forrestal Enigma: Inside Report on a Philosophy of Power," *United Nations World* 3, no. 3 (March 1949): 14–16.

76. Zacharias, "The Forrestal Enigma," 14–15.

77. Hoopes and Douglas Brinkley, *Driven Patriot*, 452.

78. George C. Herring, *America's Longest War: The United States and Vietnam, 1950–1975*, 6th ed. (New York: McGraw-Hill Education, 2020), 17.

79. "Gyrene" is slang for a US marine. See *Merriam-Webster's Collegiate Dictionary*, 11th ed. (2003), s.v. "gyrene."

80. Randy Roberts and James S. Olson, *John Wayne: American* (Lincoln: University of Nebraska Press, 1995), 209–11. "Duke's case," Roberts and Olson insist, "was not a matter of draft dodging" (209). Yet, considering everything else that they report about this time in Wayne's life, draft dodging may indeed have been "Duke's case." See also Tag Gallagher, *John Ford: The Man and His Films* (Berkeley: University of California Press, 1986), 214; and Scott Eyman, *John Wayne: The Life and Legend* (New York: Simon & Schuster, 2014), 130–32.

81. See "Iconic Artifacts," National Museum of the Marine Corps, http://www.usmcmuseum.com/iconic-artifacts.html.

82. Bradley had been identified, though perhaps mistakenly, as one of the flag raisers. See note 1 above.

83. Roberts and Olson, *John Wayne*, 321. See also Lawrence H. Suid, *Guts and Glory: The Making of the American Image in Film*, revised and expanded ed. (Lexington: University Press of Kentucky, 2002), 116.

84. Such is the "insight" that eases the guilt of Ira Hayes (Tony Curtis) in *The Outsider* (Delbert Mann, 1961). Alone at the foot of the US Marine Corps memorial in Washington, DC, Hayes has an epiphany: "It was," he tells a friend, "like God said, 'Everything's okay now. You know, this thing is just a symbol. You don't have to carry it around in your guts no more.'"

## Chapter 3

1. William Manchester, *Goodbye, Darkness: A Memoir of the Pacific War* (New York: Back Bay Books, 2002), 12.

2. Kenneth D. Rose, *Myth and the Greatest Generation: A Social History of Americans in World War II* (New York: Routledge, 2008), 169–70.

3. Randy Roberts and James S. Olson, *John Wayne: American* (Lincoln: University of Nebraska Press, 1997), 295.

4. Tobias Wolff, *In Pharaoh's Army: Memories of the Lost War* (New York: Vintage, 1994), 127.

5. Wolff, *In Pharaoh's Army*, 128.

6. Kurt Vonnegut, *Slaughterhouse-Five, or The Children's Crusade, a Duty-Dance with Death* (New York: Dell, 1969), 14.

7. Vonnegut, *Slaughterhouse-Five*, 15.

8. Roger Ebert, "Deep in the Heart of Texas," July 04, 2004, https://www.rogerebert.com/reviews/great-movie-the-last-picture-show-1971.

9. Ron Kovic, *Born on the Fourth of July* (New York: Pocket Books, 1977), 73.

10. Kovic, *Born on the Fourth of July*, 74.

11. James Webb, *Fields of Fire* (New York: Bantam, 2002), 34.

12. Webb, *Fields of Fire*, 25.

13. Webb, *Fields of Fire*, 31.

14. Webb, *Fields of Fire*, 33.

15. Webb, *Fields of Fire*, 35.

16. Webb, *Fields of Fire*, 36–37.

17. John Wayne, "A Candid Conversation with the Straight-Shooting Superstar/Superpatriot," interview by Richard Warren Lewis, *Playboy* 18, no. 5 (May 1971), 80. William Manchester, *American Caesar: Douglas MacArthur, 1880–1964* (Boston: Little, Brown, 1978), 702, says only that Wayne was MacArthur's favorite movie star.

18. Richard Slotkin, *Gunfighter Nation: The Myth of the Frontier in Twentieth-Century America* (New York: Atheneum, 1992), 514.

19. "Authorizing the President to Present on Behalf of the Congress a Gold Medal to John Wayne," *Congressional Record—House*, May 23, 1979, https://www.govinfo.gov/content/pkg/GPO-CRECB-1979-pt10/pdf/GPO-CRECB-1979-pt10-3-2.pdf.

20. Robert Jay Lifton, *Home from the War: Vietnam Veterans; Neither Victims nor Executioners* (New York: Basic Books, 1985), 219–20 (ellipses in the original).
21. John M. Del Vecchio, *The 13th Valley* (New York: St. Martin's Griffin, 1998), 7.
22. Del Vecchio, *The 13th Valley*, 126.
23. Del Vecchio, *The 13th Valley*, x–xi.
24. Del Vecchio, *The 13th Valley*, 146.
25. Lifton, *Home from the War*, 9.
26. Lifton, *Home from the War*, xi.
27. Chuck Keen, producer, and John Wayne, host, *No Substitute for Victory* (Alaska Pictures Productions, 1970; Echo Bridge Home Entertainment, 2004, DVD).
28. Paul Fussell, *The Great War and Modern Memory* (New York: Oxford University Press, 2000), 222.
29. Michael Herr, *Dispatches* (New York: Vintage, 1991), 209.
30. Fred Turner, *Echoes of Combat: Trauma, Memory, and the Vietnam War* (Minneapolis: University of Minnesota Press, 2001), 21.
31. Eric Bentley, "The Political Theatre of John Wayne," in *Theatre of War: Comments on 32 Occasions* (New York: Viking, 1972), 309.
32. Philip Caputo, *A Rumor of War* (New York: Owl Books, 1996), 6.
33. Herr, *Dispatches*, 20.
34. Gustav Hasford, *The Short-Timers* (New York: Bantam Books, 1978), 172.
35. Hasford, *The Short-Timers*, 176.
36. Christian G. Appy, *Working-Class War: American Combat Soldiers and Vietnam* (Chapel Hill: University of North Carolina Press, 1993), 281.
37. Turner, *Echoes of Combat*, 24.
38. Kovic, *Born on the Fourth of July*, 112.
39. Wayne, "Candid Conversation with the Straight-Shooting Superstar/Superpatriot," 84.
40. Slotkin, *Gunfighter Nation*, 519–20. For somewhat different definitions of the John Wayne Syndrome, see Garry Wills, *John Wayne's America: The Politics of Celebrity* (New York: Touchstone, 1998, 13). See also Lifton, *Home from the War*, 219.
41. Jonathan Shay, *Achilles in Vietnam: Combat Trauma and the Undoing of Character* (New York: Scribner, 1994), 15.
42. Shay, *Achilles in Vietnam*, 20. See also Wills, *John Wayne's America*, 11.
43. Wills, *John Wayne's America*, 110.
44. Frank Allen Patterson, ed., *The Student's Milton: Being the Complete Poems of John Milton* (New York: Appleton-Century-Crofts, 1930), 167.
45. Voltaire, *Henriade*, quoted by William James, *The Will to Believe and Other Essays in Popular Philosophy* (New York: Dover, 1956), 62.
46. Hasford, *The Short-Timers*, 172.
47. Herr, *Dispatches*, 244.
48. Lifton, *Home from the War*, 223–24.
49. Caputo, *A Rumor of War*, 128.
50. Kovic, *Born on the Fourth of July*, 204.
51. Kovic, *Born on the Fourth of July*, 205–6.
52. See Slotkin, *Gunfighter Nation*, 522. The name of this character, Mike Kirby, appears nowhere in the source text, Robin Moore's *The Green Berets* (New York: Crown, 1965).

53. For Kennedy and counterinsurgency, see Richard Drinnon, *Facing West: The Metaphysics of Indian-Hating and Empire-Building* (New York: Schocken, 1980), 369–73. See also Slotkin, *Gunfighter Nation*, 497–504.

54. Released by RCA in early 1966, eighteen months before the release of Wayne's movie. See Wills, *John Wayne's America*, 229.

55. John Hellmann, *American Myth and the Legacy of Vietnam* (New York: Columbia University Press, 1986), 36.

56. Roger Hilsman, "Internal War: The New Communist Tactic," in *The Guerrilla—and How to Fight Him*, Fleet Marine Force Reference Publication 12–25, 22–36 (Washington, DC: Department of the Navy, 1990), reprint of *The Guerrilla—and How to Fight Him: Selections from the Marine Corps Gazette*, ed. Lt. Col. T. N. Greene (New York: Praeger, 1962).

57. W. W. Rostow, "Guerrilla Warfare in Underdeveloped Areas," in *The Guerrilla—and How to Fight Him*, Fleet Marine Force Reference Publication 12-25 (Washington, DC: Department of the Navy, 1990), https://www.marines.mil/Portals/1/Publications/FMFRP%2012-25%20%20The%20Guerrilla%20and%20How%20to%20Fight%20Him.pdf.

58. Walter Cronkite, "We Are Mired in Stalemate," Transcript of broadcast, CBS Evening News, February 27, 1968, in *Reporting Vietnam, Part 1: American Journalism, 1959–1969*, 581–82 (New York: Library of America, 1998).

59. Moore, *Green Berets*, 164.

60. Moore, *Green Berets*, 6.

## Chapter 4

1. Tim O'Brien, *If I Die in a Combat Zone* (New York: Broadway Books, 1975), 11.

2. "The One Great Power," *Hearts and Minds*, chapter 1, directed by Peter Davis (Rainbow Pictures, 1974; Criterion Collection, 2003, DVD).

3. "The Unsung Soldiers," *Vietnam: The Ten Thousand Day War*, produced by Michael Maclear and Ian McLeod, written by Peter Arnett, side 3 of 3 (Canadian Broadcasting Corp., 1980, DVD).

4. Denis Johnson, *Tree of Smoke* (New York: Farrar, Straus and Giroux, 2007), 603.

5. "The Unsung Soldiers."

6. For General Westmoreland, see "Uneasy Allies," *Ten Thousand Day War*, side 1 of 3. For President Obama, see Barack Obama, "Remarks by the President at 93rd Annual Conference of the American Legion," The White House, August 30, 2011, https://obamawhitehouse.archives.gov/the-press-office/2011/08/30/remarks-president-93rd-annual-conference-american-legion.

7. Stanley Karnow, *Vietnam: A History*, 2nd ed. (New York: Penguin Books, 1997), 19.

8. Jerry Lembcke, *The Spitting Image: Myth, Memory, and the Legacy of Vietnam* (New York: New York University Press, 2000). Lembcke bases his entire argument on the following premise: "relations between veterans and the anti-war movement were empathetic and mutually supportive. On the basis of that provable truth, I argue that the image of spat-upon veterans must be false" (6). But see Lawrence A. Tritle, *From*

*Melos to My Lai: War and Survival* (London: Routledge, 2000), 197. Gary Kulik's argument contra Lembcke seems to me as dependent on plausibility, conjecture, and hearsay as he claims Lembcke's own is. See Gary Kulik, *"War Stories": False Atrocity Tales, Swift Boaters, and Winter Soldiers—What Really Happened in Vietnam* (Washington, DC: Potomac Books, 2009), 92–94.

9. Quoted in Karnow, *Vietnam*, 670.

10. Samuel Hynes, *The Soldiers' Tale: Bearing Witness to Modern War* (New York: Penguin, 1997), 177.

11. Nathaniel Hawthorne, "Young Goodman Brown," in *Nathaniel Hawthorne: Tales and Sketches* (New York: Library of America, 1982), 285–86.

12. Hawthorne, "Young Goodman Brown," 284.

13. Joseph Conrad, *Heart of Darkness*, 5th ed. (Norton Critical Edition), ed. Paul B. Armstrong (New York: Norton, 2016), 7.

14. Clint Smith, "When People Say 'We Have Made It through Worse Before,'" in *Above Ground: Poems* (New York: Little, Brown, 2023), 12.

15. "Extra Census Bulletin No. 2" (Washington, DC: Department of the Interior, Census Office, April 20, 1891).

16. W. D. Ehrhart, *Vietnam-Perkasie: A Combat Marine Memoir* (Jefferson, NC: McFarland, 1983), 246.

17. Ehrhart, *Vietnam-Perkasie*, 246–47.

18. Ron Kovic, *Born on the Fourth of July* (New York: Pocket Books, 1977), 222.

19. Robert C. Mason, *Chickenhawk* (New York: Penguin, 1983), 430.

20. Kovic, *Born on the Fourth of July*, 223.

21. "Feeling of Men Coming Back from Vietnam, before the Senate Committee on Public Relations," in "John F. Kerry: Senate Committee on Foreign Relations, April 22, 1971," Digital History, http://www.digitalhistory.uh.edu/learning_history/vietnam/kerry.cfm.

22. John Del Vecchio, *The 13th Valley* (New York: St. Martin's Griffin, 1982), 589.

23. Philip Caputo, *A Rumor of War* (New York: Henry Holt, 1996), 335.

24. Caputo, *A Rumor of War*, 220.

25. My sources for accounts of the battle are "Cursing Their Colonel, GIs Reel Bleeding off Mountain," *Lexington Herald* [Kentucky], May 19, 1969; Samuel Zaffiri, *Hamburger Hill: The Brutal Battle for Dong Ap Bia: May 11–20, 1969* (New York: Presidio, 1988); David Lamb, "Reporters at Work: Giving a Battle a Name," About Editing and Writing, Blog by Jack Limpert, September 4, 2012, jacklimpert.com/2012/09/reporter-at-work-giving-a-battle-a-name/; Guenter Lewy, *America in Vietnam* (New York: Oxford University Press, 1978); and Douglas P. Scalard, "The Battle of Hamburger Hill: Battle Command in Difficult Terrain against a Determined Enemy," in *Studies in Battle Command*, 165–75 (Fort Leavenworth, KS: Combat Studies Institute Press, 1995).

26. Zaffiri, *Hamburger Hill*, 277.

27. Albert Camus, "The Myth of Sisyphus," in *The Myth of Sisyphus and Other Essays*, trans. Justin O'Brien (New York: Vintage International, 1991), 33.

28. Camus, "The Myth of Sisyphus," 28.

29. Camus, "The Myth of Sisyphus," 50.

30. Jonathan Shay, *Achilles in Vietnam: Combat Trauma and the Undoing of Character* (New York: Scribner, 1994), 38.

31. Camus, "The Myth of Sisyphus," 42.

32. Camus, "The Myth of Sisyphus," 12 (emphasis added).

33. Camus, "The Myth of Sisyphus," 54.

34. If we have seen anything like this face before, it is when the entire platoon viciously attacks Leonard, who is bound to his bunk and gagged, with slings made of soap bars in hand towels, one whack per marine, all aimed at the torso. Joker, last in line and initially the most reluctant of the torturers, grimaces, hesitates, and then, in uncontrolled rage, lets loose with many vicious swings.

35. For the lyrics of the march that introduced *The Mickey Mouse Club* show, see https://www.youtube.com/watch?v=x4C_lUy58Rw. All other lyrics sung in *Full Metal Jacket* to the same tune seem to be specific to the movie.

36. Joker's élan in these last moments shows an affinity with reports of postcombat euphoria. "After a firefight," says the narrator in Tim O'Brien's chapter "How to Tell a True War Story," "there is always the immense pleasure of aliveness. The trees are alive. The grass, the soil—everything. All around you things are purely living, and you among them, and the aliveness makes you tremble." Tim O'Brien, *The Things They Carried* (New York: Broadway Books, 1990), 81. And consider this other one: moments after witnessing a comrade's death, Paul Baumer, the protagonist of Remarque's *All Quiet on the Western Front*, attests, "The night crackles electrically, the front thunders like a concert of drums. My limbs move supplely, I feel my joints strong. I breathe the air deeply. The night lives, I live. I feel a hunger, greater than comes from the belly alone." Erich Maria Remarque, *All Quiet on the Western Front*, trans. by A. W. Wheen (New York: Fawcett, 1958), 33.

## Chapter 5

1. See "*The Deer Hunter* and Michael Cimino winning Best Picture and Directing: 1979 Oscars," YouTube, https://www.youtube.com/watch?v=og8pywu8gbU.

2. Scott Eyman, *John Wayne: The Life and Legend* (New York: Simon & Schuster, 2014), 552.

3. Randy Roberts and James S. Olson, *John Wayne: American* (Lincoln: University of Nebraska Press, 1995), 634.

4. Eyman, *John Wayne*, 552.

5. For Wayne at the ceremony, see https://www.youtube.com/watch?v=og8pywu8gbU.

6. Eyman, *John Wayne*, 554.

7. Roberts and Olson, *John Wayne*, 633.

8. Garry Wills, *John Wayne's America* (New York: Touchstone Books, 1997), 18–19.

9. See the documentary *I Knew It Was You: Rediscovering John Cazale*, directed by Richard Shepard (Oscilloscope Laboratories, 2009), DVD.

10. John Hellmann, "Vietnam and the Hollywood Genre Film: Inversions of American Mythology in *The Deer Hunter* and *Apocalypse Now*," *American Quarterly* 34, no. 4 (Autumn 1982), 418–39.

11. Hellmann, "Vietnam and the Hollywood Genre Film," 423.

12. Keith Beattie, *The Scar That Binds: American Culture and the Vietnam War* (New York: New York University Press, 1998), holds that the Green Beret sergeant's

laconic "Fuck it!" amounts to a "failure" on Cimino's part "to invest his characters with any opportunity to speak" (70). See also Peter Lehman, "'Well, what's it like over there? Can you tell us anything?': Looking for Vietnam in *The Deer Hunter*," *North Dakota Quarterly* 51, no. 3 (Summer 1983), 131–41.

13. James Fenimore Cooper, *The Pioneers, or the Sources of the Susquehanna; A Descriptive Tale*, in *The Leatherstocking Tales*, Vol. 1 (New York: Library of America, 1985), 268.

14. William Faulkner, *Go Down, Moses* (New York: Vintage International, 2011), 5.

15. Faulkner, *Go Down, Moses*, 268.

16. Faulkner, *Go Down, Moses*, 310.

17. The conjecture that Michael learns that Nick is alive only after Steven shows him the drawer full of cash has been made before by Susan Jeffords, *The Remasculinization of America: Gender and the Vietnam War* (Bloomington: Indiana University Press, 1989), 94–96.

18. Aljean Harmetz writes that director Michael Cimino "made it clear that the singing of 'God Bless America' by the film's survivors—an ending that early reviewers considered to be ironic—was not irony but a sincere expression of faith in America." Aljean Harmetz, "Oscar-Winning 'Deer Hunter' Is under Attack as Racist," *New York Times*, April 26, 1979, https://www.nytimes.com/1979/04/26/archives/oscarwinning-deer-hunter-is-under-attack-as-racist-film-among-the.html.

19. Consider, for instance, the veteran's return in *First Blood* (Kotcheff, 1982), *Birdy* (Parker, 1984), *Born on the Fourth of July* (Stone, 1989), *Casualties of War* (De Palma, 1989), *Jacob's Ladder* (Lyne, 1990), and *Heaven & Earth* (Stone, 1993). Michael Vronsky's first impulse upon his return to Clairton is to hide from his friends. Consider also *Return* (Johnson, 2011), discussed in the introduction, in which the soldier's gender has a great deal to do with the conditions and the outcome of the return.

## Chapter 6

1. *Apocalypse Now*, directed by Francis Ford Coppola (Omni Zoetrope, 1979; "Full Disclosure Edition," Blu-ray, 2010). All cited dialogue is from the soundtrack.

2. Richard Slotkin, "Unit Pride: Ethnic Platoons and the Myths of American Nationality," *American Literary History* 13, no. 3 (Autumn 2001): 491–92.

3. In the source narrative by David Lang there are ambiguities—for example, about the chain of command, as Eriksson tells Lang (738)—that refocus the movie's perhaps too simple good-versus-evil polarities. David Lang, "Casualties of War," in *Reporting Vietnam, Part One: American Journalism 1959–1969* (New York: Library of America, 1998), 709–67. To be sure, Meserve does not enter the narrative as a thorough villain. His hatred of the Vietnamese emerges fully from his grief at the unexpected death of his buddy, the easygoing Brown (or "Brownie," played by Erik King).

4. Viet Than Nguyen, *Nothing Ever Dies: Vietnam and the Memory of War* (Cambridge: Harvard University Press, 2017), 120.

5. Joseph Conrad, *Heart of Darkness*, 5th ed. (Norton Critical Edition), ed. Paul B. Armstrong (New York: Norton, 2016), 36.

6. Conrad, *Heart of Darkness*, 48.

7. Margo Norris, "Modernism and Vietnam: Francis Ford Coppola's *Apocalypse Now*," *Modern Fiction Studies* 44, no. 3 (1998): 730–66.

8. Walter Murch, who led the efforts on the movie's sound design, sound editing, and editing, explains to Peter Cowie that "having a song called 'The End' at the beginning of the film has its own irony, . . . and yet there are images at the beginning that forecast the end, so it's telegraphic in a sense." Peter Cowie, *The "Apocalypse Now" Book* (Boston: Da Capo, 2000), 100. See also Karl French, *"Apocalypse Now" Bloomsbury Movie Guide No. 1* (New York: Mass-Market Paperback, 1999), 165–66.

9. Col. Robert Rheault—one source for Walter E. Kurtz—used the phrase "terminate with extreme prejudice" when he ordered the assassination of a suspected double agent. See Frank McCulloch, "The Fall of a 'Lost Soldier,'" *Life*, November 14, 1969, 34–40. See also Stanley Karnow, *Vietnam: A History*, 2nd revised ed. (New York: Penguin Books, 1997), 615; Cowie, *The "Apocalypse Now" Book*, 22 and 74; and French, *"Apocalypse Now" Bloomsbury Movie Guide No. 1*, 197–98.

10. Jonathan Schell, *The Real War: The Classic Reporting on the Vietnam War* (New York: Pantheon Books, 1988), 208.

11. Neil Sheehan, *A Bright Shining Lie: John Paul Vann and America in Vietnam* (New York: Vintage, 1988), 731. See also Karnow, *Vietnam*, 617. For more on the Phoenix Program, see Gabriel Kolko, *Anatomy of a War: Vietnam, the United States, and the Modern Historical Experience* (New York: New Press, 1994), 397, 398; and Frances FitzGerald, *Fire in the Lake: The Vietnamese and the Americans in Vietnam* (New York: Vintage Books, 1989), 516.

12. James George Frazer, *The Golden Bough: A Study in Magic and Religion*, new abridged ed. (Oxford: Oxford University Press, 1998), 588.

13. Transcribed from the onscreen close-ups of the document.

14. Nick Turse, *Kill Anything that Moves: The Real American War in Vietnam* (New York: Metropolitan Books, 2013), 14.

15. See Spencer E. Tucker, ed., *Encyclopedia of the Vietnam War: A Political, Social, and Military History* (New York: Oxford University Press, 1998), 264–65; and Karnow, *Vietnam*, 606.

16. Michel Foucault, *Madness and Civilization: A History of Insanity in the Age of Reason*, trans. Richard Howard (New York: Vintage Books, 1965), 66.

17. Foucault, *Madness and Civilization*, 67.

18. "The War in Vietnam (1961–1968)," *The Sixties*, produced by Tom Hanks and Gary Goetzman, CNN, first broadcast June 19, 2014.

19. Robert Jay Lifton, "Bearing Witness to My Lai and Vietnam," in *Facing My Lai: Moving Beyond the Massacre*, ed. David L. Anderson (Lawrence: University Press of Kansas, 1998), 21.

20. Tucker, *Encyclopedia of the Vietnam War*, 20–21.

21. Walter Benjamin, "Theses on the Philosophy of History," in *Illuminations*, trans. Harry Zohn, ed. Hannah Arendt (New York: Mariner Books, 2019), 200.

22. Quoted in George C. Herring, *From Colony to Superpower: U.S. Foreign Relations Since 1776* (New York: Oxford University Press, 2008), 912.

23. Calley was speaking to a jury of six US Army officers before they deliberated on his participation in the My Lai Massacre (March 16, 1968). Calley stood accused of personally killing twenty-two Vietnamese men, women, children, and babies. See

"Text of Calley Statement," *New York Times*, March 31, 1971, https://timesmachine.nytimes.com/timesmachine/1971/03/31/issue.html. See also Homer Bigart, "Calley Pleads for Understanding," *New York Times*, March 31, 1971, https://timesmachine.nytimes.com/timesmachine/1971/03/31/81878923.html?pageNumber=1.

## Chapter 7

1. *Oscar Presents: The War Movies and John Wayne*, Directed by Mel Stuart, written by Charles Champlin (Academy of Motion Picture Arts and Sciences, 1977). I screened the DVD of this two-hour presentation at the Pickford Center for Motion Picture Study in Hollywood. My thanks to Cassie Blake and May Haduong for making the DVD available for viewing at the center's facilities.

2. The screenplay writer of *Home of the Brave*, Carl Foreman, also proved problematic for Wayne. Foreman, who had written the screenplay for *High Noon* (Zinneman, 1952)—a movie that Wayne was ever ready to disparage—had been a prominent target of the McCarthy hearings. In the 1971 *Playboy* interview, Wayne maintained that he would "never regret having helped run Foreman out of the country." John Wayne, "A Candid Conversation with the Straight-Shooting Superstar/Superpatriot," interview by Richard Warren Lewis, *Playboy* no. 5 (May 1971), 90. For an account of an amicable (if chance) encounter between the two men, however, see Scott Eyman, *John Wayne: The Life and Legend* (New York: Simon & Schuster, 2014), 508.

3. Eyman, *John Wayne*, 537.

4. *The Frogmen* (Bacon 1951), though not a Wayne film, would have been among the war movies preceding *Stalag 17* by some two years.

5. *Josey Wales* opened in wide release on June 30, 1976; *The Shootist* opened on August 20, 1976. *Josey Wales* grossed $31.8 million in the United States, while *The Shootist* grossed $13.4 million. All dates and figures are from the Internet Movie Database.

6. Thao's Gran Torino also functions as symbolic reparation for the Hmong people, US allies in the Vietnam War. "We fought on your side," Sue explains to the historically unlettered Walt, "and when the Americans quit, the communists started killing all the Hmong."

7. Antonio Machuco, "Violence and Truth in Clint Eastwood's *Gran Torino*," *Anthropoetics* 16, no. 2 (spring 2011), http://anthropoetics.ucla.edu/ap1602/1602machuco/, makes much of the ubiquity of Christian motifs in *Gran Torino*.

8. Chris Kyle, with Scott McEwen and Jim DeFelice, *American Sniper: The Autobiography of the Most Lethal Sniper in U.S. Military History* (New York: Harper, 2012), 90. See also Michael J. Mooney, *The Life and Legend of Chris Kyle, American Sniper, Navy SEAL* (New York: Back Bay Books, 2015), 46.

9. James Fenimore Cooper, *The Last of the Mohicans: A Narrative of 1757*, in *The Leatherstocking Tales*, Vol. 1 (New York: Library of America, 1985), 598.

10. Cooper, *The Last of the Mohicans*, 816.

11. Cooper, *The Last of the Mohicans*, 877.

12. Cooper, *The Last of the Mohicans*, 681.

13. Cooper, *The Last of the Mohicans*, 502.

14. D. H. Lawrence, *Studies in Classic American Literature* (London: Penguin Books, 1977), 68.

15. This drab conceit is set down with undeserving gravity by Dave Grossman with Loren W. Christensen, *On Combat: The Psychology and Physiology of Deadly Conflict in War and in Peace* (n. p.: PPCT Research Publications, 2004), 176–77. See also Gregory Drobsny, "The 'Sheepdog' Analogy Is Deeply Flawed," *The Havok Journal*, October 19, 2019, https://havokjournal.com/culture/sheepdog-analogy-flawed/.

16. Percy Bysshe Shelley, "Ozymandias," Poetry Foundation, https://www.poetryfoundation.org/poems/46565/ozymandias.

17. Anthony Zurcher, "*American Sniper*: Was Chris Kyle Really a Hero?," *Echo Chamber* (blog), BBC News, January 21, 2015, https://www.bbc.com/news/world-us-canada-30923038.

18. Amy Nicholson, "Worst Movies of 2014: *American Sniper* Glosses over Chris Kyle's Lies," *Slate* (January 9, 2015). https://slate.com/culture/2015/01/worst-movies-of-2014-american-sniper-glosses-over-chris-kyles-lies.html.

19. David French, "*American Sniper* Has Created a Cultural Moment: Here's Why," *National Review* (January 19, 2015). https://www.nationalreview.com/corner/american-sniper-has-created-cultural-moment-heres-why-david-french/. See also the earlier article, David French, "Responding to the *American Sniper* Backlash: Angry, Remorseless Warriors Are Still Heroes," *National Review* (January 16, 2015). https://www.nationalreview.com/corner/responding-american-sniper-backlash-angry-remorseless-warriors-are-still-heroes-david/.

20. Dennis Jett, "The Real 'American Sniper' Had No Remorse About the Iraqis He Killed" *New Republic* (January 13, 2015). https://newrepublic.com/article/120763/american-sniper-clint-eastwood-biopic-misrepresents-chris-kyle.

21. Routh said later that if he didn't kill them, they were going to take his soul. See Mike Spies, "Inside the Tortured Mind of Eddie Ray Routh, the Man Who Killed American Sniper Chris Kyle," *Newsweek*, November 23, 2015, https://www.newsweek.com/2016/01/08/inside-tortured-mind-man-who-killed-american-sniper-chris-kyle-397299.html.

22. The body count is disputed, but 160 is the figure cited most often. Kyle, pretending not to care for the count, still pegged it at over 255 as if 160 were a piffling tally. See Terrence McCoy, "The 'Unverifiable' Legacy of Chris Kyle, the Deadliest Sniper in American History," *Washington Post*, July 20, 2014, https://www.washingtonpost.com/news/morning-mix/wp/2014/07/30/the-complicated-but-unveriable-legacy-of-chris-kyle-the-deadliest-sniper-in-american-history/. See also Matthew Cole and Sheelagh McNeill, "'American Sniper' Chris Kyle Distorted His Military Record, Documents Show," The Intercept, May 25, 2016, https://theintercept.com/2016/05/25/american-sniper-chris-kyle-distorted-his-military-record-documents-show/.

# Bibliography


Abinales, Patricio. "An American Colonial State: Authority and Structure in Southern Mindanao." In *Vestiges of War: The Philippine-American War and the Aftermath of an Imperial Dream, 1899–1999*, ed. Angela Velasco Shaw and Luis H. Francia, 89–117. New York: New York University Press, 2002.

*The American Film Institute Catalog of Motion Pictures Produced in the United States: Feature Films, 1931–1940: Film Entries, M–Z.* Edited by Patricia King Hanson. Berkeley: University of California Press, 1993.

Anderson, Carol. "Self-Defense." In *The 1619 Project: A New Origin Story*, ed. Nikole Hannah-Jones, Caitlin Roper, Ilena Silverman, and Jake Silverstein, 250–66. New York: One World, 2021.

Appy, Christian G. *American Reckoning: The Vietnam War and Our National Identity.* New York: Viking, 2015.

Appy, Christian G. *Working-Class War: American Combat Soldiers and Vietnam.* Chapel Hill: University of North Carolina Press, 1993.

Baldwin, James. "Down at the Cross: Letter from a Region in My Mind" [1963]. In *The Fire Next Time.* New York: Vintage, 1993.

Bates, Milton J. *The Wars We Took to Vietnam: Cultural Conflict and Storytelling.* Berkeley: University of California Press, 1996.

Beattie, Keith. *The Scar That Binds: American Culture and the Vietnam War.* New York: New York University Press, 1998.

Benjamin, Walter. "Theses on the Philosophy of History." In *Illuminations*, trans. Harry Zohn, ed. Hannah Arendt, 196–209. New York: Mariner Books, 2019.

Bentley, Eric. "The Political Theatre of John Wayne." In *Theatre of War: Comments on 32 Occasions.* New York: Viking, 1972.

Beschloss, Michael. *Reaching for Glory: Lyndon Johnson's Secret White House Tapes, 1964–1965.* New York: Simon & Schuster, 2001.

Bigart, Homer. "Calley Pleads for Understanding." *New York Times*, March 31, 1971. https://timesmachine.nytimes.com/timesmachine/1971/03/31/81878923.html?pageNumber=1.

Bishop, Jim. *FDR's Last Year: April 1944–April 1945.* New York: William Morrow, 1974.

Bogdanovich, Peter. *John Ford.* Berkeley: University of California Press, 1968.

Bradley, James, with Ron Powers. *Flags of Our Fathers.* New York: Bantam Books, 2000.

Bud Bagsak, Massacre at [June 11–15, 1913]. Contemporaneous Documents Relating to the Massacre. https://web.archive.org/web/20120522073018/http://www.moroland history.com/Home%20Page/Home%20Page%20content.htm.

Bullard, R. L. "Preparing Our Moros for Government." in *The World's Story: A History of the World in Story, Song, and Art*, Vol. 1, *China, Japan, and the Islands of the Pacific*, ed. Eva March Tappan, 542–62. Boston: Houghton Mifflin, 1914.

Burrell, Robert S. *The Ghosts of Iwo Jima.* College Station: Texas A&M University Press, 2006.

Calley, William. "Text of Calley Statement." *New York Times*, March 31, 1971. https://timesmachine.nytimes.com/timesmachine/1971/03/31/issue.html.

Camus, Albert. "The Myth of Sisyphus." In *The Myth of Sisyphus and Other Essays*, 2–138. Translated by Justin O'Brien. New York: Vintage International, 1991.

Caputo, Philip. *A Rumor of War.* New York: Owl Books, 1996.

Church, Benjamin. "Entertaining Passages Relating to Philip's War . . . with Some Account of the Divine Providence towards Benj. Church Esqr." In *So Dreadfull a Judgment: Puritan Responses to King Philip's War, 1676–1677*, ed. Richard Slotkin and James K. Folsom. Hanover, NH: Wesleyan University Press, 1978.

Clifford, Charles L. *The Real Glory.* London: William Heinemann, 1937.

Cole, Matthew, and Sheelagh McNeill. "'American Sniper' Chris Kyle Distorted His Military Record, Documents Show." Intercept, May 25, 2016. https://theintercept.com/2016/05/25/american-sniper-chris-kyle-distorted-his-military-record-documents-show/.

Conrad, Joseph. *Heart of Darkness.* 5th ed. Edited by Paul B. Armstrong. New York: Norton, 2016.

Cooper, James Fenimore. *The Deerslayer: or, The First War-Path.* In *The Leatherstocking Tales*, Vol. 2, 483–1030. New York: Library of America, 1985.

Cooper, James Fenimore. *The Last of the Mohicans: A Narrative of 1757.* In *The Leatherstocking Tales*, Vol. 1, 467–878. New York: Library of America, 1985.

Cooper, James Fenimore. *The Pioneers, or the Sources of the Susquehanna; A Descriptive Tale.* In *The Leatherstocking Tales*, Vol. 1, 1–465. New York: Library of America, 1985.

*Correspondence Relating to the War with Spain Including the Insurrection in the Philippine Islands and the China Relief Expedition, April 15, 1898, to July 30, 1902.* 2 vols. Reprint ed. Washington, DC: US Government Printing Office, 1993.

Cowie, Peter. *The "Apocalypse Now" Book.* Boston: Da Capo, 2000.

Cronkite, Walter. "We Are Mired in Stalemate." Transcript of broadcast, CBS Evening News, February 27, 1968. In *Reporting Vietnam, Part 1: American Journalism, 1959–1969*, 581–82. New York: Library of America, 1998.

Davis, Ronald. *Duke: The Life and Image of John Wayne.* Norman: University of Oklahoma Press, 1998.

Davis, Ronald. *John Ford: Hollywood's Old Master.* Edited by Richard Etulian. Norman: University of Oklahoma Press, 1997.

Debo, Angie. *Geronimo: The Man, His Time, His Place.* Norman: University of Oklahoma Press, 1976.

Del Vecchio, John M. *The 13th Valley*. Reprint ed. New York: St. Martin's Griffin, 1998.

Deocampo, Nick. "Imperialist Fictions: The Filipino in the Imperialist Imaginary." In *Vestiges of War: The Philippine-American War and the Aftermath of an Imperial Dream, 1899–1999*, ed. Angela Velasco Shaw and Luis H. Francia, 225–36. New York: New York University Press, 2002.

Didion, Joan. "John Wayne: A Love Song" [1965]. In *Slouching towards Bethlehem: Essays*, 29–41. New York: Farrar Straus and Giroux, 2008.

Dippie, Brian W. *Custer's Last Stand: The Anatomy of an American Myth*. Lincoln: University of Nebraska Press, 1994.

Drinnon, Richard. *Facing West: The Metaphysics of Indian-Hating and Empire Building*. New York: Schocken, 1980.

Drobsny, Gregory. "The 'Sheepdog' Analogy Is Deeply Flawed." *Havok Journal*, October 19, 2019. https://havokjournal.com/culture/sheepdog-analogy-flawed/.

Egan, Timothy. *A Fever in the Heartland: The Ku Klux Klan's Plot to Take over America, and the Woman Who Stopped Them*. New York: Viking, 2023.

Egerton, John. *Speak Now against the Day: The Generation before the Civil Rights Movement in the South*. New York: Knopf, 1994.

Ehrhart, W. D. *Vietnam-Perkasie: A Combat Marine Memoir*. Amherst: University of Massachusetts Press, 1995.

"Extra Census Bulletin No. 2." Washington, DC: Department of the Interior, Census Office, April 20, 1891.

Eyman, Scott. *John Wayne: The Life and Legend*. New York: Simon & Schuster, 2014.

Eyman, Scott. *Print the Legend: The Life and Times of John Ford*. New York: Simon & Schuster, 1999.

Faulkner, William. *Absalom, Absalom!* 1936; Corrected edition: New York: Vintage International, 1990.

Faulkner, William. *Go Down, Moses*. New York: Vintage International, 2011.

"Feeling of Men Coming Back from Vietnam, before the Senate Committee on Public Relations." In "John F. Kerry: Senate Committee on Foreign Relations, April 22, 1971," *Digital History*. https://www.digitalhistory.uh.edu/active_learning/explorations/vietnam/kerry.cfm.

FitzGerald, Frances. *Fire in the Lake: The Vietnamese and the Americans in Vietnam*. New York: Vintage, 1989.

Fleming, Thomas. "Pershing's Island War." *American Heritage* 19, no. 5 (August 1968). https://www.americanheritage.com/pershings-island-war.

Ford, Daniel. *Incident at Muc Wa*. Portsmouth, NH: William Heinemann, 1967.

Foucault, Michel. *Madness and Civilization: A History of Insanity in the Age of Reason*. Translated by Richard Howard. New York: Vintage, 1965.

Frazer, James George. *The Golden Bough: A Study in Magic and Religion*. New abridged ed. Oxford: Oxford University Press, 1998.

French, David. "*American Sniper* Has Created a Cultural Moment: Here's Why." *National Review*, January 19, 2015. https://www.nationalreview.com/corner/american-sniper-has-created-cultural-moment-heres-why-david-french/.

French, David. "Responding to the *American Sniper* Backlash: Angry, Remorseless Warriors Are Still Heroes." *National Review*, January 16, 2015. https://www.nationalreview.com/corner/responding-american-sniper-backlash-angry-remorseless-warriors-are-still-heroes-david/.

French, Karl. "*Apocalypse Now*" *Bloomsbury Movie Guide No. 1*. New York: Mass-Market, 1999.
Frost, Robert. "The Gift Outright." In *Robert Frost: Collected Poems, Prose, and Plays*, 316. New York: Library of America, 1995.
Fussell, Paul. *The Great War and Modern Memory*. New York: Oxford University Press, 2000.
Gallagher, Tag. *John Ford: The Man and His Films*. Berkeley: University of California Press, 1986.
Garand, George W., and Truman R. Strobridge. *Western Pacific Operations: History of U.S. Marine Corps Operations in World War II*, Vol. 4. Washington, DC: US Government Printing Office, 1971.
*Glimpses of the Louisiana Purchase Exposition and the Famous Pike*. Chicago: Laird and Lee, 1904.
Goodwin, Michael, and Naomi Wise. *On the Edge: The Life and Times of Francis Coppola*. New York: Morrow, 1989.
Gowing, Peter Gordon. *Mandate in Moroland: The American Government of Muslim Filipinos*. Quezon City: New Day, 1983.
Graham, Don. *No Name on the Bullet: A Biography of Audie Murphy*. New York: Viking Penguin, 1989.
Grossman, Dave. *On Killing: The Psychological Cost of Learning to Kill in War and Society*. New York: Back Bay Books, 1996.
Grossman, Dave, with Loren W. Christensen. *On Combat: The Psychology and Physiology of Deadly Conflict in War and in Peace*. n.p.: PPCT Research Publications, 2004.
Hannah-Jones, Nikole. "Democracy." In *The 1619 Project: A New Origin Story*, edited by Nikole Hannah-Jones et al., 7–36. New York: One World, 2021.
Hansen, Matthew. "New Mystery Arises from Iconic Iwo Jima Image." *Omaha World-Herald*, November 23, 2015, https://omaha.com/new-mystery-arises-from-iconic-iwo-jima-image/image_b9c97612-5c3b-11e7-b10e-a34b95d0f3b6.html.
Hasford, Gustav. *The Short-Timers*. New York: Bantam Books, 1978.
Hawthorne, Nathaniel. "Young Goodman Brown." In *Nathaniel Hawthorne: Tales and Sketches*, 276–89. New York: Library of America, 1982.
Hellmann, John. *American Myth and the Legacy of Vietnam*. New York: Columbia University Press, 1986.
Hellmann, John. "Vietnam and the Hollywood Genre Film: Inversions of American Mythology in *The Deer Hunter* and *Apocalypse Now*." *American Quarterly* 34, no. 4 (Autumn 1982): 418–39.
Herr, Michael. *Dispatches*. New York: Vintage, 1991.
Herring, George C. *America's Longest War: The United States and Vietnam, 1950–1975*. 6th ed. New York: McGraw-Hill Education, 2020.
Herring, George C. *From Colony to Superpower: U.S. Foreign Relations since 1776*. Oxford: Oxford University Press, 2008.
Hilsman, Roger. "Internal War: The New Communist Tactic." In Fleet Marine Force Reference Publication 12–25, *The Guerrilla—and How to Fight Him*. Washington, DC: Department of the Navy, 1990. Reprint of *The Guerrilla—and How to Fight Him: Selections from the Marine Corps Gazette*, ed. Lt. Col. T. N. Greene. New York: Praeger, 1962.

Hofstadter, Richard. "The Paranoid Style in American Politics." In *The Paranoid Style in American Politics and Other Essays*. Cambridge: Harvard University Press, 1964.

Hofstadter, Richard. "The Pseudo-Conservative Revolt—1954." In *The Paranoid Style in American Politics and Other Essays*. Cambridge: Harvard University Press, 1964.

Hoopes, Townsend, and Douglas Brinkley. *Driven Patriot: The Life and Times of James Forrestal*. New York: Knopf, 1992.

Hurley, Vic. *Swish of the Kris: The Story of the Moros*. New York: E. P. Dutton, 1936.

Hutton, Paul Andrew. "Correct in Every Detail." In *The Custer Reader*, ed. Paul Andrew Hutton, 488–524. Lincoln: University of Nebraska Press, 1992.

Hynes, Samuel. *The Soldiers' Tale: Bearing Witness to Modern War*. New York: Penguin, 1997.

James, William. *The Will to Believe and Other Essays in Popular Philosophy*. Reissue ed. New York: Dover, 1956.

Jeffords, Susan. *The Remasculinization of America: Gender and the Vietnam War*. Bloomington: Indiana University Press, 1989.

Jett, Dennis. "The Real 'American Sniper' Had No Remorse about the Iraqis He Killed." *New Republic*, January 13, 2015. https://newrepublic.com/article/120763/american-sniper-clint-eastwood-biopic-misrepresents-chris-kyle.

Johnson, Denis. *Tree of Smoke*. New York: Farrar, Straus and Giroux, 2007.

Kakehashi, Kumiko. *So Sad to Fall in Battle: An Account of War*. Translated by Giles Murray. New York: Presidio, 2007.

Karnow, Stanley. *Vietnam: A History*. 2nd ed. revised. New York: Penguin Books, 1995.

Kennan, George F. [as "X"]. "The Sources of Soviet Conduct." *Foreign Affairs* 25, no. 4 (July 1947): 566–82.

Kenworthy, E. W. "Kennan Bids U.S. 'Dig In' and Await Talks in Vietnam." *New York Times*, February 11, 1966, 1 and 3.

King, Gilbert. *Devil in the Grove: Thurgood Marshall, the Groveland Boys, and the Dawn of a New America*. New York: HarperCollins, 2012.

Kolko, Gabriel. *Anatomy of a War: Vietnam, the United States, and the Modern Historical Experience*. New York: New Press, 1994.

Kovic, Ron. *Born on the Fourth of July*. New York: Pocket Books, 1977.

Kulik, Gary. *"War Stories": False Atrocity Tales, Swift Boaters, and Winter Soldiers—What Really Happened in Vietnam*. Washington, DC: Potomac Books, 2009.

Kyle, Chris, with Scott McEwen and Jim DeFelice. *American Sniper: The Autobiography of the Most Lethal Sniper in U.S. Military History*. New York: Harper, 2012.

Lamb, David. "Reporters at Work: Giving a Battle a Name." About Editing and Writing, Blog by Jack Limpert, September 4, 2012, jacklimpert.com/2012/09/reporter-at-work-giving-a-battle-a-name/.

Lane, Jack C. *Armed Progressive: General Leonard Wood*. San Rafael, CA: Presidio, 1978.

Lang, David. "Casualties of War." In *Reporting Vietnam, Part One: American Journalism, 1959–1969*, 709–67. New York: Library of America, 1998.

LaRocca, David, ed. *The Philosophy of War Films*. Lexington: University Press of Kentucky, 2014.

Lawrence, D. H. *Studies in Classic American Literature*. London: Penguin Books, 1977.

Lee, Trymaine. "Inheritance." In *The 1619 Project: A New Origin Story*, ed. Nikole Hannah-Jones, Caitlin Roper, Ilena Silverman, and Jake Silverstein, 293–305.

Leguebe, Eric. *John Wayne: Le cow-boy et la mort*. Paris: Éditions France-Empire, 1989.

Lehman, Peter. "'Well, what's it like over there? Can you tell us anything?': Looking for Vietnam in *The Deer Hunter*." *North Dakota Quarterly* 51, no. 3 (Summer 1983): 131–41.

Lembcke, Jerry. *The Spitting Image: Myth, Memory, and the Legacy of Vietnam*. New York: New York University Press, 2000.

Lewy, Guenter. *America in Vietnam*. New York: Oxford University Press, 1978.

Lieberman, Robbie. "Communism, Peace Activism, and Civil Liberties: From the Waldorf Conference to the Peekskill Riot." *Journal of American Culture* 18, no. 3 (Fall 1995): 59–65.

Lifton, Robert Jay. "Bearing Witness to My Lai and Vietnam." In *Facing My Lai: Moving beyond the Massacre*. Edited by David L. Anderson. Lawrence: University Press of Kansas, 1998.

Lifton, Robert Jay. *Home from the War: Vietnam Veterans; Neither Victims nor Executioners*. New York: Basic Books, 1985.

Machuco, Antonio. "Violence and Truth in Clint Eastwood's *Gran Torino*." *Anthropoetics* 16, no. 2 (Spring 2011). https://anthropoetics.ucla.edu/ap1602/1602machuco/.

Manchester, William. *American Caesar: Douglas MacArthur, 1880–1964*. Boston: Little, Brown, 1978.

Manchester, William. *Goodbye, Darkness: A Memoir of the Pacific War*. New York: Back Bay Books, 2002.

Mason, Robert C. *Chickenhawk*. New York: Penguin, 1983.

McBride, Joseph. *Searching for John Ford: A Life*. New York: St. Martin's, 2001.

McCallum, Jack. *Leonard Wood: Rough Rider, Surgeon, Architect of American Imperialism*. New York: New York University Press, 2005.

McCulloch, Frank. "The Fall of a 'Lost Soldier.'" *Life*, November 14, 1969, 34–40.

Michallon, Clemence. "Was One of the Soldiers in Iconic Flag-Raising Photo Wrongly Identified? Marine Corps Investigate New Claims by Two Amateur History Buffs." *Daily Mail*, May 2, 2016. https://www.dailymail.co.uk/news/article-3570165/Marines-investigating-claim-men-Iwo-Jima-photo.html.

Milius, John, and Francis Ford Coppola. *Apocalypse Now, Redux: The Screenplay*. Prepared by Anahid Nazarian. New York: Hyperion, 2000.

Miller, Stuart Creighton. *"Benevolent Assimilation": The American Conquest of the Philippines, 1899–1903*. New Haven, CT: Yale University Press, 1982.

Mooney, Michael J. *The Life and Legend of Chris Kyle, American Sniper, Navy SEAL*. New York: Back Bay Books, 2015.

Moore, Robin. *The Green Berets*. New York: Crown, 1965.

Morrison, Toni. *Beloved*. New York: Vintage Books, 2004.

Morrison, Toni. "Mourning for Whiteness." *New Yorker*, November 14, 2016. https://www.newyorker.com/magazine/2016/11/21/aftermath-sixteen-writers-on-trumps-america#anchor-morrison.

Murphy, Audie. *To Hell and Back: The Classic Memoir of World War II by America's Most Decorated Soldier*. New York: Henry Holt, 2002.

Nadel, Alan. *Containment Culture: American Narratives, Postmodernism, and the Atomic Age*. Durham, NC: Duke University Press, 1995.

Nguyen, Viet Than. *Nothing Ever Dies: Vietnam and the Memory of War*. Cambridge: Harvard University Press, 2016.
Nicholson, Amy. "Worst Movies of 2014: *American Sniper* Glosses over Chris Kyle's Lies." *Slate*, January 9, 2015. https://slate.com/culture/2015/01/worst-movies-of-2014-american-sniper-glosses-over-chris-kyles-lies.html.
Norris, Margo. "Modernism and Vietnam: Francis Ford Coppola's *Apocalypse Now*." *Modern Fiction Studies* 44, no. 3 (1998): 730–66.
Obama, Barack. "Remarks by the President at 93rd Annual Conference of the American Legion." The White House, August 30, 2011. https://obamawhitehouse.archives.gov/the-press-office/2011/08/30/remarks-president-93rd-annual-conference-american-legion.
O'Brien, Geoffrey. "John Ford: Superstar." *Village Voice* 31, no. 42 (October 21, 1986): 41–43.
O'Brien, Tim. *If I Die in a Combat Zone*. New York: Broadway Books, 1975.
O'Brien, Tim. *The Things They Carried*. New York: Broadway Books, 1990.
*Official Guide to the Louisiana Purchase Exposition*. Compiled by M. J. Lowenstein. St. Louis, MO: Official Guide Co., 1904.
Orosa, Sixto Y. *The Sulu Archipelago and Its People*. Yonkers-on-Hudson, NY: World Book, 1923.
Patterson, Frank Allen, ed. *The Student's Milton: Being the Complete Poems of John Milton*. New York: Appleton-Century-Crofts, 1930.
Pearce, Roy Harvey. *Savagism and Civilization: A Study of the Indian and the American Mind*. Berkeley: University of California Press, 1988.
*The Pentagon Papers: Defense Department History of U.S. Decisionmaking on Vietnam*. Senator [Mike] Gravel Edition, 4 vols. Boston: Beacon, 1971.
Philippines Embassy. *The Story of Our Flag, Coat of Arms, and National Anthem*. Washington, DC: Philippine Library of Information, 1949.
Poague, Leland. "'All I Can See Is the Flags': *Fort Apache* and the Visibility of History." *Cinema Journal* 27, no. 2 (Winter 1988): 8–26.
Puller, Lewis B., Jr. *Fortunate Son: The Autobiography of Lewis B. Puller, Jr.* New York: Grove, 1991.
Reagan, Ronald. "Peace: Restoring the Margin of Safety." Speech delivered at the Veterans of Foreign Wars Convention, Chicago, August 18, 1980. https://www.reaganlibrary.gov/archives/speech/peace-restoring-margin-safety.
Remarque, Erich Maria. *All Quiet on the Western Front*. Translated by A. W. Wheen. New York: Fawcett, 1958.
Roberts, Randy, and James S. Olson. *John Wayne: American*. Lincoln: University of Nebraska Press, 1995.
Roosevelt, Theodore. *The Winning of the West*, Vol. 2, *Louisiana and the Northwest, 1791–1807*. Lincoln: University of Nebraska Press, 1995.
Rose, Kenneth D. *Myth and the Greatest Generation: A Social History of Americans in World War II*. New York: Routledge, 2008.
Ross, Bill D. *Iwo Jima: Legacy of Valor*. 1st Vintage Books ed. New York: Vintage, 1986.
Rostow, W. W. "Guerrilla Warfare in Underdeveloped Areas." In *The Guerrilla—and How to Fight Him*, Fleet Marine Force Reference Publication 12–25. Washington, DC: Department of the Navy, 1990. https://www.marines.mil/Portals

/1/Publications/FMFRP%2012-25%20%20The%20Guerrilla%20and%20How %20to%20Fight%20Him.pdf. Reprint of *The Guerrilla—and How to Fight Him: Selections from the Marine Corps Gazette*, ed. Lt. Col. T. N. Greene (New York: Praeger, 1962), 54–61.

Sarris, Andrew. *The John Ford Mystery*. Bloomington: Indiana University Press, 1975.

Scalard, Douglas P. "The Battle of Hamburger Hill: Battle Command in Difficult Terrain against a Determined Enemy." In *Studies in Battle Command*. Fort Leavenworth, KS: Combat Studies Institute, 1995.

Schell, Jonathan. *The Real War: The Classic Reporting on the Vietnam War*. New York: Pantheon Books, 1988.

Serwer, Adam. *The Cruelty Is the Point: The Past, Present, and Future of Trump's America*. New York: One World, 2021.

Shay, Jonathan. *Achilles in Vietnam: Combat Trauma and the Undoing of Character*. New York: Scribner, 1994.

Sheehan, Neil. *A Bright Shining Lie: John Paul Vann and America in Vietnam*. New York: Vintage, 1988.

Shelley, Percy Bysshe. "Ozymandias." Poetry Foundation. https://www.poetryfoundation.org/poems/46565/ozymandias.

Slotkin, Richard. *Gunfighter Nation: The Myth of the Frontier in Twentieth-Century America*. New York: Atheneum, 1992.

Slotkin, Richard. "Unit Pride: Ethnic Platoons and the Myths of American Nationality." *American Literary History* 13, no. 3 (Autumn 2001): 469–98.

Smith, Clint. *How the Word Is Passed: A Reckoning with the History of Slavery across America*. New York: Little, Brown, 2021.

Smith, Clint. "When People Say 'We Have Made It through Worse Before.'" In *Above Ground: Poems*, 12. New York: Little, Brown, 2023.

Smith, Holland M., and Percy Finch. *Coral and Brass*. New York: Scribner, 1949.

Smythe, Donald. *Guerrilla Warrior: The Early Life of John J. Pershing*. New York: Scribner, 1973.

*The Standard Guide of the World's Fair*. St. Louis: Blattner Brothers, 1904.

Starkey, Marion. *The Devil in Massachusetts: A Modern Inquiry into the Salem Witch Trials*. New York: Knopf, 1950.

Stone, Oliver, and Richard Boyle. *Oliver Stone's "Platoon" and "Salvador": Original Screenplays*. New York: Vintage, 1987.

Suid, Lawrence H. *Guts and Glory: The Making of the American Image in Film*. Revised and expanded ed. Lexington: University Press of Kentucky, 2002.

Swindell, Larry. *The Last Hero: A Biography of Gary Cooper*. Garden City, NY: Doubleday, 1980.

Tritle, Lawrence A. *From Melos to My Lai: War and Survival*. London: Routledge, 2000.

Tucker, Spencer C., ed. *Encyclopedia of the Vietnam War: A Political, Social, and Military History*. New York: Oxford University Press, 1998.

Turner, Fred. *Echoes of Combat: Trauma, Memory, and the Vietnam War*. Minneapolis: University of Minnesota Press, 2001.

Turse, Nick. *Kill Anything That Moves: The Real American War in Vietnam*. New York: Metropolitan Books, 2013.

The Vietnam Veterans against the War. *The Winter Soldier Investigation: An Inquiry into American War Crimes*. Boston: Beacon, 1972.

Vonnegut, Kurt. *Slaughterhouse-Five, or The Children's Crusade, a Duty-Dance with Death*. New York: Dell, 1969.
Wayne, John. "A Candid Conversation with the Straight-Shooting Superstar/Superpatriot." Interview by Richard Warren Lewis. *Playboy* 18, no. 5 (May 1971): 75–92.
Webb, James. *Fields of Fire*. New York: Bantam, 2002.
Weston, Jessie L. *From Ritual to Romance*. Mineola, NY: Dover, 1997.
Wheeler, Richard. *Iwo*. Annapolis, MD: Naval Institute Press, 1980.
Whitehead, Colson. *The Underground Railroad*. New York: Doubleday, 2016.
Whitman, James Q. *Hitler's American Model: The United States and the Making of Nazi Race Law*. Princeton, NJ: Princeton University Press, 2017.
Whitman, Walt. "Facing West from California's Shores." In *Walt Whitman: Complete Poetry and Collected Prose*, ed. Justin Kaplan, 266–67. New York: Library of America, 1982.
Whitman, Walt. "From Far Dakota's Cañons (June 25, 1876)." In *Walt Whitman: Complete Poetry and Collected Prose*, ed. Justin Kaplan, 592–93. New York: Library of America, 1982.
Whitman, Walt. "From Pent-up Aching Rivers." In *Walt Whitman: Complete Poetry and Collected Prose*, ed. Justin Kaplan, 248–50. New York: Library of America, 1982.
Whitman, Walt. "Specimen Days." In *Walt Whitman: Complete Poetry and Collected Prose*, ed. Justin Kaplan, 689–926. New York: Library of America, 1982.
Williams, Roger M. "A Rough Sunday at Peekskill." *American Heritage Magazine* 27, no. 3 (April 1976). https://www.americanheritage.com/rough-sunday-peekskill.
Wills, Garry. *John Wayne's America: The Politics of Celebrity*. New York: Touchstone, 1998.
Woolf, Tobias. *In Pharaoh's Army: Memories of the Lost War*. New York: Vintage, 1994.
X [Kennan, George F.]. "The Long Telegram." National Security Archive, February 22, 1946. https://nsarchive2.gwu.edu//coldwar/ documents/episode-1/kennan.htm.
Zacharias, Admiral Ellis M. "The Forrestal Enigma: Inside Report on a Philosophy of Power." *United Nations World* 3, no. 3 (March 1949): 14–16.
Zaffiri, Samuel. *Hamburger Hill: The Brutal Battle for Dong Ap Bia, May 11–20, 1969*. New York: Presidio, 1988.
Zurcher, Anthony. "*American Sniper*: Was Chris Kyle Really a Hero?" Echo Chamber (blog), BBC News, January 21, 2015. https://www.bbc.com/news/world-us-canada-30923038.

# Filmography

*Advance of Kansas Volunteers at Caloocan*. Thomas A. Edison, Inc., 1899. Paper Print Collection, Library of Congress. https://www.loc.gov/item/98501192.

*Allegheny Uprising*. William A. Seiter, dir. Featuring Claire Trevor and John Wayne. RKO Radio Pictures, 1939; Warner Home Video, 2007, DVD.

*American Sniper*. Clint Eastwood, dir. Featuring Bradley Cooper and Sienna Miller. Warner Bros., 2014; Warner Bros, 2015, DVD.

*Anzio*. Edward Dmytryk, dir. Featuring Robert Mitchum and Peter Falk. Columbia Pictures, 1968; Sony Pictures Home Entertainment, 2005, DVD.

*Apocalypse Now*. Francis Ford Coppola, dir. Featuring Marlon Brando, Martin Sheen, and Robert Duvall. American Zoetrope, 1979; Lionsgate Home Entertainment, packaged as *Apocalypse Now: Final Cut*, 40th Anniversary, 2019, Ultra HD Blu-ray, 2 of 6.

*Back to Bataan*. Edward Dmytryk, dir. Featuring John Wayne and Anthony Quinn. RKO Radio Pictures, 1945; Warner Home Video, 2006, DVD.

*Bataan*. Tay Garnett, dir. Featuring Errol Flynn and George Murphy. Metro-Goldwyn-Mayer, 1943; Warner Archive, 2020, DVD.

*Bat 21*. Peter Markle, dir. Featuring Gene Hackman and Danny Glover. TriStar Pictures, 1988; Kino Lorber, 2006, DVD.

*The Battle of the Bulge*. Ken Annakin, dir. Featuring Henry Fonda and Robert Shaw. Warner Bros., 1965; Warner Home Video, 2005, DVD.

*The Beguiled*. Don Siegel, dir. Featuring Clint Eastwood and Geraldine Page. Malpaso Co., 1971; Universal City Studios, 2017, Blu-ray.

*The Best Years of Our Lives*. William Wyler, dir. Featuring Myrna Loy, Dana Andrews, and Fredric March. Samuel Goldwyn Co., 1946; MGM Home Entertainment, 2000, DVD.

*Birdy*. Alan Parker, dir. Featuring Matthew Modine and Nicolas Cage. TriStar Pictures, 1984; Sony Pictures Home Entertainment, 2000, DVD.

*The Birth of a Nation*. D. W. Griffith, dir. Featuring Lillian Gish, Mae Marsh, and Henry B. Walthall. David W. Griffith Corp., 1915; Kino Video, 2002, DVD.

*The Blinding of Isaac Woodard: How a Horrific Incident of Racial Violence Became a Powerful Catalyst for the Civil Rights Movement*. Jamila Ephron, dir. Aired March 30,

2021, PBS, VOD, https://www.pbs.org/wgbh/americanexperience/films/blinding-isaac-wwoodard/#part01.

*Born on the Fourth of July*. Oliver Stone, dir. Featuring Tom Cruise, Bryan Larkin, and Kyra Sedgwick. Universal Pictures, 1989; Universal Pictures Home Entertainment, 2004, DVD.

*The Boys from Co. C.* Sidney J. Furie, dir. Featuring Stan Shaw, Andrew Stevens, and James Canning. Columbia Pictures, 1978; Henstooth Video, 2008, DVD.

*Brannigan*. Douglas Hickox, dir. Featuring John Wayne and Richard Attenborough. United Artists, 1975; Kino Lorber, 2017, DVD.

*The Bridges at Toko-Ri*. Mark Robson, dir. Featuring William Holden, Grace Kelly, and Fredric March. Paramount Pictures, 1954; Paramount Home Video, 2006, DVD.

*Buck Privates*. Arthur Lubin, dir. Featuring Bud Abbott and Lou Costello. Universal Pictures, 1941; Universal Pictures Home Entertainment, 2012, DVD.

*The Caine Mutiny*. Edward Dmytryk, dir. Featuring Humphrey Bogart, Jose Ferrer, and Van Johnson. Columbia Pictures, 1954; Sony Pictures Home Entertainment, 2008, DVD.

*Casualties of War*. Brian De Palma, dir. Featuring Michael J. Fox and Sean Penn. Columbia Pictures, 1989; Columbia TriStar Home Entertainment, 2001, DVD.

*Col. Funston Swimming the Bagbag River* [Library of Congress correction of onscreen title]. Thomas A. Edison, Inc., Library of Congress, The Spanish-American War in Motion Pictures, Paper Print Collection, https://www.loc.gov/item/99407593/.

*Coming Home*. Hal Ashby, dir. Featuring Jane Fonda, John Voight, and Bruce Dern. Jerome Hellman Productions, 1978; Twentieth Century Fox Home Entertainment, 2007, DVD.

*Coogan's Bluff*. Don Siegel, dir. Featuring Clint Eastwood and Lee J. Cobb. Universal Pictures/Malpaso Co., 1968; Universal Pictures Home Entertainment, 2021, Blu-ray.

*Da 5 Bloods*. Spike Lee, dir. Featuring Delroy Lindo, Jonathan Majors, and Clarke Peters. 40 Acres & A Mule Fireworks, 2020, distributed by Netflix, 2020.

*The Dead Pool*. Buddy Van Horn, dir. Featuring Clint Eastwood and Liam Neeson. Warner Bros.–Malpaso Productions, 1988; Warner Home Video, 2009, DVD.

*The Deer Hunter*. Michael Cimino, dir. Featuring Robert De Niro, Christopher Walken, John Cazale, and Meryl Streep. EMI/Universal Pictures, 1978; Universal Pictures Home Entertainment, 2011. Blu-ray.

*Destry Rides Again*. George Marshall, dir. Featuring Marlene Dietrich and James Stewart. Universal Pictures, 1939; Criterion Collection, 2020, Blu-ray.

*The Dirty Dozen*. Robert Aldrich, dir. Featuring Lee Marvin, Ernest Borgnine, and Charles Bronson. Metro-Goldwyn-Mayer, 1967; Warner Home Video, 2006, DVD.

*Dirty Harry*. Don Siegel, dir. Featuring Clint Eastwood, Harry Guardino, and Andy Robinson. Malpaso Productions, 1971; Warner Home Video, 2008, Blu-ray.

*Django Unchained*. Quentin Tarantino, dir. Featuring Jamie Foxx, Christopher Waltz, and Leonardo DiCaprio. Weinstein Co./Columbia Pictures, 2012; Lionsgate Home Entertainment, 2019, DVD.

*Dodge City*. Michael Curtiz, dir. Featuring Errol Flynn and Olivia de Havilland. Warner Bros., 1939; Warner Home Video, 2017, Blu-ray.

*Drums along the Mohawk*. John Ford, dir. Featuring Claudette Colbert and Henry Fonda. Twentieth Century Fox, 1939; Twentieth Century Fox Home Entertainment, 2005, DVD.

*84 Charlie MoPic*. Patrick S. Duncan, dir. Featuring Jonathan Emerson and Nicholas Cascone. Charlie MoPic Co., 1989; RCA/Columbia Pictures Home Entertainment, 1989, VHS; New Century/Vista Film Company, DVD.

*The Fighting Seabees*. Edward Ludwig, dir. Featuring John Wayne and Susan Hayward. Republic Pictures, 1944; Lionsgate Home Entertainment, 2007, DVD.

*First Blood*. Ted Kotcheff, dir. Featuring Sylvester Stallone, Brian Dennehy, and Richard Crenna. Anabasis N.V., 1982; Lionsgate Home Entertainment, 2015, Blu-ray (as *Rambo: First Blood*).

*A Fistful of Dollars*. Sergio Leone, dir. Featuring Clint Eastwood and Gian Maria Volontè. Jolly Film, 1964/1967; King Lorber Studio Classics, 2018, Blu-ray.

*Flags of Our Fathers*. Clint Eastwood, dir. Featuring Ryan Phillippe and Barry Pepper. Dreamworks Pictures, 2006; Paramount Home Entertainment, 2008, DVD and Blu-ray.

*The Flying Leathernecks*. Nicholas Ray, dir. Featuring John Wayne and Robert Ryan. RKO Radio Pictures, 1951; Warner Home Video, 2014, DVD.

*Fort Apache*. John Ford, dir. Featuring John Wayne and Henry Fonda. Argosy Pictures, 1948; Warner Home Video, 2012, DVD and Blu-ray.

*For a Few Dollars More*. Sergio Leone, dir. Featuring Clint Eastwood and Lee Van Cleef. Produzioni Europee Associate, 1965/1967; Twentieth Century Fox Home Entertainment, 2013, DVD and Blu-ray.

*The Frogmen*. Lloyd Bacon, dir. Featuring Richard Widmark and Dana Andrews. Twentieth Century Fox, 1951; Twentieth Century Fox, 2005, DVD.

*Frontier Marshal*. Allan Dwan, dir. Featuring Randolph Scott. Twentieth Century Fox, 1939; Twentieth Century Fox, 2012, DVD.

*Full Metal Jacket*. Stanley Kubrick, dir. Featuring Matthew Modine, R. Lee Ermey, and Vincent D'Onofrio. Warner Bros., 1987; Warner Home Video, 2012, DVD and Blu-ray.

*Go Tell the Spartans*. Ted Post, dir. Featuring Burt Lancaster and Craig Wasson. Mar-Vista Entertainment and Spartan Productions, 1978; Scorpion Releasing, 2015, DVD.

*The Good, the Bad, and the Ugly*. Sergio Leone, dir. Featuring Clint Eastwood, Eli Wallach, and Lee Van Cleef. Produzioni Europee Associate, 1966/1967; Warner Bros. Home Entertainment, 2020, DVD and Blu-ray.

*Gran Torino*. Clint Eastwood, dir. Featuring Clint Eastwood and Bee Vang. Matten Productions, 2008; Warner Home Video, 2009, DVD.

*The Green Berets*. Ray Kellogg and John Wayne, dir. Featuring John Wayne and David Janssen. Batjac Productions, 1968; Warner Home Video, 2010, DVD and Blu-ray.

*The Guns of Navarone*. J. Lee Thompson, dir. Featuring David Niven, Gregory Peck, and Anthony Quinn. Highroad Productions, 1961; Sony Pictures Home Entertainment, 2011, Blu-ray.

*Hamburger Hill*. John Irvin, dir. Featuring Anthony Barrile, Michael Boatman, and Don Cheadle. RKO Pictures, 1987; Lionsgate Home Entertainment, 2012, DVD and Blu-ray.

*Hang 'Em High*. Ted Post, dir. Featuring Clint Eastwood and Inger Stevens. Leonard Freeman Productions, 1968; Warner Bros. Home Entertainment, 2020, DVD and Blu-ray.

*The Hanging Tree*. Delmer Daves, dir. Featuring Gary Cooper, Maria Schell, and Karl Malden. Baroda and Warner Bros., 1958; Warner Home Video, 2018, DVD and Blu-ray.

*The Harder They Fall*. Jeymes Samuel, dir. Featuring Jonathan Majors, Regina King, and Idris Elba. Overbrook Entertainment, 2021; Netflix VOD.

*Hearts and Minds*. Peter Davis, dir. Featuring Tin Chan, Chau Diem, and Ngo Dihn Diem. Audjeff, 1974; Criterion Collection, 2014, DVD and Blu-ray.

*Heaven and Earth*. Oliver Stone, dir. Featuring Hiep Thi Le, Tommy Lee Jones, and Haing S. Ngor. Alcor Films, 1993; Warner Home Video, DVD.

*High Noon*. Fred Zinnemann, dir. Featuring Gary Cooper and Grace Kelly. Stanley Kramer Productions, 1952; Lionsgate Home Entertainment, 2008, DVD and Blu-ray.

*Home of the Brave*. Mark Robson, dir. Featuring Douglas Dick and Steve Brodie. Stanley Kramer Productions, 1949; Olive Films, 2012, DVD and Blu-ray.

*I Knew It Was You: Rediscovering John Cazale*. Richard Shepard, dir. Oscilloscope Labs, 2009, DVD.

*I Married a Communist* (aka *The Woman on Pier 13*). Robert Stevenson, dir. Featuring Robert Ryan and Laraine Day. RKO Radio Pictures, 1949.

*Jacob's Ladder*. Adrian Lyne, dir. Featuring Tim Robbins, Elizabeth Peña, and Danny Aiello. Carolco Pictures, 1990; Artisan Entertainment, 1998, DVD.

*Jesse James*. Henry King, dir. Featuring Tyrone Power and Henry Fonda. Twentieth Century Fox, 1939; CBS/Fox, 1991, VHS.

*The Last Picture Show*. Peter Bogdanovich, dir. Featuring Timothy Bottoms, Jeff Bridges, and Cybil Sheppard. Columbia Pictures, 1971; Criterion Collection, 2010, DVD.

*Lawless Range*. Robert N. Bradbury, dir. Featuring John Wayne. Paul Malvern Productions, 1935; Republic Pictures Home Video, 1993, VHS.

*Letters from Iwo Jima*. Clint Eastwood, dir. Featuring Ken Watanabe and Kazunari Ninomiya. Dreamworks Pictures, 2006; Warner Home Video, 2010, DVD.

*Little Dieter Needs to Fly*. Werner Herzog, dir. Featuring Dieter Dengler, Werner Herzog, and Eugene Deatrick. Werner Herzog Filmproduktion, 1997; Shout! Factory, 2014, Blu-ray, DVD.

*Magnum Force*. Ted Post, dir. Featuring Clint Eastwood and Hal Holbrook. Malpaso Co. and Warner Bros., 1973; Warner Home Video, 2010, Blu-ray.

*Man from Utah*. Robert N. Bradbury, dir. Featuring John Wayne. Paul Malvern Productions, 1934; Passport International Entertainment, 2006, DVD.

*Man of the West*. Anthony Mann, dir. Featuring Gary Cooper, Julie London, and Lee J. Cobb. Ashton Productions, 1958; MGM Home Entertainment, 2001, DVD.

*McQ*. John Sturges, dir. Featuring John Wayne, Eddie Albert, and Diana Muldaur. Warner Bros., 1974; Warner Bros. Home Entertainment, 2016, Blu-ray.

*Memories of a Forgotten War*. Camilla Benolirao Griggers and Sari Raissa Lluch Dalena, dirs. Kawayan Films, 2002; Plan Z Media, 2001, DVD.

*Missing in Action*. Joseph Zito, dir. Featuring Chuck Norris and M. Emmet Walsh. Cannon Group, 1984; MGM Home Entertainment, 2000, DVD.

*Mister Roberts*. John Ford and Mervyn Le Roy, dir. Featuring Henry Fonda, James Cagney, and William Powell. Orange Productions, 1955; Warner Home Video, 2005, DVD.

*Mt. Suribachi Flag Raising*. Combat color camera by William Genaust, Iwo Jima, Japan, February 23, 1945. 6:33 minutes; flag raising at 1:47–2:13 mins. VOD. https://www.youtube.com/watch?v=vI2LxSVWp90.

*No Substitute for Victory*. Robert P. Slatzer, dir. Featuring John Wayne. Alaska Pictures, 1971; Echo Bridge Home Entertainment, 2001, DVD.

*Paint Your Wagon*. Joshua Logan, dir. Featuring Lee Marvin, Clint Eastwood, and Jean Seberg. Alan J. Lerner Productions, 1969; Paramount Home Video, 2013, DVD.

*Pale Rider*. Clint Eastwood, dir. Featuring Clint Eastwood, Michael Moriarty, and Carrie Snodgress. Malpaso Co., 1985; Warner Home Video, 2000, DVD.

*Patton*. Franklin J. Schaffner, dir. Featuring George C. Scott and Karl Malden. Twentieth Century Fox, 1970; Twentieth Century Fox Home Entertainment, 2012, DVD and Blu-ray.

*Platoon*. Oliver Stone, dir. Featuring Charlie Sheen, Tom Berenger, and Willem Dafoe. Hemdale and Cinema '84, 1984; Warner Bros. Home Entertainment, 2020, DVD and Blu-ray.

*Play Misty for Me*. Clint Eastwood, dir. Featuring Clint Eastwood, Jessica Walter, and Donna Mills. Malpaso Co., 1971; Kino Lorber Studio Classics, 2020, Blu-ray.

*Rambo: First Blood Part II*. George P. Cosmatos, dir. Featuring Sylvester Stallone and Richard Crenna. Estudios Churubusco Azteca S.A. and Anabasis N.V., 1985; Artisan Entertainment, 2002, DVD.

*The Real Glory*. Henry Hathaway, dir. Featuring Gary Cooper and David Niven. Samuel Goldwyn Company, 1939; Warner Home Video, 2016, DVD.

*Red River*. Howard Hawks, dir. Featuring John Wayne, Montgomery Clift, and Joanne Dru. Monterey Productions, 1948; Criterion Collection, 2014, DVD.

*Rescue Dawn*. Werner Herzog, dir. Featuring Christian Bale, Steve Zahn, and Jeremy Davies. Metro-Goldwyn-Mayer, 2007; MGM Home Entertainment, 2007, Blu-ray and DVD.

*Retreat, Hell!* Joseph H. Lewis, dir. Featuring Frank Lovejoy and Richard Carlson. United States Pictures, 1952; Olive Films, 2012, Blu-ray.

*Riders of Destiny*. Robert N. Bradbury, dir. Featuring John Wayne, Cecilia Parker, and Forrest Taylor. Paul Malvern Productions, 1933; Alpha Video Distributors, 2008, DVD.

*Rio Grande*. John Ford, dir. Featuring John Wayne, Maureen O'Hara, and Ben Johnson. Argosy Pictures, 1950; Olive Films, 2012, DVD.

*Sands of Iwo Jima*. Allan Dwan, dir. Featuring John Wayne, John Agar, Lt. Harold G. Schrier, Pfc. Rene A. Gagnon, Pfc. Ira Hayes, and PM3c John H. Bradley. Republic Productions, 1949; Olive Films, 2012, Blu-ray and DVD.

*Saving Private Ryan*. Steven Spielberg, dir. Featuring Tom Hanks, Matt Damon, and Tom Sizemore. DreamWorks Distribution, 1998; DreamWorks Home Entertainment, 2010, Blu-ray and DVD.

*The Searchers*. John Ford, dir. Featuring John Wayne, Jeffrey Hunter, and Vera Miles. C. V. Whitney Pictures, 1956; Warner Home Video, 2007, DVD.

*Sergeant York*. Howard Hawks, dir. Featuring Gary Cooper, Walter Brennan, and Joan Leslie. Warner Bros., 1941; Warner Home Video, 2006, DVD.

*Shane*. George Stevens, dir. Featuring Alan Ladd, Jean Arthur, and Van Heflin. Paramount Pictures, 1953; Warner Home Video, 2013, Blu-ray and DVD.

*She Wore a Yellow Ribbon*. John Ford, dir. Featuring John Wayne, Joanne Dru, and John Agar. Argosy Pictures, 1949; Warner Archive Collection, 2016, Blu-ray and DVD.

*The Shootist*. Don Siegel, dir. Featuring John Wayne, Lauren Bacall, and Ron Howard. Paramount Pictures/Dino De Laurentiis Presents, 1976; Warner Home Video, 2013, DVD.

*Since You Went Away*. John Cromwell, dir. Featuring Claudette Colbert, Jennifer Jones, and Joseph Cotten. Selznick International Films, 1944; Kino Lorber, 2017, Blu-ray and DVD.

*Soldier Blue*. Ralph Nelson, dir. Featuring Candice Bergen and Peter Strauss. AVCO Embassy Pictures, 1970; Lionsgate Home Entertainment, 2006, DVD.

*Soldiers in Hiding*. Malcolm Clarke, dir. Narrated by Bob Gunton. Filmworks, Inc./HBO America Undercover Series, 1985, VHS; YouTube, https://www.youtube.com/watch?v=oSP2wtcBRjU, VOD.

*Stagecoach*. John Ford, dir. Featuring John Wayne and Claire Trevor. Walter Wanger Productions, 1939; Criterion Collection, 2010, DVD and Blu-ray.

*Stripes*. Ivan Reitman, dir. Featuring Bill Murray, John Candy, and Harold Ramis. Columbia Pictures, 1981; Sony Pictures Home Entertainment, 2011, Blu-ray.

*Sudden Impact*. Clint Eastwood, dir. Featuring Clint Eastwood and Sondra Locke. Warner Bros./Malpaso Co., 1983; Warner Home Video, 2008, Blu-ray.

*They Came to Cordura*. Robert Rossen, dir. Featuring Gary Cooper, Rita Hayworth, and Van Heflin. Columbia Pictures, 1959; Columbia TriStar, 2004, DVD.

*This Is the Army*. Michael Curtiz, dir. Featuring George Murphy, Joan Leslie, and Ronald Reagan. Warner Bros., 1943; Critics' Choice Video, 2016, DVD.

*Thunderbolt and Lightfoot*. Michael Cimino, dir. Featuring Clint Eastwood, Jeff Bridges, and George Kennedy. Malpaso Co., 1974; MGM Home Entertainment, 2000, DVD.

*Tigerland*. Joel Schumacher, dir. Featuring Colin Farrell and Matthew Davis. Twentieth Century Fox, 2000; Twentieth Century Fox Entertainment, 2011, Blu-ray and DVD.

*To Hell and Back*. Jesse Hibbs, dir. Featuring Audie Murphy, Marshall Thompson, and Charles Drake. Universal International, 1955; Universal Pictures Home Entertainment, 2004, DVD.

*Twilight's Last Gleaming*. Robert Aldrich, dir. Featuring Burt Lancaster and Richard Widmark. Bavaria Atelier, 1977; Olive Films, 2015, Blu-ray.

*Two Mules for Sister Sara*. Don Siegel, dir. Featuring Clint Eastwood and Shirley MacLaine. Universal Pictures/Malpaso Co., 1970; Kino Lorber, 2020, Blu-ray.

*Ulzana's Raid*. Robert Aldrich, dir. Featuring Burt Lancaster, Bruce Davison, and Jorge Luke. Universal Pictures, 1972; Universal Pictures Home Entertainment, 2013, DVD.

*Unforgiven*. Clint Eastwood, dir. Featuring Clint Eastwood, Gene Hackman, and Morgan Freeman. Malpaso Productions, 1992; Warner Home Video, 2006, HD DVD and DVD.

*Union Pacific*. Cecil B. DeMille, dir. Featuring Barbara Stanwyck and Joel McCrea. Paramount Pictures, 1939; Kino Lorber, 2021, Blu-ray.

*Vietnam: The Ten Thousand Day War.* Produced by Michael Maclear and Ian McLeod. Narrated by Richard Basehart. Canadian Broadcasting Corporation, 1980, DVD, 4-disc set.

*The Vietnam War.* Ken Burns and Lynn Novick, dir. Narrated by Peter Coyote. 10 episodes. Florentine Films, 2017; Public Broadcasting Service, 2017, DVD and Blu-ray.

*The Virginian.* Victor Fleming, dir. Featuring Gary Cooper, Walter Huston, and Mary Brian. Paramount Pictures, 1929.

*Wagon Master.* John Ford, dir. Featuring Ben Johnson, Joann Dru, and Harry Carey Jr. Argosy Pictures Corporation, 1950; Warner Home Video, 2009, DVD.

*The Westerner.* William Wyler, dir. Featuring Gary Cooper, Walter Brennan, and Doris Davenport. Samuel Goldwyn Co., 1940; Twentieth Century Fox Home Entertainment, 2008, DVD.

*Westward Ho.* Robert N. Bradbury, dir. Featuring John Wayne and Sheila Bromley. Republic Pictures, 1935; Olive Films, 2012, Blu-ray.

*We Were Soldiers.* Randall Wallace, dir. Featuring Mel Gibson, Madeleine Stowe, and Greg Kinnear. Icon Entertainment International, 2002; Paramount Home Entertainment, 2008, Blu-ray.

*Winchester '73.* Anthony Mann, dir. Featuring James Stewart and Shelley Winters. Universal International Pictures, 1950; Universal Pictures Home Entertainment, 2008, DVD.

*The Young Lions.* Edward Dmytryk, dir. Featuring Marlon Brando and Montgomery Clift. Twentieth Century Fox, 1958; Twentieth Century Fox Entertainment, 2002, DVD.

# Index

*Italicized references indicate illustrations.*

www.ingramcontent.com/pod-product-compliance
Ingram Content Group UK Ltd.
Pitfield, Milton Keynes, MK11 3LW, UK
UKHW040432220926
475848UK00002B/201

9 780806 197487